Imperfect Encounter

William Rothenstein and Rabindranath Tagore, 1912

Imperfect Encounter

Letters of William Rothenstein
and Rabindranath Tagore
1911–1941

Edited, with an Introduction and Notes by Mary M. Lago

Harvard University Press, Cambridge, Massachusetts, 1972

© Copyright 1972 by the President and Fellows of Harvard College
Library of Congress Catalog Card Number 73-182182
All rights reserved

SBN 674-44512-0
Printed in the United States of America

To my friends
Doris and Gerald Selinger

Preface

All letters and manuscripts quoted in this book have been transcribed by me from original materials, or, unless otherwise identified, from microfilms or photocopies of original materials. I conducted the interviews cited; they are quoted by permission.

William Rothenstein's letters to Rabindranath Tagore are among the Tagore Papers in the Rabindra-Sadana, Tagore archives at Santiniketan, West Bengal, with the exception of Letters 112, 114, 116, 119, and 139; Mr. Krishna Kripalani supplied these from his personal papers. Tagore's letters to Rothenstein are among the Rothenstein Papers in the Houghton Library, Harvard University. Tagore's letters quoted in notes to Letters 35, 100, and 172 are parts of this series still among personal papers of the Rothenstein family.

I have omitted from the numbered sequence of letters forty of the Rothenstein and the Tagore letters preserved in the Houghton Library and the Rabindra-Sadana. Those omitted are Tagore's letters to members of the Rothenstein family other than William; notes of invitation, of introduction, or of instruction about travel and other arrangements; and a few letters containing commentary that is essentially repeated in the numbered sequence. Passages omitted, as indicated, from numbered letters are repetitions of subject matter or are detailed accounts of family news. In all cases, I have omitted only those letters and passages peripheral to a full account of the association of the two principal correspondents. Addresses and dates of the letters have been made consistent in style and in most cases are arranged on a single line.

In transcribing William Rothenstein's letters I have silently corrected obvious errors and slips of the pen where they do not alter meaning. Where meaning or essential information is involved, additions or corrections are enclosed within brackets. Tagore's letters have been transcribed unaltered; additions or corrections are supplied within brackets only where a serious question of meaning arises. Thus, it is hoped, these letters may help to answer the question that persists in discussions of his translated works: how well did Tagore know English? These are his informal letters to an old friend, not intended for publication but written in haste or in illness, in health and high spirits, amid the confusions of travel, and during crises of political stress and personal grief. Because Rothenstein was a painter, not a poet, Tagore perhaps wrote to him in a manner more relaxed than that in which he wrote, for example, to W. B. Yeats or Robert Bridges. The letters to Rothenstein may therefore stand as a fair sample of Tagore's English in its most natural state.

Letters and other materials supplied by The Macmillan Company, New York, and Macmillan and Company, Limited, London, are from three separate sources: Macmillan Company Records in the Manuscript Division of the New York Public Library; Macmillan Papers in the Department of Manuscripts, British Museum; and office files of Macmillan and Company, Limited, to which I was given access in London. Photocopy or microfilm copies of original letters from the two Macmillan firms to Tagore and his assistants proved to be unobtainable; therefore letters written by George P. Brett, for the New York firm, and by members of the London firm have been cited from carbon copies in the various Macmillan archives. Letters from Tagore and his assistants to the New York firm are usually identifiable as having been received and answered by Mr. Brett. Letters to the London firm, however, are for the most part addressed "Dear Sir," "Dear Sirs," or "Dear Mr. Macmillan," and receipt is acknowledged in the Macmillan manner, that is, with the stamped initials of that member of the firm who received a particular letter. Whether in every case that recipient also wrote the reply is impossible to determine without reference to signatures on original letters. Whenever possible, I have identified writers of letters for the London firm, but so strong is the sense of a corporate personality that this synthesis of correspondents in no way interferes with the course and coherence of the exchange.

Passages in the Introductions and notes translated or paraphrased from Bengali texts are, unless otherwise identified, my own work.

Transliteration of Bengali presents peculiar problems because there is as yet no general and full agreement upon a uniform system of transliteration. Therefore the use of diacritics is limited here to the important distinction between the Bengali short *a* and long *ā;* this is a very frequent basis for distinctions between meanings and spellings of Bengali words. The Bengali consonants চ and ছ are transliterated here as *c* and *ch,* a formula that differentiates clearly between them, yet reserves the form *cch* for transliteration of the conjunct consonant চছ.

Variations will be noted in the spelling of some names of persons, places, and, in a few cases, of the titles of published works. For the names of persons the spelling used is that preferred, to the best of my knowledge, by the individual, although even this sometimes varied from time to time and varies considerably in the usage of the letter writers. Place names are transliterated directly from the Bengali spelling except where variants appear in established English usage or in the usage of the letter writers. Titles of published works conform generally to prior publication.

Tagore's works are cited, as appropriate, in the following order in the notes: Bengali title; literal translation of title; date of first publication in Bengali volume form; volume and page reference in *Rabindra-Racanābali* [Rabindranath's Works]; title of translated version and translator; place of publication and date of first English translation; page reference in his *Collected Poems and Plays.* In the notes and bibliography, dates of first publication of Tagore's works in Bengali volume form conform to those listed in *Rabindranath Tagore: A Centenary Volume, 1861–1961* [comp. Sahitya Akademi], pp. 504–511.

For permission to publish these letters of Rabindranath Tagore I wish to thank his daughter-in-law, the late Mrs. Pratima Tagore. For permission to publish William Rothenstein's letters I am indebted to his sons, Sir John Rothenstein and Mr. Michael Rothenstein, and for such sustained kindness, confidence, and hospitality as cannot be quantitatively assessed I am indebted to all the members of the immediate Rothenstein family: Sir John and Lady Rothenstein, Mr. and Mrs. Alan Ward, Dr. and Mrs. Ensor Holiday, and Mr. and Mrs. Michael Rothenstein.

I am grateful to the American Philosophical Society for assistance in the early and crucial stages of the project, in the form of two grants for travel and research in 1967 and 1968.

I thank all those persons, known and unknown to me, who forwarded my letters, answered my questions, corrected my errors, and thus helped to direct the course of my work. I should like to mention especially Lady Albery, Professor G. M. Almy, Lady Anderson, Mr. and Mrs. W. G. Archer, Mrs. Supriya Bari, Miss Sunanda Basu, Dr. and Mrs. Leslie Bates, Mrs. Mary Bennett, Mr. and Mrs. Asit Bhattacharyya, Mrs. Noel Blakiston, Miss Margaret Campbell, Mrs. Melinda Campbell, Miss Mollie Cohen, Mr. and Mrs. Stanley Cooke-Smith, Professor Carlo Coppola, Mr. A. W. N. Cowper, Mr. Mitchell Crites, the Lord Brooke of Cumnor, Sir Arthur Dash, Miss Elizabeth de Haas, Mr. R. St. L. Deraniyagala, Mrs. Pamela Diamand, Mr. Lovat Dickson, Mr. and Mrs. William Dockar-Drysdale, Dr. Carl Dolmetsch, Mrs. John Drinkwater, Mr. Leonard Elmhirst, Mr. Vivian Fox Strangways, Mrs. Jeannie Geddes, Mrs. Iris Gould, Lady Green, Professor Allan Gwynne-Jones, Sir Rupert Hart-Davis, Mrs. Robert H. Hole, Mr. Frank Howes, Mr. E. X. Kapp, Dr. Stella Kramrisch, Mr. Robert Lutyens, Sir Francis Meynell, Mrs. Curtis Moffat, Miss Ria Mooney, Mr. Henry Moore, Mrs. Beryl Newman, Mrs. Jeanette Powell, Mrs. Eva Reichmann, Miss Stella Rhys, Miss Margaret Richards, Mrs. Minnie Roberts, Mr. and Mrs. David Rutherston, Dr. Anil Seal, Dr. S. C. Sen, Cecilia Lady Sempill, Mrs. Olivia Sowerby, Mr. Robert Speaight, Mr. M. M. Stuart, Miss Riette Sturge Moore, Dr. Amitendranath Tagore, Mr. Nicholas Taylor, Mr. and Mrs. Julian Trevelyan, the Reverend Vincent Turner, S.J., Mr. John Vickers, Mrs. Igor Vinogradoff, Mrs. Gillian Wilkinson, Lady Wilson, Mrs. Yvor Winters, and Senator Michael Yeats.

I am especially indebted to Dr. Amiya Chakravarty of the State University of New York; to Dr. W. H. Bond, Mr. Rodney

G. Dennis, and Miss Carolyn Jakeman of the Houghton Library at Harvard University; to Mr. Sobhanlal Ganguli of the Rabindra-Sadana, Santiniketan; to Mr. Krishna Kripalani of the Sahitya Akademi, New Delhi; to the Lord Bridges and to his father, the late Lord Bridges; and to Miss Sylvia Moore of Macmillan and Company, Limited, London, all of whom patiently helped me to gather materials central to this book.

Valuable assistance and advice have been given by libraries, art galleries, government archives, and other agencies in many countries, and to all of these I am most grateful. Special thanks are owed to Mr. M. R. Dudley and Mrs. Caroline Carpenter of the Photographic Department, Ashmolean Museum, and Mr. D. S. Porter of the Bodleian Library, Oxford; Mr. L. J. Gorton and other staff members of the Department of Manuscripts, British Museum; Miss Mary Thatcher of the Cambridge University Centre for South Asian Studies; Miss Jane Bebbington of the India Office Library and Miss Sally Johnson of India Office Records; Mr. Patrick Henchy and members of his staff of the National Library of Ireland; M. Carlos van Hasselt, Institut Néerlandais, Paris; Miss Joan Gibbs and Mr. Timothy Rogers, Palaeography Room, University of London Library; Mrs. Agnes Moran and Mr. Gerald Gross of The Macmillan Company, New York; Dr. Roger Highfield and Mr. John Burgass, Merton College Library, Oxford; Mrs. Ann Todd Rubey and Dr. Murari Nagar, Library of the University of Missouri at Columbia; Mr. Paul Rugen and his assistants in the Manuscript Division, New York Public Library; the staff of the Royal Society for India, Pakistan, and Ceylon; Dr. D. G. C. Allan of the Royal Society of Arts; Miss M. E. Barber of the Society of Authors; Mr. G. D. A. Macpherson of the Victoria and Albert Museum Library; and Mr. Michael Horniman of A. P. Watt and Son, London.

I am indebted to the following for their kind permission to publish copyrighted materials: Professor G. M. Almy for a letter to myself; the Right Reverend William Anderson for letters of J. D. Anderson; Mr. Henry Baker for letters of Sir Herbert Baker; Mrs. Eva Reichmann for an excerpt from "Enoch Soames," by Max Beerbohm (William Heinemann & Co.); Mrs. Nicolette Gray for letters of Laurence Binyon; Mr. George P. Brett, Jr., and The Macmillan Company, New York,

xii   Preface

for letters of George P. Brett; the Lord Bridges for letters of Robert Bridges and for quotations from his "Humdrum & Harum-Scarum: A Lecture on Free Verse" (Oxford University Press); the Lord Brooke of Cumnor for letters of Stopford Brooke; Mr. Chanler Chapman for letters of John Jay Chapman; the late Mrs. Ananda Coomaraswamy and Dr. Rama Coomaraswamy for letters of Ananda Coomaraswamy; Mrs. Clare Chapman for letters of Frances Cornford; Sir Arthur Dash for a letter to myself; Mr. Leonard Elmhirst for excerpts from his transcript of his diaries and for letters to myself; Mrs. Mary Bennett for letters of H. A. L. Fisher; the Lord Ilchester for letters of A. H. Fox Strangways; Mr. David Garnett for letters of Constance Garnett; Lady Wilson for letters of E. B. Havell; Mr. A. W. N. Cowper and Mrs. Robert H. Hole for letters of Lady Herringham; Jonathan Cape Limited for letters of Laurence Housman; Dr. Stella Kramrisch for a letter to William Rothenstein; Mr. Mark Longman for letters of C. J. Longman; Macmillan and Company, Limited, London, for editorial correspondence and for letters of Sir Frederick, George, and Maurice Macmillan; Society of Authors as the literary representative of the Estate of John Masefield, for a letter of John Masefield; *The New Statesman and Nation* for editorial correspondence of Henry Massingham; Mr. Niel Pearson for letters of W. W. Pearson; Mr. Harry Pieris for a letter to myself; Miss Stella Rhys for letters of Ernest Rhys; the late Brigadier A. G. Rolleston and Mrs. Honor Dockar-Drysdale for diaries of T. W. Rolleston; Mr. Richard Sadler for letters of Sir Michael Sadler; Professor P. C. Mahalanobis for letters of Sir Brajendranath Seal; Dr. S. C. Sen for letters of D. C. Sen; Messrs. Jonas and Parker and the Trustees Department of the Westminster Bank, London, for a letter of Sir Harry Stephen; Miss Riette Sturge Moore and Mr. Daniel Sturge Moore for letters of Thomas Sturge Moore; Mr. Alokendranath Tagore for letters of Abanindranath Tagore; Mr. Nicholas Taylor for a letter to myself; Mrs. Edward J. Thompson and Mr. Edward P. Thompson for letters of Edward J. Thompson; Society of Authors for letters of G. H. Thring; Mrs. Gillian Wilkinson for letters of Evelyn Underhill; Mr. John Vickers for a letter to myself; Mrs. Alan Ward for letters to Rabindranath Tagore; Mrs. Yvor Winters for letters to myself; Senator Michael Yeats and Miss Anne Yeats for letters of W. B. Yeats.

All materials from the Houghton Library quoted in this book are used by permission of the Harvard College Library, and William Rothenstein's letters at Santiniketan are used with the approval of the Rabindra-Sadana. The Bodleian Library, the British Museum, and the India Office Library have allowed me to use papers from several collections. A letter of Sir Alan Green is unpublished Crown-copyright material in the India Office Library transcribed for this book and appearing by permission of the Controller of Her Majesty's Stationery Office. A letter from William Rothenstein to Max Beerbohm is quoted by permission of the William Andrews Clark Memorial Library of the University of California at Los Angeles. The University of London Library has approved my use of materials from the Thomas Sturge Moore Papers, and materials among the Macmillan Company Records are used by permission of the Manuscript Division, the New York Public Library, Astor, Lenox and Tilden Foundations.

It gives me particular pleasure to record my thanks to friends who have given me much encouragement and helpful criticism: Amiya Chakravarty, an unfailing source of the assistance that he is uniquely qualified to give; Karl Beckson, John Broomfield, Edward C. Dimock, Jr., P. N. Furbank, Michael Holroyd, and William Peden.

Finally, I must thank all those who have supplied the books and instruction in the Bengali language that helped me to gain access, however partial, to a splendid literature of which I would otherwise have no direct knowledge. The staff of Marlborough Court, residence club of the Middlesex Hospital, London, have facilitated my work in countless ways during my visits to England. My daughter Jane has been my only research assistant. Above all, I wish to thank my husband and both my children for bearing with my absences from home and even more frequent absences of mind during the preparation of this book.

Mary M. Lago

Columbia, Missouri
February 1971

Contents

Introduction   1
Royal Society of Arts and The India Society, 2. Rothenstein in 1911, 8. Tagore in 1911, 13. *Gitanjali:* The Paradigm, 17.

Prologue   25

I	Rothenstein in India, 1910–1911	27
II	Tagore in the West, 1912–1913	37
III	Nobel Prize and After, 1913–1914	133
IV	Hesitations and Losses, 1915	177
V	Marking Time, 1916–1919	217
VI	"A Passing Breeze," 1920–1922	267
VII	The Teacher and the Traveler, 1923–1935	299
VIII	Afterthoughts, 1936–1940	357

Epilogue   371

Bibliography   375

Index   389

ILLUSTRATIONS

William Rothenstein and Rabindranath Tagore, London, Summer 1912. Courtesy of Mrs. Alan Ward. Photograph by John Trevor, Hampstead. *frontispiece*

Ernest B. Havell, about 1910. Courtesy of India Office Library and Records, London, and Lady Sonia Wilson. 3

William Rothenstein in India, about November 1910. Courtesy of Mrs. Ensor Holiday. 29

London, Summer 1912. Front: Somendra Dev Burman, Rabindranath Tagore, Rathindranath Tagore; rear: Dr. D. N. Maitra, John Rothenstein, William Rothenstein. Courtesy of Mrs. Alan Ward. Photograph by John Trevor, Hampstead. 45

London, Summer 1912: Rabindranath Tagore with Betty, Rachel, and William Michael Rothenstein. Courtesy of Sir John Rothenstein. Photograph by John Trevor, Hampstead. 60

William Orpen, oil, "Selecting Jury. N[ew] E[nglish] A[rt] C[lub] 1909." Courtesy of National Portrait Gallery, London. 72

William Rothenstein, pencil drawing, 1912: Thomas W. Rolleston. Courtesy of Lady Una Albery. 91

William Rothenstein, pencil drawing, 1912: Rathindranath Tagore. Courtesy of Brian Gould. Photograph by Ashmolean Museum, Oxford. 114

William Rothenstein, pencil drawing, about 1912: Arthur H. Fox Strangways. Courtesy of Sir John Rothenstein. Photograph by M. R. Dudley, A.I.I.P., F.R.P.S. 137

Alice Rothenstein, about 1913. Courtesy of Mrs. Alan Ward. 149

W. W. Pearson at Santiniketan. Courtesy of Mrs. Ensor Holiday. 158

C. F. Andrews, M. K. Gandhi, and W. W. Pearson in South Africa, about December 1913. Courtesy of Niel Pearson and Miss Margaret Richards. 181

Jyotirindranath Tagore, pencil drawing, January 30, 1914: Rabindranath Tagore. Courtesy of Sir John Rothenstein. Photograph by M. R. Dudley. 193

William Rothenstein, oil, "St. Martin's Summer," 1915. Courtesy of Manchester City Art Gallery: Rutherston Collection. 200

Max Beerbohm, drawing: "Mr. William Rothenstein warns Mr. Tagore against being spoilt by occidental success," 1913. Courtesy of Mrs. Eva Reichmann and Richard Spiegelberg. 205

Frances D. Cornford and Francis M. Cornford at Vattetot, France, with the Rothensteins, about 1910. Courtesy of Sir John Rothenstein. 210

William Rothenstein, pencil drawing, Sir Edward Elgar, 1919. Courtesy of National Portrait Gallery, London, and Sir John Rothenstein.	261
Edmond X. Kapp, pastel, 1921: Rabindranath Tagore in London. Courtesy of Edmond X. Kapp. Original owned by Barber Institute of Fine Arts, Birmingham, England.	270
Sylvain Lévi and Rabindranath Tagore at Santiniketan, about 1923. Courtesy of Mrs. Ensor Holiday.	289
Sir William Rothenstein, painting out-of-doors at Far Oakridge, about 1935. Courtesy of Mrs. Alan Ward.	323
William Butler Yeats, about 1935. Courtesy of Sir John Rothenstein.	348
Sir William Rothenstein at Far Oakridge, in uniform of R.A.F. War Artist, about 1940. Courtesy of Mrs. Ensor Holiday. Photograph by Ensor Holiday.	359

Imperfect Encounter

Abbreviations

BrP	Robert Bridges Papers: Bridges Family Papers
CPP	Rabindranath Tagore, *Collected Poems and Plays*
MCP	Macmillan Company Papers: Macmillan and Company, Limited, London
MM I	William Rothenstein, *Men and Memories, 1872–1900*
MM II	William Rothenstein, *Men and Memories, 1900–1922*
MP:BM	Macmillan Company Papers: British Museum
MP:NYPL	Macmillan Company Records: New York Public Library
MR	*The Modern Review* (Calcutta)
RP	Rothenstein Family Papers
RP:HL	Rothenstein Papers: Houghton Library, Harvard University
RP:IOL	Rothenstein Papers: India Office Library, London
R-R	Rabindranath Tagore, *Rabindra-Racanābali* [Rabindranath's Works]
R-S	Rabindra-Sadana (Tagore Archives): Santiniketan
SF	William Rothenstein, *Since Fifty: Men and Memories, 1922–1938*
TSM	Thomas Sturge Moore Papers: University of London Library

Introduction

The thirty-year correspondence of William Rothenstein, a painter, and Rabindranath Tagore, a poet, is a history of the friendship of two men who reached out, the one from England toward India, the other from India toward the West. Their letters record the elements and stages of this friendship: curiosity and admiration; a happy sharing of interests and efforts; weariness, exasperation, and reconciliation; and, underlying all and enduring to the end, a mutual respect and deep affection.

Acting upon and reacting to this friendship were the forceful personalities of their friends. The personalities of Rothenstein and Tagore were nothing if not forceful, and many—indeed, most—of their mutual acquaintances were cultural movers and shakers. It was inevitable that they should not always move together in one direction or agree as to which foundations of society needed shaking; the resulting confusion was frequently exasperating and sometimes disabling. How pictures are to be painted and poetry written despite this confusion is an endlessly troublesome question that becomes a leitmotiv of these letters.

The correspondence traces the patterns of accident and coincidence that determined the manner of Tagore's introduction to readers in the West and his unexpected honor of a Nobel Prize. It records also the gradual formulation of certain questions that were crucial to his role as a writer whose works must travel abroad in translation. During his lifetime these questions went unanswered; they go essentially unanswered today.

About William Rothenstein's role as prime mover of Tagore's career as an international figure, however, there can be no question. This correspondence documents and confirms the magnitude of his contribution to Tagore and to the history of cultural exchange between India and the West—in Rothenstein's crowded life, one contribution among many, to other friends and other causes.

2   Imperfect Encounter

ROYAL SOCIETY OF ARTS AND THE INDIA SOCIETY

The cultural chain reaction that brought Tagore to the attention of readers in the West began on Thursday afternoon, January 13, 1910, when the Indian Section of the Royal Society of Arts, London, met to hear a paper, "Art Administration in India," read by Ernest B. Havell, former Principal, School of Art, and Keeper of the Art Gallery, Calcutta. Sir George Birdwood was in the chair.[1]

Havell's paper was a heartfelt protest against administrative policy then prevailing in the four Government-sponsored art schools in India, one each in Madras, Calcutta, Bombay, and Lahore, all founded between 1850 and 1875 to improve the natives' taste with regard to articles in daily use. This policy, he reminded his audience, harked back to "Lord Macaulay's view of the worthlessness of all Indian culture." In art education the result had been a disastrous division between the "applied" arts and the "fine" arts, with the latter virtually ignored on the assumption that India had no fine arts worth preserving. Havell felt that even in the teaching of applied arts, all was not well. By 1910 administrators disapproved in theory the force-feeding of Indian artists on European notions about art. The schools, however, were in the cities, and neither teachers nor students ventured from these Anglicized centers in search of "real Indian art, that is, the art which enters into the religion, life, and work of the great mass of the Indian people." Havell described the students as, "for the most part, the flotsam and jetsam of the Anglo-Indian university system," who went to art school because they could find nothing better to do, and as a result rarely did do better. The few who triumphed over art-school mediocrity found themselves tied to an ill-defined foreign tradition and uncertain of employment or recognition.[2]

---

1. E. B. Havell, "Art Administration in India," in "Proceedings of the Society," *Journal of the Royal Society of Arts*, 58 (1909–10), 274–285. Ernest B. Havell (1861–1934), Superintendent, Madras School of Art, 1884–1892; Principal, Calcutta School of Art, 1896–1906; attaché, British Legation, Copenhagen, 1916–1923. Sir George Birdwood (1832–1917), Bombay Medical Staff, 1854; Persian Expedition, 1856–57; Royal Commissioner for Indian and Colonial Exhibition, 1886; Revenue and Statistics Department, India Office, 1871–1902.

2. Havell, in "Proceedings," *RSA Journal*, 58:274, 275. See also T. B.

Ernest B. Havell

4   Imperfect Encounter

Havell was replying to a paper given in 1909 by Cecil Burns, Principal of the Bombay School of Art. Burns considered the fine arts "but the development and higher expression of kindred crafts, [and] it is unfortunately true that in India, as in Europe, the teaching of those branches of art has become separated in modern practice from the teaching of the crafts." The opening of the Suez Canal had increased the pressure of Western influence upon India; now Indian artists and artisans must acquire practical (that is, industrial) expertise in order to succeed (compete with Western workmen). It was Government's function to supply this industrial expertise.[3]

Not so, Havell retorted in 1910. There are technical differences between arts and crafts, but, aesthetically, "all art is one"; in Europe and in Asia one aesthetic philosophy controls the weaver's fingers, the painter's brush, and the sculptor's chisel. At the Madras school Havell had been unable to depart from prescribed policy, but the Calcutta school offered something that Madras did not: a gifted student, Abanindranath Tagore, to whom Havell's interest in Indian art came as a revelation. In 1905 Abanindranath had become Havell's Vice Principal, and, after Havell's departure, the first Indian to be even Acting Principal of any Government School of Art. He and his brother Gaganendranath now led a revival of interest in Indian traditions of painting and sculpture. "It is a school of idealists," Havell said, "for otherwise it would not be Indian. The idealist is popularly supposed to be an unpractical person, and in our Indian administration is generally regarded with grave suspicion." But, he went on, "It is the practical men who, in the name of scientific progress, have helped to ruin Indian handicrafts, and still continue to do so, in spite of the lessons they might learn from the industrial history of modern Europe." Government now wished to fasten this discredited system onto India. "I shall not cease," Havell declared, "to protest against this recommendation and this propaganda as long as I live."[4]

Macaulay, "Minute on Education" (1835), quoted in *Sources of Indian Tradition*, comp. W. T. de Bary et al. (New York, 1958), p. 601; W. G. Archer, *India and Modern Art* (London, 1959), p. 24.

3. Cecil Burns, "The Functions of Schools of Art in India," in "Proceedings," *RSA Journal*, 57 (1908–9), 629–641.

4. Havell, in *ibid.*, 58:275, 276, 277, 285. Abanindranath Tagore

The Chairman responded by invoking the shades of Fergusson, Pugin, Ruskin, and Saint Francis of Assisi. He reminded Havell that "a strong man would never raise a quarrel with his superiors," and categorized every product of Indian art that he had ever seen as either a "sacrosanct article of utility" or "a ritualised, and generally monstrous representation of the high gods, and epic heroes of the race of the Brahmanical Hindus"; these might be "perfected examples of 'applied art,' but never of 'fine art.'" Sir George discharged his heaviest gun at the traditional figure of the Buddha: "This senseless similitude, in its immemorial fixed pose, is nothing more than an uninspired brazen image, vacuously squinting down its nose to its thumbs, and knees, and toes. A boiled suet pudding would serve equally well as a symbol of passionless purity and serenity of soul!"[5]

William Rothenstein was one of the few who rose to the defense of Havell, Indian art, and the Lord Buddha. "If artists had only realised earlier in their Western art the value of Eastern ideas," he argued, "Western art would have had an entirely different character." Western artists now began to see that "reality and realism were not the same thing, and that the essence of art was reality." The West, Rothenstein said, owed Asian art even exaggerated attention, "if it were possible to exaggerate it," to compensate for whole centuries of neglect; and English artists owed Mr. Havell a "very great debt of gratitude."[6]

A journalistic exchange was the second link in this chain

(1871–1951), Gaganendranath Tagore (1867–1938), artists and art teachers.

5. "Proceedings," *RSA Journal*, 58:286, 287.

6. *Ibid.*, pp. 290–291. Rothenstein recalled that he, Havell, and Ananda Coomaraswamy "went to hear a lecture by Sir George Birdwood" at the Royal Society of Arts. (*Men and Memories: Recollections of William Rothenstein, 1900–1922* [London, 1932], p. 231.) Perhaps Sir George's remarks loomed as large as a lecture in Rothenstein's memory. Coomaraswamy had written, "I shall be there to support [Havell]. I very much wish you could too." (Coomaraswamy to Rothenstein, December 22, 1909. Rothenstein Papers: Houghton Library, Harvard University.) Ananda Coomaraswamy (1877–1947), Director, Mineral Survey of Ceylon, 1903–1906; Director, Art Section, United Provinces Exhibition, 1910–11; Fellow for Research in Indian, Persian, and Muhammedan Art, Museum of Fine Arts, Boston, 1917–1947.

of events. "Fine Art in India," a letter drafted by Rothenstein and signed by him and twelve other artists, art teachers, and art critics, appeared in the *Times*. It quoted from and disavowed Sir George's statements on Indian art in general and the Buddha figure in particular, asserted that Indian art could assimilate Western influence without losing its individual character, and assured Indian artists that they had understanding friends among artists in the West.[7] This aroused the *Times* to an editorial, "Art in India," a masterpiece of either-or journalism. It, too, focused on the Buddha image but sidestepped the artistic issue; this interesting controversy, the newspaper noted, revealed the gulf between Oriental and European ideas of art. The East was too easily satisfied with symbolism, the West with photographic representation: "What is needed is that art in both continents shall become more expressive, using in each case the natural means of expression."[8]

The *Times* missed the point of both Havell's paper and Rothenstein's letter. Neither wished the art of East and West homogenized, a bland and characterless mixture. Havell had asked precisely what the *Times* asked: that English art administrators allow Indian artists to discover their "natural means of expression." Rothenstein underlined this by exhorting Indian artists to "jealously preserve the individual character" of their traditions. When Havell had said that "all art is one," he meant art for the sake of art and artists, not art for the sake of industrial expansion, a point that the *Times* overlooked.

Reaction in Calcutta was prompt and emphatic. Abanindranath Tagore wrote at once to Havell: "All of us read with great interest the full account of your lecture in the Royal Society [of Arts]. What a storm of discussion it has raised! Who is this Sir T. H. Holdich and alphabets who after 36 years in the East and India has such *superfine* ideas of our art! Sir G. B.—in spite of his resolve—re-resolves—is grand even when he is tottering, he will always command respect, the dear old man."[9]

7. Rothenstein, "Fine Art in India," *Times* (London), February 28, 1910, p. 6.
8. "Art in India," *Times,* March 1, 1910, p. 11.
9. Abanindranath Tagore to Havell, February 24, 1910. Havell Papers: India Office Library. Col. Sir Thomas Holdich, K.C.M.G., K.C.I.E., C.B.,

Others were less charitable. Sister Nivedita's letters to Havell bristled with indignation and exclamation marks.[10] The Calcutta English-language journal, the *Modern Review,* reprinted both Rothenstein's letter and the *Times*'s editorial. It admonished the cultural high priests and elders to behold how and why they had been misled, then concluded: "It is not for us to blame Sir George Birdwood, who is today what he has always been. We must despise ourselves for our want of penetration in the past." On a resoundingly nationalist note the journal observed that Europe was already orphaned by wealth and mad extravagance, while impoverished India had a firm hold on the eternal verities: "INDIA is the burden which [Indian art] will strive continually to express, always with a growing force, and by this shall it be made worthy to enrich the world."[11]

The most consequential outcome of the meeting at the Royal Society of Arts was the founding of The India Society in London. Rothenstein recalled that the suet pudding simile "so disgusted me that, there and then, I proposed we should found an India Society."[12] Two days later Havell wrote to him, "I hope, too, that your idea of an India Society may take definite shape—it is really scandalous that so little should be known of Indian art compared with Chinese and Japanese."[13] On June 11, alongside charity, bankruptcy, and auction notices, the *Times* announced that the Executive Committee of The India Society "desires to promote the study and appreciation of Indian culture in its aesthetic aspects, believing that in Indian sculpture, architecture, and painting, as well as in Indian literature and music, there is a vast unexplored field, the investigation of which will bring about a better understanding of Indian ideals and aspirations, both in this country

---

D. Sc., Royal Engineers ret. (See "Proceedings," *RSA Journal,* 58:294–295.)

10. Sister Nivedita to Havell, March 3, April 7, 1910. Havell: IOL. Margaret Noble (1867–1911), Irish teacher who turned Theosophist, joined the Ramakrishna Mission in India in 1899, and took the name "Nivedita": "Devoted One."

11. Editorial, "Eastern Art Makes Events in the West," *The Modern Review: A Monthly Review and Miscellany* (Calcutta), 7 (1910), 517, 519.

12. *MM* II, 231.

13. Havell to Rothenstein, February 15, 1910. RP:HL.

and in India."¹⁴ The newspaper took no further notice, and no letters recalled the editor's attention to the event.

The *Modern Review*, however, remained alert: "It may be that at last we are to have in England a society non-official and non-political for the study of Indian art and culture in the newly founded 'India Society.'" Readers learned that a distinguished company assembled on June 15 at the old hall of Clifford's Inn and that the chairman, "Will Rothenstein, the artist," made an "earnest introductory speech."¹⁵

By April 1911 the Society had 193 members in Great Britain, India, and the United States. T. W. Rhys Davids, eminent Pali scholar, was its President. The Treasurer was T. W. Rolleston, an important link with groups similarly interested in rediscovering "real Irish art." The Secretary was A. H. Fox Strangways, whose role would become crucially important to Tagore. On these foundations, designed by Rothenstein, Tagore's literary career in the West would be built.¹⁶

ROTHENSTEIN IN 1911

The Rothenstein who met Rabindranath Tagore in India in 1911 differed in important respects from that Will Rothenstein who sparkles and pontificates in Max Beerbohm's story, "Enoch Soames":

> In the Summer Term of '93 a bolt from the blue flashed down on Oxford. It drove deep, it hurtlingly embedded itself in the soil. Dons and undergraduates stood around,

14. "The India Society," *Times*, June 11, 1910, p. 18.
15. Editorial, "The India Society," *MR*, 8 (1910), 161–163.
16. T. W. R. Davids (1843–1922), founder, Pali Text Society; Professor of Pali and Buddhist Literature, University College, University of London, 1882–1912; Professor of Comparative Religion, Manchester University, 1904–1915. T. W. Rolleston (1857–1920), editor, *Dublin University Review*, 1885–86; First Honorary Secretary, Irish Literary Society, London, 1892–93; Assistant Editor, New Irish Library, 1893; Managing Director, Irish Industries Association, 1894–1897; Honorary Secretary, Irish Arts and Crafts Society, 1898–1908; organizer, Irish loan collection to St. Louis Exposition, 1904. Arthur Fox Strangways (1859–1948), schoolmaster, Wellington College, 1887–1910; appointed music critic for the *Times*, 1911; for the *Observer*, 1925; founder-editor, *Music and Letters*, 1920–1936.

rather pale, discussing nothing but it. Whence came it, this meteorite? From Paris. Its name? Will Rothenstein. Its aim? To do a series of twenty-four portraits in lithograph. These were to be published from the Bodley Head, London. The matter was urgent. Already the Warden of A, and the Master of B, and the Regius Professor of C, had meekly "sat." Dignified and doddering old men, who had never consented to sit to any one, could not withstand this dynamic little stranger. He did not sue: he invited; he did not invite: he commanded. He was twenty-one years old. He wore spectacles that flashed more than any other pair ever seen. He was a wit. He was brimful of ideas. He knew Whistler. He knew Edmond de Goncourt. He knew every one in Paris. He knew them all by heart. He was Paris in Oxford.[17]

This was the wool merchant's son from Bradford, Yorkshire, who at the age of seventeen persuaded his parents to let him study art, first in London and then in Paris, where his precocious talent and energies attracted the attention of artists like Degas and Rodin, Toulouse-Lautrec and Whistler. By 1911 this *wunderkind* was thirty-nine years old, married, the father of four children, a recognized London artist, but, like that Will Rothenstein who dazzled Oxford in 1893, he remained closely identified with the New English Art Club and with other groups and individuals who tried to be all that the Royal Academy was not: curious about new departures in art; adventuresome in giving them a showing; above all, sympathetic to the influences emanating from France since the advent of Impressionism.

Yet Rothenstein's family and friends sensed a change in him that was more than the sedateness of middle age. He was no less dynamic; his wit still sparkled; he was still brimful of ideas and a tireless organizer; but he had taken some inward turning, as yet unmapped, that made him outwardly restless. Christmas of 1910 found him in India, Christmas of 1911 in the United States, painting, meeting old friends and making new ones, storing up kaleidoscopic impressions, and always,

17. Max Beerbohm, "Enoch Soames," *Seven Men* (New York, 1920), p. 10. Rothenstein's lithographs: *Oxford Characters* (London, 1896).

everywhere, weighing relative values against absolutes: art as perfect order, the artist as a man with a mission to see and explain the extraordinary that lies within and beyond the ordinary.

Rothenstein was not the only English artist who felt restless in those years. Virginia Woolf observed later that "in or about December 1910 human character changed."[18] On November 8, 1910, London's first Postimpressionist exhibit, organized by Roger Fry, had opened at the Grafton Galleries. It was a revelation. It was an artistic revolution. It was not quite human character that had changed, but Postimpressionism changed many persons' visual approach to the real world, and it is no accident that the word "vision" recurs in explications of Postimpressionist painting. It was literally a "re-vision," and a profound uneasiness seeped in among the protests and the ridicule heaped upon the French painters and their English admirers.[19]

Meanwhile, where was William Rothenstein, who had been "Paris in Oxford"? He was painting beside the Ganges at Benares, getting the news of the Grafton Galleries through his friends.[20] He was less concerned with national art—English, French, or even Indian—than with the universal art that had prompted Havell to say that "all art is one."

The founding of The India Society had coincided with a major decision that had profound effects on Rothenstein's career. In 1910 Herbert Fisher urged him to apply for the vacant Slade Professorship of Fine Art at Oxford. Rothenstein demurred, for he did not wish to compete with Roger Fry, and responded to Fisher's continued urging with a statement of aesthetic creed:

> Honours, dear Master, no one knows better than yourself are not for those who hold them to be used for their individual advantage, nor are they to be regarded as a reward

18. Virginia Woolf, "Mr. Bennett and Mrs. Brown," *Collected Essays* (New York [1967]), I, 320. Roger Fry (1866–1934), painter and critic; a director, Metropolitan Museum of Art, 1905–1910; appointed Slade Professor of Fine Art, Cambridge, 1933.

19. See, for example, a review, "The 'Post-Impressionists' at the Grafton Galleries," *The Academy* (London), 79 (1910), 546–547.

20. See Eric Gill to Rothenstein, December 5, 1910. RP:HL. Quoted in part in *MM* II, 213–214.

for services rendered, but rather as an opportunity of rendering still greater ones in the service of mankind. I am one of those who hold that it is not critics we want, but criticism, and it is the duty of those who care to suggest a basis from which something in the nature of public criticism may be forthcoming. The expert is the devil, who in the dress of a high priest takes the offerings, once intended for the divine spirit of light and life, for his own table. If you elect a mere critical weigher and balancer of schools and opinions, you get no further in the direction of inspiring people with respect for the eternal struggle for the expression of what is best and sanest in men's aims; if you can get some one who will inspire young people with a sense of the significance of life, using the past to illumine the present, you will indeed do well.[21]

If Rothenstein's feelings were mixed, this letter is nevertheless the clearest possible statement of the high principles and deep misgivings that shaped his attitudes toward all the arts. Fry, who was also a painter, was becoming, in Rothenstein's view, a "mere critical weigher and balancer of schools and opinions." When the Oxford electors met, Fry, to his great disappointment, was passed over.[22]

Rothenstein also had had disappointments. In May 1910 his one-man show in London attracted few purchasers. Fry wrote an appreciative article for the *Nation,* but this kind gesture brought few results. The critical consensus was that Rothenstein's pictures were too realistic, not charming enough to have popular appeal. As Fry had indicated, Rothenstein dispensed with chiaroscuro and left the viewer no place to hide; his pictures had to be accepted as an uncompromising presentation of reality.[23]

Both the Slade appointment and this show figured in the

21. Rothenstein to Fisher, March 8, 1910. Fisher Papers: Bodleian Library, Oxford. H. A. L. Fisher (1865–1940), Fellow and Tutor, New College, Oxford; Member, Royal Commission on Public Services of India, 1912–1915; Vice-Chancellor, Sheffield University, 1912–1916; President, Board of Education, 1916–1922; President, British Academy, 1928–1932.

22. See Virginia Woolf, *Roger Fry: A Biography* (London, 1940), p. 151.

23. See Fry, "The Art of Mr. Rothenstein," *The Nation* (London), 7 (1910), 382.

background of Rothenstein's Indian tour, but it was not a quixotic journey. Since his Paris days, Asian art and aesthetic theory had interested him. An Apsaras figure (the celestial nymph of Hindu mythology) in Degas' studio remained a touchstone of the mythic quality, the massive yet vital style of Indian sculpture and painting. Long before 1910, friends and acquaintances had found in him an esoteric quality, which they characterized as "Eastern," lightened and brightened by a refreshing dryness of wit and of manner.[24]

In 1911, after his return from India, Rothenstein showed his Indian drawings and two of his Indian paintings in London. Again Roger Fry commended him for work distinguished by dignity and forthrightness rather than souvenir prettiness.[25] But Mrs. Christiana Herringham, a pillar of The India Society and the organizer of two artistic safaris to India to copy the Ajanta Cave paintings, was severely critical: "I thought myself that he would also *paint* Indian pictures with that intense humanity which he put into those early pictures—and the doll's house. I would *not* go to India I think. I would do what can be done here. He will find his life dreadfully broken up—if that spell comes on him. Ruskin says you never paint well except what you have known from your childhood."[26]

Fry also had felt "that spell" of India. He belonged to The India Society at least through 1912, and Mrs. Herringham's Ajanta drawings made him envy Rothenstein his trip to India.[27] But events moved the two men apart. In 1911 Fry was offered the directorship of the Tate Gallery; it paid poorly, and he refused it and took instead an offer to use the Grafton Galleries again that autumn. He hoped to begin a series of annual shows with progressive English painters and Conti-

24. See *The Letters of Sir Walter Raleigh, 1879–1922*, ed. Lady Raleigh (New York, 1926), I, 270–271.
25. Fry, "Plastic Design," *Nation*, 9 (1911), 396.
26. Christiana Herringham to Alice Rothenstein, July 7, 1911. RP:HL. Lady Herringham (1853–1929), artist and translator, wife of Sir Wilmot Herringham (1855–1936), distinguished physician, Vice-Chancellor, University of London, 1912–1915. Her Ajanta expeditions, 1909–10 and 1910–11; in 1910–11, Abanindranath Tagore sent, at his own expense, five Indian student assistants. "The Doll's House": oil by Rothenstein (1899);Tate Gallery, London.
27. Fry to Rothenstein, April 2, 1910. RP:HL.

nental Postimpressionists side by side, and he asked Rothenstein to exhibit. Again Rothenstein declined. He felt that Postimpressionism was abandoning that "reality" for which he had expressed such concern at the Royal Society of Arts.

On September 30, 1911, Rothenstein set off for the United States while Fry labored on at the Grafton Galleries. There were obstacles and delays, alarums and excursions, but the second Postimpressionist Exhibition opened on October 5, 1912, and the uproar was greater than before.[28] Rothenstein by then was back in London, but he devoted most of that summer to Tagore, and in his letters to Tagore written that autumn and winter there is not a word of events at the Grafton Galleries. Not a word, that is, about the exhibition itself, but almost every letter reflects aesthetic and personal issues raised by the advent of Postimpressionism, while Rothenstein settled down to the long process of examining them after his own forthright and uncompromising fashion.

TAGORE IN 1911

If Postimpressionism dominated London's art circles between 1910 and 1912, in Bengal the great fact of 1911 was the Coronation Durbar during which King George V canceled Lord Curzon's 1905 order for Bengal Partition and announced Government's plan to move the capital from Calcutta to a new center at Delhi. This was a stunning psychological and political victory for the Bengali *bhadralok*—the "cultured people," in effect and in fact the educated elite of Bengal. Since 1903, when Curzon as Viceroy proposed Partition, the Government of India, Whitehall, and Parliament had been held at bay by this miscellany of middle-class groups bound by cultural ties that often frayed and sometimes parted altogether.

In the forefront of the protesters had been the patrician Bengali poet, Rabindranath Tagore, making speeches, writing articles, marching through the Calcutta streets at the head of crowds who sang his patriotic songs. Foreigners might not catch all the Bengali words, but the tunes were unmistakably incendiary. Speeches, articles, processions, and songs were

28. See Michael Holroyd, *Lytton Strachey: A Critical Biography* (New York, 1967–68), II, 70–71.

banned as seditious, but this did little to curb "Indian unrest" in Bengal.[29]

The title of J. H. Broomfield's study, *Elite Conflict in a Plural Society*, neatly summarizes the predicament of the bhadralok in this situation. Centuries before the British Raj, Bengal had had a recognized elite distinguished by mores, modes of behavior, and above all by "belief in the inferiority of manual occupations."[30] In the nineteenth century this group had virtually exclusive access to English-language education and a maximum exposure to English books that imported the ideas of the Utilitarian philosophers; of Shakespeare, Milton, and the Romantic Poets; of Emerson, Whitman, and Thoreau. Some rode this cultural tidal wave joyfully and not too cautiously; others closed their eyes and clung to conservative absolutes; still others, among them the Tagores, tried to harness its powers by making deliberate choices and syntheses of old and new, indigenous and foreign traditions. Amid this intellectual and emotional confusion, Lord Curzon's Partition order raised an issue upon which the educated bhadralok could unite for a time and argue eloquently—in English—with the English.

The really serious "elite conflict" was still to come, for if Bengal was not actually cut in two, Bengali society in 1911 was decidedly "plural." In addition to divisions between British and Bengalis, Hindus and Muslims, a schism now deepened between bhadralok Extremists—the terrorists and bomb-throwers—and parliamentarian Moderates. For decades this controversy would hamper even the most intelligent and sympathetic efforts to heal wounds inflicted during the long fight against Partition.[31]

Where was Rabindranath Tagore when Partition was annulled in 1911? Like Rothenstein, who had helped to carry the news of Impressionism from Paris to London in the 1890's but stood aside when Postimpressionism arrived, Tagore was

29. "Indian unrest": comprehensive term for disturbances in India, formalized by Valentine Chirol in *Indian Unrest* (London, 1910).

30. J. H. Broomfield, *Elite Conflict in a Plural Society: Twentieth-Century Bengal* (Berkeley and Los Angeles, 1968), p. 6.

31. Broomfield follows this controversy from Partition projected in 1903 to Partition accomplished in 1947.

standing aside, certain of his convictions but joining no faction. He had repudiated Extremist terrorism; he had criticized Moderate lack of a coherent program; his Santiniketan school, with its unorthodox educational philosophy and methods, was suspect among both British officials and conservative Bengalis. This isolation may explain why, when Rothenstein visited the Tagores' home in January 1911, no one told him that this extraordinarily attractive member of the family was a leading exponent of the "real Indian literature" in Bengal.[32]

Tagore was first and last a poet. He habitually expressed himself by metaphor and symbol. The lyric, that most Romantic, most personal mode of poetic expression, was the genre most congenial to him. He had been brought up in a tradition avowedly and unabashedly Romantic; he responded instinctively to the Vaishnava lyricists and the Bāul singers who were the authentic individual voice of medieval Bengal. This voice still sounded, faint but familiar and reassuring, amid forced introductions to modernity and industrialization.[33]

Contrasts and contradictions of temperament and training had intensified Rabindranath's need for a uniquely personal mode of expression. He was the youngest of fourteen children, his childhood a mixture of extreme loneliness and vicarious stimulation as observer of the literary, musical, and theatrical activities of his elders. He hungered for knowledge and new experiences, but rebelled utterly against formal schooling and was so chronic a truant that his elders finally educated him at home. He was both attracted and disconcerted by his patriarchal father, Debendranath, who was a mixture of ascetic and hardheaded pragmatist. The Tagores, although prominent in Calcutta, were somewhat outside the mainstream of community life, a fact of his own life that Rabindranath bore continually in mind. As Brahmans, they were said to be impure because an ancestor supposedly smelled meat cooked for Muslims. As or-

---

32. See *MM* II, 249. "Santiniketan school": small experimental school on a tract owned by the Tagores, near Bolpur, north of Calcutta. "*Santi*": peace; "*niketan*": abode.

33. On Bengali Vaishnava tradition, see Edward C. Dimock, Jr., Introduction to *In Praise of Krishna: Songs from the Bengali,* trans. Edward C. Dimock, Jr., and Denise Levertov (Garden City, N.Y., 1967), pp. vii-xx. On Bāul singers see Dimock, "Rabindranath Tagore, 'The Greatest of the Bāuls of Bengal,'" *The Journal of Asian Studies,* 19 (1959–60), 33–51.

thodox Hindus, identification with the Brahmo Samaj, Ram Mohun Roy's Hindu reform movement, put them beyond the pale.[34] As Bengalis, they were often suspect because they were too fascinated by Western ideas. Rabindranath's withdrawal from the anti-Partition protest made hardcore nationalists regard him as a turncoat.

The course of his personal life had been erratic. A stay in England from October 1878 to February 1880, which the family hoped might make a barrister of him, disappointed them; he found the climate cold and the law repellent. A brief visit in 1890 quickened but did not focus his curiosity about life in the West. Until the age of thirty he remained the precocious young man of letters in Calcutta, writing, discussing poetry, editing and contributing to journals launched and largely supported by the Tagores. In 1891 Debendranath despatched this grown son, now married and the father of three children, to supervise family estates in East Bengal. For the first time Rabindranath was close to Bengali peasants; here he began to write the short stories that mark the beginning of modern Bengali short fiction.[35] He was still his father's subordinate, but with a freedom and a financial security enjoyed by few poets in East or West. After 1901 he lived away from Calcutta, and away from his father, at Santiniketan, where he concentrated upon providing his sons and a few other pupils with the freedom and delight in learning so deplorably absent from his own formal schooling.

Rabindranath's intensely personal, intensely Romantic outlook and his comparatively independent life style contributed to a pattern repeated, with variations, throughout his life: a restless search for like-minded persons, an impetuous emotional response often leading to equally impetuous rejections, and a dislike for administrative detail. Like a very long pendulum, his moods swung between restlessness that drove him out to see the world, and a gnawing homesickness that seized him whenever he felt that foreign involvements had driven him beyond his depth. In his poems, essays, fiction, and letters, the bird and

34. See de Bary, *Sources of Indian Tradition*, pp. 604–615.
35. See Mary M. Lago, "Modes of Questioning in Tagore's Short Stories," *Studies in Short Fiction*, 5 (1967), 24–36; "English Literature and Modern Bengali Short Fiction: A Study in Influences," unpub. diss. University of Missouri, 1969.

the nest are a recurring metaphor: the bird winging away beneath the open sky, and the nest receiving the weary wanderer at dusk.

After 1912 Tagore undoubtedly justified his travels by idealizing their purpose. This idealization, increasingly marked after 1920, was itself justification for a flight from sheer loneliness. His wife had died in 1902, his daughter Renuka in 1903, his father in 1905, and his younger son Somendranath in 1907. Rabindranath never went abroad alone. Companions must, he insisted, attend to practical details of travel, but some of those whose passage he paid needed more guidance than Tagore did. For a time new surroundings would divert him. Then the world was suddenly too much with him; the pendulum would swing and the reaction set in; the trip was all a terrible mistake, and he longed for the nest that was Santiniketan. But sometimes even he could not break away, and this was at the heart of his dilemma, for he knew that a time would come when he must have the stimulation of society.

In 1915, a crucial year in his literary relations with the West, he published a poem whose title, "The Freedom of Separation," summarized his desires and his predicament.[36] But continued separation from society is not freedom for the artist and certainly was not for Tagore, for Bengal was his subject: Bengal past, present, and future; Bengal in all her relations at home and abroad. Separation from Bengal was not the path to freedom but, as for Shelley's Alastor, to artistic death by stagnation. Tagore fretted and worried and longed for a simple solution to the problem, but he knew in his heart that this could never be.

GITANJALI: THE PARADIGM

In the summer of 1912 Thomas Sturge Moore wrote to Robert Trevelyan about an evening party at the Rothensteins':

> Yeats and Rothenstein had a Bengalee poet on view during the last days I was in London. I was first privileged to see him in Yeats' rooms and then to hear a translation of his poems made by himself and read by Yeats in Rothenstein's drawing room. His unique subject is "the love of

36. See Letter 90, note 1.

God." When I told Yeats that I found his poetry preposterously optimistic he said "Ah, you see, he is absorbed in God." The Poet himself is a sweet creature beautiful to the eye in a silk turban, he likes Keats and Wordsworth best of English poets, has read everything including my work. It is a pleasure merely to sit beside him, he reposes the mind and the body. Speaks very little, but looks beneficent and intelligent. The poems read were little pieces. Dealing each one with some image in a narrative biographical way. "He felt very nice all day and suddenly realised that his friend God had been walking about with him unperceived" or suchlike themes sometimes vastly fetching. The elect like children play by the sea building castles making boats of leaves (their dreams and hopes) the sea goes on causing wrecks and disasters far and wide but they are always glad of him as a background to their play. The stars sang together everybody listened, suddenly snap a string of an instrument broke. Some one cried one of the stars had disappeared. And all began to hunt about for the missing star. Such is the origin and nature of evil but the stars sing to one another "Why is there all this hunting and turmoil among our listeners" the Choir of Perfection is complete now as ever it was. He is popular in Bengal, his brother is a Rajah, his name Tagore, he makes a poem every day when he can, sets it to a tune and beckons to a friend who learns it from him then goes away from house to house teaching it to all who want to learn it over the countryside. He is the wrong side of 50. The poems (translations by himself) will be published in the autumn.[37]

More than all the panegyrics published later, this candid, hastily written account captures the simplicity, the tranquil good will of that evening. Here are the elements of the incipient Tagore legend: his radiant appearance, his familiarity with the English poets, the Blakean overtones of his own poems, his prolific output of lyrics and their popularity in Bengal. It is all here, fresh and unhackneyed, but also oversimplified and over-

37. Sturge Moore to Trevelyan [June 30? 1912]. Thomas Sturge Moore Papers: University of London Library. Sturge Moore (1870–1944) and Robert Trevelyan (1872–1951), poets and neoclassical dramatists.

romanticized. It is the stereotyped Tagore, the sage from the East. He had only to sit quietly, with mixed feelings of diffidence and curiosity, and the stereotype dropped neatly, snugly into place around him.

There can be no doubt that he projected a unique aura. Frances Cornford met him in Cambridge in July 1912, and her impression of him would be echoed by countless others in years to come:

> I must write and tell you both what a wonderful thing it has been to see Tagore. I now understand all you say. He *is* like a saint, and the beauty [and] dignity of his whole being is wonderful to remember . . . [and] made me feel that we in the West hardly know what real gentleness and tenderness are. With us they are so often mixed with sentimentality and weakness. But with them it goes with power and dignity and is most extraordinary—a sort of revelation. I can now imagine a powerful and gentle Christ, which I never could before. He says [that] in India for 10 years except you he never saw an English person. *What* are the English doing? We are blind barbarians sometimes.[38]

"A saint," "revelation," "powerful and gentle Christ": a conditioned Western response to the appearance of sanctity and uncommon knowledge. Long exposure to Biblical and Hellenic tradition had given rise to notions that beards and long robes are *de rigueur* the apparel of prophets, and the relation with India had intensified in many Englishmen, sometimes very sophisticated ones, suspicions that India knew something that England did not know and ought, for her own good, to learn. Tagore loved fun and laughter—he had a sparkling wit—but, alas, there in the drawing room he was the wisdom of the East personified! He lacked the courage, or the discourtesy, to break up this stereotype. Politely, unwisely, he accepted the West's demand that he symbolize something missing from its own cul-

---

38. Frances Cornford to Rothenstein [July 15, 1912]. RP:HL. Frances Darwin Cornford (1886–1960), granddaughter of Charles Darwin, wife of Francis Cornford (1874–1943), Cambridge classicist. " . . . for 10 years . . . an English person": unlikely in a literal sense; he perhaps meant that he had not cultivated friendships with Englishmen.

ture. Rothenstein learned to detest this popular image of his friend, but to many who never felt the direct warmth of Tagore's personality, to would-be mystics and idealists who sat solemn and dependent at his feet, a symbol he remained.[39]

Like the poet, the poems had an immediate appeal. Rothenstein sent some to Stopford Brooke, who replied,

> I have been deeply impressed by the poems. Mysticism of this lofty and profound kind is at root similar all over the world and this accounts for the strange unity of the East and West in these poems, and makes them ready to find a sympathetic home among that large, quiet and silent group of English people who do not talk against any form of materialism, but think and feel apart in stillness of the eternal matters. I wonder if he would let them be published. They would not make a stir, but the book would be loved by a great number whose love would be worth having, and would be a delicate companion of quiet hours. Now it is full of poetry—"bright shoots of everlastingness"— and I am often carried away into the infinite with a whirling pleasure.[40]

At first glance the poems seemed like the poet, gentle, otherworldly, and, as the *Athenaeum* noted, "of a trance-like beauty." But the poems of *Gitanjali* are strung upon interrelated themes inherited from the Vaishnava lyricists, and these have the affective power that Western critics have since rediscovered in Donne's religious poems, in the gentle George Herbert, in Blake's mystical lyrics. They speak of the elusive relation between man and God, of the paradox of the sacred and the profane, of the desperate loneliness of the human condition. In 1912 not only the general public but many poets did not fully comprehend this, and *Gitanjali* fell without a struggle into the category of ascetic and decidedly anemic devotional literature. The reviewer for the *Athenaeum* thought that "their negation of movement and colour, and the deliberate flavourlessness of

---

39. See *MM* II, 301–302.
40. Brooke to Rothenstein, July 16, 1912. RP:HL. Stopford Brooke (1832–1916), ordained in Church of England, 1857; appointed Honorary Chaplain to the Queen, 1876; seceded from Church of England, 1880. "Bright shoots": Henry Vaughan, "The Retreat," line 19, in his *Silex Scintillans*.

their simplicity are appropriate to the vein of essentially Oriental mysticism which supplies throughout the poet's inspiration." It was Mr. Yeats in his Introduction who supplied life and breath by being "eloquent" and "impetuous."[41]

Yet warning signs were posted at the outset of Tagore's career that he would become more than The India Society's protégé. By far the most important of these was the report in which Charles Whibley, as reader for the London Macmillans, recommended that they issue a commercial edition of *Gitanjali* to succeed The India Society's small private one. *Gitanjali* came to Whibley as one among many manuscripts, and he commented as follows:

> I think I had better consider the work of this poet separately.
> The book, whose title stands at the head of this page, is the book already published by the India Society. I may say at once that I think it is very good. Rabindra Nath is a real poet, and he has translated his own poems into beautiful English. He is obviously a student of the English Bible, and has modelled his style upon the Song of Solomon and other books of the Old Testament. He is also not without a knowledge of Western poetry, and he makes excellent use of the refrain and other artifices. He has a very real sympathy with children, and if you would like to read what seems to me an admirable specimen of his work, turn to Number 60, "On the seashore of endless worlds" etc. . . .
> The unpublished manuscripts of the same author, which you sent me yesterday, vary greatly in kind and value. In the first place there is a mass of poems, resembling in character those already printed. These are of great worth. Then there is a collection of essays and short stories, badly

---

41. *"Gitanjali (Song-Offerings)," The Athenaeum* (London), November 16, 1912, p. 583. Tagore, *Gitānjali* [Song-Offering] (1910), in his *Rabindra-Racanābali* [Rabindranath's Works] (Calcutta, 1964–66), XI, 1–124: fifty-one poems selected for inclusion in *Gitanjali (Song-Offerings)* (London, 1912): in his *Collected Poems and Plays* (New York, 1958), pp. 1–37. *Gitanjali (Song-Offerings)* comprises selections from ten volumes of Tagore's Bengali poems and therefore does not parallel *Gitānjali*.

translated, which I think may for the present be neglected. Then there are a certain number of plays or dramatic dialogues which consciously or unconsciously recall Maeterlinck, which are of undoubted interest.

Obviously you cannot publish all these at once. A large volume of poems, delicate as these, would be an artistic mistake. Here, indeed, the half is greater than the whole. What I would suggest to you is this: I would take the already printed volume and publish it with Yeats's preface. Then if that were a success, you might publish another volume of verse, carefully edited by the author and possibly also a volume of dramatic dialogues. In the meantime I do not think you could run any risk by publishing Gitanjali, and you could have the satisfaction of introducing to English readers a real poet.⁴²

Like Sturge Moore's description of Tagore at the Rothensteins', Whibley's report mixes accuracies, inaccuracies, and unintended forecasts. The Vaishnava lyric, not the English Bible, was Tagore's model. Tagore, a song writer, was a master of "the refrain and other artifices." Whibley was quite correct about his sympathy with children, and "Number 60" is the poem that Sturge Moore had paraphrased for Trevelyan as "The elect like children play by the sea."⁴³ The "mass of poems" comprised the unpublished translations that Tagore was sending periodically to Rothenstein. The "essays and short stories" were probably translations published at intervals since 1907 in the *Modern Review* and, perhaps, lectures that Tagore was even then writing in English. "Dramatic dialogues" is apt, but it is unlikely that Tagore recalled Maeterlinck or any other Western playwright.

By all odds Whibley's most important statement is his prophetic warning that "the half is greater than the whole" and that publishing too much too quickly would be "an artistic mistake."

42. Whibley to Macmillan, Macmillan Reader's Reports, vol. F [November 1912], pp. 484–485. Macmillan Company Papers: Macmillan and Co., Ltd., London. Charles Whibley (1859–1930), journalist and critic.
43. Tagore, prefatory poem, *Shishu* [Child] (1903), in *R-R*, IX [3–4]: "On the Seashore," *The Crescent Moon* [*Shishu*] (London, 1913): in *CPP*, pp. 41–42.

John Masefield, when asked to read Tagore's plays, had already said much the same thing:

> I doubt if we have a sufficiently delicate instrument for them on our stage; they would need the most subtle handling: and then all, with the exception of the Post Office, are exceedingly brief, and would play not more than twenty or twenty five minutes; the Post Office perhaps half an hour, not more. If they could be done by children, I think their delicacy and grace could be kept, if the theatre were small; but I fear that they would lose so much, if done in the accustomed London way, that the production would be a failure. . . .
>
> I keep in this to the two or three practical points which occur to me, that the plays are short and difficult to do fittingly, and also that they are written for a stage and an audience strangely unlike our own; a great deal of the Chitra play would have to be cut. Our people could not get effects out of dialogue of that kind; the plant won't transplant.[44]

"The plant won't transplant": in later correspondence about the plays, Yeats would say that only *The Post Office* would appeal to a Western audience.[45]

J. D. Anderson, a man of wit, perception, and personal experience of Bengal that included a knowledge of Bengali literature, pointed out that the principal hazard in the reception of Tagore's translated works came not from those who knew the ways of poetry and poets, but from those who did not. From Cambridge, Anderson wrote Rothenstein:

> I am glad to know that the most distinguished of Bengali men of letters is having a good time and is appreciated by

---

44. Masefield to Rothenstein, October 7, 1912. RP:HL. John Masefield (1878–1967), poet and playwright, Poet Laureate, 1930–1967. "Post Office": Tagore, *Dākghar* [Post Office] (1912), in *R-R*, XI, 379–406: *The Post Office*, trans. Devabrata Mukerjea (Dundrum, County Dublin, 1914): in *CPP*, pp. 177–200. "Chitra play": Tagore, *Citrāngadā* [Chitrangada] (1892), in *R-R*, III, 157–200: *Chitra: A Play in One Act* (London, 1913): in *CPP*, pp. 119–138.

45. See Letter 20, note 1.

his English friends. Only yesterday I met a lady who had travelled widely if not wisely in India and had never heard that there was any modern literature in India at all. One cannot well blame her, for the Tower of Babel has borne bitter fruit for those to whom the learning of languages is a toilsome task, and even such linguists as the late E. H. Palmer cannot master *all* languages. That is where *your* art has the advantage of appealing to all races—more or less, though even in painting there are national idiosyncrasies and national prejudices.[46]

Anderson had summarized the future. The West's stereotype of the sage from the East, the knowledge of the knowledgeable and the ignorance of the ignorant, the artistic idiosyncrasies and prejudices of India and of the West, all would converge upon Tagore's delicate poems. The plant that would not transplant, the half that was greater than the whole, must now justify its presence on foreign soil.

46. Anderson to Rothenstein, June 29, 1912. RP:HL. James D. Anderson (1852–1920), Indian Civil Service, 1875–1900, then University Lecturer in Bengali, Cambridge. E. H. Palmer (1840–1882), brilliant non-academic linguist who went to Egypt in 1882 on a secret mission, and was captured and shot by Arabs.

Prologue   August 9, 1941

William Rothenstein to Rathindranath Tagore

> Far Oakridge, Gloucestershire
> August 9, 1941

My dear Rathindranath—to-day I read of your dear father's peaceful end in The Times, & my mind goes back over the years to the days when I first knew him at your family house, when he came to England & joined us, that wet but happy summer, here at Oakridge. Since then he has become a world figure, symbol of all that is noble & great in India, the interpreter of India's soul. But I think of him as the genial & inspiring friend & companion, with whom I spent some of the happiest hours of my life, witty, wise & delightfully fanciful; & the friend, too, with whom I could exchange my deepest thoughts, who gave me the riches of his own mind with complete generosity. That meeting at Jorasanko brought 31 years of a wonderful friendship. Only once was this disturbed by a passing breeze, when, after the war, your dear father preferred German to English support for his great scheme for a model University.

One memorial of our close friendship remains—the letters I had from him over the space of years, which will, so long as I live, keep his enchanting sense of life fresh & vital, & will prove a precious legacy to my children, & their children.

But what memories you must all have! So rich & fruitful a life, so much love given & received! and upon his single shoulders the genius & honour of India! Tributes to the inspiring influence he had the world over will be coming to you from all sides. You will be glad to know that England does full justice to his greatness, in public expression & in private homage.[1] I send you & your dear wife, as to Abanindranath, the expression of deep affection from us all. Ever yours, dear Rathindranath

William Rothenstein

1. See "Sir Rabindranath Tagore, Death in Calcutta," *The Times* (London), August 8, 1941, p. 4.

I 1910-1911 Letter 1

Rothenstein in India

Travel arrangements were the least of the complications attending Rothenstein's journey. "Unrest in India" caused officials to review the credentials of all travelers to South Asia. The India Office was frankly afraid, Rothenstein discovered, "that my sympathy for Indians and for things Indian would encourage the Nationalists . . . ; I must promise to keep in touch with the officials and to this end [Sir Richmond Ritchie] provided me with letters to Provincial Governors."[1]

It was as well that the India Office knew nothing of Rothenstein's connection with a celebrated sedition case of 1910, a connection altogether innocent, but probably sufficient to put an end to his plans. In April, Constance Garnett asked him to help resist the extradition to India of a young Nationalist agitator, Vinayak Savarkar. She had heard, Mrs. Garnett wrote, "that you are much interested in the Indian national movement. This encouraged me to try to enlist your sympathies." Her own sympathies had been enlisted by her son David, who had met the agitator in London. "[Savarkar] has been living in England since 1906," Mrs. Garnett told Rothenstein, "and so cannot be regarded as a 'fugitive from justice,' since the 'sedition' is alleged to have been committed recently. This makes it important as a test case, for if the extradition law is interpreted so as to enable Indians to be tried in India—under the special laws now in force there—for acts committed here, it comes practically to extending that repressive legislation to England as well." Would Rothenstein help, "either with money or by writing to other people who might be willing to help"? He responded with a "good warm letter about Savarkar." He must have collected money too, for Mrs. Garnett advised him to send it to her or to the young man's lawyer: "It is just possible that you may prefer

1. *MM* II, 232. Sir Richmond Ritchie (1854–1912), Permanent Under Secretary of State for India.

not to have your help and sympathy in this case spoken of too freely—as you are intending to go to India. It is extraordinary how blind the official world is, how wanting in any feeling [of] English honour in the Indian question."[2]

For nearly four months Rothenstein observed the Indian question on its home ground. He spent two days at Mrs. Herringham's camp near the Ajanta Caves, then moved on to Udaipur, Jalgaon, and Chitor. One must, he told one friend, "take the physical beauty of the world as the whole world, if one is to travel in peace. To look at other aspects of life is to be faced by the insurmountable difficulties, not of the British Government of India, but of life itself. I always find when travelling alone that one's views become very much more abstract; the things which bind us to the more intimate sides of life are no longer there—that is why, I suppose, travel is regarded as an educational thing."[3]

At Chhatarpur, in Central India, Rothenstein's propensity for the abstract earned him a warm welcome from the Maharaja, who was a cultural hybrid with the Western elements very imperfectly assimilated. Discussions of religion and philosophy took priority at court; lesser officials more or less looked after mundane matters. "The M. is a touching person," Rothenstein wrote to his wife, "very intelligent, I fear not very moral, and distinctly neurotic. His devan—his first minister—has an awful time, as the M. won't listen to business or be bothered by affairs unless he is just in the mood." He was in a mood, however, to entertain Rothenstein, who

> found a stage set up, a cushion and a mattress in front of it, where I was shown, and behold, a religious passion play was produced for my benefit, I alone forming the audience.

2. Constance Garnett to Rothenstein, April 20, 26, May 13, 1910. RP:HL. Vinayak Savarkar (1883–1966), Maharashtrian Nationalist and Hindu revivalist; London resident, 1906–1910; President, Hindu Mahasabha, 1919–1925. The Garnetts: Edward (1868–1937), writer and editor; Constance (1861–1946), first English translator of Gogol, Turgenev, Dostoevsky; David (1892–   ), novelist, editor, critic. David's sympathies drew him into a preposterous scheme to rescue Savarkar from Brixton Gaol; Indian accomplices abandoned him in Paris, whence Edward rescued his exhausted and disillusioned son. (See David Garnett, *The Golden Echo* [New York, 1954], pp. 136–162.)

3. Rothenstein to Margaret Woods, November 25, 1910. RP:HL.

William Rothenstein in India

What would Craig—or Albert—have given to see it? It was a mystery play, with dancing and wonderful music—the life of Krishna; there was beautiful dancing and most moving hieratic acting and the dresses were magnificent. It seemed so absurd that no one else should be there—and to-night another play is to be acted again for my benefit![4]

He was seeing Vaishnava belief personified as the Lord Krishna—not the warrior Krishna, Arjuna's divine charioteer of the *Bhagavad Gita,* but Krishna the mischievous boy of Vrindavan and lover of the milkmaid Radha. Rothenstein would encounter this pair again, lyrically transmuted into the dialogue of God and the human soul, in the poems of *Gitanjali.*

Nevertheless, his emotions became very mixed. Although "this is like a wonderful summer," with Christmas approaching Rothenstein began to feel twinges of homesickness. He "has never known a moment's boredom" in India, but begged for more news of home and Hampstead neighbors: "I don't think anyone realises how absolutely cut off one is from news in a place like this; at Benares, I shall be in touch with the world again." His expenditures nagged at his conscience and reminded him that a recent exhibition of his work at Manchester had brought in less than he had hoped for: "I am a little disappointed about Manchester of course; one can't help having hopes and dreaming dreams of comfort and peace." He was exhilarated by the Indian scene and depressed by everyone else's apparent disregard of it: "I have met no single person who has any notion of the beauty of India—everyone is surprised at the statement of the existence of anything in that direction outside Cashmere." And then the subject of Manchester returned to vex him: "I am disappointed about Manchester—thus far and no farther is always my fate. I never seem to get beyond the point of hand to mouth existence—there I stick. And again, the

4. William to Alice Rothenstein [November 1910], quoted by Robert Speaight in *William Rothenstein: The Portrait of an Artist in His Time* (London, 1962), p. 238. Gordon Craig (1872–1966), stage designer. Albert Rothenstein (later Rutherston) (1881–1953), William's younger brother, painter, theater designer; Ruskin Master of Drawing at Oxford, 1929–1949. (See also J. R. Ackerley, *Hindoo Holiday: An Indian Journal* [London, 1932], pp. 45–47. Journal of a stay at Chhatarpur, renamed Chhokrapur, December 28, 1923, to May 8, 1924.)

2nd largest city in England, and none of one's work attracting anyone. A hard life, but a pleasant one, as Albert would say."[5]

On December 8 he left Chhatarpur to visit Coomaraswamy, who was at Allahabad, and by December 11 he was in Benares, "the final object of my pilgrimage."[6] With a big umbrella and some biscuits he settled himself to paint on one of the river landings and promptly became an object of curiosity. A household functionary of the Maharaja of Benares asked why Rothenstein was paying passing sweepers to sit for him, instead of being paid himself to paint maharajas. But he was not interested now in maharajas. He was at last closer to the "real India" that Havell spoke of, and he found new meaning in Coomaraswamy's remark about the architecture of Udaipur: "I find the indigenous element in this art even larger than I surmised, and the Persian element very much smaller. People have a mania for thinking that everything comes from somewhere else than where you find it. I am beginning to see that the best things are always *well* rooted in the soil."[7]

Rothenstein was happy at Benares, intoxicated, almost, by the sweep and color of the riverfront scene and overwhelmed by the abundance of artistic materials. But again his feelings were mixed. He missed the "sylvan and lyrical" charm of Chhatarpur. Benares away from the riverfront was ugly and smelly, as lacking in spirituality as any Western city. He was depressed by the Americans trooping through without a backward glance on their way to or from Delhi and Agra, Lucknow and Cawnpore. He hated returning at night to the hotel filled with smug tourists: "My days here are wonderful but my evenings dreary enough. I never feel lonely when I am alone—it is this hotel life that depresses me." Rothenstein, a brilliant conversationalist when with the right people, was not a hotel-lounge type: "But I am not a hotel favourite, that is quite certain; I haven't the proper manner, or appearance, and as usual, all the people to whom I have letters are away."[8]

Not quite everyone, for Sir Harry Stephen, Lady Stephen, and

5. William to Alice Rothenstein, December 5, 1910. RP:HL.
6. William to Alice Rothenstein, December 11, 1910. RP:HL. (See *MM* II, 241.)
7. Coomaraswamy to Rothenstein, October 10, 1910. RP:HL.
8. William to Alice Rothenstein, December 13 [1910]. RP:HL.

Sir John Woodroffe came to Benares from Calcutta as his guests for Christmas.⁹ But he went back to work almost at once, and ecstasies alternated with feelings of frustration:

> I am literally working all day; but I feel I am doing everything but just what is most worth doing—things are quite hopelessly noble and grand, and I don't seem to get near what I see when I am not working. You know my abominably pedantic method of matching tones and colours and trying to get solidity; and painting stones on a wall in the sun when the most wonderful figures are passing up and down all day seems a fearsome waste of my opportunities. But getting people to sit quietly is very difficult, and I am always attracted by figures and architecture combined. Unhappily the most impressive things are difficult of approach —as usual I know, after 3 weeks painting, what I ought to have begun; but to leave what one has laboured over seems difficult—it is the old old story, but this time it seems such a serious one. Here I am in living Greece and living Egypt, and there is no reason in the world why I should not do what is all ready waiting round me—of course I hope I may still touch the fringe of some sari, but it bruises my heart to see what I see and feel I express so little of it.¹⁰

Rothenstein did not intend to visit Calcutta. He asked Abanindranath Tagore to join him or send a pupil to Benares. Abanindranath replied that it was examination time and no one could come. Instead, he urged, "Do visit Calcutta, many members of our Art Society are really anxious to meet you and get your advice regarding the *working of this art movement* of ours. Calcutta is most uninteresting city but we will show you collections of old Indian pictures and Bronzes which are unique in India. All of us expecting to meet you, we have heard of you from so many friends in England that I am sure you will be quite at your ease in this wretched *metropolis!*"¹¹

  9. Sir Harry Stephen (1860–1945), Judge of the High Court, Calcutta, 1901–1914. Sir John Woodroffe (1865–1936), Puisne Judge of the Calcutta High Court, 1904–1922.
  10. William to Alice Rothenstein, December 28, 1910. RP:HL.
  11. Abanindranath Tagore to Rothenstein, December 16, 1910. Rothenstein Papers: India Office Library.

Rothenstein was there during part of January and early February of 1911. He met not only Abanindranath and Gaganendranath but their uncle Rabindranath, as well. Rabindranath sat silently while the others talked art. "I felt an immediate attraction," Rothenstein recalled, "and asked whether I might draw him, for I discerned an inner charm as well as great physical beauty, which I tried to set down with my pencil."[12]

Many of Rothenstein's most portentous and enduring friendships began thus, based upon art and instinct and needing no prompting from third parties. Rabindranath Tagore represented a type of congenial personality and an aspect of India to which the artist responded. However, their contacts in 1911 were brief and passing. On February 17 Coomaraswamy both telegraphed and wrote to Rothenstein, urging him to visit Santiniketan: "It is peculiarly attractive to know Rabindranath in his own world. The Santals are nothing much to see and will not provide good models, but some of the teachers sitting under trees with their classes out of doors will."[13] Abanindranath wrote twice, urging Rothenstein to visit Santiniketan.[14] But Rothenstein was in Darjeeling, and when he returned to Calcutta it was time to leave India. He was never to see Tagore's school under the trees at Santiniketan.

If India impressed Rothenstein, he himself had a profound effect upon many who met him there. Sir Harry Stephen found him "one of the few people my wife and I have met who really like India on its merits."[15] The Maharaja of Chhatarpur wrote, in tones of one who recalls bygone ecstasies, of his pleasure in Rothenstein's philosophical discussions.[16] The most touching, most prophetic letter came from Abanindranath, who commented obliquely upon the vacuum left by Havell's departure and the dearth of Englishmen genuinely sympathetic toward Indian art and artists. He and his students, Abanindranath wrote, would not soon forget Rothenstein: "I can not tell you how we feel toward you. Before you came I was feeling very

12. *MM* II, 249
13. Coomaraswamy to Rothenstein, February 17 [1911]. RP:HL.
14. Abanindranath Tagore to Rothenstein [February 14?], February 15, 1911. RP:IOL.
15. Harry Stephen to Rothenstein, January 7, 1911. RP:HL.
16. Shahu Chhatrapati, Maharaja, to Rothenstein, January 14, 1911. RP:HL.

very discontented with everything around me and dissatisfied with all my work but your visit has cleared all doubts and hesitations. I feel young again, see my way better and go to work with renewed life. We were both so far apart and I wonder who made us meet and why?"[17]

Who indeed? In 1945 Max Beerbohm would repeat Abanindranath's estimate of Rothenstein's worth. His friend of more than fifty years, Max Beerbohm said at the Memorial Service for Will Rothenstein, had been "a giver, a giver with both hands, in the grand manner."[18] In 1911 Rothenstein's first letter to Rabindranath Tagore began a thirty-year record of his giving full value to India, with both hands, in the grand manner.

17. Abanindranath Tagore to Rothenstein, April 26, 1911. RP:IOL.
18. Max Beerbohm, "William Rothenstein," Address at the Memorial Service, St. Martin-in-the-Fields, London, March 6, 1945 (London [1945]), p. 2.

1
Rothenstein to Tagore

4 Camac Street, Calcutta[1]
February 21, 1911

Dear Mr Tagore—I had a desperate hope that I should be able to catch the mid-day train yesterday but failed to do so. When I got back here I found a note from Mr Abanindra telling me to take the night train. Unfortunately I caught a slight chill coming away from Darjeeling which, becoming evident during the afternoon made it unwise for me to take to the train again in the evening. I don't think you can know how real my regret is & how much I looked forward to spending a few quiet hours with you. Unfortunately I leave Calcutta for Bombay to-morrow, so that I fear I shall not be seeing you again before leaving.

I do not like leaving India, now that the time has come. I have spent perhaps the fullest months of my life here & not a day has passed without my having been stirred by the beauty of the world. I feel it is not exactly India I have been seeing, not Indians, but life and my fellow men. I can't so far dissociate myself from these as to observe coldly from the outside; it is not what is curious & exceptional I have been aware of but what is touching & beautiful & above all I have felt the physical dignity of men & women wherever I have been, & the wonderful beauty of what man has been able to make out of his faith & his hope & his skill. So I feel I am going away richer by far than when I came here. It has been for me a real privilege & joy to have had the advantage of meeting you all, & I feel in going away that I am leaving kind friends behind whom I may look forward to greeting again, either here or in England.

Yourself I shall always allow myself to regard with reverence & affection, & I hope you will allow me to write to you sometimes & that you will perhaps remember that I shall be grateful for any translations of poems or stories which may appear at any time. I shall think of you often & am happy to have had the good fortune to find myself so generously welcomed by your household. Believe me with homage & sympathy most sincerely yours

W. Rothenstein

1. Address of Sir Harry Stephen, Rothenstein's Calcutta host.

II 1912-1913   Letters 2-65

Tagore in the West

Rothenstein returned to England in the middle of March 1911. In September he left for the United States, but his thoughts already turned again toward India. "I want to go back there next year," he told Bernard Berenson, "if it can be done. What I saw and felt there has had I think more effect upon my work than I expect I shall be able to show others—at any rate it has convinced me and strengthened my own intuitions about art."[1]

In 1912, however, it was not Rothenstein who went to India, but Tagore who came to England. His arrival was delayed by one of the spells of total collapse that were to punctuate all his travels abroad. Instead of leaving on March 19 he retired to the family estate at Shilaidaha in East Bengal. By mid-May he felt, not well, but well enough to travel; on May 27, with his son Rathindranath, daughter-in-law Pratima, and Somendrachandra Dev Burman, a Santiniketan student, he sailed from Bombay for Marseilles. They spent a day in Paris, which Tagore described as *shamasta ieuroper khaelāghar*, "the playroom of all Europe."[2] On June 2 they crossed from Calais, and when English began to predominate in conversations on the boat-train, Tagore felt that he was among his own people.[3] He felt he knew France through his eyes only, and therefore imperfectly, but in England his were the peculiarly intensified feelings of the person who has long envisioned a foreign country through its poetry.

This euphoria of the abstract soon yielded to the realization that he was a stranger in a strange land. Tagore had last seen England in 1890. In 1912 a roar of mechanized traffic filled the streets. Londoners had a hectic, hunted air; they were so ab-

1. Rothenstein to Bernard Berenson, September 17, 1911. RP:HL.
2. Tagore, "Landane" [In London], *Pather Shancay* [Travel Notes] (1939), in *R-R*, XXVI, 514.
3. *Ibid.* The word is *ātmiya*: "kinsman," "belonging to one's self."

sorbed in dodging motorcars that they seemed unable really to look, listen, or think about anything. He was dismayed by their singlemindedness, their relentless perseverance.

The Tagores took shelter in the Bloomsbury hotel to which Thomas Cook and Son assigned them. Hotel life, too, seemed mechanized. People came and went like puppets moved by invisible pressures of anxiety. A bell rang. The puppets went to the dining room and ate behind open newspapers. Mechanically they looked at their watches, jumped up, clapped their hats on their heads, and disappeared. Tagore tried to do as the Londoners did; he looked at his watch—but he had nothing to do, nowhere except the hotel room to disappear to, and he was not sleepy.[4] In this vast urban machine a poet was not even a spare part. He seemed to fit in nowhere.

On the second day the Tagores set out to find Hampstead.[5] Rothenstein at once found a place for the poet, within a week had moved the Tagores to Hampstead, and was introducing them to his friends from Oxford and Cambridge, London and Dublin. Very soon Rabindranath was being considered for a kind of public recognition that had inescapable political connotations. The first such gesture was the initial attempt to persuade Oxford University to give him an honorary degree. Rothenstein recalled that this was Fox Strangways' idea, and that Lord Curzon, returned from India and Chancellor of Oxford, rejected it because "there were more distinguished men in India than Tagore."[6] Fox Strangways had reported to Rothenstein as follows:

> I only had time yesterday to tell you the fact contained in the Vice Chancellor's letter. I understand that he has consulted Lord Curzon, and though I have no idea what may have passed between them, I think one may guess that the latter did not wish a University of which he is Chancellor to

---

4. Tagore, "Bandhu" [Friend], *Pather Shancay*, in *R-R*, XXVI, 516–521. A description of arrival in London and of the Rothensteins' home.

5. Tagore later gave Edward Thompson a slightly different impression. (See Thompson, *Rabindranath Tagore: Poet and Dramatist* [London, 1926], pp. 231–232.) E. J. Thompson (1886–1946), missionary teacher in Bengal, 1910–1918; later Lecturer in Bengali at Oxford.

6. *MM* II, 266. Fox Strangways wanted Oxford or Cambridge to honor Tagore, but does not mention Cambridge. The Oxford rejection may have discouraged an approach there.

take public notice of one who had added politically to the labours of the Viceroy. I feel sure the Vice Chancellor would not have written so shortly if it had been a question of deciding the case on its own merits.

I don't know exactly what the political question is—perhaps you do. But whether it is a grave one or not, I think there are many Anglo Indians who thought it so. In that case, I have been wondering since last night whether we ought to make [an India Society dinner honoring Tagore] a *public* dinner, and *advertise* it, without first putting ourselves right with the authorities. It seems to me not impossible that if Lord Curzon happens to hold strong views on the matter he might on the announcement of the dinner write and protest publicly, which would raise an unpleasant situation for R.N.T. which we should all regret.

But there would be no objection I imagine to our circularizing the members of the Society, with a view to a private dinner, or to our inviting to it any quasi-public guests we chose.

I know the idea of having the dinner at all is to bury political hatchets; but that simple motive will not necessarily be believed either by the governors or the governed in India if the dinner is advertised. But perhaps you will think me unduly sensitive in the matter of advertisement. I must confess I dread it in almost any form, and in the present case there seems to me to be a more substantive ground for the dread than mere feeling.[7]

This letter reflects a fateful anomaly in relations between England and India. Arthur Fox Strangways' brother Maurice spent thirty-one years in the Punjab, and Arthur had stayed there while he prepared to write *The Music of Hindostan*.[8] How could he have failed to understand "the political question" that caused Curzon to reject Tagore? If Arthur Fox Strangways, alert, sympathetic, and well-informed about India, was unaware of political cause and effect in events connected with Bengali Partition politics, how much more unaware was the average Englishman?

7. Fox Strangways to Rothenstein, June 12, 1912. RP:IOL.
8. Fox Strangways, *The Music of Hindostan* (Oxford, 1914).

The India Society dinner was eventually brought off in style on the evening of July 10. Keeping it a private affair obviated another political impasse: Yeats had refused to take the chair if it meant, as at a public dinner it would, proposing a toast to the King.[9] Graciously he proposed the toast to "Our Guest" and said, "To take part in honouring Mr. Rabindra Nath Tagore is one of the great events of my artistic life." His brief remarks amounted to a précis of the preface he would write two months later for *Gitanjali*. Mr. Tagore, the *Times* reported, was received "with the warmest enthusiasm."[10] Fox Strangways went home and happily wrote Rothenstein:

> The dinner was a very perfect thing—and I don't forget that it was your design, and that it worked out on the whole on the lines on which you conceived it. I feel quite sure it has done a great deal—the most that has been done yet—for the object we have at heart. What makes me think so as much as anything is that Hornell—who takes no truck with the arts—I mean quite simply, not as a gird—was very obviously pleased—if he were just a little more emotional I should have said bowled over by it. And that is a gain, because it will permeate through the Board of Education to the India Office. Also Thomas expressed himself warmly: and Walter Ford and Vaughan Williams spoke as those speak who have a window suddenly opened: Mackail said little, but I know his face, and I know he liked talking to old R.N.T. Gupta is of the earth, earthy; but he said nothing offensive and that was a great thing. But we have to thank Yeats a lot for establishing the key (if you were a musician you would know what I mean, but you will find your own analogy). I simply loved his Irish "friend" and the like, and the mystic waving of arms over the victim of the evening. And, my dear man, you were very nice; so direct and jolly, and so much what wanted saying and what I didn't know I felt till you said it. I dined with Curzon the night before, and I'll tell you about it (in private).

9. Rolleston told Yeats that the dinner would be private, whereupon Yeats promised to preside. (Yeats to Rothenstein [June 22, 1912]. RP: HL.)

10. "Dinner to Mr. Rabindra Nath Tagore: A Bengali Poet," *The Times* (London), July 13, 1912, p. 5.

I'm glad to think the old fellow will go back to his country with warm feelings in his heart: simply that, because I like him, not for any ulterior axe grinding. I'm *sure* he reached the point of view beyond these bickerings and suspicions, or not-quite-sure-nesses. And I'm bound to say I could never have conceived the sort of success this thing has been.[11]

If political frictions had to be smoothed over gently, so also did frictions generated by the collisions of forceful personalities. There was trouble between Yeats and Fox Strangways as soon as The India Society undertook to publish *Gitanjali*. Fox Strangways suggested changing a word in one of Tagore's poems, whereupon Yeats fired a broadside from Coole Park at Rothenstein:

> I have had an interminable letter from a man called Strangways suggesting alterations in Tagore's translation. He is the sort of man societies like the India Society fatten. He is a manifest goose. I want you [to] get the society to understand that I am to edit this book and that they are to send me proofs as any other publisher would. I cannot argue with a man who thinks that "the ripples are rampant in the river" should be changed because "rampant" suggests to his goose brains "opposition to something." I am very busy—I work like a clerk—and I cannot carry on a correspondence with this man. I have replied politely saying I would go carefully through the text in proof but do please see that he goes back to his pond.[12]

Fox Strangways had trodden on the tender prerogatives of a poet-editor, and Yeats was unaware that Fox Strangways also worked as hard as any clerk to get *Gitanjali* into English print.

---

11. Fox Strangways to Rothenstein, July 10, 1912. RP:IOL. W. W. Hornell (1878–1950), Professor of English, Presidency College, Calcutta, 1902–1908; appointed to Board of Education, Whitehall, 1908; Assistant Director of Special Inquiries and Reports, 1910; Director of Public Instruction, Bengal, 1913–1924. F. W. Thomas (1867–1956), India Office Librarian, 1903–1927. Walter Ford (1861–1938), Professor of Singing, Royal College of Music. Ralph Vaughan Williams (1872–1958), composer. J. W. Mackail (1859–1945), Professor of Poetry, Oxford. Sir Krishna Gupta (1851–1926), Member, Indian Council of the India Office.

12. Yeats to Rothenstein, September 7 [1912]. RP:HL.

Two months later a new controversy arose, this one involving Ezra Pound. Yeats wished to see Tagore elected to the newly constituted Academic Committee of the Royal Society of Literature, a prestigious body of which Yeats was a member. But he had received only one copy of *Gitanjali* in The India Society's edition, and he had hoped to supply copies to influential Committee members like Henry Newbolt, Gosse, and Shaw.[13] Unfortunately, *Gitanjali* cost ten shillings sixpence, Yeats's funds were low, and he could not afford the extra copies. Pound discovered that this was the case and said so to Rothenstein. This elicited a reply from Rothenstein that brought forth in turn a detailed explanation from Yeats:

> I have certainly no quarrel with you or the Society, and never asked Pound to write to you. If I had anything to say I should have written myself. I can imagine what has happened. I was ill and Pound came round to look after me. I showed him the Tagore book. We talked about your drawing and I remember praising it and praising the printing and arrangement of the book. I then discussed an old project of mine to get Tagore elected to the Academic Committee, but said the book cost 10/6 and I have been sent only one copy and so would not be able to get the people on our Committee to read it. I said "I think it very shabby of the India Society but societies are always shabby. We are all rascals in our collective capacity" or some such phrase. Pound was vehement and some days after when he came again he said, "I had to write to Rothenstein about something and I told him they should have given you more than one copy." I assumed that he had done it in the way that is customary among the faint energies of our dying European civilization, and thought no more of it. I forgot that he was an intrepid American and also at that moment full of zeal. We had had a quarrel. He had altered some poems of mine which I had given him for a review, he was London correspondent for, and I had been in a fury and threatened to wire to his editor to withdraw the poems. Then I had forgiven him. He was zealous therefore in my service. He is a headlong ragged

---

13. Sir Henry Newbolt (1862–1938), Professor of Poetry, Oxford, and Vice-President of the Royal Society of Literature.

nature, is always hurting people's feelings, but he has I think some genius and great good will. I am delighted to find by your letter that I am it seems to get two more copies —Fox Strangways had not mentioned this in the letter he sent with this one I have—but if I could have three more instead of two more I could do all I want.[14]

Then Yeats discovered that Rothenstein had enclosed Pound's letter, which referred to his Introduction to *Gitanjali*, and added a postscript:

I had written the foregoing before I discovered that you had enclosed Pound's letter. The phrase about your having "persuaded" me to do "the introduction for nothing" is most exasperating. No one persuaded me. I was very proud of the opportunity of praising so great a poet. I am very sorry you have been troubled in this way. I assure you that the sentence I gave in my letter about my being sent only one copy was all I said on the subject and I never blamed you for that, or indeed anybody in particular. I never complained of discourtesy and there has most certainly been none. I thought your secretary was being a little over economical, and that is the way of secretaries, out of zeal for the welfare of the India Society.[15]

What passed between Yeats and Pound thereafter was not relayed to Rothenstein. Ten days later Yeats wrote to Gosse, proposing Tagore for the Academic Committee. His efforts went for naught, since the Committee passed over Tagore.[16]

14. Yeats to Rothenstein, November 14 [1912]. RP:HL. "Your drawing": Rothenstein's drawing of Tagore, *Gitanjali* frontispiece. "He had altered some poems": see Noel Stock, *The Life of Ezra Pound* (New York, 1970), p. 123.

15. Yeats to Rothenstein, November 14 [1912]. RP:HL. "Pound's letter": Pound to Rothenstein, one undated page, perhaps a fragment of this letter. RP:HL.

Yeats and Rothenstein apparently gave Introduction and frontispiece for almost nothing: "I do not suppose that Yeats, any more than myself, would care to add to the expenses of the publication of Gitanjali. I myself would ask no more than the nominal fee of one guinea for the use of any portrait Macmillan would care to select." (Rothenstein to Fox Strangways, February 6, 1913. Macmillan Papers: British Museum.)

16. See *The Letters of W. B. Yeats,* ed. Allan Wade (London, 1954),

44   Imperfect Encounter

The import of the apparently trivial incident reflects the fact that Yeats expended so much time and energy trying to get Tagore admitted to a body whose recognition was a signal honor. If Pound in his peppery way was overzealous in seeking extra copies of the book for Yeats, this same zeal resulted in the first American publication of Tagore's poems and in the first genuinely critical appraisal of his work to appear in a Western journal.[17] Yeats, Pound, and Rothenstein were self-employed creative artists whose voluntary distribution of their time determined their incomes, and these were not enhanced by efforts to get a Bengali poet into the Royal Society of Literature.

An episode in the summer of 1913, after Tagore's return from the United States, illustrates what proved in the long run to be one of the most serious weaknesses in his method of dealing with his translated works: his lack of confidence in himself and in his collaborators. The principal characters in this little drama were Sturge Moore, keeping house in Hampstead with his infant daughter while his wife was on the Continent; Yeats, who made one fateful appearance in the wings; and Tagore. Events were reported by Sturge Moore in communiqués from Hampstead to Marie Sturge Moore in Lausanne and Torre Pelice.

JULY 28, 1913[18]

"Shortly after lunch Tagore and his son turned up. He wanted me to help him correct the proofs of his poems Yeats has been preparing. He said Yeats worked so slowly and missed over so many little incorrections so we worked away till tea and after tea till nearly suppertime and then he asked me to go there to lunch tomorrow to finish them. The motor car was waiting for them all the time outside. I am going tomorrow and shall press

---

pp. 572–573. In Sturge Moore's opinion, "Tagore has not been elected to the Academical Committee thanks to Gosse's malice." (Thomas to Marie Sturge Moore [July? 1913]. TSM.) See also *The Letters of Ezra Pound*, ed. D. D. Paige (New York, 1950), p. 106.

17. See Tagore, "Poems," *Poetry: A Magazine of Verse* (Chicago), 1 (1912–13), 84–86. See also Pound, *Letters*, pp. 10–11; "Rabindranath Tagore," *The Fortnightly Review* (London), 99 (1913), 571–579.

18. This and dated passages following, from postcards and letters, Thomas to Marie Sturge Moore. TSM.

London, Summer 1912
front: Somendra Dev Burman, Rabindranath Tagore, Rathindranath Tagore; *rear:* Dr. D. N. Maitra, John Rothenstein, William Rothenstein

for you to translate the children's poems. It was all hard work today and we had no ordinary conversation and only spent about 10 minutes over tea. He said Baby reminded him of Bengali little girls, no doubt a superlative compliment."[19]

JULY 29, 1913

"I have been from lunch till after 6 P.M. with Tagore, and working hard at his corrections. I think we understood each other very well indeed and that he was pleased and satisfied with the results. He says you shall translate the children's poem and he is going to dedicate the book in English to me."

JULY 30, 1913

"If you translate the children's Poems successfully I should not wonder if you could not get the new volume of Love poems etc. to translate and then the next series of Gitanjali. So you have only to go ahead. I think Tagore is quite simple and has real confidence in me, and that he wishes I had had the editing of his books rather than Yeats. I may be mistaken and it may be the effect of his politeness but I don't think I am. He had no need to bring his proofs over to me on Sunday. I had never even hinted a desire to see them or to have any say in the matter.

19. "Yeats . . . preparing": poems for Tagore's book *The Gardener* (London, 1913). Yeats had commented on these: "I have only had time to read a few so far but of these few some are of great beauty. I find some words to be changed. It is again the old difficulty 'the words that have not got their souls yet and the words that have lost their souls.'" (Yeats to Tagore, April 25 [1913]. Tagore Papers: Rabindra-Sadana, Santiniketan.) Yeats quotes a letter from Tagore to Pound; see Stock, *Ezra Pound*, p. 129. "Motor car": probably property of Harriet Moody (1857–1932), widow of the American poet, William Vaughan Moody, and the Tagores' London hostess. "Children's poems": Marie Sturge Moore hoped to translate *The Crescent Moon* into French. This introduces a project that became a fourteen-year publishing nightmare for all concerned, except, perhaps, Tagore, who seemed unaware of its complications. Rothenstein and Fox Strangways had arranged for André Gide to translate *Gitanjali*, but Yeats recommended Iseult Gonne, who thought of learning Bengali. (Yeats to Rothenstein [August 19, 1912]. RP:HL.) Then, at the Sturge Moores' request, Yeats endorsed Marie Sturge Moore's claim. (Yeats to Fox Strangways, June 16 [1913]. RP:HL.) Nevertheless, he arranged a meeting between Tagore and Iseult. (Yeats to Tagore, July 25 [1913]. R-S.)

He has given me The King [of the Dark Chamber] his other play to read . . . It is all symbolist the whole way through and I am very doubtful whether it can be possible to produce the best effects with that method."[20]

AUGUST 1, 1913

"When I got home from the dentist's yesterday I found Tagore here waiting for me. He is rather frightened about Yeats and my corrections. They are going over them together now. I shall be very curious to learn how Tagore manages. It will require great tact. It really is not at all my fault if Yeats is vexed because I never even suggested doing anything till I was asked, but I may get into hot water with Yeats all the same if Tagore is a little cowardly. 'The King' that I do not like represents what Tagore is doing now, it is more like some of Goethe's things that he did in old age than anything else."

AUGUST 2, 1913

"I am going to Tagore's on the way [to dinner on August 5 with Yeats and Iseult Gonne] to learn how matters stand between him and Yeats. . . . I am working on Tagore's children's poems."

[AUGUST 4, 1913]

"Yesterday Tagore sent a telegram to ask me to lunch there today. I had written to him because Yeats had invited me for tomorrow night and I wanted to know what had passed between them. It seems Tagore never mentioned my name and Yeats accepted all my corrections showing surprise often that he had missed over such obvious errors and apparently strengthened Tagore's confidence in me. . . . We had a little talk after tea. I like him very much and I am sorry he has so soon to go back to India."

20. "Next . . . Gitanjali": Tagore's *Fruit-Gathering* (London, 1916), before publication often referred to as "the second *Gitanjali*." Tagore, *Rājā* [King] (1910), in R-R, X, 191–266: *The King of the Dark Chamber* [trans. Kshitish Chandra Sen] (London, 1914).

This episode summarizes the pitfalls in Tagore's translation projects. There were too many translators, too many editors, and too little communication between them and the author, and the author was much too willing to dispense permissions without reference to prior agreements with his publisher. All, together with the qualities that endeared Tagore to his friends —his artless simplicity, his willingness to trust in them— established an uneasy balance of negatives and positives, of antipathies and sympathies: an imperfect encounter of cultures and individuals.

2
Tagore to Rothenstein

> 3 Villas on the Heath
> Vale of Health, Ham[p]stead
> June 7, 1912

Dear Mr Rothenstein

I send you some more of my poems rendered into English. They are far too simple to bear the strain of translation but I know you will understand them through their faded meanings. Very sincerely yours

> Rabindranath Tagore

3
Tagore to Rothenstein

> 3 Villas on the Heath [Hampstead]
> July 16, 1912

Dear Mr Rothenstein

I just heard the sad news. You know my heart is with you in your present trial. I do not know what made me sit down to translate three of my poems, all on the subject of death, directly I came back from Cambridge yesterday.[1] It seems to me that the sympathetic chords of heart are touched at some unseen communication. I feel I must send you the first one of those translations—the original of which sprang from a direct experience of death   Very sincerely yours

> Rabindranath Tagore

In desparate hope I go and search her in all corners of my room; I find her not. My house is small and what once is lost from there can never be regained. But infinite is thy mansion, My lord, and seeking her I have come to thy door. I stand under the golden canopy of thine evening sky and I lift my eager eyes to thy face. I have come to the brink of Eternity from which nothing can vanish—no hope, no happiness, no vision of a face seen through tears. Oh, dip my emptied life into that ocean, plunge it into the deepest fulness. Let me for once feel that lost sweet touch in the allness of thine universe.²

1. Rothenstein's mother had died in Bradford. "Cambridge yesterday": Goldsworthy Lowes Dickinson (1862–1932), historian, Fellow of King's College, Cambridge, entertained Tagore there on July 15. J. D. Anderson was also a guest; he told Rothenstein: "The poet's quiet dignity and modesty are very delightful, and it is easy to see why he has such extraordinary influence over the rising generation in Bengal. I am very grateful to you for having given me the chance of making the acquaintance of so distinguished and attractive a being." (Anderson to Rothenstein, July 15, 1912. RP:HL.)

2. Probably the first-draft translation, no. 5, *Smaran* [Memory] (1903), in *R-R*, VIII, 84: no. 87, *Gitanjali*: in *CPP*, p. 32. Poems on the death of Tagore's wife, Mrinalini Devi, in 1902.

4
Rothenstein to Tagore

6 Walmer Villas, Bradford
July 18, 1912

My dear Rabindro nath Babu—your letter was a comfort to me, & the poem you sent me a thing so poignantly real in its understanding that it was able to serve as a real help to my father, when I read it to him. It was a true instinct of friendship that prompted you to send it to me. It is strange that my feeling about the reality of your work should have so soon been put to the test. All I can tell you is that I have repeated things to myself which I have learned from your songs more often than any other things read, since I came here, & always with comfort. When my mother's face was hidden for the last time & my poor father & my sisters & brothers had to say goodbye to the physical aspect of my mother's touching & familiar form, I read some of your songs on death to them, & they were greatly moved by them.

We cannot, save at rare moments of insight, love the whole world. We concentrate this upon a few individuals—those who will allow us to care for them we call friends. It is not because of what we ask from them but on account of that which we give them that we need friends. A few people there are who will take nothing from us, & these we regard as our enemies & if we are wise, avoid them, for hostility is a sense which is unbalancing & destructive. One's mother is the cathedral, the mother roof, but all round lie other roofs sheltering thousands. She never wanted my love for herself alone, but she did ask with her whole nature for what it was a joy to give her, & the more I gave to her the more I found over for others. Charm & the qualities which draw men's affections to us are given to a few favoured ones only, but the power to give is in us all, & I am happy in having had the privilege of knowing so many who allow me to care for them. That I have been permitted to count you among them is something I value more than I care to tell you.

I had a dear letter from Mrs Cornford, telling me of meeting with you at Cambridge, & I am sending you two letters, one from Andrew Bradley & the second from Stopford Brooke, which you may care to read. You will be good to keep them for me, as they are not yet answered.[1]

Please remember me very kindly to your son & his wife—it is such a pleasure to us to have had the chance of getting to know them.

We return to Hampstead at the end of the week. Yours always most sincerely

W. Rothenstein

1. "Mrs. Cornford": see Introduction, note 38. A. C. Bradley (1851–1935), Professor of Poetry, Oxford, expressed pleasure at having met Tagore. (Bradley to Rothenstein, July 15 [1912]. RP:HL. See also *MM* II, 262–263.) Brooke: see Introduction, note 40.

5

Tagore to Rothenstein

> Butterton Vicarage, Newcastle, Staffordshire
> August 5, 1912

Dear Mr Rothenstein

From the above you will know my address. I am still waiting for yours, having lost the little note I got from Mrs Rothenstein.

The weather here is not an ideal summer weather but the

country round is beautiful and our host and hostess are nice people.[1] So I have nothing to complain of. But I have made a discovery since I came here that I had grown fond of Hampstead without being aware of it. The reason of it was that while there I could easily go to a place which was dear to me and it gave me a purpose in my daily life in London. You must have a central attraction if you want to save yourself from the distraction of having nothing particular to look forward to. It is really this one definite attraction that makes everything else attractive. I miss here that nucleous of love that made each of my London days so complete. I am sure that the best thing I could carry back home from my travels would be the memory of those happy days in your dear neighbourhood.

My daughter in law has the knack of making herself loved by all with her quiet ways and sweet manners. And I can see she is making her way into the heart of these good people here. The country air has done her good and all traces of the fever she had in London has left her.

I hope you are enjoying your holidays and shaking off your fatigue. I am sure the dear children are having a jolly time of it in the country.[2] When last evening the people of this house went to church leaving Pratima and myself alone in the drawingroom to have a good long talk in Bengali after a long time, the first objects of our conversation were your children. Give them our love, and kindly remember us to Mrs Rothenstein. Ever yours

Rabindranath Tagore

1. The Reverend and Mrs. William Outram, friends of C. F. Andrews (1871–1940), Fellow of Pembroke College, Cambridge, in Delhi since 1904 as a member of the Cambridge Brotherhood, in England in 1912 on home leave. Andrews arranged the Butterton visit when he found Tagore looking ill and worn in London. (See Andrews, "With Rabindra in England," *MR*, 13 [1913], 70–75.)

2. The Rothensteins were at Oakridge Lynch, a hamlet near Stroud, Gloucestershire. Tagore joined them there (see Letter 6), and, while out walking with him, William, Alice, and John Rothenstein found Iles Farm, a little farther along the valley at Far Oakridge.

6
Tagore to Rothenstein

> Butterton Vicarage, Newcastle
> August 6, 1912

Dear Mr Rothenstein

Hope you have got my telegram. Kindly write to me if it would be possible for us—myself and my daughter-in-law—to get some kind of accommodation somewhere near you, if we start from here by the afternoon train next Saturday? Our host Rev. Mr Outram has kindly volunteered to accompany us up to Birmingham where we have to change. Do you think you can come to Gloucester to guide us to the train that goes to Stroud? You know my helplessness and in a big Junction Station it is so bewildering, specially when crowd of holidaymakers are abroad.   Ever yours

> Rabindranath Tagore

7
Rothenstein to Tagore

> 6 Walmer Villas, Bradford
> October 18, 1912

My dear Rabindra Babu—what can I say to you? For months I have had something no one else could give me but yourself & now it is going to be a memory. I can't quite believe that when I come back on Sunday you will not be there.[1] You have walked so quietly into my life, yet somehow you have filled it with a new essence & I don't feel it will ever be quite the old life I shall live again. To me they have been wonderful days, these days I have spent with you. I have never I think been so near to another man, or looked so deep into the well of another's soul. What I have seen there will help me to respect & love my fellows more than ever before. So long I hope as I live this vision will remain with me. They were happy days, days I shall never forget. Your poems & your personality will bring you the love & admiration of many men & women, but somehow I feel that no one will ever know better than myself, that in loving & admiring you they are paying their homage to life itself. To have lived so closely to any one as I have been able to do to you & to have seen nothing but things that have given me faith & courage in mankind is the most wonderful of all my experiences. I can only send you all the love I have to give—this not for you alone, but for your dear son & his no less dear wife who has won the affection of all who have met her. Your name will ever be a household word among us & when you return you will I hope find as warm a fire burning in our hearth as when you left us. Ever your affectionate friend

William Rothenstein

I read your play coming down—I have had to write this in haste to catch the post—I will write you to N. York at leisure.[2]

1. Tagore sailed for New York on October 19, 1912.
2. Perhaps "plays": Rothenstein had those read by Masefield and Yeats. (See Introduction, note 44; Letter 20, note 1.)

8
Rothenstein to Tagore

11 Oak Hill Park, Hampstead
October 23, 1912

My dear Rabindra Babu—I look for you each day when my work is done—I am still not used to the idea of your being a few hundred miles away. As for thinking of you, I do a good deal of that, for you have filled my life during these last months & I go over many things in the quiet of my studio of which we talked. To-night it is so quiet & peaceful, & it seems difficult to realise that you are in an uncomfortable ship; but I can fancy your looking out upon a vast sea in the starlight, & we are all hoping daily that your voyage will be a fair one & that you will not be suffering discomfort. I cannot yet see you in New York, but I can fancy that you will find much to impress you. I wrote you a letter to the hotel which I hope you will have received, for Dr Carroll Dunham;[1] my wife was greatly upset & deeply disappointed at having to go to rehearsal on Saturday morning.

In fact she has discovered that the undertaking is too wearing & exigent a task for a householder & has reluctantly decided to give up the idea of returning to the stage.² The children speak of you daily. You all of you won their hearts. I have been going through all the translations & putting them in order. Directly Gitanjali appears I propose going to see Macmillan. I will see that all copies are sent out to your friends. You may be sure of one thing, that I will do all I can to look after your affairs here while you are away. I hope you will meet Chapman & find the Flexners in New York, & above all, that you will get the benefit from the homoeopathic doctors you hoped for.³ It is a comfort to feel that you have the good Dr Maitra with you to look after you—I have little faith in your capacity to look after yourself.⁴ Please give our affectionate greetings & love to your dear daughter-in-law, & to your son. We all look to the day when you will return to us. Kalimohon was here to-day—I have asked him to bring Ramananda Babu's son & other friends of his here next week.⁵ My regards to Dr Maitra, & my wife sends you again her deep regrets at not having been able to get to you on Saturday. Ever your friend

William Rothenstein

1. Carroll Dunham II (1858–1922), homeopathic physician who lived at Irvington-on-Hudson, New York.

2. Alice Rothenstein (1870–1958) before marriage used the stage name of Alice Kingsley.

3. John Jay Chapman (1862–1933), New York lawyer who retired in 1898 to be full-time essayist, playwright, and social critic. Dr. Simon Flexner (1863–1946), distinguished pathologist, Director of Laboratories for the Rockefeller Institute for Medical Research.

4. Dr. D. N. Maitra (1878–1950), Resident Surgeon, Mayo Hospital, Calcutta. He is the "distinguished Bengali doctor of medicine" whom Yeats quotes in his Introduction to *Gitanjali* (pp. vii–x).

5. Kalimohon Ghose (1882–1940), teacher of agriculture at Santiniketan. "Ramananda Babu": Ramananda Chatterji (1865–1943), editor, *The Modern Review*. His son Kedar Nath was enrolled at the Royal College of Medicine.

9
Tagore to Rothenstein

Herald Square Hotel, New York
October 27, 1912

Dear Friend

The first half of our voyage was frightfully rough. I promised a sonnet to the sea god if he behaved decently but I suppose he had no faith in human nature and knew I would forget all about it directly I reached land safely. However he made amends at last and we had some very beautiful days. Altogether our voyage across the Atlantic was as unsatisfactory and uninteresting outwardly as it possibly could be, still I had some moments of most profound peace and sweetness which my physical sufferings seemed to intensify than otherwise. Misery has the effect of creating a sort of a night of intense loneliness through which shine all the true lights which have been gathered in the depths of one's life. One should have occasions to know them.

We have landed in New York this morning and passed through the ordeals of the custom house. My turban attracted the notice of a newspaper interviewer and he attacked me with questions but I was almost as silent as my turban. This was my first taste of America—the custom house and the interviewer.

Each time I come to a city like New York or London I discover afresh that in my veins courses the blood of my ancesters who were forest-dwellers. The thick solitude of the crowd is oppressive to me. In London your friendship was the only refuge I had, and I clung to you with all my heart. If I had not known you I should have gone back to India not knowing Europe. It fills me with wonder when I think how by a merest chance I came to know you and in what a short time your friendship has become a part of my life.

Give our love to dear children and our warmest regards to Mrs Rothenstein.   Ever yours

Rabindranath Tagore

Mr Chapman is not in town. Dr Flexner is on his way to Europe.

10
Tagore to Rothenstein

> Herald Square Hotel, New York
> October 31, 1912

Dear Friend

Off we go to the west—to Illinois. I hope I shall get rest there for which I long. Though it is too early for me to pronounce any opinion on this country I must say I do not like it. America, like an unripe fruit, has not got its proper flavour yet. It has a sharp and acid taste. Anyhow, it hasn't proved attractive to me yet. I haven't tried to see the people to whom you have given me introduction for fear of being drawn into engagements. I am too tired to face that. You know how absurdly helpless I am in most things, that is why it takes such a long time for me to accommodate myself to strange surroundings. Either I must have a friend or solitude. To me, the crowd, like the sea, is enjoyable from a distance, but to navigate myself through it is beyond my power.

I am eagerly waiting to have some news of Dr Seal. I do hope it will be possible for him to stay in England and do his work there. I gathered from Mr Arnold that it would be quite easy for Dr Seal to get the appointment at Cromwell Road if he would only accept it.[1]

Kindly send ten copies of Gitanjali to my Illinois address when it is out. My love to you all.   Ever yours
> Rabindranath Tagore

1. Sir Brajendranath Seal (1864–1938), Principal, Victoria College, Cooch-Behar, 1896–1913; George V Professor of Mental and Moral Science, Calcutta University, 1914–1920; Vice-Chancellor, Mysore University, 1920–1930. Seal and Rothenstein had met in London during the First Universal Races Congress in 1911. (See E. Willis, "Contemporary Thought and Life: The Races Congress," MR, 10 [1911], 275–281.) In 1912 Dr. Seal went quietly to London for medical treatment, and Thomas Arnold (1864–1930), India Office adviser to Indian students in England, offered him a post at the Cromwell Road Centre for Indians. Seal wanted to stay in England but was reluctant to forego his Cooch-Behar pension.

11
Tagore to Rothenstein

508 High Street, Urbana
[November 4?, 1912]
(The above is our permanent address)

My dear friend

It is little over two weeks since I left England and it seems to me as if I have not seen you for ages. Do write to me giving me all your news.

I am staying here with Professor Brooks, and they are very kind to me. Mrs Brooks is a nice woman—I feel quite at ease with her.[1] Rathi and his wife have been staying with Professor Seymour and they have just removed to a house which they have rented for a year. It is a very attractive house, full of all kinds of convenience. Rathi has already taken his course of Biology in the college here and Mrs Seymour is helping Pratima in her English.[2] Most of the professors here are genuinely fond of Rathi and they are glad to have him back among them. That is the chief consideration for us to choose this place. This is a quiet place—has all the advantage of a village and conveniences of a town. The country round is flat and open, which has a great attraction for me, reminding me of our own scenery. It has no pronounced features in the shape of hills and valleys and for that very reason it seems to me so full of repose—and the simplicity and obvious monotonousness of the physical aspects here have the effect of setting ones mind free. It reminds me of Mr Craig's arrangement of the stage where materials are few and simple and unaggressive.[3] I have plenty of blue sky and sunlight and leisure in this little place. . . . With love to you all   I am   ever yours

Rabindranath Tagore

1. Morgan Brooks (1861–1955), Professor of Electrical Engineering and Cosmopolitan Club adviser, University of Illinois.
2. Rathindranath had received a B.Sc. degree in agriculture at Illinois in 1909. (See Mayce [Mrs. Arthur] Seymour, "That Golden Time," *Visva-Bharati Quarterly*, 25 [1959], 1–15.) Arthur Seymour (1872–1955), Professor of Spanish and French and a pioneer in the movement to provide special advisers for foreign students on American campuses. At Illinois he was Adviser, then Assistant Dean for Foreign Students, 1909–1921.

3. Gordon Craig's efforts to unclutter British stages had met with little success in England, but Tagore's use of the word "unaggressive" shows admirable grasp of his intentions.

12
Rothenstein to Tagore

11 Oak Hill Park, Hampstead
November 6, 1912

Dear friend—your letter came to give us news of you ill—not very joyful news as yet, seeing your account of the stormy voyage, but still news of your well-being. Your letter made me realise again all day long how much I am missing you. We say this, alas, to many people when we don't altogether mean it, but in your case your absence has left a very definite blank in my life. It is not merely the absence of a friend with whom I am on terms of affection, but you must remember that you brought to me certain things no man has ever given me, & no mere memory makes up for what you have taken away with you. There are many gifts we can give to one's friends, but only one is of actual value—the one of allowing him to be *himself*, & that gift you put into my hands. The quiet exaltation in which I lived with you & to which I had in a way become so accustomed cannot now so easily be kept alive. Twenty times a day I think of you & wish you here. I don't think I realised even when I thought of your leaving how much I would miss you. I am sorry that you should have missed Dr Flexner. I sent a letter to Dr Dunham, brother to my friend Dr Carroll Dunham,[1] to Dr Maitra, & another to Dr Carroll Dunham for yourself to the Hotel St Andrews, & I fear you may not have sent to enquire after any letters there. By this time none will, I take it, reach you in New York, but I hope they will find you in the peace of a college town. I don't visualise you in New York. Chapman will I trust somehow have got into touch with you. I shall await further news of you eagerly. The book is out, & looks very pure & virginal in its covering of white & gold. Directly reviews appear I shall go to see Macmillan.[2] Andrew Bradley writes with enthusiasm of the new poems—he will also by this time have

London, Summer 1912
Rabindranath Tagore with Betty, Rachel, and William Michael Rothenstein

had Gitanjali.³ Dr Seal has left, the dear man, for Mentone. Nothing has been settled yet by Arnold. Kalimohon still sits in patient contemplation—what a sweet creature he is! Your portrait is practically finished, & will be exhibited this month.⁴ In the meanwhile I will send you any reviews which may appear.

I am spending Sunday with Herbert Fisher at Oxford, & expect to see Gilbert Murray there too.⁵

The children send their dear love to you all—they speak of you so often & ask me when Mr and Mrs Tigore are coming back. My wife sends many affectionate greetings.   Yours ever

William Rothenstein

1. Edward Dunham (1860–1922), Professor of Pathology and Bacteriology, Bellevue Hospital Medical College, New York City.
2. The India Society edition appeared November 1, 1912: 500 copies for members, 250 for public sale.
3. Bradley was enthusiastic but cautious. He reminded Rothenstein that a pattern of variations on a theme is the essence of both Indian poetry and Indian music, and that many readers unused to the style might weary of the theme if suddenly surfeited with variations. (Bradley to Rothenstein, November 5 [1912]. RP:HL.)
4. See Letter 15, note 2.
5. Gilbert Murray (1866–1957), Regius Professor of Greek, Oxford.

13
Rothenstein to Tagore

11 Oak Hill Park, Hampstead
November 7, 1912

Dear friend—need I tell you with what joy I read the first review—perhaps the most important that could appear—in the Times supplement this morning?¹ Nothing I think could please you more than the quiet & emphatic appreciation of your work. It is really more than I had dared hope for from our great Tory organ, & this will show the way to other reviewers & make my talk with Macmillan, I hope, a fairly easy one. It is a great delight to us to feel that what we felt at once is shared by others, & that you have once and for all gained the ear of the West for your literature. I wonder whether Bengal will realise what your simple visit has done for its history.

I cannot help looking upon your decision to cross the seas as a momentous and blessed thing. My warm regards to your son & his dear wife. All send their greetings to you all. Ever your friend

W. R.

1. Review, "Mr. Tagore's Poems," *Times Literary Supplement,* November 7, 1912, p. 492.

14
Tagore to Rothenstein

508 High Street, Urbana
November 10, 1912

My dear friend

The quietness of this place and the sunny leisure are sinking deeper and deeper in my heart every day. I feel like a bee that has found the hidden honeycell of the flower and has completely shut up its wings and settled down to get into the centre of the store of sweetness. The veil of my smaller self has been drawn aside and the great in me, the ancient, the true has today been able to make its voice heard. Its insistent claim to let it live that life which transcends birth and death, pleasure and pain, which comprehends all, has reached me.

The living butterfly is gnawing at its prison woven of innumerable silken threads—it must spread its wings and float free in the light. All the cares of my selfish life, my desire for recognition and worldly chances appear utterly pale and small to me. I must be free—free in the bosom of God who is all love and all beauty. This wish comes to me like an anguish, like wails of the violin chords when being tuned, but it carries a hope that this [is] a prelude to the music to come. I feel I must not fritter away my life in idle ceremonies of society any longer. The golden shade of evening is upon me and it is time for me to go, by the lonely path, to the stream to fill my pitcher. I do not know what makes me write you all this—but I want you to understand me and I know that you will do so. Ever yours

Rabindranath Tagore

15
Rothenstein to Tagore

11 Oak Hill Park, Hampstead
November 14, 1912

My dear friend—I hope you have found a haven at last. The thought of you being pushed & buffetted about the streets & subways of New York was a distressing one & I like to think of your reaching the shelter of a peaceful place where the good things of life are treated with tenderness and respect. I stopped at Oxford last week end on my way back from Oakridge & stayed a night with my friend Herbert Fisher.[1] I found many people asking me about you—news of the book had reached them & Gilbert Murray was especially keen to read it. I am sorry you did not meet Chapman, & that Flexner, that excellent doctor, was away in Europe. I fear the good Dr Maitra will have been disappointed. Peace I know is what you really want, & by the time this reaches you I hope you will all have settled down to a quiet & regular life. I am sending away your portrait & the large picture next week to the exhibition & am starting fresh work.[2] I am corresponding with the house of Macmillan in relation to your poems, & have sent down the book & the ms. Dr Seal went off to Mentone to join his son & left the question of his appointment still undecided.[3] No parcels have yet come from India, but I had a charming letter from your brother & when the new books come I will set about getting the reproductions made.[4]

November 17

The Nation notice I have just seen will I think give you great pleasure.[5] I can imagine it to be of the character you would like, being so impersonal in its attitude. It seems to me very beautifully written & done with great sincerity. Will you, I wonder, find Illinois a fruitful soil for work. I loved "The King [of the Dark Chamber]," perhaps the most daring play ever conceived & as profound & inspiring as is everything you fashion. I hope in a few days to have news from Macmillan's firm to give you. Not a day passes without your names coming up in our house—all beg me to send their love to Mrs Tagore.

We hope to hear news of you soon—in the meanwhile ever your friend

William Rothenstein

Mr Jacks, editor of the Hibbert Journal, was deeply impressed by Gitanjali & asked me to write a review for the H. J. I will get someone really competent to do it.[6] Ramananda Babu wrote me last week, & I will try to find time to write something for the Modern Review.[7]

1. Fisher was to go to India with a Royal Public Services Commission. (See editorial, "Indian Public Services: A Royal Commission to be Appointed," *The Times* [London], July 25, 1912, p. 5.)
2. "Exhibition": New English Art Club. "Large picture": "Panel for a Hypothetical Decoration to Symbolize the Religions of East and West." Reviewers thought that "Mr. Rothenstein, attempting new tasks of expression, . . . is still conscientious just where he ought to be unscrupulous." (Review, "New English Art Club: A Memorable Exhibition," *Times*, November 23, 1912, p. 11.) He showed a drawing, "Study for a Portrait of Rabindranath Tagore," and an oil, "Babu Rabindranath Tagore." Present owners unknown.
3. Dr. Seal's son: B. N. Seal (1892–1953), Indian Educational Service, 1921–1947.
4. Rothenstein recruited Emery Walker (1851–1933), distinguished typographer and designer, to make plates from drawings of eminent Bengalis by Jyotirindranath Tagore. "New books": Jyotirindranath's portfolios.
5. [Evelyn Underhill] review, "An Indian Mystic," *The Nation* (London), 12 (1912–13), 320–322.
6. Rothenstein recruited Rolleston. (See T. W. Rolleston review, "*Gitanjali [Song-Offerings],*" *The Hibbert Journal*, 11 [1913], 692–694.) L. P. Jacks (1860–1955), its editor, 1902–1947; Principal, Manchester College, Oxford, 1915–1931.
7. Rothenstein, "A Basis for the Appreciation of Works of Art: A Lecture Delivered Before the Cambridge University," *MR,* 13 (1913), 125–136.

16
Tagore to Rothenstein

508 W. High Street, Urbana
November 19, 1912

My dear Mr. Rothenstein

Your two letters of the same date amply made up for the long delay and eager waiting. They are delightful. I thought I had come to that age when doors to my inner theatre must be closed and no more new admission could be possible. But the impossible has happened and you have made my life larger by your friendship. I feel its truth and its preciousness all the more because it came to me so unexpectedly and in a surrounding not familiar to me at all. That I should, while travelling in a foreign land, meet with some experience of life which is not temporary and superficial fills me with wonder and gratitude. It is to me a gift from the divine source and I shall know how to value it.

I am so glad to learn from your letter that my book has been favourably criticized at the Time's Literary Supplement. I hope the paper has been forwarded to me and I shall see it in a day or two. My happiness is all the more great because I know such appreciations will bring joy to your heart. In fact, I feel that the success of my book is your own success. But for your assurance I never could have dreamt that my translations were worth anything and up to the last moment I was fearful lest you should be mistaken in your estimation of them and all the pains you have taken over them should be thrown away. I am extremely glad that your choice has been vindicated and you will have the right to take pride in your friend, supported by the best judges in your literature. Remember me kindly to Mrs Rothenstein and give our love to the children   Ever your affectionate friend

Rabindranath Tagore

17
Tagore to Rothenstein

508 W. High Street, Urbana
November 23, 1912

Dear friend

I send you with this letter a translation of a prose speech of mine. It reminded me when I got it of a rainy evening at Bolpur and the eager faces of the boys listening to me in that hall of the temple, dimly lit by a few hurricane lanterns.[1] I can not tell you how intense with emotion was that hour and how deep was our communion with nature around us. Of course the speech was not written down at that moment and it gives you only the outline.

Many thanks for the Time's Supplement you sent to me. The review of my book is more than I could hope for. Indeed, it is very generous.

But I have not yet got the parcel of my books which I am expecting every day. I hope they have been sent before this.

The evening is cloudy and it is cold. It is so still and quiet. I have been thinking of you all and that is my only excuse for writing you these few lines. I am, dear friend,   Ever yours

Rabindranath Tagore

1. Tagore, "Visvabodh" [World-Knowledge], *Shāntiniketan* (1909–1916), in *R-R*, XIV, 507–519: incorporated in "The Relation of the Individual to the Universe" [trans. Satishchandra Ray; rev. Rabindranath Tagore], *Sādhanā: The Realisation of Life* (London, 1913), pp. 3–22. This was the "prose speech" entitled "World-Realisation," read in Urbana. (See Letter 19, note 1.)

"The temple": prayer hall at Santiniketan, which a Bengali pilgrim described as comparable in style, if not in size, to the Crystal Palace. (See L. S. S. O'Malley, *Bengal District Gazeteer: Birbhum* [Calcutta, 1910], pp. 111–113.)

18
Rothenstein to Tagore

11 Oak Hill Park, Hampstead
November 26, 1912

My dear friend—your letters are a great joy to me. Only at times am I able to shelter the moods that came to me as it were automatically when I had you sitting near me in the studio. That mood comes too the moment I find myself in the country, when I see good works of art & read good books—less certainly at other times, & sometimes I realise that for a day or two it has not come at all. So many people drive it away, & with these one finds one's nerves uncertain & jumpy, & one is prone to say things with impatience & to feel one's life untidied & fruitless.

How well I can understand what you have been going

through. I think that desire for some kind of perfection comes to us all—a passionate wish to wear the livery of God, not as a form of ostentation or piety, but to tell men openly what one cares for alone. We have to appear to countenance so much cruelty, indifference, gossip & injustice, so that we may not appear priggish & superior to our fellows, & then comes that longing to throw off everything—the things one hates to carry in one's heart, on one's shoulders, & have done with all these things once & for all. There seems to be a conspiracy always to prevent us from being quite ourselves. The Devil does represent something quite actual—something bitter dragging always at our feet. Mediaeval literature spoiled the idea, took it from the realm of reality, made something unnatural of it. The curious thing is that men constantly criticise one another's imperfections, yet if we would try to rid ourselves of them we find them putting every difficulty in our way. Had it been otherwise we should never have had either priests or monks. I think the desire to show men at least that one cares for perfection made men adopt rules & a habit—that is why in spite of all that people say the figure of the sannyasi always touches me. I have just spent 3 days at Oakridge, such happy days. I wish you could have seen the place as it is now, with men & horses all busy in the fields ploughing the rich brown earth & going into the woods to do a hundred things. There is something about the autumn & winter which always moves me very much, when nature has thrown aside her green & gold garments & appears in all her slender nakedness. England is very sweet at this time, so pensive & delicate in her moods.

 I don't like coming back to town, after staying alone, spending the night in my builder's little house, sitting up chatting over the kitchen fire with him & his wife & a very delicate natured boy whom they have adopted.[1] My picture is done & away, & I am setting about my western panel, & soon I hope too to be painting some country pictures.[2] Wherever I go I hear things said of Gitanjali that warm my heart. People have felt your work more than ever I dared to hope & more than you yourself will readily believe. A friend sent the book as a gift to Mrs Watts, the wife of G. F. Watts, the painter, & she wrote that your book had brought her closer to her great husband (dead now some dozen years) than ever since she lost him. I am sending you a letter from Mrs Stuart Moore enclosed.[3] As for Malini & The Post Office, my own copy of The Post Office is with Macmillans, but I sent Yeats a copy & I will write him for it at once. In the meanwhile I send Malini. How pleasant to know that your plays are to be acted by the students.[4] I am so happy to know of your being in peaceful surroundings that inspire you & bring you rest. I think not a day passes but we speak of you & wish you with us. I had a charming letter from your brother, but so far no drawings nor Sannyasi clothes have reached me—many thanks for writing for these. I have heard nothing from Dr Seal. Yeats is still in Ireland. The Winter's Tale is over, & has been replaced by Twelfth Night, which has been greatly praised. Mr Galsworthy has produced a new play, but I have been to no theatre.[5]

I still hope you may meet Chapman. Ghose comes regularly —what a really good creature he is. The irrepressible Das Gupta is putting on Sakuntala at the Albert Hall.[6] The children send their dear love to you all—I think letters are in slow preparation. My wife asks me to send you hers too—she met Andrew Bradley last week, who spoke most gratefully of you. Macmillans have all your mss, having asked for everything I had of your work to give to their reader, & I hope before long to let you know of any arrangements proposed. I am so glad to know you are with good & simple people. In the meanwhile I am ever your friend—

William Rothenstein

1. Rothenstein had bought Iles Farm. (See Letter 5, note 2; *MM* II, 272–275.)

2. Perhaps for a set of allegorical panels; the painting at the New English Art Club may have been one of these. (See Letter 15, note 2.)

3. She wrote: "I am *delighted* that my review of Mr Tagore's poems did not displease you, and that you even think he may like it. Myself, I felt it to be horribly inadequate although I tried my best. It was deliberately made as detached as possible, partly because it seemed to me that the personal note was much overdone in the Introduction and partly because he is too big to sentimentalize over. And I hoped by being objective to help those out of touch with these subjects to understand his poems." (Evelyn Underhill to Rothenstein, November 23, 1912. R-S.) Evelyn Underhill (Mrs. Stuart Moore) (1875–1941), poet and writer on mysticism.

4. Mrs. Brooks hoped that Illinois students might produce a Tagore play. (Tagore to Rothenstein, November 12, 1912. RP:HL.) *The Daily Illini* (Urbana) notes no performances during his stay there. His *Mālini*

[Malini] (1896), in *R-R*, IV, 137–178: *Malini*, in *Sacrifice and Other Plays* (London, 1917), pp. 43–82; in *CPP*, pp. 387–402.

5. Granville-Barker productions, *The Winter's Tale* and *Twelfth Night* at the Savoy Theatre; Galsworthy's *The Eldest Son* at the Kingsway.

6. Kedar Nath Das Gupta, London-based Bengali organizer, writer, producer. A 1919 Das Gupta production of *Sakuntala* involved Laurence Binyon, who asked Rothenstein to design scenery and costumes: "K. N. Das Gupta, who gets up performances of Indian plays, asked me to revise his version; and it was so bad I had to rewrite it entirely." (Binyon to Rothenstein, February 24, 1919. RP:IOL.) (See Kalidasa, *Sakuntala: Prepared for the English Stage by Kedar Nath Das Gupta in a New Version Written by Laurence Binyon* [London, 1920].) R. L. Binyon (1869–1943), poet, art historian; Department of Prints and Drawings, British Museum, 1895–1933, and Deputy Keeper, Oriental Prints and Drawings, 1913–1932.

19
Tagore to Rothenstein

508 W. High Street, Urbana
December 2, 1912

Dear Friend

You will be surprised to learn that I have read four papers in the Unity Club here on four consecutive Sundays.[1] It has not been an easy task for me to express my thoughts in English, especially thoughts which are not familiar to the audience here. My papers have been admired by my hearers but understood by very few. We have a German professor of Physics here, a newcomer from Europe, who has a great vitality of mind and whose great enthusiasm for the ideas I have expressed in my papers is very encouraging to me. American people have an unhealthy appetite for sugarcandy and for lectures on any subject and from anybody. I am afraid they have spotted me—I am being stalked. I have already invitations from different quarters. Being an oriental I am expected to talk. I am planning escape but I don't think I shall be altogether successful. I am too good humoured to say "no" to anybody if persistently pressed. I am sure I will succumb to this weakness of mine before long. Once you lose all feeling of shame you know not to what length you may not go. I hope

I shall be able to find out some way of escape before I become completely brazen.

I have been fortunate to meet some really nice people in this little town. Mr Vale is one of them. He is a Unitarian Minister, very broad minded—with no tinge of sanctimonious pretentiousness about him. He is very simple and sweet-natured and his religion has nothing professional about it.[2] For Dr Seymour also I have a great admiration. He is the professor of Spanish here. In him all the foreign students of this University have their best friend. His genuine love for Rathi is simply touching.

Rathi has joined his classes in the college here. Pratima has got quite a number of friends in this place. She gets her lessons in English from Mrs Seymour. By the way, shouldn't Pratima and Rathi be called by you by their personal names? We have had beautiful weather last month. The American November has made good all the debts of the English August, in sunshine. With my love to you all I am ever yours

Rabindranath Tagore

P.S. The review that appeared in the Nation has been very gratifying to me.

1. Urbana Unitarian group. On November 10, "World-Realisation"; November 17, "Self-Realisation"; November 24, "Realisation of Brahma"; December 1, "The Way of Action." All were included in *Sādhanā* (see Letter 17, note 1). According to Prabhatkumar Mukhopadhyay, Tagore had the Ray translation at hand and revised it for reading to the Unity Club, whose request for more readings encouraged him to produce more such papers. (See Mukhopadhyay, *Rabindrajibani o Rabindrashāhitya-Prabeshak* [Life of Rabindranath and Introduction to Rabindranath's Literature], rev. ed. [Calcutta, 1960–64], II, 335–336.) According to Rathindranath, his father had already begun *Sādhanā* in Urbana and read "all the chapters" to the club, whose response made him think that each might "serve as subject matter for a separate discourse." (See Rathindranath Tagore, *On the Edges of Time* [Calcutta, 1958], pp. 123–124.)

2. The Reverend Albert R. Vail (1880–   ), Urbana Unitarian minister from 1907, when he was ordained, to 1918, when he left after a clash with that congregation, to form a new church in Chicago, a synthesis of Unitarianism and the Bahai faith already hinted at in his missionary education text, *Heroic Lives* (Boston, 1917), pp. 289–303, 311–321. Mr. Vail left the American Unitarian Association in 1918. The Chicago church was never formed, and Unitarian archives have no record of him after 1931.

20
Rothenstein to Tagore

11 Oak Hill Park, Hampstead
December 2, 1912

My dear friend—herewith the two plays. Yeats thinks The Post Office a masterpiece, & would like the Dublin theatre people to produce it. He is talking the matter over with the Irish theatre people—he thinks the other plays need more knowledge & understanding than an English or Irish audience is likely to possess.[1] Macmillan are to republish Gitanjali & to follow it up with the new poems & the plays.[2] The terms have only been touched upon—I am consulting Yeats & Fox Strangways.[3] In any case you are to have half the profits after the expenses have been paid & I hope a sum in advance, & the book will I think be published in America & in India. . . . I try to visualise you all in your quiet little town, wooden housed & neat in the bright winter sunlight. When the snow comes the sleighs will be brought out, & very gay & pretty they are, & Mrs Tagore will enjoy driving in them. I am reading von Hügel's Mystical Element in Religion, a very remarkable book I think, perhaps the profoundest I have read on the subject.[4] The preface—the 3 elements of religion—is a most searching & sincere exposition of religion in its relation to creed. I only wish he would say simply & frankly "to us, living in a Christian tradition, the Christ represents this thing of which I am writing" instead of putting the teaching of Christ so far above that of any other teacher. You cannot measure pain or ecstasy with a foot rule or weigh them in scales, nor can you say—this man's apprehension of the divine & human is greater than that [man's]. The accidents of time & place give one colour or another to our perception of God, & it is somehow absurd to suppose that the light of the sun is brighter in one century than in another. I think however that you will find the book a deep well of inspiration. Your own beautiful sermon you send me makes me feel richer than I have felt for many days. I have been through a period of depression which is I am glad to say beginning to lift, & you & von Hügel have both helped.[5] Our country home is getting completed, & when you come back

72   Imperfect Encounter

William Orpen, "Selecting Jury. NEAC 1909."
Courtesy of National Portrait Gallery, London

we can at any moment escape from people & go & seek quiet at Oakridge. I am planning much work to be done there, & each time I do I feel the better for the beauty & the solitude. My wife promises to write, & so do the children. I send you all my affectionate greetings. Ever your friend

W. Rothenstein

   1. Yeats returned *Malini* with the verdict that neither it nor *The King of the Dark Chamber* would play well for Western audiences. (Yeats to Rothenstein, December 1 [1912]. RP:HL.)
   2. Macmillan's acceptance followed Whibley's recommendations and concluded: "We shall be glad to carry out this suggestion [of publishing Tagore's work by stages] and to publish the volume in question at our own risk giving the author half of any profits that may be realised. We should of course do our best to work the book in the Indian market as well as here and in America." (George Macmillan to Rothenstein, November 26, 1912. RP:HL.)
   3. Fox Strangways now took over negotiations. Yeats disapproved of The India Society as publisher and felt that Theosophical Society activity made possible a larger initial sale through a commercial publisher. He suggested John Murray, publisher of the Wisdom of the East Series. (Yeats to Rothenstein, August 10 [1912]; [August 19, 1912]. RP:HL.)
   4. Friedrich von Hügel, *Eternal Life: A Study of Its Implications and Applications* (Edinburgh, 1912).
   5. Rothenstein had resigned from the New English Art Club because he felt that it disapproved of his current work, but he was deeply hurt when his resignation was promptly accepted. (See Speaight, *William Rothenstein*, pp. 262–264.)

21
Tagore to Rothenstein

508 W. High Street, Urbana
December 8, 1912

My dear Friend

The author's copy of Gitanjali has just reached me. It is beautiful to look at and I must thank you and Mr Fox Strangways for this gift....

The house we have engaged is a cosy little place and the locality is very quiet. Pratima is doing the housekeeping. We have been trying to find somebody to help her in the kitchen but have not been successful yet. We had a Japanese student for a few days. We discovered that he had a very fair knowledge of Jujutsu but not the faintest notion of cooking. So we had to abandon that experiment soon enough. As there is no restaurant anywhere near our house we depend upon the unsophisticated skill of Rathi and Pratima for our meals and we take our daily nourishment with uncomplaining resignation. We have an Indian student to help us in dusting rooms and washing dishes. He had been a teacher of mathematics in our school. Being brought up as a poet, the only help I can offer our party is never to try to assist them in their work. Our household here is a most bright example of selfhelp—certainly not very bright in its effect upon the external of our surroundings. I wish Mrs Rothenstein could come and see us. I should not ask her to dinner, for that would be asking too much. But I am sure she would enjoy the sight of our professor of Mathematics bravely tackling the problems of brooms and mops. Somendra is living with us. He is cheerful and lazy, always humming songs out of tune in perfect unconcern. He has all the qualifications of a poet except the gift of the metre and music. With love to you all I am, dear friend   Ever yours

Rabindranath Tagore

22
Tagore to Rothenstein

508 W. High Street, Urbana
December 15, 1912

My dear Friend,

I have got the manuscripts you sent to me.[1] Last night I read The Post Office before a friendly audience here and it was heartily appreciated. My reputation as a poet is fast spreading here but it has not made my stay here impossible as yet. I am left pretty much to myself. People connected with papers came to me to ask for my portrait and materials of my life but I held them at bay—but I believe they had better satisfaction from Rathi. Rathi has a natural affection for the people here and he does not like to disappoint them.

I have read the review of my book that appeared in the Athenaeum. Do you know, that is the kind of criticism I expected all along. It is not hostile, you can even call it appreciative, but you feel that the reviewer is at a loss how to estimate these poems. He has not got a standard by which to judge these productions, quite strange to him. He sees some beauty in them but they arouse no real emotion in him, so he imagines them as cold—he thinks they have no red life blood in them. He can not believe that they are quiet and simple, not because there is lack of enthusiasm in them but because they are absolutely real. I can assure you they are not literary productions at all they are life productions.

My writings have met with a very generous appreciation in your country. I never could believe it to be possible. So much so that sometimes it oppresses me. That his works should be accepted by men is the highest reward that can come to an artist. Yet we should be strong enough not to have to depend upon it. Reward should not be made a necessity to us. This fame in a foreign land has a strange fascination and I am afraid it was growing upon me; I was unconsciously getting into the habit of expecting it more and more. But I must get out of it. It is like using your own best works as chains to shackle you. I have a poem which I translated when I was in London. I do not know if it is in your collection. I give it below.—

Free me from bonds of praise and blame of men and guide me only by the beckons of your right hand, my lord. Let all the forces of my life take the one great course, made irresistable by one supreme love, even as the river that ever flows through its bounderies yet ever loses its limits in the sea, led by the hidden call and the inmost impulse of its own.[2]

I send you herewith the translation of a poem, story of which is based upon an episode of the Rāmāyana[3]   Ever your friend

Rabindranath Tagore

1. See Letter 20, note 1.
2. Tagore, no. 84, *Naibedya* [Offering] (1901), in *R-R*, VIII, 64.
3. Perhaps, Tagore, "Ahalyār Prati" [To Ahalya], *Mānashi* [She of the Imagination] (1890), in *R-R*, II, 263–265: no. 7, *Poems*, ed. Krishna Kripalani et al. (Calcutta, 1942), pp. 15–17, 216–217.

23
Rothenstein to Tagore

Hampstead December 15, 1912

My dear friend—alas, that the peace & pleasantness of your days should be threatened! The American (usually a lady) has a most delicate scent for charlatans & men of genius, but being unable to discriminate between them, dare not let one or the other go by unaccosted; & you are now fish for the pot. Perhaps you understand now why I was not sorry to escape, despite the most generous treatment & affecting kindness. And don't you find yourself closer to your German? the something more solid & professional that the European has? I found my respect for Europe grew large & stout during my sojourn. I do hope you will however, meet my friend Chapman. The enclosed was sent me from a friend, & I think it will throw some light on the stuff of which he is made. Don't you think the situation most dramatic, & the spirit of the man most noble? This means America to me, & his figure remains as the most living & substantial memory of the American scene.[1] The light was wonderful to me too, & although the landscape was magnificent, somehow it remains anonymous through lack of that association history & folk lore give to our soil & to yours. That you are meeting with dear & kindly people it is delightful to know, & it must touch you very much to discover the love your son sows in the heart of his professor & other friends.

We do speak so often of you all. If I miss you often I have you often too, for words grow finer & more radiant when they are thought over & remembered as does the memory of people who have left us for ever, & those happy days we spent together have as it were deposited crystals which I rejoice over daily.

Yesterday I saw Yeats, just returned to London, full of new theories of life & death, of literature & language, & I propose taking Kalimohon & Babuananda's son, whom I met the other day, to see him to-morrow night. This week I go to Oakridge to put the house in order, & look forward with joy to spending many days there, with new work planned. Your struggle with the word no I know so well myself—yes is the word which comes most readily to our lips, despite the warning finger of experience. My wife can say no but I cannot, & at times I am able to shelter behind the walls she can so emphatically set up. At the same time there is that within us which prompts us, while we are alive, to pour such treasures as we have upon the ground. If pearls be scattered before swine there are always gleaners who know what they gather, & have learned to prefer them to truffles. If we have slender purses, we can at least be generous with ourselves—this we have ever been & always will be, so long as we deserve the name of artist. So there will be, here & there, some souls which you will enrich, for it is with souls as it is with worldly wealth—to those who have shall be given. How delightful it is, however unpalatable to you at times, to think of your leaving Bengal to bring so much light to people who, in your country, are regarded as the superior races; there is a gentle irony in the situation which tickles one, although there is mirrored within it a story as sad as it is old.

From Brajendra Nath [Seal] I have no news—I have written him to-day to ask him how he fares. Of your health you say nothing—may I take it that you are less troubled than you were? I have no books yet from your brother, & look forward to getting them soon. I propose sending a few poems to reviews after Xmas—it will not be a bad thing in view of the second volume, for I fancy Gitanjali will be published by Macmillan early next year.

Directly the agreement is drafted I will send it to you for your approval. If you make any more translations I hope you will send them. I enclose a letter from a young artist & poet of promise.[2] I see that Mrs Stuart Moore has just published a book of poems & will get them & send them on to you.[3] It was she who wrote the review in The Nation. My wife & the children are writing. I send you my Xmas greetings & happy to know you will spend this pleasant feast with good & sweet natured people. Believe me ever your affectionate friend—

W. Rothenstein

1. On August 13, 1911, a lynching occurred at Coatesville, Pennsylvania. A year later no one had been charged. Chapman observed the anniversary by holding a public prayer meeting in Coatesville; he read

Scripture and delivered a moving address to a friend from New York, a lady from Boston, and an unidentified man who seemed to be a local informer. (See John Jay Chapman, "Coatesville," *Memories and Milestones* [New York, 1915], pp. 225–232; M. A. DeWolfe Howe, *John Jay Chapman and His Letters* [Boston, 1937], pp. 215–220.)
  2. Unidentified.
  3. Evelyn Underhill [Moore], *Immanence* (London, 1912).

24
Tagore to Rothenstein

> 508 W. High Street, Urbana
> December 23, 1912

Dear Friend

    Christmas holidays have commenced. Rathi and Pratima have gone to Chicago. I am left here under the guardianship of Somendra. I have been invited by some people at Chicago but I am best left alone.[1] Yesterday was the day of the anniversary festival of our Bolpur Ashram. Early in the morning while it was still dark we five of us had our quiet service and my day passed in gladness of heart. We are still having beautiful sunshine, quite unusual for this time of the year. I have been reading some papers to a circle of friends here. They have been quite enthusiastically received. They ask me to publish these to the leading magazines here. But I must submit them to your judgment first before I should think about their publication. So I shall wait till I go back to England. They also want to publish some of my translations in the periodicals here—but I have not yet consented to that. My friends here are trying to push me into publicity but I must resist that.

    Don't you think I should carefully go through the translations that are ready for the next book? Good many of them have been done in a very slovenly manner. I hope you wouldn't require them before I go to England. I could revise them here—but just now this fever of prose writing has got hold of me and I do not know when it will be over. . . . Ever your friend

                                        Rabindranath Tagore

  1. The invitation was from Dr. Edwin Lewis of the Lewis Institute, Chicago, which enrolled a number of Indian students. (See K. C. Chow-

dhury, "The Lewis Institute," *MR*, 11 [1912], 395–401.) Tagore declined because big cities bewildered him. (Tagore to Lewis, December 25, 1912. Janet L. Winters Papers.) Dr. Lewis' daughter, Mrs. Yvor Winters, thinks that all three Tagores visited them in January 1913; she recalls "those three people standing in our doorway in the cold, waiting to come in. Tagore handed me a gift—perhaps as from the oldest to the youngest (I must have been thirteen) but clearly a hospitality gift for the whole family. It was a wicker basket lined with satin and filled with candied fruits. I was awfully impressed." (Janet L. Winters to the editor, January 3, 1970.) E. H. Lewis (1866–1938), between 1899 and 1935 Professor of English, Dean of College Students, and Dean of the Faculty of Lewis Institute, now incorporated in the Illinois Institute of Technology; author of texts on composition and rhetoric.

25
Rothenstein to Tagore

11 Oak Hill Park, Hampstead
December 25, 1912

My dear friend—the picture you have painted for us of your American interior is most living & illuminating. I can hear Somendra's gay songs & see our dear Pratima bustling from pot to frying pan while you, robed in the golden inefficiency of the poet await, radiant & patiently expectant, the triumph of other men over the almost insuperable difficulties of nature. It is always a wonder to me how things can ever be cleaned up & the world made reasonably neat & tidy. Imagine what we have been going through at Oakridge, when I tell you that my wife & I were only able to pic-nic in one room last week, & not for another ten days at least will the rest of the family be able to join John & myself, who go back to-morrow. But what charming fellows all these country workmen are! I have enjoyed being with them more than I can say, staying with the old builder himself (well over 70, but working all day with the best of them) & hearing all the gossip of the country side. I think you will all like the place when you come & will find it transformed & seemly. We do so love our wood, which is quite extensive & full of noble trees. We will build you a wattled shelter there, where you can sit all day alone & watch the rooks flying in & out of their nests, & the rabbits scurrying through the undergrowth, & there perhaps inspiration may come to you. I take it that in America you have become the man of action, lecturing, receiving, answering ten thousand conundrums; this day a year I was staying up the Hudson River with Chapman, the year before I was at Benares, sitting down to my Xmas dinner with an almost unbearable headache & two High Court judges from Calcutta, garlanded with an enormous wreath of orange flowers which my servant had hung upon my shoulders.[1] This year I have been with the children & their joy yesterday evening was immense. For us I think the Xmas tree is the most beautiful thing connected with the family ceremony—half made by God & half by men, a symbol, if you will, of our own souls. We have the green branches with all the wealth of gold & silver, of red & white & blue, or miniature images of the things we find about us, that we can command, until the simple tree becomes a glittering marvel, shining with an hundred lights. But Billy was more intent upon an engine & train of carriages running upon lines, Rachel & Betty were able to inform me that I was now a grandfather, as they hugged their new dolls to their bosoms & John exulted in a box of tools & a pile of books.[2]

I hope you will be seeing something of a similar kind—I have the pleasantest recollection of my American Xmas—indeed I had a party in my own studio there for all the children I met there. We do so deeply wish you were with us, for all miss you all, & I am with you in thought always. . . . I had a touching letter from Dinesh Chandra Sen, who sent me a translation of "Sati," a charming story, but which requires a good deal of correction so far as the English is concerned.[3] I am very sorry to hear that he has had a stroke of some kind— he writes so charmingly & takes such pride in your success here. I think I told you Gitanjali is long sold out. Fox Strangways is still in communication with Macmillan, as we wish your interests to be safeguarded in every possible way.[4] I won't tell you all the things that are said about you & the book, but when you return you will really have to build glacis & wire entanglements, & put Krupp guns behind your trenches.

Dr Maitra leaves this week for Germany & Italy, he is full of passionate enthusiasm for America & I hope Europe, & will have many things to say I fancy on his return. You will have been sorry to read of the attack on the Viceroy, I know. Power means always risk, but I find myself always depressed on these occasions by the fear that they mean less generous treatment & a less fair attitude towards legitimate Indian claims, & a more difficult position for fair minded patriots.[5]

I do hope your health is better than it was here, & that all of you flourish in the keen cold air of America. My love & my wife's & the children's to all of you. Ever your friend

W. R.

1. Chapman lived at Barrytown-on-Hudson, New York. The judges were Sir Harry Stephen and Sir John Woodroffe. (See Introduction to Part I, "Rothenstein in India," note 9.)

2. William Michael (Billy) Rothenstein was four years old, Betty was seven, Rachel nine, and John eleven.

3. D. C. Sen (1866–1939), Bengali literary historian, had heard of Rothenstein through the Tagores. He wrote, "The kindness with which you received Rabindra Babu in England has laid the whole Bengali race under a deep debt of gratitude to you." He asked Rothenstein to find an English publisher for *Sati*, a story based on Puranic legend, to make revisions, and to write a preface: "I venture to make this request to you knowing you to be a good man who has love for India sincerely at his heart." (Sen to Rothenstein, December [7?] 1912. RP:HL.) His *Sati*, 2nd rev. ed. (Calcutta, 1909): *Sati: A Mythological Story*, trans. by the author (Calcutta [1916]).

4. Fox Strangways promised to consider Macmillan's draft agreement; he returned the "half-profit agreement," asked for a specimen page and binding, and inquired about list price and whether Macmillan would use Yeats's Introduction and Rothenstein's frontispiece. Reminding Macmillan that he could do nothing unless the firm answered his letters, he returned the draft agreement with itemized comments and queries, all designed for Macmillan's minimum risk and Tagore's maximum liberty and profits. He then inquired about a cheap Indian edition, commented on the specimen page, offered to call at the office to discuss anything hitherto overlooked, and promised to consider the suggestion that The India Society approach Yeats about his Introduction. (Fox Strangways to Macmillan, December 17 [two letters], 19, 20, 21, 1912. MCP.)

5. On December 23 a bomb was thrown into the elephant howdah in which Lord and Lady Hardinge rode into Delhi to accept the city as India's new capital. An attendant was killed; the Viceroy was injured but survived. "His helmet," the *Times* reported, "was found to be full of screws." (See "Details of the Outrage," *The Times* [London], December 24, 1912, p. 4.)

26
Tagore to Rothenstein

> 508 W. High Street, Urbana
> December 30, 1912

My dear friend,

How glad I am to get your letter! Round me I have an abundance of sunshine and quiet hours and your friendly greetings seem to make them brilliantly alive to me.

Rathi and Pratima have gone to Chicago. I had several invitations to go there but I have succeeded in warding them off.[1] I have not come to discover America or to be discovered by Americans. All I want is a few months of restful obscurity if possible. So just now I am busily active in rescuing myself from all kinds of possible engagements. Fortunately my ill health has been a real help to me—has almost acted like a wife in bluntly saying no to all intruders. I passed some very bad days lately and went through acute physical sufferings. But it had its compensation. It seemed to me like an embrace which shut off everything else except the presence which was nearest, and a fountain of sweetness sprung up from the hidden depth because the opening was narrowed from all sides.

Please thank Mrs Moore for me for her review in the Nation. I appreciate it very much for she has written it with true understanding. These poems of mine are very different from other literary productions of the kind. They are revelations of my true self to me. The literary man was a mere amanuensis —very often knowing nothing of the true meaning of what he was writing. . . .

The news of the outrage at Delhi has come to us with a great shock. The man who is too lazy for earning honest livelihood takes to burglery and only those who are disinclined to serve their country with useful works and patient heroism try these violent and cowardly methods and bring down fearful nemesis upon their countrymen. . . . Ever your friend

> Rabindranath Tagore

1. In addition to the Lewis invitation, from Harriet Monroe, editor of *Poetry.* (See her *A Poet's Life: Seventy Years in a Changing World* [New York, 1938], pp. 320–321.) Tagore told her, too, that he hoped to come

to Chicago later. (Tagore to Harriet Monroe, December 25, 1912. University of Chicago Library: Special Collections.)

27
Rothenstein to Tagore

Iles Farm, Far Oakridge
January 3, 1913

My dear friend—your news is delightful. After the conquest of Europe you receive the homage of the new world. You need not be afraid that all this homage is going to disturb you. Artists are never vain in the true sense, though they are so often said to be so—give the world indeed an excuse for thinking it. Anyone who really gives himself up to the thing or feeling he wishes to represent & succeeds in allowing the spirit of this to creep into the nooks & crannies of his work believes that there is truth & beauty in it; not because he has done it himself, but, to be paradoxical, because he has not done it himself. No insincere artist can cooperate with nature, & sending no tap roots into the ground can draw no sustenance from the earth. No, we are not vain about our work, but we do have moments of intense exaltation in doing it, when we feel we have caught truth on the wing, as it were, for one brief moment, & our habit of pursuit makes us aware of sincerity or insincerity in the work of others & at times it is hard to see the world entirely unable to distinguish between the two. It is in moments of depression that we doubt the value of our work —Heaven knows these come uninvited under our doors—not when the world withholds its approval or reward, & we are at heart ashamed only of these moments, as being unworthy of ourselves & of the truth we worship, never of our joy & exaltation.

I think you may reasonably, then, take some pleasure in the delightful appreciation given to your work by every one whom it reaches. I know that it warms my heart most gratefully & that those dear & near to you must get great joy from the homage given you. I greatly liked your poem on the subject, as the noble "—take back your coins, King's minister."[1]

These will go to swell the second volume.² I look many times into your box here & think of the happy drenching days we spent among these soft green slopes. London & its insistent calls upon one's time seems far away, & I am giving myself up entirely to the pleasures of country life. I think you will like our farm house when you come here—we have one vast room in which to live, & I believe we have been able to make the house look very fresh & beautiful. But there is so much to do, with the sheds & barns in bad repair & the garden to make, & every minute of my time is filled up delightfully. Every wall, every hedge, as well as barns and cottages carry touching indications of the care & intelligence of man & of his presence & strength & weakness far back in time, & I never tire of the woods & fields about here & when you come back I can show you many lovely corners. My wife & the children join John & myself to-morrow. If they were here they would all send their love to all. Ever yours

W. Rothenstein

1. Rothenstein misquotes. See Tagore, "Patitā [The Fallen], *Kāhini* [Tales] (1900), in *R-R*, V, 84–93: no. 60, *Lover's Gift and Crossing* (London, 1918): in *CPP*, pp. 211–212.

2. Rothenstein anticipates. In London, Fox Strangways still wrote almost daily to Macmillan, insisting on a royalty basis while reiterating that "fully appreciating the great advantage to the book of being brought out by a firm of your high standing and reputation, I am willing to withdraw all alterations which do not seem to me to be essential." (December 27, 1912. MCP.) He asked 15 percent of the list price on the first 1,000 copies, 20 percent on the second 1,000, 25 percent thereafter. (December 31, 1912. MCP.) Macmillan must have declined this on New Year's Eve. Fox Strangways began 1913 by writing: "I have to say that the terms I particularized in my letter of yesterday are final. If you cannot see your way to embodying these in the agreement I must with regret transfer the work to other hands." (January 1, 1913. MCP.) In a more conciliatory mood he sympathized with Macmillan's wish not to be "bound by agreement not to do those things which you have no intention of doing . . . You asked the author, in effect, to trust you; and, on his behalf, I have in effect replied . . . that in my opinion such trust is justified. I very much prefer things to be on that basis, and the agreement is so far satisfactory to both parties." (January 2, 1912. MCP.) By January 8 they had terms Fox Strangways felt Tagore could accept. Yeats's Introduction still dangled: "I do not know Mr Yeats well enough to ask a favour, and it does not lie with me to make it a matter of business with him. Mr Rothenstein who knows him better declines to make the application. In these circumstances I do not see how I can be of assistance in the matter." (January 4, 1913. MCP.) Yeats and Rothenstein apparently settled their affairs separately. Yeats reserved the right to reprint his Introduction. (Yeats to Macmillan, February 5, 1913. MP:BM.) The frontispiece was

put in hand shortly thereafter. (Rothenstein to Macmillan, February 13, 1913. MP:BM. See Introduction to Part II, "Tagore in the West," note 15.)

28
Tagore to Rothenstein

508 W. High Street, Urbana
January 6, 1913

Dear Friend

I have just got a beautiful letter from Mr Stopford Brooke and it has given me a great joy. That my works should be welcomed not into the library but into the life is the highest reward that a poet I could ever hope for.[1] Mere praise makes one feel proud but appreciation like this has the opposite effect. It makes me aware that these writings have not come from that person who tries to appropriate to himself all the praise and the remunerations of the authorship. It was a different personality which sang these songs. He is the lord of the mansion who asked his friends to a feast and it is the servant who gets tips from the guests.

I am sending you some more of my translations. My friends here think that some of these should be published in American Magazine to whet the appetite of the would be buyers of my books when they are ready. Dr Lewis of Lewis Institute Chicago advised my son to have some of these sent to editors here through Mr Ezra Pound or Mr Yeats. He thinks that America is the place where books can have gigantic sale if properly introduced. I believe it is true and it is fully worth trying for the sake of my institution. I have sent some translations to Mr Ezra Pound. I think he will come to you for consultation, for I have asked him to avoid those pieces that you might have selected for English periodicals.[2]

Dinesh Babu has sent me proofs of his translation of "Sati," and asked my advice if it could be published in England. It is difficult for me to judge. But, I think the story should be much more simply told and much of its prolixities cut down. Would it be possible for the Everyman's Library people to take it up and to include it in their series, after having thouroughly revised it? Or perhaps, Mr Cranmer-Byng might be tempted to take it in his hands.³

I have told you about my German friend here. He is really a Swiss.⁴ His childlike simplicity and his boundless enthusiasm for all kinds of ideas are very refreshing to me. His great vigour and freedom of mind at once distinguishes him from his fellow professors in this University. He also has a liking for me and he bursts upon my room at unlikely hours like a storm with a great gust of heartiness. He thinks Europeans like him have a great mission in America, to rouse her from her dreams of dollers to a higher reality. Ever your friend

Rabindranath Tagore

    1. Tagore struck out "a poet." Brooke's letter to Tagore, December 18, 1912. R-S. (See "Mr. Stopford Brooke on the 'Gitanjali'," *MR*, 13 [1913], 479.)

    2. "American Magazine": apparently, American periodicals in general. "Dr Lewis . . . advised my son": see Letter 24. Fox Strangways commented, "I did not personally attach much importance to the remark made to Mr Tagore's son by Dr Lewis of Chicago." (Fox Strangways to Macmillan, February 11, 1913. MCP.) Mrs. Winters writes, "If my father advised Tagore, I imagine that it would have been in conversation, and I cannot imagine that such advice went very far, probably no farther than the comment you have found." (Janet L. Winters to the editor, November 23, 1969.)

    3. Ernest Rhys (1859–1946), dedicated editor of J. M. Dent's Everyman's Library, makes no mention of this in letters to Tagore (R-S). L. Cranmer-Byng (1872–1945), editor of the John Murray Wisdom of the East Series.

    4. Jakob Kunz, mathematical physicist, University of Illinois, 1909–1938. The present head, Physics Department, writes, "Jakob had the spirit of a poet and I am not surprised that he and Tagore interacted vigorously." (G. M. Almy to the editor, April 17, 1970.) (See Joel Stebbins, "Jakob Kunz, 1874–1938," *Popular Astronomy*, 47 [1939], 1–5.)

29
Tagore to Rothenstein

508 W. High Street, Urbana
January 13, 1913

My dear friend

I send you some more of my translations of which Nos 6, 7, 8, 9 and 13 have been sent to "Poetry" in Chicago for publication. They specially requested me to send them some of my love lyrics and that made me to translate these from my earlier writings. I hope these will be enough for this paper and Mr Ezra Pound need not supply them with more of my things.

Last week after a heavy fall of rain at night the roads have become coated with ice and they have become quite impassable for me. Even for those who are accustomed to such things walking is not altogether safe on these roads. So I have been keeping indoors last few days which is not a very great calamity for me. But I have got to sign a document before the notary public empowering Mr Fox Strangways to negociate with Messrs MacMillans on my behalf. His office is not nearby, cabs or motor cars are not available and as I must take care of my limbs with which I have to sign I don't know what I am to do. Day or two ago I did make a sortie but I am sorry to say the progress I made was not considerable and the fall I had was hardly dignified for a man of my age. Fortunately there was only one other pedestrian in the street and he was not in a mood to enjoy the misfortune of a fellow being, being himself anxiously concerned about his own safety.

I had the curiosity to try the forbidden path, ate the fruit of knowledge and had the fall. But Satan has not left off tempting me and it is urging me that with better caution I am sure to evade consequences. But from the little experience I had I could see that caution is hardly a help in a slippery path, where dashing recklessness is a much better guide. Unfortunately caution is within ones means but recklessness is a divine gift not to be had for asking. So I will have to wait till the ice melts. But the sky is clear, the sun is bright and the colourless white of widowhood of the wintry nature is beautiful to me.

I have an invitation to Rochester to some Congress of Liberal religious bodies where I am requested to read a paper on Race Conflicts. I have accepted the invitation and I must be ready with my paper before the end of this month. But, as the time allotted for reading it is not more than thirty minutes the paper is not going to be a formidable one. Ever yours

Rabindranath Tagore

30
Tagore to Rothenstein

508 W. High Street, Urbana
January 16, 1913

My dear friend

I have got a disquieting letter by this mail from Bolpur giving me details of the debts and liabilities incurred by my school. Some of the debts are of urgent nature. If publishers could be had in America for my children's poems or some of my plays offering better terms than I could expect from English publishers should I close with them. Dr Lewis of Chicago told my son that publishers here are much more liberal and prompt with their cash than they are on your side. Of course I should go by your advice and won't do anything rash.

But I will have to run back home as soon as the publication of my books are arranged. I was planning of staying on in Europe for two or three years. But this will not be possible. I hope I shall be able to spend my summer in England and then I will leave for India.

Please don't be the least anxious about this financial difficulty with regard to my school. My master claims more sacrifice from me, and I must gladly prepare myself for that. It will increase the value of my work and my life will gain strength. My offering will not be cheap and my path will not be easy, of that I am feeling more and more sure. My Beggar has come to my door, and he calls me and my whole heart comes out in response.

I am going out of my retirement next Sunday, when I am starting for Chicago. After spending a week there I will go to Rochester where I have an appointment. From thence I go to Boston and possibly to New York where I am sure to meet Mr Chapman this time.

I have got a very kind letter from him asking me to see him when I next come to New York.

I do not know when I am to come back to this town or whether I shall at all come back but please address my letters to the care of Dr Seymour 909 W. Nevada Street.

I have a plan of going to England next March leaving my son and daughter in law behind. But the burden of my helplessness will be heavy upon you which makes me hesitate. Ever your friend

          Rabindranath Tagore

The condition of the roads here, if anything, is worse.

31
Rothenstein to Tagore

        Far Oakridge January 17, 1913

My dear friend—I was indeed sorry to hear in your last letter that your health has not been good. We had hoped, since you said nothing about it in your earlier letters, that the dry climate of America had cured you. I am sure you are most wise not to take unnecessary tasks upon yourself—I can imagine how people will be pressing you to lecture & write. So long as you can get sufficient leisure for your own thoughts & your own work a little of your time may fairly be asked by your good hosts of a winter, but travelling in America is a tedious affair, was to me certainly, & you do well to save yourself the racket of the American pilgrimage. With the exception of a rare visit of a night to Hampstead, I have been leading the life of peace. Every moment of the day seems eventful here, either working with my brushes or with my hands—how often have I wished you with me! We have had wonderful moonlight nights of late; the night can see no meanness in life; what man makes & the works of the Gods are alike to her, & everything becomes grand & noble under her eyes. The night alone is kind, even to our middle class civilisation, & to the jerry built villas gives the same romance as to cathedral & castle. I think our civilisation has suffered from knowledge of "the ugly" & "the beautiful" & has produced too many men whose notion of passion is a fine frenzy; and that power of looking with a passion that outwardly is the sister of calm, which has been the priceless possession of many noble artists & poets, is understood by very few of those who follow in the wake of the arts. If people will understand that the passion of such poetry as yours has nothing in common with the pretence which so many of our poets make of feeling things implied by the subject, then they will learn much from reading it. People are so easily deceived, just as children are, by make believe, & make believe is so natural a thing to most artists, that they often themselves think that there is nothing beyond this in art. I enjoyed the last poems you sent me as I enjoy all your work, for to me you have to an unique degree that quality of the night I care for, & hope always some touch of it may creep into my own. I am revelling in the beauty of trees here, & trying to draw them as faithfully & tenderly as I would draw men. The days when I must take train for London are the only prosaic days of the week, . . .

You will have heard from the zealous Fox Strangways who has conducted the difficult negociations with Macmillan with patience & firmness, & obtained for Gitanjali I fancy the best terms possible.[1] He & Havell are on strained terms I fear; Havell wants the India Society to take up a more active polemical attitude over the Delhi affair, & the rest of us are disinclined to interfere unless we have more precise knowledge than any of us can have of the government's intentions, or the actual genius for building still lingering among Indian builders.[2] I myself dislike exaggeration, & think it our duty to admit that the powers of Indian craftsmen have suffered from the same blight that has come over the rest of the world, & that although much is still left, their work cannot be placed beside the work of their ancestors. Havell says quite definitely it is as good as ever it was, & only the machinations of the British officials are keeping Indians from showing their genius. Alas, what artists have ever depended upon the active support of any government? We have to put our little treasure into the world as we may, & think ourselves lucky if men will bring us food for our platters. I see struggles on the horizon, if the Society is to continue with the work it set itself, that of showing people something of what has been done & is being done in India, this being to most of us the most forcible answer to the detrimental things so often said in the immediate past regarding Indian art and letters.

Thomas W. Rolleston, drawing by Rothenstein

I have only been up in London one day a week, & have seen very few people, & intend working here all through the winter. I look forward even now to the day when you will come back to us, & your room is ready for you here, cool & white, whenever you come. That you can manage to remain in your Adrianople with the armies of all the Americas besieging your stronghold fills me with amazement. I have heard from Chapman lately, he read your book as I knew he would with deep interest & he writes that he hopes to get into touch with you.[3] My love to our dear Pratima & Rathindranath. Ever your friend—

W. Rothenstein

1. Fox Strangways told Tagore: "you may feel yourself *safe*. The royalty was all they would give—not so much I think as the book is worth, but I am told the terms would be considered very good indeed for an ordinary book of poems, so I think you may be *satisfied*. . . . I hope you are not *idle!!* We want to read much more of you. And as you know of course, now is the time one success should be followed up by another." (Fox Strangways to Tagore, January 15, 1913. R-S.)

2. "Delhi affair": designs for New Delhi. Davids, Rothenstein, and Fox Strangways, as India Society officers, appealed for participation by Indian artists. (See Davids, et al., "The Architecture of Delhi," letter to *The Times* [London], December 17, 1912, p. 5.) They hesitated to press harder in the face of Havell's convictions. Rolleston recorded: "Went down to Havell's this afternoon—to talk over my letter of Friday. He was very good humoured—pointed out quite correctly that the Society had a 'craft' programme at the beginning, and that it was the Society, not he, which had changed its position in the matter. But he seemed to realize that as a governing member of a Society he was out of place when also acting as a free lance in the same field, and he practically placed his resignation in my hand." (Rolleston diary, entry for March 16, 1913. Honor Stopford Drysdale Papers.)

Abanindranath Tagore also resigned: "Perhaps I owe an apology and explanation to you and my other friends in England for giving up the 'India Society' so suddenly. Mr. Havell my 'Guru' has left the Society under most unfortunate circumstances and as his 'Chela' I have no other way left open but to follow my 'Guru' in this affair. Perhaps many will laugh at this exhibition of childish devotion of a 'Chela' to his 'Guru,' but you my friend who knows India and the Indians better than any one else will I hope understand my feeling and excuse me for committing this folly." (Abanindranath Tagore to Rothenstein, July 3, 1913. RP: IOL.) Rolleston recorded: "India Soc. . . . when we had the Rothenstein v. Havell trouble in full [word illegible]. R. badly prepared—no resolution to propose—When one was finally evolved it was covered with contradictions." (Rolleston diary, entry for April 15, 1913. Drysdale.)

3. Chapman found the poems "very extraordinary. They are the only Eastern things which I have ever understood,—or feel as if I did . . . I

hate everything that Yeats says at the beginning (but that is of no importance)." (Chapman to Rothenstein, December 21, 1912. Chapman Papers: Houghton Library, Harvard.)

32
Rothenstein to Tagore

Far Oakridge   January 28, 1913

My dear friend—the French have a saying "the best is enemy to the good"—I have been waiting for leisure in order to write you a long & full letter, & so time has slipped away, & though you have been in my thoughts each day I am shocked to find your last letter & your poems unacknowledged still. So I must sit down without more ado, & send you such news as I can. I think you are most wise to consider the pressing offers of American magazines. I went over to see Ezra Pound in London on receipt of your letter, & we are all agreed on the subject. Only the actual *book* must be published here, only serial rights given to the magazines, & an American edition can easily be arranged from here. I wrote to Fox Strangways, suggesting that Macmillan should arrange for an American edition of Gitanjali, which would precede the second book there as well as here. Both Yeats & Pound think this should wait until Gitanjali has reached people who have not been able to get the India Society book, & they have agreed to edit & take charge of the second book when the time comes. The poems you sent me will make a notable addition to those I have already. I love no. 8 & no. 13 as much as anything you have translated. Ezra Pound tells me he has sent some of the poems out already, & is looking after the practical side of the publication. In the meanwhile I hope you are keeping as well as possible, & that the life you are leading in Urbana allows of your keeping a serene and cheerful mind. You are missing much rain & mud, but we have had little cold, & work out of doors has, except on wet days, been all the while possible. . . . I am delighted to hear of our dear Stopford Brooke writing to you—it is many weeks since I have seen him, but next time I travel to town I shall go to [his home, Number One]

Manchester Square. Seeing no one but country folk I have little news to give you. One seems to do nothing, yet each day is full, & if one does little good to one's fellows, at least one does little harm. Chapman wrote me that he hoped to see you—I shall be interested to hear what you think of him. I heard from Ramananda Babu that my complete MS has at last reached him, & that he intends to publish it in the Modern Review—I read a pleasant article about you by Mr Andrews in the last number, & others I gather are to appear over here during the next month or two. You will however have had your fill of fame by now, & your curiosity regarding people's views of your work will be a little less lively. . . .

. . . You I take it are beginning to sound the depths of American hospitality—one needs a very long line, for surely they are among the kindest people in the world. I will make up for my ten days neglect by writing you again during the next few days. . . . Ever your devoted friend—

W. Rothenstein

33
Rothenstein to Tagore

Far Oakridge   January 31, 1913

My dear friend—your letter telling me of your setting out upon your travels & of the news that has been making you uneasy has reached us. First let me make you quite clear upon one point—if it should happen that you are considering coming over to England you come to us. There must be no hesitation in your mind—if you come alone, whether here or at Hampstead we can without any trouble to ourselves give you a roof for shelter. You know the life we lead, & if you will share it you may be sure of a welcome, & we may take it that you will not feel called upon to join us should you wish to be alone & that you will consider yourself free to do exactly as you please regarding other invitations at any time. I myself am likely to be here more than at Hampstead, but the house there will be at your service whenever you may wish to stay in London, & I do beg of you to put away from your mind any hesitation you may be feeling. I shall do my own work & your being with us will not interfere with it, & my wife will delight to minister to your simple wants in the way of physical comforts. I do want you then to feel quite easy upon the subject of coming to England alone—I would meet your boat & bring you safely to your destination, whether it be here or Hampstead.

I quite understand the importance of the American approach, & have written to Fox Strangways to put the matter at once before Macmillan. It is possible that they may put the matter into the hands of the Macmillan Co in New York. At any rate, as they have been approached regarding the second volume, I feel it only fair to put the serious inducement the American publishers offer before them. If they will not at once offer very definite terms, I cannot see why your book should not appear first in America, if they are willing to make really favourable terms with you. Yeats & Ezra Pound seemed to think that your work should appear first in Europe, but in view of what you tell me of practical offers they may be inclined to change their minds. I am writing Yeats to-night.

I hope you are not letting the difficulties of your school worry you too much. What you tell me of the exaltation these difficulties can give you I do indeed understand, & from all that I have heard no sacrifice can be too great for the sake of an institution which must be a pride & a touching delight to your heart. I do love the thought of all those dear, pure minded, gentle & enthusiastic boys living a beautiful life, with your influence to inspire them & to mould them; when I think of the influences most of the more liberal youths are subjected to, both in Bengal & in London, it makes your school an immensely important & necessary counter force. If—alas, that if—I had nor wife nor family how gladly I would join you at Bolpur—I can imagine no more attractive task than this. I should also like to do a little begging for you—I feel that if I were in Calcutta I could raise some of your rich lawyers to a sense of things, but that is probably only my vanity. A little angry I do get, however, at their indifference. Such a thing as is happening in that little village has not often been seen in the world before & may not easily be seen

for many a decade. It is the old story—men are blind to the vivid realities & seem only to care for shadows. They will sit & read lives of great men, hold their bibles on their knees & pore over printing ink, but are deaf to the knocking on the door of their own hearts. In the meanwhile something must be done, I quite see, in the way of turning poems into practical help. The house here is more in working order, I am almost alone here now, John having gone back to school with his mother, & shall have more time in the evenings during the next weeks. I will therefore gird up my loins & do what I can do to help over here. In the meanwhile you will wait for Macmillan's reply to Fox Strangways' suggestion, & I will keep you informed the moment I hear from him. I hope your peregrinations in America to conferences & the like will prove fruitful & profitable to many, & that you will not be tempted into doing a great deal too much—a little too much I know you will do. I am glad you are to meet Chapman—he I am sure will help to look after you. I shall await further news anxiously. In the meanwhile I am ever your devoted friend
W. Rothenstein

P.S. I have just been rereading your letter. I think the idea of publishing the children's poems alone a very good one, also the plays. These last you must give Chapman to read. Then you could keep the more personal ones for publication here, to follow on Gitanjali, & I have suggested to Fox Strangways that Macmillan publish Gitanjali simultaneously in America next March. The more I think of publishing only the plays & the children's poems, the more does the idea appeal to me Perhaps Rathindranath could get some idea of what a publisher would pay for the rights of these—there could be two volumes, one for the children's poems, & the other containing the plays. He will of course get someone—you mention Prof Lewis—to advise him. Above all, look after yourself travelling, & when you have nothing to do, practise saying the word "no" at odd moments, or you will be worn out before you get to New York . . .

34
Rothenstein to Tagore

Far Oakridge   February 6, 1913

My dear friend—I have just heard from Fox Strangways who communicated what I wrote him to Macmillans. They write "—in regard to Mr. R's letter, we told him at the time when he first sent us the book & the unpublished manuscripts that we should be very glad to bring out a second volume of poems if the sale of 'Gitanjali' were satisfactory, & our attitude on the subject is still the same. We think therefore nothing in the meantime should be done either in America or elsewhere in regard to these poems, for if Gitanjali is as successful as we should wish it to be we should no doubt be able to arrange to copyright the new poems in the United States & to publish them on both sides of the Atlantic on a royalty basis similar to that which has been arranged for Gitanjali. We ought perhaps to add that as Gitanjali has been published in England for some two or three months it is too late now to secure American copyright for it, but we shall hope to arrange to put the book on the American market through our New York house and as our American agent, Mr Brett, is shortly to be in England we shall then take the opportunity of discussing the matter with him."[1]

As I told you in my last letter, I am very much inclined to support Macmillan's plea; but I gather they have less feeling about the plays & the children's poems, for they say

"In regard to the children's poems & plays, if Mr. T. has had definite offers from American publishers we should be sorry to stand in his way—it ought, however, to be pointed out that if these are published in the States before they are published in this country the English copyright would be lost."

If then, dear friend, you have a really generous offer, I can see no reason why you should not accept it, for these children's poems & the plays, but only if the offer be a really worthy & substantial one, made by a reputable publisher, under an agreement upon which you shall get the best possible advice.

The other poems you must, I think, (except for serial publication in reviews) keep for a really noble book with which to follow up Gitanjali. I have absolute faith in its ultimately paying you well. You are to get a cheque in advance from Macmillan now, & I hope in the meanwhile that Pound's efforts are bringing you some small profit.[2] Of Gitanjali you may be quite sure—demands for it pour in on every hand, I am told. Your last poems have been a great joy to me—I have read & reread them with ever greater pleasure. I am writing you again shortly. This will just carry you the message you will be waiting for, which is I hope, agreeable to you.

I hope too it is fixed in your mind that whenever you choose to return to England that we look upon it as a foregone conclusion that we are responsible for your welfare. Ever yours
W. R.

1. George P. Brett, Sr. (1858–1936), with the New York firm since 1874, later President and Chairman of the Board.
2. *Poetry* sent Tagore thirty dollars. (See Pound, *Letters*, p. 13.)

35
Tagore to Rothenstein

Felton Hall, Cambridge, Mass.
February 14, 1913

Dear friend

I have been rushing through this vast land for the last few weeks going from town to town reading lectures and shaking hands with new acquaintances. I was in New York last week and came to Boston last evening. I am invited to read two lectures in the University here and two others in clubs connected with it. As my lectures were appreciated in Chicago I hope they will be received here with attention. Other invitations have come to me but I do not think I will be able to accept them.[1] I am longing to go back to Urbana and settle down to my quiet work.

I met Mr Chapman in New York and I was at once struck with his personality. It was his vigorous sincerity which attracted me to him and I wish I could have opportunity to see him more. It was entirely my fault that I did not have it. You know very well that exploration of new places is not in my power, and the idea of going about visiting people, however estimable they may be, scare me. But I still have the desire in my heart to know him better, but I doubt very much if it will ever be realised.²

In Chicago I was the guest of Mrs Moody. She is the widow of William Vaughan Moody, one of the most famous of modern American poets. Mrs Moody has been extremely kind to me. She has volunteered to pilot me safe through my tour in American cities and I was living under her protection in New York. She has sheltered me from all kinds of intrusion and publicity and within a very short time she has been able to make me feel quite at ease with her which is a difficult feat you know. Had it not been for her I could not have come out of my shell at all as long as I remained in this country. I feel I have been of some help to her—for she was gradually drifting towards the vague region of Christian Science and its allied cults which are in vogue here and which are so destructive of spiritual sanity and health.³

I have been experimenting with translation of various kinds of my poems, some, and perhaps, most of them have to be rejected. Only those that can sustain the spirit of the Gitanjali poems should be retained. You will have to maintain a severely critical attitude towards them and be uncompromisingly fastidious in your selection for the next publication. Please do not for a moment think that it will hurt me at all. I am going to have type written all the translations I have done, in some kind of order, and then send them to you.

Mr Yeats is not satisfied with some of the corrections that have been made without his knowledge. I have promised him to submit to him the proofs of the second Edition of Gitanjali, for him to make necessary restorations. Will you ask MacMillans to arrange it?⁴ With my love to you all I am your affectionate friend

                    Rabindranath Tagore

Yesterday I read my paper on the Problem of Evil in the Emerson Hall before the University people. You will be glad to learn that it was enthusiastically received. Prof. Woods has been urging me to have all these papers published here in a book form and he thinks he can arrange with some publishers who are reliable. He is sure of its having a fairly good sale. What do you advise me to do?⁵

1. For his itinerary see Stephen N. Hay, "Rabindranath Tagore in America," *American Quarterly*, 14 (1962), 443–444; Sujit Mukherjee, *Passage to America: The Reception of Rabindranath Tagore in the United States, 1912–1941* (Calcutta, 1964), pp. 210–211. Tagore spoke twice to the philosophy class of Professor James Woods. "Other invitations": from Wisconsin, Michigan, Purdue, and Iowa universities. (See Rabindranath to Jyotirindranath Tagore, Bengali letter, February 13, 1913, *Cithipatra* [Letters] [Calcutta, 1942–60], V, 15.)

2. The meeting was not a success. Tagore was fatigued, and Chapman found him "a little unhealthy . . . and his moral being, *hot house*." (Chapman to Rothenstein, March 8, 1913. RP:HL. Quoted in Howe, *John Jay Chapman and His Letters*, p. 260.)

3. Tagore arrived at a crucial juncture in Mrs. Moody's life, which was cruelly distorted by a divorce, family financial failure, an accident that left her lamed, and Moody's death in 1910. (See Olivia Dunbar, *A House in Chicago* [Chicago, 1947], pp. 93–106.)

4. Yeats found a change in number 52 of *Gitanjali*, which he thought ruined the poem. (Yeats to Tagore, January 9 [1913]. R-S.) Tagore explained that Andrews' insistence on this change had overborne his own objections when it was too late to consult Yeats. He apologized and begged Yeats to re-revise proofs of the Macmillan edition. (Tagore to Yeats, January 26, 1913. Michael Yeats Papers.) Andrews disliked Yeats's Introduction from the start and had demanded a second proof of the India Society edition. (Andrews to Rothenstein, October 6, 1912. RP:HL.)

5. Professor Woods was perhaps the friend who offered to print *Gitanjali* at his expense and give Santiniketan the profits. Tagore later quoted a letter from the London Macmillans advising him that profits would be as great or greater if he allowed their New York firm to print and distribute the book. (Tagore to Woods, June 1, 1913. David G. Williams Papers.)

Tagore told Alice Rothenstein: "I am now and again approached by the women's clubs to give them readings and be made much of by them in return but I am not made to be a drawingroom pet and so far I have been successful in escaping their snares." To John Rothenstein he wrote: "I wish you could come to America with us, for this country is full of engines and engineers—and nothing else." (Tagore to Alice and to John Rothenstein, February 14, 1913. Rothenstein Family Papers.)

"My paper on the Problem of Evil": see Letter 40, note 2.

36
Rothenstein to Tagore

> Far Oakridge   February 15, 1913

My dear friend—I am wondering where you are, among what people you are staying & hoping that you are not doing too much

& overtaxing your strength. I am a little anxious knowing the American appetite for culture & the "higher life"; you will be devoured many times, I fear, & all with the best & kindest intentions. The old jest of the lion saying how kind of my keepers to put bars up to prevent the ravening people from getting too near me has some point in the great country where you are now sheltering—I can hear the questions & see the eager circle round you. Some protector I hope you have with you—some one who can say no once or twice a day at least. I thought of you to-day, when I discovered a few miles from here a little old church, dating back from Norman times, standing by itself in a sloping field, built in the simplest & most touching way, just like a barn, with a loosely tiled roof & nothing to tell you that God's house differs in any way from the humblest man's. When you come here we will drive out together to see some of the old villages round Oakridge. . . .

I am awaiting further news of you anxiously. Letters I decided not to send you—you will have quite enough amenities to enjoy & endure without help from me. . . . Ever yours—
W. R.

37
Tagore to Rothenstein

2970 Groveland Avenue, Chicago
February 28, 1913

Dear friend

I am on my way to Urbana from my lecturing engagement at Harvard University. Just at present I am staying with Mrs Moody in Chicago till the end of this week.

I think I have told you in my last letter that my lectures have been very well received and I am requested to print them in a book form. In the meanwhile I have sent my paper on the Problem of Evil to the Editor of the Hibbert Journal.

I do wish to go back to England[1] as soon as could be arranged and then go over to India. I feel I am very much needed in my school this moment—for a wave of depression seems to have come over the people in charge of the institution in my absence. So I think I should not delay any longer. You know I have my post of the flute player—and I have been absent too long from my work. My school-people think it is the money that they are most in need of, but, I am sure, it is the music which they really want. I have almost persuaded Rathi to wind up his affairs here and accompany me to England by the end of March or beginning of April.

I have given up the idea of publishing any of my poetical works in this country. At least, I will not think of it at all till I go to England and discuss it with you. I feel happy to think it will not be long before I shall see you.   Yours
Rabindranath Tagore

1. Tagore originally wrote "India," then struck it out and wrote "England."

38
Rothenstein to Tagore

Far Oakridge   March 4, 1913

My dear friend—your courage is wonderful; indeed your experience of active public life in England was but a preparatory exercise for an infinitely busier career, & looking back it must seem to you as though you led an almost Arcadian life with us. I do view with delight your triumphant progress through the States, & now that I know you have come through the strain without ill effects of any kind, & are returning to harbour again, I am most happy you were persuaded to say wise, simple & noble things to the American people. The faddists & cranks have had it all their own way, so far as India is concerned, in America as well as here, & you will have done much to show that throwing ropes up into the air, & climbing up them, does not take men to God. I am delighted that you should have lectured before Harvard University—that is after all a very pleasant practical acknowledgement—& as there is just a note of something raw & aggressive in the Indian student element of America (I gather this only from the pages of the Modern

Review) upon which your sane & balanced thought should act fruitfully.¹ I gather from your last letter that you do not propose returning to Europe so soon as you at least half intended. . . .

I gather many more were expectant than you were able to satisfy—there were hopes of a longer feasting & celebration which your return to peaceful Urbana must have dashed. I gather Gitanjali is very nearly ready & is to appear in the immediate future. I have sent a poem to the Fortnightly [Review], & your noble paper which Kalimohon gave me to the Hibbert Journal.² Directly Gitanjali appears I will send some more poems to the Reviews, & Macmillan will doubtless begin to prepare for the second book. . . .   Ever yours

W. R.

1. *The Modern Review* served notice ("Indians in America," MR, 13 [1913], 492) that it would now require certification of contributors' characters before accepting articles on Indian students' activities in America.

2. Tagore, "Kritārtha" [Success], *Kshanikā* [Momentary] (1900), in *R-R*, VII, 304–307: "At the Fair," *The Fortnightly Review* (London), 99 (1913), 790. Verses 1 and 4 of the Bengali poem are omitted in the English version. His paper, "The Problem of Evil," evidently submitted in duplicate. (See Letter 37; Letter 40, note 2.)

39
Rothenstein to Tagore

Far Oakridge   March 14, 1913

My dear friend—I am greatly touched by what you tell me of Mrs Moody. It is a great relief to us to know of your having found so kindly & rich a nature to take charge of you, & I can tell from the way in which you write that you have found a real friend, & that Mrs Moody knows the value of her charge. I feel personally very grateful to her for her generous offices—evidently she is both proud & happy to serve you. The warmth of the appreciation shown you by Americans must be very grateful to you—how much you have lived through during these last months. One stays at home & one year passes like another, but to travel for a few weeks means pressing the experience of years into days. I can imagine you will feel as I did after my months in India—a wild desire to get away from the concrete happenings, so that one might chew the cud of the new experience, alone & at leisure. It is like a man who buys something he cares for greatly in a shop, & hurries home to unpack it & enjoy it for the first time as his own. . . . Shall I, I wonder, ever see your beloved country again? I met Arnold last week when I was in London & he told me that Dr Seal has definitely refused the London appointment, his reason being that he has been approached regarding some position in India. I am very disappointed, personally, as I believe his influence would have been a most important one among the students here. I do think it imperative that young India should get itself out of two dangerous ruts, for they either wish to throw overboard all their familiar habits of mind & practise, taking, very self consciously, European ones upon themselves, or they criticise Europeans with bitterness & great lack of imagination & through another kind of self consciousness are inclined to repress their natural spirit of joy & interest in the world about them. Of course I am speaking only of students in England. How hard it is for people to escape excess, in one direction or another! Passion is not temperamental outburst in one direction or another, but is the concentration of a mind bent upon perfection. It is a stable & eternal striving to attain truth. The needle of the compass moves continually & to the uninitiated seems restless & inconsequent, but in reality this striving for the north, this passion for the perfect point of the compass, is a light by which all men can guide themselves from haven to haven. Young India must outgrow its bitterness before it can produce fruitful works. . . . Gitanjali is to appear, I gather, at once. I sent your message to Fox Strangways & hope Yeats had the proofs. If we can do anything for your arrival please command us . . . Ever your friend—

William Rothenstein

40
Tagore to Rothenstein

508 W. High Street, Urbana
March 15, 1913

Dear Friend

We are getting ready to leave this country, and the momentum of the force of my desire to be once more among my friends in England is increasing every day. We shall start from New York either on the 12th or the 17th of the next month so we shall not miss much of the pageantry of the coming of the spring in your country. I have done revising all my translations I had in hand and Rathi is busy typing them. I will send you the first instalment which consists of the Gitanjali series of poems next Monday. You will find among them a large number of new ones and most of the old ones considerably altered. I will send you my love poems and other lyrics of the earlier time a week or two later. Carefully go through them and make your selection.[1]

I have sent to the Hibbert Journal a paper of mine on the Problem of Evil. I have not heard from the editor yet. The paper on the Race Problem I sent to the Modern Review. If it is also published in the April Number of the Hibbert Journal I don't think there could be any objection.[2]

Mr Alfred Noyes, the English poet, is lecturing in this University. I have not been able to be present at any of his lectures. I am invited to meet him at a dinner tomorrow. Unfortunately I do not know his works.[3] My love to you all.   Yours
Rabindranath Tagore

1. "Gitanjali series": i.e. *Fruit-Gathering*. "Lyrics of the earlier time": poems written earlier than those for *Gitanjali*.
2. Tagore, "The Problem of Evil," *The Hibbert Journal*, 11 (1913), 705–716. "The Problem of Race" appeared as "Race Conflict," *MR*, 13 (1913), 423–426.
3. Alfred Noyes (1880–1958) lectured March 14, 1913, on militarism; March 15, on poetry, materialism, and radicalism. Edward Thompson, in his *Rabindranath Tagore: Poet and Dramatist*, comments (pp. 305–308) on limitations of Tagore's acquaintance with the poetry of his English contemporaries.

41
Rothenstein to Tagore

> Far Oakridge   March 27, 1913

My dear friend—this is indeed good news. Need I tell you how much I look forward to the pleasure of seeing you all again? You I hope to find not too burdened with the weight of bay & laurels you have had placed upon your brow by the quick & appreciative Americans. . . . When you last came, it was as a stranger, with only our unworthy selves to offer our friendship; now you come as a widely recognised poet & seer, with friends, known & unknown, in a hundred homes. You must be prepared then, for a more clamorous reception than you met with before. At least you will always have this harbour to retire to whenever the calls upon you become too insistent. I see that Gitanjali is out, & I expect a copy by every post from Macmillans. I am delighted to hear of new poems on the way. When you are here we can at once settle the details of the second book of poems with Macmillans. Ever since Christmas I have been living here, going up to London very rarely, & for years I have not been so happy as these last months. I find my relations with the people here of the pleasantest, & the physical work I have found to occupy my leisure every day more fruitful to myself at least than any I can find to do at Hampstead. I do hope you will care for this place as you did before, & will find it as inspiring. . . . Ever yours

> W. R.

42
Tagore to Rothenstein

> [2970 Groveland Avenue, Chicago
> April 1?, 1913]

Dear friend

Our date of departure has been fixed. Our steamer Olympic will start from New York on 12 April, so we shall reach London by the middle of this month. I cannot tell you how glad I feel to be once again near you, for which I always had a longing since I came to this country. But for the dread of the cold weather I should have been back to your place long before this. Except for lapses of very short durations I passed my time like a recluse in the little town of Urbana. I have had my ample compensation for this life of seclusion and I am glad that I have been able to protect myself from the dissipations of social success. I have gone through a series of public engagements but I have been deaf to the alluring calls of drawingrooms. I have refused to be handled and passed on from one show to the other by the connoisseurs of genius. The people in this country are hearty in their kindness but there is a rudeness in their touch, it is vigorous but not careful. Their admiration is not convincing therefore I could not take any delight in it as I did in your country. However, I have met with some sincere friends in America and I am deeply grateful to them. I feel sure if I had courage to come out and know the people here I should have loved them with all my heart. But I did not have the opportunity and I am certain I have not the right to judge them at all excepting through those few friends of mine whose deep earnestness and transparent simplicity have won my love. Somehow, I have an impression that America has a great mission in the history of the Western civilisation; for it is rich enough not to concern itself in the greedy exploitation of weaker nations. Its hands are free and perhaps it will hold up the torch of freedom before the world.   Affectionately yours

             Rabindranath Tagore

43
Tagore to Rothenstein

        c/o Messrs Thomas Cook & Son
        Ludgate Circus
        April 28, 1913

My dear friend

 I do not know why I am in London at all—it has lost its flavour and has become all South Kensington to me. I would have fled from here, but very unfortunately I have bound myself to this place till the middle of June by my lecturing engagements. It was foolish on my part to agree to this, for after all it is very unimportant—My poems are my best works and these papers will be of very little use to anybody. But wisdom comes too late and I must go through my weekly penance till I am purged of my *karma.*

I am waiting for you to come to London when I shall hand over to you my prose papers and perhaps I shall accompany you to your country home for a few days till I am required here for my lectures.

I am spending quiet days but very little work is being done. What I most want is a little more sunshine and the presence of loving friends.   Ever yours

Rabindranath Tagore

Is there anybody in your house to whom we can come for our letters which must be waiting there? Thanks for the cheque.

44
Rothenstein to Tagore

Far Oakridge   [May 6?, 1913]

My very dear friend—I am deeply moved by your lectures which I have just read—there must be no question about whether they be published or no over here. Published they must be, for nothing so clear, so direct & so inspired by experience has to my knowledge at least, been written about the unity of man with God, a subject so often dealt with, either by abstruse metaphysicians whom we poor untrained thinkers cannot follow, or by vague & not very convincing amateurs of religion. Of course it is your poetry over again, the same power of sending a line to bring up active personal experience & inspiration, without which no writing can possess a spark of true life. The examples you use to make your points clear are most beautiful; there is not a word with which I do not personally most passionately agree, & reading such work makes me feel the absolute necessity of art & poetry as a step to the sense of the immense value of life, a sense few men can get without a ladder the physical beauty of the face of the world does, for those who can see, provide. I do, reading these papers, feel again how great my personal debt to you is, a debt which can, I am almost happy to say, never be repaid. . . . Please do not think I am paying you compliments—I am not. I only want you to feel that there are people who are deeply moved by the shining sincerity of your thought, & that I know is in a way all that an artist wants in the way of acknowledgement. I know that dozens of people will tell you how grateful they are to you & speak of their admiration, but you will not always be sure that they have understood how serious a matter it is to agree with the things you speak of. . . . In one or two rare cases I believe you can improve the expression [in the lectures]—when I come next week we shall I hope get a little time together. . . . I would love to hear you read *Chitra*, had I known what the weather was going to do to-day I would have stayed, but I am glad to be in the peace & quiet of this place, & think of you none the less.[1] Ever your friend

W. R.

. . . Is it true you will come to Cambridge with me? That would be delightful.[2]

1. On May 9 Tagore lectured and read *Chitra* for the Indian Art, Dramatic and Friendly Society at the Cromwell Road Centre. Stopford Brooke commented: "I see Tagore has been reading before a London audience his play. I don't see—in my soul's eye—him in that crew. I suppose it was sure to be, that he had to do this. If London gets hold of a Lion, it [is] certain to pinch his tail until he roars for them, but the noble beast must shiver, at least a little. Did Tagore write that Shiva would turn his awful eye on them? I fancy not. He is too good for that; he would take refuge in the thought that the whole thing was illusion. Yet, I did not like it. Flee from the press & dwell with steadfastness. I hope it is not priggish to say this." (Brooke to Rothenstein, May 1913. RP:HL.)

2. Late in May Rothenstein spoke to Indian students at Cambridge. J. D. Anderson decided not to attend: "I was going to offer to be present on that occasion, but perhaps I had better not. I have few prejudices, political or other, but I am, after all, an old retired Civilian, and the lads you address might find my presence a nuisance." (Anderson to Rothenstein, May 12, 1913. RP:HL.)

45
Tagore to Rothenstein

>37 Alfred Place [West], South Kensington
>May 9, 1913

My dear friend

   I cannot tell you what a great happiness it has caused me to know that my papers have moved you so deeply. Though they had some kind of appreciation in America I was not quite sure that they could be of any real value to the people in this country. Most of these ideas were expressed in Bengali to my students in Bolpur and they can boast of no erudition or philosophical acumen but they came straight from my heart and they are parts of my life. In fact, in course of giving them expression I came to know them. They were being manifest to me the moment I was holding them to others. When I spoke them they were more than mere ideas, they were flowering of my life. I was not quite sure if this quality was still there in these English writings of mine—the spontaneous revelation of my spirit's growth—which is the only element that could be of any value to others. But your letter has given me the assurance that these have not been written in vain. Looking forward to meeting you next week   I am ever yours

>Rabindranath Tagore

46
Tagore to Rothenstein

>37 Alfred Place West, South Kensington
>May 29, 1913

Dear friend

   Could you invite Yeats at your house to lunch next Wednesday so that I can have an opportunity of discussing with him my translations that he is revising. MacMillans are ready to publish my next book of poems and also my lectures, and they want the Mss. as soon as possible so as to be in time for the next autumn publication season.¹   Yours always

Rabindranath Tagore

Yeats will come back from Ireland next Sunday.

    1. Fox Strangways told Macmillan: "Don't draw up the agreement for the *poems* just yet, please. I should like to be sure first that the others (Tagore and Rothenstein) agree to the terms being the same as for Gitanjali. My own view is that they should be the same, with the understanding that if the book turned out a real success you should give some of the profits in the form of a donation to Tagore's school. . . . it would be more than the money if it came as a gift from you." He signed the agreement, however, for October publication of the lectures as *Sādhanā*. (Fox Strangways to Macmillan, May 29, 1913. MCP.)

47
Rothenstein to Tagore

Far Oakridge   May 31, 1913

My dear friend—I am delighted to hear you have already arranged with Macmillan for the immediate publication of your lectures—this is the best of news, for I regard them as the most important contribution to religious-ethical thought we have had from East or West this century at least. . . . My wife writes that you enjoyed your time with Shaw—I felt sure you would like him, for he is the most genial of all the men of talent I know, with a largeness of personality & radiance of wit which endears him to us very much.¹ My wife also writes that you are to read the King [of the Dark Chamber] to us on the evening of the 10th. That is a noble proposition, & we will ask the most worthy company we can get together.² Your success & the admiration which is expressed on all sides is naturally very dear to me. I believe that in spite of the strain all this homage must entail upon you that there must be some joy to you too in a way, & that when you are back in India the more distressing side of this personal toasting & feasting will be forgotten. . . . You are not often out of my thoughts—my only fear is lest you overtax your strength. I felt often last year that I seemed to be a kind of watch dog, frightening many passersby away, but this year no

one can complain of your being difficult of access, or that your wisdom is being monopolised unduly by a few.   Ever yours—
W. R.

Sunday

I open this to say that Alice has just come to see me for a day & gives me good news of you, telling me you are looking well externally, though suffering as I feared within. I long to come & carry you off but I know it cannot be. If you would care to see me to-morrow before the lecture I could come & fetch you, but I expect you will want to be alone up to the last moment. Anyway, a line to Hampstead would find me at five thirty when I shall reach home. I am looking forward greatly to seeing you.

   1. See *MM* II, 265. Rothenstein seems to imply here that Shaw and Tagore met in 1912, but Tagore had left England by the end of Shaw's "solid month" of moratorium on engagements in 1912. In 1913 Mrs. Shaw asked Tagore and the Rothensteins to lunch, but William could not attend. (Charlotte Shaw to William and Alice Rothenstein. May 19, 1913. RP:HL.)
   2. The Rothensteins did their best, but it was holiday time and many were away. However, Tagore swelled the guest list with suggestions of his own. (Tagore to Rothenstein, June 6, 7, 1913. RP:HL.) This play was read more than once, for Evelyn Underhill heard it on May 8. (Evelyn Underhill to Tagore, May 9, 1913. R-S.)

48
Rothenstein to Tagore

Far Oakridge   June 13, 1913

My dear friend—here is a letter which will prove to you that there were people of understanding listening to you on Tuesday evening last. I think you will not be averse to letting Massingham have one or two of your poems for the Nation—it was there you made your first bow to the British public.[1] I shall miss you this week, as I am staying down here to go on with my work quietly, the more especially as I am suffering from a very disagreeable complaint called hay fever which does not make my appearance bear a stronger resemblance to Apollo than usual. I wish I could carry you off here for a rest; I feel that you will be badly in need of one, for there are few who can stand the racket of a London season. I hope things are going well with you otherwise—I shall look to seeing you next week—perhaps you will keep either Tuesday evening or Wednesday morning free for me. Please tell your nephew that I should be delighted to have him any time, should he feel inclined to come down here—of course when the car is in working order there will be no excuse for you not coming, all of you.[2] The flags shall be flying from all the houses, & all the artillery of Oakridge will be requisitioned to welcome you.   Ever yours

W. R.

(Shall I write Massingham or will you?)[3]

1. H. W. Massingham (1860–1924), editor, *The Nation*, Liberal left-wing spokesman. He met Tagore in 1912 and told Rothenstein: "I welcome the idea of his making 'The Nation' [his] present means of expression. He is a very great master, . . . and I propose that every fortnight Mr Tagore, if he is willing, should write us a poem . . . I should not like to work for lengthy studies; I am sure that what he writes in the way of brief poetic allegories will sink into many minds. Their form seems to me wonderful: nothing like 'Gitanjali' has ever appeared in an English [dress?] since Wordsworth." (Massingham to Rothenstein [June 1912]. RP:HL.)
2. Surendranath Tagore (1872–1940), Tagore's nephew and translator.
3. Tagore wrote. See Letter 49, note 3.

49
Tagore to Rothenstein

37 Alfred Place West, South Kensington
June 17, 1913

Dear Friend

I am glad indeed to read Mr Massingham's letter which you have kindly sent to me. Not because I am hankering for appreciation but because I do want the message embodied in this particular play to reach your people. This play has come out of my innermost experience, almost unconsciously almost inspite of myself. Therefore it has its message for me as much for others and I have almost an impersonal love for it.[1]

Directly I have done with my lectures I shall run to your

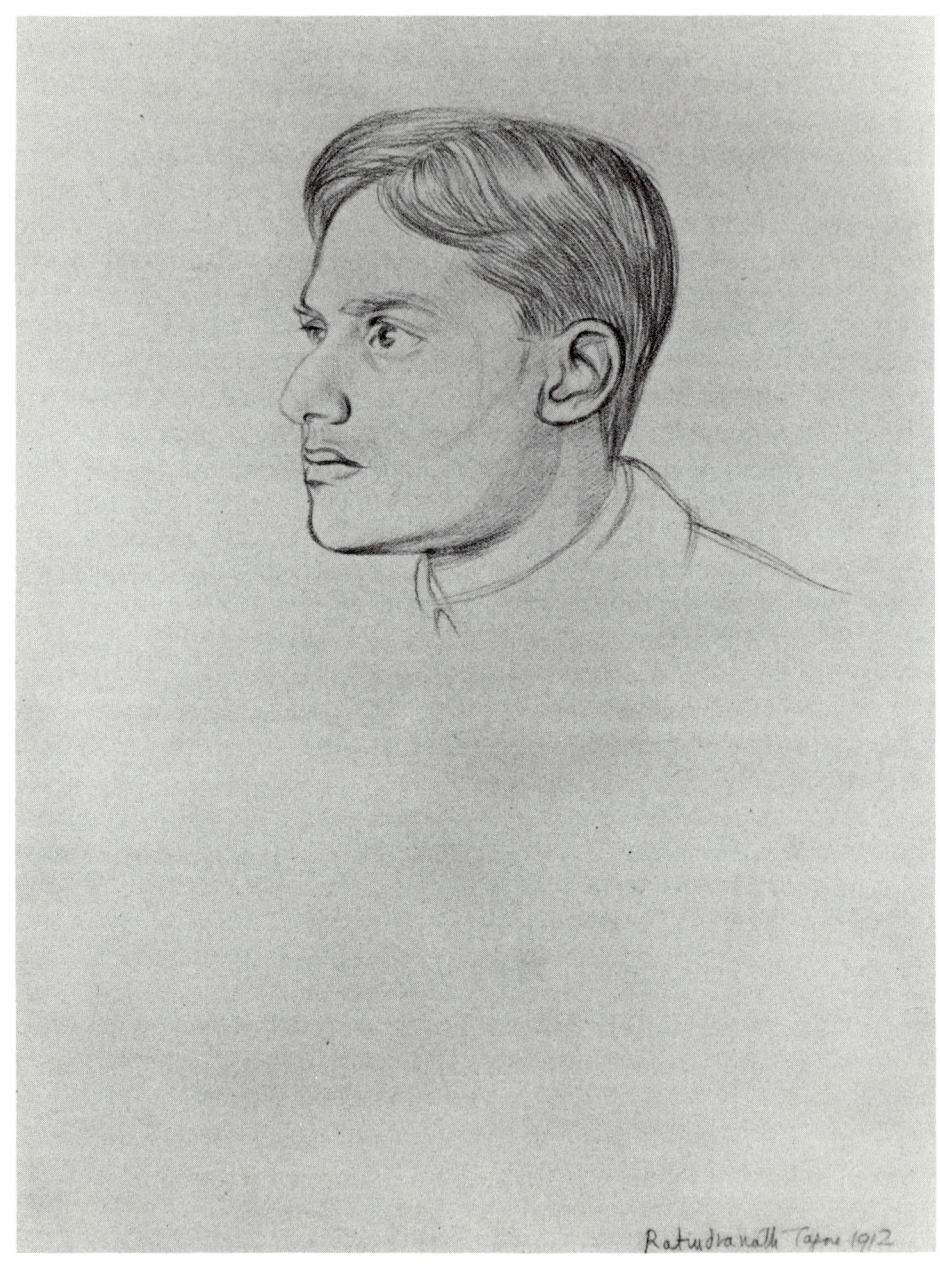

Rathindranath Tagore, drawing by Rothenstein

country home and rest for a few days before I submit myself to the surgical operation which doctors recommend.

Suren is leaving England next Thursday for India and it will not be possible for him to visit you before that. He sends you his kindest regards.[2]

I will select a poem of mine and send it to the Editor of The Nation, perhaps, tomorrow.[3]   Yours

Rabindranath Tagore

  1. I.e., *The King of the Dark Chamber.*
  2. Surendranath, Rathindranath, and Pratima left on June 19.
  3. Tagore, no. 10, *Utsharga* [Dedication] (1914), in *R-R*, X, 19–21: "The Woman in Sorrow," *The Nation* (London), 13 (1913), 498: no. 57, *Fruit-Gathering:* in *CPP*, p. 164.

50
Rothenstein to Tagore

Far Oakridge   June 17, 1913

My dear friend—of course the King must lie very near your heart—is it not your own life, as it is in fact everyman's? For do we not all lust after painted toys & even when wisdom has come the temptations at times can be as great as ever before? For an artist the play is peculiarly moving, for there is always something tempting us to leave our work & yet it is, we know anew each time we come back to our task, this work which alone brings one certain joy. More than this, the temptation to adopt a formula which is in the air, so to say, is ever at our elbow, yet we know that absolute concentration upon our task of interpretation, singleminded & absolutely sincere, will alone convince our souls that we are obeying absolute commands. It is because your plays, like the rest of your work, deal with these essential realities that they move me so deeply. I have seen so many pictures & read so many books in my life, & now I have come to a time when a picture or a book must mean everything to me, or nothing. If a book is a good book, it can be a bible for any man who responds to it, & any picture should contain within itself all that a thousand pictures can give. The serious thing is not that so many pictures are painted & books written, but that one person reads so many books & looks at so many pictures. At least I feel that those who care for your work do read it carefully, & perhaps when the plays are printed they will be as well understood as the poems. To me they are infinitely precious & I hope when you have more leisure that you will take upon yourself the burden of further translations. . . . I greatly regret not seeing Surendranath again. I would have written him had I known he was leaving to-morrow. It is impossible to know such a man & not to love him & he will always be remembered with the greatest affection by all of us. I am glad you are sending a poem to Massingham.   Ever yours—

W. R.

51
Tagore to Rothenstein

Duchess Home, 2 Beaumont Street [London]
July 6, 1913

The forced cheerfulness of your letters are sadly pathetic, my friend,—for I know you had to go through all this interminable series of outrages not very long ago. It is dreadful to have to watch helplessly the indignity that is being daily offered to my poor body in the name of the science of healing, as if the body were no more than a mere peace of flesh and bones. Surely she has her claims to be treated with the utmost delicacy and respect, considering that it is her noble privilege to initiate our soul into the double mystery of life and death. But your brute science is no respecter of persons, it rudely tramples upon her tender susceptibilities and desecrates her beautiful sanctuary of privacy into which she has taken shelter since her banishment from the Eden of the primitive innocence. I suppose the end justifies the means in this case, but all the same, it is difficult to summon up gratitude for this pitiful means so long as it solely occupies the field. Unfortunately we have to submit to its tyranny, but we must lie in wait for our revenge, and massacre it at the first opportunity and bury it in the subterranean vault of Archeology where all the well meaning ineptitude of the past

ages find their rest. I am eagerly waiting to see you and I am sure you know that your visit is not likely to tire me   Ever yours
Rabindranath Tagore

52
Tagore to Rothenstein

[16 More's Garden, Cheyne Walk[1]
August 6?, 1913]

I have got a letter from Mr Drinkwater expressing great satisfaction at the result of the interview he had with Mrs Rothenstein. Evidently they want to reserve the right of performance of Chitra and as they have the first refusal they have gained their object without having to pay for it. I am sure they have not the least doubt in their minds that nobody else than themselves is ever likely to be willing to put this play on the stage.[2]

I must come and see you when I get my release from the doctor and also from the pair of sculptors who are plying me with their attention at the same time. I do not think they will be long over it.   Ever yours
Rabindranath Tagore

Have you made any special arrangements with The Nation about the payment for my poems? I have not yet received anything from them. Kalimohan has heard from home that his family is suffering privation from want of funds. I want to help him when I am paid by The Nation for the poems published.

1. One page only and letter perhaps incomplete. Place and approximate date from reference to "the pair of sculptors." Mrs. Moody had arrived by June 22 and commissioned Jo Davidson to do a bust of Tagore in her London flat. Davidson may have had an assistant but mentions only May Sinclair, poet and novelist, who came from her studio upstairs to talk to Tagore and prevent his falling into private meditations. (See Jo Davidson, *Between Sittings: An Informal Autobiography of Jo Davidson* [New York, 1951], p. 92. The bust: The Knoedler Galleries, New York, current custodians. See also Dunbar, *A House in Chicago*, pp. 99–102.)

2. John Drinkwater (1882–1937), poet and playwright; "they": Birmingham Repertory Company. Drinkwater's biographer writes: "They were very interested in producing worthwhile but little known works, in-

cluding a number of world premieres. Also, they were interested in verse drama. I've no doubt whatever that they would be interested in a play by Tagore, and would have welcomed the opportunity of giving it a first performance, especially if it had little hope of being put on elsewhere. . . . but it appears that for some reason the negotiations came to nothing, and no production of *Chitra* took place there during the first ten years of the theatre's history." (John Vickers to the editor, December 19, 1969.) Alice Rothenstein's only role was apparently that of go-between.

53
Tagore to Rothenstein

16 More's Garden, Cheyne Walk
August 12, 1913

Dear friend

I have got my release from the doctor and next Thursday I shall have my last sitting with the sculptors. It is still uncertain when Mrs Moody will be able to leave her bed so I have made up my mind to visit you some day next week.[1] I was putting it off till I could get complete leisure but that will not be possible before I leave this country. I have to go over my proofs which has to be done with the help of Ernest Rhys and get my other mss ready for the press which requires some help of either Sturge Moore or Yeats.[2] But I must not wait till they are done—for my intention is to leave England by the end of this month and spend a month travelling on the continent and then take my steamer at some Italian port and sail for India. So I must go and take my farewell from you next week.

I am not the least anxious about Chitra never having any great expectation from it and being quite sure you will do what could be done   Ever yours

Rabindranath Tagore

1. Mrs. Moody was prostrated by overindulgence in English strawberries; the flat was "made over to the Tagores and their stream of visitors." (See Dunbar, *A House in Chicago*, p. 101.) Tagore went to Far Oakridge on August 16.

2. According to Tagore, Macmillan "gladly" accepted his suggestion that Rhys revise *Sādhanā* for publication; he knew of no one better qualified to give his English the considerable attention it required. (Tagore to Rhys, May 31, 1913. R. St. L. Deraniyagala Papers.)

54
Tagore to Rothenstein

16 More's Garden, Cheyne Walk
August 17, 1913

My dear friend

I am still occupied with my proofs and my manuscripts and I hope I shall be free by the end of the next week when I shall come and see you. The nature of my work is fitful though it keeps me tied and I am thoroughly tired of this enforced idleness which robs me of my true leisure. I can assure you, since you are away from here London has no attraction for me and my life has become desultory. The difference is very great for me, the difference between the last summer and this—the difference between the time when I was translating my "children" series of poems one by one and reading them to you and the time when I am getting the Ms. ready for publication. Now it is a mere business and it tires me. This cold blooded literary craftsmanship, this weighing of words and expressions is utterly wearisome. I am pining for touch of life, for the warmth of reality—and that is the reason why the call of my Bolpur school is getting to be more and more insistent. I have drained dry my wine cup here and now I must go back there where my food is waiting for me. Give my love to Mrs Rothenstein and to the dear children.   Ever yours

Rabindranath Tagore

55
Tagore to Rothenstein

S.S. City of Lahore   September 7, 1913[1]

Beloved friend, this is just to let you know that it is an uninterrupted delight to me, these days on the sea, full of the sunlight and leisure. The first two days were grey but now that the curtain has been raised I am listening to the duet of the gold and blue, of the silence and sound, of the sky and the sea. This dancing sea seems to me like a maiden heartfree laughing at the lavish gold of love offered at her feet by the pale sky. My heart is like a greedy bee wallowing in the honeycells of a gorgeous cluster of forget-me-nots—its wings have grown languid and silent. Kalimohan and myself, two solitary souls take our chairs in the loneliest corner of the deck and pass our days in silence while our fellow passengers are busy with their endless schemes of amusements. They do not molest us in any way except a missionary who takes every opportunity of impressing upon my mind the superiority of Christianity over Hinduism. He is after my immortal soul, lying in wait for it, like a cat for a bird. I can see from this window poor Kalimohan is caught; I should come to his rescue but that would only add to the number of victims.

We are just passing through Gibralter—the rock looks like a dozing sentry, in the early morning light. My love to you all. Ever yours

Rabindranath Tagore

Have you asked for Macmillan's consent for publishing The King in The Nation?[2] I do not know where Mrs Moody is—I am sending a letter to her addressing it to your care.[3]

    1. Tagore and Kalimohon had planned to leave England on August 27 and sail from Trieste on September 1. (Tagore to Rothenstein, August 21, 1913. RP:HL.) Rothenstein apparently persuaded them to stay longer in England and sail from Liverpool. The *City of Lahore*, however, passed Gibraltar on September 8; Tagore is very likely mistaken about the date.

    2. Massingham wanted *The King of the Dark Chamber* as a *Nation* supplement. This had to be approved by Macmillan, who now wished to consider all new Tagore translations.

    3. Mrs. Moody and her secretary rented Rothenstein's Hampstead house until she was well enough to leave for the United States early in October.

56
Rothenstein to Tagore

Far Oakridge   September 11, 1913

My dear friend—when this reaches you you will have had your welcome home. I can fancy it a triumphant one—did ever any one leave, slipping away so quietly & come back with such crowns of bay & laurel as yourself? If Bengal is especially proud of you you must bear with ovations, however noisy, & having done so you will then again slip away & anchor in your own beloved haven of Bolpur. Your boys' welcome will be dearer to you I imagine than all the clamour of the Calcutta crowd—I should like to witness it myself. It is difficult to realise that you have indeed left us, but your presence does in a manner remain—it certainly lingers among us here—& makes the thought of you something quite vital & actual. That you will come back to us I feel pretty sure & when you do you will find us, in heart at least, as you left us. They were good & rich days, were they not, the days we spent together? It is not every man who has the good fortune to meet a fellow being whose mind is so wonderfully in sympathy with his own that he feels himself cleansed & strengthened by his friendship & intercourse. That we practise different arts is perhaps a happy thing; it certainly allows me to enjoy yours without that technical interest which sometimes acts as blinkers. I have been reading Chitra carefully & later am going to make one or two suggestions regarding a return to your original translation. For the moment you will not want to be bothered with matters of the kind—indeed letters of any kind at this time are likely to be more of a nuisance, given the surfeit of correspondence you will have, than anything else. . . . I enclose report of Sir Oliver Lodge's presidential address —you will see that he quotes you twice in it.[1] . . . I know you will think of us sometimes, & you will know that we will watch over your interests as well as cherish the warmest love for you all. . . . Ever your friend

           William Rothenstein

1. Sir Oliver Lodge (1851–1940), physicist, past President of the Society for Psychical Research, President of the British Association in 1913, opened its Birmingham meeting on September 10 with a plea for refusal to shut the gates of science against psychic and philosophical imponderables. (See "British Association: The Presidential Address: Sir O. Lodge on Scientific Dogmatism," *The Times* [London], September 11, 1913, p. 11. On Lodge's position athwart science and religion, see Samuel Hynes, *The Edwardian Turn of Mind* [Princeton, 1968], pp. 143–146.)

57
Rothenstein to Tagore

Far Oakridge   September 17, 1913

My very dear friend—your letter came as a great relief. I felt the responsibility I bore in your long sea journey & would have had the consequences of a rough crossing of the Bay [of Biscay] on my conscience, & I was delighted to learn from you of your peaceful time on board. I knew you would be happy provided the weather were fair, & so it turned out. I love your account of the missionary lying in wait for your soul—dear Kalimohon, his is so simple & transparent & is at the disposition of any one, even a missionary. I have written Massingham re the King, & suggested either he or Fox Strangways approach Macmillan.[1] . . . I think of you daily, passing smoothly & with patient regularity over the waters, with the rising & setting of the sun as the two great events of the day. How well do I remember them when I took the same journey! and each day brings you nearer your own wonderful country, so radiant & yet so woeful. You have at least served her well, better perhaps than any one realises. But the whole world is in travail, & there must be much pain & lamenting before a new era can dawn. There are moments when one gets an awful vision of what our children & their children must go through, but at bottom one knows justice must be done, & the cry of the poor may be shut out from our ears, but it never ceases. I hope at least for myself that I may anchor here & help in some little way the life of this little corner of the world. Your own path shines white & clear before you, & therein are you blessed.

. . . Please tell Surendra Babu that he must by all means hurry on with his translations of your stories—those recently published are too monstrously ill done for words.[2] I am delighted with your Kabir translations—they are priceless.[3] I hope by the time this reaches you the strain of your reception will be over. Ever yours—

W. R.

1. Massingham must have approached Macmillan. Fox Strangways was falling behind events. He had heard that in addition to *The Gardener*

and *The Crescent Moon,* a second *Gitanjali* (i.e., *Fruit-Gathering*), *Chitra,* and perhaps *The Post Office* would be published. "Are you undertaking any of these?" he asked. "And if so can you give me a rough date at which you hope to produce it or them?" (Fox Strangways to Macmillan, September 21, 1913. MCP.) He requested copies of new agreements signed by Tagore and added, "I remember now that we arranged (he and I) that he should sign these, (or his son) so that I have no bone to pick with him over *that.*" (Fox Strangways to Macmillan, September 29, 1913. MCP.)

2. Tagore, *Glimpses of Bengal Life,* trans. R. R. Sen (Madras, 1913), short stories not to be confused with Tagore's *Glimpses of Bengal,* trans. Surendranath Tagore [rev. Thomas Sturge Moore] (London, 1921), from his *Chinnapatra* [Torn Leaves] (1912), letters written in the 1890's. Tagore tried in 1913 to block Sen's book, but Sen proceeded on the basis of a promise made in 1909. Tagore felt that his new fame in England had altered circumstances, and Sen ought to have reconfirmed that earlier permission. Tagore later asked Macmillan to apprise other London publishers of these facts. (Tagore to Macmillan, through Andrews. December 28 [1914]. MP:BM.)

3. Lyrics by the fifteenth-century Benares mystic, a synthesis of Vaishnava and Sufi thought. Evelyn Underhill was to collaborate as editor and commentator. It would finally emerge as *One Hundred Poems of Kabir,* trans. Rabindranath Tagore, assisted by Evelyn Underhill (London, 1914), and *Songs of Kabir,* trans. Rabindranath Tagore with the assistance of Evelyn Underhill (New York, 1915).

58
Rothenstein to Tagore

Far Oakridge October 3, 1913

My very dear friend— . . . Need I tell you how much you are missed, & how constantly your name is on our & others' lips? All that remains to us is to have patience, & await news of you. It seems long since you left already, yet we must still remain expectant for some weeks longer. I have had a day, in London for an India Society meeting, & saw Mrs Moody— much better, I think, & on the very edge of the sea, leaving London I think to-morrow. She told us of your safe arrival & pleasant voyage.

The Society would like to publish Kabir, of course. I think the good Fox Strangways will write to some of you on the subject.[1] We are putting the Ajanta reproductions in hand & expect to have the work out next autumn.[2] Fox Strangways tells me Macmillan object to the previous publication of the "King" by Massingham, so I fear that pleasant scheme is knocked in the head.³ He seems also to have had some difficulty with Gide & is a little irritable over affairs.⁴ He tells me things are all well forward with Macmillan, but he appears to think you ought to get better terms, now that your sale is so settled a thing, for future books. I am looking forward to the Gardener & the Crescent Moon, but have had no proofs of the illustrations sent me nor indeed of the reproductions of your brother's drawings. People need a deal of prodding, & prodding unfortunately takes time. . . . All send their most affectionate greetings. Ever yours

W. R.

1. Rothenstein wanted the Kabir poems published at once. Evelyn Underhill thought this "quite impossible, . . . till I have a great deal more information about K's position in Indian literature, his relation to the Sufi poets, etc., than I at present possess." She was "glad and proud to be able to help with it: but I feel it a great responsibility to have it left entirely in my hands." (Evelyn Underhill to Tagore, August 19, 1913. R-S.)

2. Lady C. J. P. Herringham, *Ajanta Frescoes: Being Reproductions in Colour and Monochrome of Frescoes in Some of the Caves at Ajanta . . . , with Introductory Essays by Various Members of the India Society* (London, 1915). (See above, Introduction, note 26.)

3. The good Fox Strangways still lagged behind: "I have got a little confused about the plays. I think you said you wanted to publish 'The King of the Dark Chamber' and 'The Post Office' but not 'Chitra.' Was this so? And are there any other plays, or works (besides the 2nd series Gitanjali) that you contemplate doing or would like to do?" (Fox Strangways to Macmillan, October 3, 1913. MCP.) Beside his mention of *Chitra* is a Macmillan notation: "Pause."

4. See Introduction to Part II, "Tagore in the West," note 19. Gide translated *Gitanjali* as *L'Offrande Lyrique* (Paris, 1913), but dispute arose over similar intentions by Jean de Rosen. (See de Rosen, "Rabindranath Tagore" and "*Gitanjali* [*L'offrande des chants*]," *La Revue* [Paris], 101 [1913], 496–498, 499–503.) Fox Strangways had introduced Alexis Léger (St.-John Perse) who intervened on Gide's behalf. (Fox Strangways to Tagore, October 14, 1912. R-S; to Macmillan, September 18, 1913. MCP.)

59
Rothenstein to Tagore

Far Oakridge   October 8, 1913

My very dear friend— . . .

Doubtless you yourself are thankful to be in your beloved Bengal; Oakridge is a very tame affair in comparison with the fiercer grandeur of your sun & storms, but I hope & believe you will think of us all sometimes. I have been reading the second Gitanjali—[Sturge] Moore has in many cases made some good suggestions I think, but in others I feel emphatically that your own words, if possibly less correct, are infinitely more pregnant.[1] I am sorry to say Fox Strangways tells me Macmillans are averse to "The King" appearing as a Nation supplement. I think it would have been possible had you yourself written to them expressing your own strong desire to let Massingham carry out his suggestion. I have written Massingham, proposing that he should approach you for a translation of some unpublished play for the purpose.[2] I hope your friend Kshiti Mohan Sen will let The India Society publish the Kabir translations at once, as they wish. You & Mrs Moore have done wonders with Ajit's rather hurried work & the more I read the more do I care for your great mystic.[3] I see The Gardener is announced—also your father's autobiography, & I hope Surendra is working on the prose translations [of the short stories].[4] I send you my warmest greetings, dear friend, & hope you have by this time escaped from the caresses of your admiring country & are sitting at peace—with new & fruitful visions passing before you. Ever your devoted—

W. R.

Many greetings to Pearson & Andrews at Bolpur.[5]

1. See Letter 78, note 6.
2. Massingham seems to have given up. No Tagore play appeared in the *Nation*. When another magazine offered £15 for *The King of the Dark Chamber*, Tagore judged it unsuited to serial publication. (Tagore to Macmillan, April 2, 1914. MP:BM.)
3. Kshiti Mohan Sen and Ajit Kumar Chakravarty, Santiniketan teachers who did first-draft translations of the Kabir poems from Hindi. Pound and Kalimohon Ghose edited ten of these. (See "Certain Poems of Kabir, translated by Kali Mohan Ghose and Ezra Pound. From the edition

of Mr. Kshiti Mohan Sen," *MR*, 13 [1913], 611–613.) Tagore and Evelyn Underhill were thus the fifth and sixth persons to take Kabir in hand.

4. "Your father's autobiography": *The Auto-Biography of Maharshi Devendranath Tagore*, trans. Satyendranath Tagore and Indira Devi [Chaudhuri] (London, 1914).

5. W. W. Pearson (1881–1923), formerly with the London Missionary Society at Bhowanipur, Calcutta. He was in England on sick leave in the summer of 1912, returned that winter to a teaching post in Delhi, and in 1913 moved to Santiniketan. He and Andrews left on November 30, 1913, for South Africa, to observe Gandhi's efforts on behalf of indentured Indian laborers.

60
Rothenstein to Tagore

Far Oakridge   October 15, 1913

My dear friend—"The Gardener" has reached me & I have to thank you for the copy which was sent me. Need I tell you what a delight it is to have a second noble volume to lie beside Gitanjali on my bookshelf? It still seems a kind of miracle that all this fruitful work should have been done since you came to us in Europe. Three years ago I was longing to get the chance of reading some of your work & it seemed almost impossible to find it, & now every man may read what he pleases. Please tell Gaganendranath & your brother how excellent the portrait is.[1] If I cover up the beardless chin it is yourself to-day. Emery Walker has at last sent—not the proofs, but photographs of the drawings, which require fitting to the page. Walker is a dear fellow, but a very snail at his work.[2] You will have heard from Fox Strangways that Macmillan has given the India Society permission to publish a limited large paper edition of Chitra.[3] This is joyful news to me, & I know when we first talked of a fine edition you were yourself pleased with the idea. I am hoping to hear direct news of you in a few days' time—it seems a long time since I last heard, but we are glad to know that your journey was so agreeable. We are enjoying a Heavenly autumn—to-day the sky is as serene & cloudless as an Indian sky. I send you my affectionate greetings, in which all join. Ever yours

W. R.

1. Tagore, *The Gardener,* frontispiece by Gaganendranath Tagore, after a drawing by Jyotirindranath of Rabindranath aged sixteen.
2. For Jyotirindranath's book; see Letter 15, note 4.
3. Fox Strangways was instructed to ask whether an India Society edition sold privately, or printed privately and sold through Macmillan, might enhance the sales of other Tagore plays about to be published. (Fox Strangways to Macmillan, June 14, 1913. MCP.) *Chitra*'s trials dragged on into the winter. Granville-Barker gave up a plan to produce the play: "From private sources I learn that Barker cannot come to terms for your play—'Chitra.' He has lost heavily on Shaw's 'Androcles,' it seems." (Rhys to Tagore, November 24, 1913. R-S.)

61
Tagore to Rothenstein

Shanti Niketan   October 20, 1913

My dear friend

I wish I had not to write to you letters but could have you by my side—for I know you would have enjoyed everything I have here around me. It has already become difficult for me to bring before my mind your October landscape dim with mist and numb with creeping cold. As I sit writing to you all the doors of my room are wide open and the stainless golden light of this late autumn is pouring in from all sides flooding my brains with its quivering stream of radiance. The glistening green of the heavy foliage of the tall *sal* trees soaring in the clear blue sky seems to me like an outburst of music from the heart of the earth. I can assure you this is the most beautiful spot of land that I can ever hope to find anywhere. I do not expect every stranger to share my enthusiasm for this place, for until one's life is in harmony with his surroundings one can never see nature in her truth. The life I have been living here for years has helped me to understand the language of the spirit of this place. In spite of the admiration I have for your civilisation I cannot but wish from the depth of my heart that you could come to us in our *āshrama* and share our simple lives filling your leisure with utmost peace and beauty. Of all the friends I have in the west I think of you as the one who ought to have been born as my brother in this country, know-

ing that you have the power to utilise to their best purposes the opportunities that India, of all countries in the world, offers to men. But with all my attractions for India in its various aspects I cannot but marvel at the fact that my best friends are in England and it took some weeks for me to adjust my mind to my old familiar surroundings where you were absent. With my best love to you   I am   ever yours
Rabindranath Tagore

62
Rothenstein to Tagore

Far Oakridge   October 29, 1913

My dear friend—just a line to send you our greetings—also the enclosed which my wife culled from her favourite organ, The Daily Mail.¹ I have been hoping to hear from you, but at any rate your friends have given me the best of news regarding you & I know how great will be the calls upon your time these first weeks. That you are so well after your journey is the best possible news & that, whatever criticisms you have to offer of your European experiences, you have only kind things to say of your many friends here is very pleasant reading. You at least have won their whole hearted devotion & there stands a shrine to Rabindranath in many a home in this island of ours. . . . I had a delightful letter from Dr Seal telling me of your reception at Calcutta, but I have heard nothing yet of your reception at Bolpur.² I think that would be a subject for one of my Indian decorations—"Gurudev being met by his chelas on the banks of the Ganges." I see by the by that an Indian master builder is to be appointed to work with Lutyens & Baker, & that it is intended to place the workshops under the supervision of Indian craftsmen.³

. . . I have heard . . . from Dinesh Babu. You know how sorry I am to disappoint my Indian friends. I am but a poor reed in this great stream of London, & there is little altruism in the vision of a publisher.⁴   I am ever yours
W. R.

I hope Surendranath is working on your prose stories. That little book I bought was too bad to pass on to anyone.[5]

1. Review, "A Great Man from Bengal," *The Daily Mail* (London), October 29, 1913, p. 6.
2. Seal wrote: "I had the privilege of garlanding Rabindranath the other day [October 6] at the Howrah Station, where a large number of our people gathered to give him an ovation on his return—the people's homage." (Seal to Rothenstein, October 8, 1913. RP:HL. See editorial, "Rabindranath's Return," *MR*, 14 [1913], 427–428.)
3. See editorial, "The Building of New Delhi," *MR*, 14 (1913), 212. Edwin Lutyens (1869–1944), widely experienced in designing for the Empire. The Royal Institute of British Architects had recommended him as designer for New Delhi; he accepted on condition that he be allowed to do the central buildings in European classical style. Herbert Baker (1862–1946), codesigner for New Delhi, architect for Government buildings in Cape Town, Pretoria, and London.
4. See Letter 25, note 3.
5. See Letter 57, note 2.

63
Tagore to Rothenstein

Shanti Niketan   November 7, 1913

Dear friend

Mr Fox Strangways wrote to me asking for a preface to Chitra. . . . The name of the heroine in Mahabharata is Chitrāngadā but as you have no soft dental d in your alphabet and as your readers are sure to put accent in the wrong place making it sound very unmusical I have ventured to cut it short, retaining the first portion of it which I am sure was the only portion used by her parents if she ever did have any name and parents to boot. You will also find that very little has been left of the original story in my play for which I need not apologize if the result be at all satisfactory.

I find that The Gardener is not having very warm reception from your critics but as I have had in Gitanjali much more than my deserts could be I can afford to climb down a great deal this time to reach my normal level which is the safest resting place for a man.[1]

I wish I could see you working at your canvas by yonder

group of trees—often and often I think of you, my dear friend, and I have a longing to have a quiet talk with you, specially when things go wrong and my mind is weighed down with responsibilities which no one else shares with me. Yours

Rabindranath

1. Reviewers nonplussed by the mysticism of *Gitanjali* seemed to feel better qualified to comment on the love poems of *The Gardener;* many found them wanting in originality. (See, for example, review, "The Gardener," *The Athenaeum* [London], November 1, 1913, p. 485.) Ezra Pound, however, still defended him. (See Pound, "Rabindranath Tagore: His Second Book into English," *The New Freewoman: An Individualist Review* [London], 1 [1913], 187–188.)

64
Rothenstein to Tagore

Far Oakridge   November 11, 1913

My very dear friend—at last I hear news of your welfare. That you should be so happy in your own dear & familiar surroundings is not surprising—I know something of the restlessness & sense of something rootless that comes upon one even among the most zealous of hosts when one is away from one's own. I like to hear of this happiness you are getting & to feel that you can still think so affectionately of your many friends here. . . . Your year with us must seem like a dream to you; a dream in a way it seems to me too—happily I can visualise it with absolute clearness & through letters we can still converse, when the mood is on us. I thought of you last night as the rain came down in torrents, & I heard the loud wailing of the wind over the hillside, & thought how your boys might run out into the storm, all joyous under the lash of the rain. . . . So in a manner, though yours is so much more ample & beautiful, our lives are not so dissimilar, for I take it you are no less inclined to respond to the alluring ogle of Calcutta than I to be inveigled into the coils of committees in London. I know these days will be fruitful ones for you & that the sun will ripen many thoughts into golden poems. Ever your affectionate—

W. R.

65
Rothenstein to Tagore

[Telegram received at Bolpur,
November 15, 1913]

Leo [*sic*] Tagore
    Bolpur

Nobel congratulations affectionately Rothenstein

III   1913-1914   Letters 66-90

Nobel Prize and After

Tagore's world changed dramatically in November 1913, but his nature did not consort well with international fame. He was attuned to what Ernest Rhys called "the paradox of the lyric impulse which seems so egoistic, but is really so bountiful, pouring out its pleasure for all created things, and transcending the smaller self to attain the greater."[1] Tagore was a writer who must respond to the lyric impulse immediately and unreservedly. He once described for a friend the wild swans, *balākā*, on the Lake of Jhelum taking suddenly to the air. This, he said, was how his poems came to him, " 'with a rush of sound and a flutter of wings.' " He must write and write until this lyric force had spent itself, not in one poem, but in a series born of this single impulse. He felt that he could not attain such heights, achieve such impact through conscious effort or with "the stroke of genius" often associated with sudden feats of technical prowess. This method Tagore found very difficult, even distasteful.[2]

Such a writer is seriously threatened by the interruptions that accompany sudden fame, and whenever Tagore mourned that he had forsaken his true vocation, he spoke a sad and sober truth. The interruptions, not the lyric impulse, began to control his life. The Nobel Prize forced him into artificial situations, and eventually separated him from some of the friends he needed most. It fastened onto him once and for all the West's stereotype of the sage from the East.

He suffered also from a vast naïveté or unawareness of publication procedure. With almost total disregard for the time and money required for preparing manuscripts and negotiations with publishers, he assigned these tasks to Rothenstein and to other friends. He would make simultaneous agreements with

1. Rhys to Rothenstein, July 11, 1914. RP:HL.
2. Interview with Amiya Chakravarty, New York City, August 30, 1965.

separate publishers, and he remained apparently oblivious to deadlines and to exigencies imposed by copyright regulations.[3] He took a hand spasmodically in such matters, but, when they became too intricate, took refuge in the fact that he was after all only a poet. The Nobel Prize, which could not change his nature, did change the world's way of looking at him. Accepting the Prize meant accepting new responsibilities and new relationships with old friends. By failing to take the initiative in this, Tagore sometimes forced his friends to do so.

These shifting balances are illustrated by his relationship with Fox Strangways. Arthur Fox Strangways was a member of an old and distinguished family, a bachelor, urbane and reserved, with great reserves as well of humor and affection. For more than a year he was Tagore's agent, legal representative, business manager. For a nominal fee which he himself requested, partially in repayment for expenses incurred, he did

---

3. The 1911 Copyright Act looms large in the background of negotiations with Tagore. It left unclear the application to British India, and whether it applied at all in Native States. At least one commentator considered this a point "quickly dismissed." (See review, "The Copyright Question," *The Edinburgh Review*, 212 [1910], 320.) Publishers like Macmillan and Longman, with large Indian interests, could not dismiss it. They urged the Publishers' Association, the Board of Trade, the Society of Authors, the India Office, and all available Parliamentary support, to press for clarification, since rights of both publishers and authors were unclear. Just before the India Society published *Gitanjali*, C. J. Longman told Sir Frederick Macmillan, "You will remember that in September I raised the question as to whether the new Copyright Act was actually in force in India. . . . it is clear that the Act is not yet in force, and, what is more, there is some idea of amending it. This is a most monstrous proposal, and, if I had not understood that the Act would come into force in India, I should certainly have met it with further opposition." (Longman to Frederick Macmillan, October 28, 1912. MP:BM.) On October 30 the Act was declared in force in India, but Longman, who wrote that very day to Sir Frederick (MP:BM), did not learn this until late in November, when he wrote: "It now remains to see that the India Office take the necessary steps to get the Act adopted in the Native States. If this is not done they will become Alsatias from which printed vernacular translations of British Copyright books will issue, and be spread over British India." (Longman to Frederick Macmillan, November 23, 1912. MP:BM.) The India Office advised the publishers to get one Native State to set a precedent by adopting the new Act. Not until February 1913 did Longman and Macmillan learn through the Society of Authors that the Maharaja of Jhalawar would propose such legislation. (Longman to F. H. Skrine, February 20, 1913; copy dated February 22, 1913. MP:BM.)

work that professional agents and writers would consider full value given and received.

Among the florid encomiums that followed Tagore's Nobel award, Fox Strangways' simple tribute stands out: "Best congratulations on the Nobel Prize. It is a great feather in your cap, and all your friends, here and in India, will be so glad." In this same letter Fox Strangways began trying to extricate himself from a burden that that award had made too heavy for even his good will: "But [your agency] is not the sort of business for which I really exist: my job is music. I think therefore I must ask you to find someone else, and pay him." He would try to find someone known to Tagore; otherwise it must be a professional agent who would charge a 10 percent fee, but "at that distance you will not be able to control him, and you may get badly swindled." Rather than allow that to happen, Fox Strangways would continue, but Tagore must pay him the professional fee. "The fact of getting the Nobel Prize makes a great difference to your position, and I see several signs, both in England and on the Continent, that people are out to make money out of you if your affairs are not in the hands of someone you can absolutely trust."[4]

When no substitute appeared, Fox Strangways offered to keep the power of attorney but insisted upon being relieved of the correspondence "because I have no clerk," because of the expense, and because of "the unpleasantness in which I am involved when you say one thing to me and another to someone else." Or, Tagore might put his affairs into Macmillan's hands entirely.

Tagore countered by suggesting that Fox Strangways enlist Ernest Rhys. Tagore forgot that Rhys was a legal amateur, must earn his own living, and had no clerk. Rhys *must*, Fox Strangways reiterated, be offered the professional 10 percent fee, or Tagore might accept Macmillan's offer to be his agent at 5 percent "on all profits *other than on books*." He told Tagore, "It is not as a rule a good thing to bind oneself to a publisher,

4. This and the following quotations are: Fox Strangways to Tagore, November 21, 28, 1913; January 2, February 20, 1914. R-S. In his January 2 letter Fox Strangways asked for £55: £5 to repay expenses, plus 5 percent of Tagore's publication profits to date, which Fox Strangways estimated at £1,000. Tagore instructed Macmillan accordingly (January 22, 1914. MP:BM).

but I think I should not mind doing so in this instance if it were my own case. I have seen a good deal of George Macmillan, in whose hands your matters are, and I am impressed by the straightforwardness and fair dealing of him and his firm." The royalty might be pushed a little higher elsewhere, but it would be hard to find a publisher with better intercontinental distribution facilities.

Thus it was arranged. In February 1914 Fox Strangways reminded Tagore, "You will remember that by this agreement things are definitely in your own hands."

Fox Strangways kept the power of attorney until, as India Society Secretary, he had settled the American rights to the Kabir volume. His contribution had been unique and invaluable; he had saved Tagore a sum of money that no one bothered to calculate; but in accounts of Tagore's career he became a minor satellite referred to in passing as "Fox Strangways and others."[5]

C. F. Andrews took up what Fox Strangways had laid down. Where Fox Strangways was reserved, Andrews was openly emotional. The style of Fox Strangways' letters is polished and finespun, with humor and controlled feeling always just beneath the surface. Andrews' letters are headlong and humorless. Fox Strangways was self-sufficient and dignified in his self-sufficiency. Andrews was a satellite badly in need of a sun; he found it in Rabindranath, whose name means "Lord of the Sun."

Andrews was not suddenly drawn to Tagore when both were in England in 1912; he had already addressed admiring poems to him from Delhi.[6] Early in 1914 Andrews moved to Santiniketan and gladly shouldered Tagore's burden of clerical detail. His commitment to the poet was deep and genuine, but it was primarily an emotional commitment to an India in whose political struggle Andrews sought to discover his own identity, an India Tagore seemed to personify. He thus imposed a new

---

5. Krishna Kripalani, *Rabindranath Tagore: A Biography* (New York, 1962), pp. 218–219. See also Mukhopadhyay, *Rabindrajibani*, II, 323. Rathindranath Tagore, who knew the facts about Fox Strangways' role, does not mention him in *On the Edges of Time*.

6. See Andrews, "To Rabindranath Tagore," *MR*, 11 (1912), 292; "On Reading the Translation of *Gitanjali*," *ibid.*, 13 (1913), 397.

Arthur H. Fox Strangways, drawing by Rothenstein

burden on Tagore at a time when the poet needed most desperately to fight free of extraliterary pressures.[7]

The Nobel Prize made Tagore a symbol not primarily of literary excellence but of the West's recognition of Asian excellence by Western standards. Although he knew that this posed both political and literary imperatives, he allowed himself to be torn between them and began to live under a compulsion to serve both at once. When added to his low aptitude for practical matters, this compulsion consumed his energies, distracted his mind, and played havoc with his responses to the lyric impulse.

7. See Andrews, "An Evening with Rabindra," *ibid.*, 12 (1912), 225–228, an account, punctuated by political digressions, of Tagore in London.

66
Rothenstein to Tagore

Far Oakridge   November 15, 1913

My very dear friend—I open the Times & a great shout comes from it—Rabindranath has won the Nobel Prize![1] I cannot tell you of the delight this splendid homage gives me—the crown is now set upon your brow. Surely this, the greatest honour which can come to a man during his lifetime, must make your own heart swell a little, & then happily the prize is materially substantial, & you will at last I think be rid of all anxiety regarding the school. We here made a holiday of this day—all rejoice in the robe of honour in which you have been invested before the eyes of Europe. I took the children for a drive, a long promised one; we had a glorious day, & as it is not often I play truant, the children were like a peal of bells. My dear friend, from the heart I send you my full congratulations. Never I think did ampler reward fit ampler merit; your pilgrimage is one of the romances of literature. It should awaken the East like a trumpet blast & at last turn the minds of the young men to something more noble & fruitful than political intrigue. For yourself it will be an incentive to a new faith in your own great powers; you are not of those whose heads can be turned by much praise, & in the solitude of Bolpur you will see still deeper into the mysteries of all those common things amongst which men live so unheeding. Poet of the sun, you will sit in the sun, poet of the night, you will go forth into the night, poet of the human heart, you will bring warmth & comfort to a thousand cold & dispirited. Is not this even a greater prize than any man can bestow? to be chosen to serve your fellows, & your neighbours now reach across the world. We send our love from house to house. Ever yours—

W. R.

1. Rothenstein's delight greatly amplified the voice of the *Times*. (See "The Nobel Literature Prize: Honour for an Indian Poet," *Times* [London], November 14, 1913, p. 8.)

67
Tagore to Rothenstein

Shanti Niketan   November 18, 1913

My dear friend

The very first moment I received the message of the great honour conferred on me by the award of the Nobel prize my heart turned towards you with love and gratitude. I felt certain that of all my friends none would be more glad at this news than you. Honour's crown of honour is to know that it will rejoice the hearts of those whom we hold the most dear. But, all the same, it is a very great trial for me. The perfect whirlwind of public excitement it has given rise to is frightful. It is almost as bad as tying a tin can at a dog's tail making it impossible for him to move without creating noise and collecting crowds all along. I am being smothered with telegrams and letters for the last few days and the people who never had any friendly feelings towards me nor ever read a line of my works are loudest in their protestations of joy. I cannot tell you how tired I am of all this shouting the stupendous amount of its unreality being something appalling. Really these people honour the honour in me and not myself. The only thing that compensates for this is the unfeigned joy and pride that the boys of my school feel at this occasion. They are having festivities and making the most of me.

I know how glad Mrs Rothenstein must have been at my great good fortune—please give her my kindest remembrances and love to the children   Yours

Rabindranath Tagore

68
Rothenstein to Tagore

Far Oakridge   [late November 1913]

My dear friend— . . . I am still under the spell of your glorious Nobel adventure. Never I think did one slender little sheaf of poems win more for itself & the material gain must be so delightfully unexpected. At least the courage with which you envisaged Europe has had its reward! I am sending you a little book from A.E. I spent a most interesting week in Dublin.[1] I never realised before how complicated the political and social conditions are in Ireland. The group to which Yeats & A.E. belong is so very small in Dublin, & so much more famous outside than within the Irish domestic circle—this must always be the case, but it is especially striking over there, for no one thinks anything of Irish ability in Ireland. They talk almost as much as Americans! I got a few words in when I lectured, otherwise it was no easy matter—& no one could call me a silent man!

I often wished you with me & thought how amused you would be. A.E. is a nice large wooly bear, very gentle & wide & fat. I myself am more impressed by the splendour of the vision of things which are—the vision of things which are not always seems a little weak & attenuated to me, but I liked A.E. very much; he is the dearest middle aged lamb one could meet.

You write that fame has brought restlessness—do not worry about that I beg, but put work fearlessly aside for a while. Peace & serenity will come back to you unassisted, & then the springs will gush out as before. In the meanwhile do not fret if people become too insistent for a time—they will take their proper place in time. . . . Ever yours

W. R.

1. George William Russell, Æ (1867–1935), poet, painter, editor of *The Irish Statesman*. His book: perhaps *Co-operation and Nationality: A Guide for Rural Reformers from This to the Next Generation* (Dublin, 1912), particularly relevant to Tagore's interest in rural reconstruction, since it suggests remedial measures for the bleakness of Irish rural life. Rothenstein arrived in Dublin, November 16 to deliver the four Hermione Lectures endowed by Alexandra College, a Church of Ireland school for girls. (See *MM* II, 260–261.)

69
Rothenstein to Tagore

Far Oakridge   December 4, 1913

My dear friend—just a few lines to acknowledge the preface to Chitra. I have sent it to Fox Strangways & he writes that the text is being set up in type & the book itself will be out early in the year. Also to thank you for the two new books [*The Gardener* and *The Crescent Moon*]. . . . I have just had a copy too of André Gide's translations. Let me tell you that I have seen nothing so remarkable in the way of translation since Baudelaire's translation of Poe's poems, I mean from English into French. Gide has got the spirit of your own English translations in a most surprising way—indeed I can find no difference in sentiment between the French & English versions. The French are a little inclined to overpoetise in their more sentimental work—Pierre Loti is an example of this, but Gide has interpreted your vision in the most perfect manner & I think you owe a cock to Fox Strangways for his sturdy resistence to the other man's pretensions. Gide has touched upon these with a delicate irony in his preface, & I am grateful to have your work in this exquisite form.[1] At least you will see, dear friend, that if we have seemed, some of us, a little fussy & difficult where your work was concerned, that we had some justification. There are so many literary & artistic leeches & if we cannot keep them off our own bodies we can save our friends from some of them. You have now four solid works upon our shelves—not a bad harvest for the first year's sowing.

India has been much before us of late. It has been interesting to see how quick our people have been to sympathise where others have been unjust—the criticism they resent they are now, happily, willing to make on the conduct of other officials, & at least it is they themselves who have broken the ice. I think these events will have important results in consequence. The door can no longer be kept so narrowly opened & I think if your people are wise & will walk steadily the future will bring many things.[2]

Our love from house to house. Ever yours

W. R.

1. See Letter 58, note 4; Tagore, *L'Offrande Lyrique*, pp. 7–9.
2. Newspapers were filled with reports of investigations by the Public Services Commission in India, of reforms for Indian universities, and of the disabilities of Indian laborers in South Africa.

70
Tagore to Rothenstein

Shanti Niketan   December 10, 1913

My friend, my days are riddled all over with interruptions, they are becoming perfectly useless to me. I am worn out writing letters, distributing thanks by handfuls and receiving visitors. I cannot tell you how unsuitable this sudden eruption of honour is to a man of my temperament. The winter sun is sweet, the green is luxuriant all around me—I want to be gloriously idle and let my thoughts melt and mingle in the blue of the space. I am beginning to envy the birds that sing and gladly go without honour. I was watching a calf this morning, tired of browsing, basking in the sun on the grass, supinely happy and placid; it made my heart ache with the desire to be one with the great life that surrounds this earth and to be able to be peacefully joyous in the simple enjoyment of the wealth lavished everywhere without being asked. But my mind is invaded and my time is wasted with things that are of the least significance to the inner. Perhaps you will smile and think this mood of mine as absurdly oriental—but still it has its truth which must not be overlooked.

With love   I am   ever yours

Rabindranath Tagore

71
Tagore to Rothenstein

Shanti Niketan   December 16, 1913

My dear Friend, . . .

My ordeal is not yet over. I still have dinners to attend to, and listen to speeches in praise of my genius, and to answer them in a becoming spirit of modesty. This has brought me to Calcutta and kept me in our Jorasanko lane, while the mustard fields are in bloom in Shilida and wild ducks have set up their noisy households in the sandbanks of the Padma. I have already raised a howl of protests and vilifications in our papers by saying in plain words what was in my mind to a deputation who had come to Bolpur to offer me congratulations. This has been a relief to me—for honour is a heavy enough burden even when it is real but intolerable when meaningless and devoid of sincerity. However, I must not complain. Let me patiently wait for the time when all this tumult will be a thing of the past and truth will shine and peace will come even to a man whom West has thought fit to honour. Ever yours

Rabindranath Tagore

72
Rothenstein to Tagore

Far Oakridge   January 7, 1914

My dear friend—I hope the long line of deputations will not be unending—I do not like to think of you as a gloriously famous personage, admired as the Taj is admired merely because of universal fame, without discrimination & natural love. . . . Here at least there is no personal element in the admiration your work brings forth—I find everywhere a real love & understanding for what underlies it, & you must not think that this only applies to Gitanjali. You have genuinely won the hearts of people over here, & they are finding out the beauties you have given them for themselves. In this lies the real delight one takes in the appreciation shown you—you are really giving & people are generously taking.

And there is something delightful in your sitting in a remote village, living the most seemly & simple life possible, thinking your thoughts & setting them down in that beautiful Bengali handwriting of yours, & then all over the world thousands will respond to those visions of sun & moon, of rivers & thatched roofs, of sea & sky that come to you.

Now the exquisite Chitra has appeared, in sable sari ornamented with the splendid red of an angry sunset. Indeed I think her dress worthy of her mind, & I do not imagine you will be ashamed of her as she leaves the hands of her servant, the humble little India Society. It was a generous & kindly thought which prompted you to place the name of our dear Christian scientist, that touching & amusing medley of all that is good in a woman's heart, of new & old, raw & ripe that makes the American mixture so odd & uncertain a prospect to our eyes.[1] ...

John is back from school, greatly improved I think—he tells me there is a hero worship for you amongst the "intellectuals" at Bedales![2]

Do give our affectionate wishes for the New Year to dear Pratima & to Rathi—I hope they have found life the more full for their visit to Europe. . . . Ever yours—

W. R.

1. Tagore dedicated *Chitra* to Harriet Moody. (See Dunbar, *A House in Chicago*, p. 106.) Benefits of her friendship must be credited also to Harriet Monroe and the milieu created by *Poetry*. To a question about the relation between them, Mrs. Winters replies: "As for the two Harriets, they were both remarkable people and most remarkably different and I suspect that there may have been a little acrimony between them from time to time. They pulled together for the large causes. Harriet Moody's generosity was enormous. It may sometimes have been possessive. I don't know. But it was so great that small things might be forgiven her. And Harriet Monroe, nicknamed Aunt Harriet by a number of exasperated young poets, was irritating beyond words in her attempt to dictate to the young, but she kept the magazine going with a devotion that was phenomenal, and we all owed her a great deal on that account. I found her delightful in her sour way." (Janet L. Winters to the editor, January 25, 1970.)
2. Bedales School, near Petersfield, Hampshire.

73
Rothenstein to Tagore

Far Oakridge   January 24, 1914

My dear friend—Walker has at last sent me eight proofs of your brother's drawings which I am sending out to you. . . . Walker is an excellent person but extremely slow; fortunately his work is very good & I think you will all be pleased with the proofs.

. . . Edward Carpenter is here staying with us & we have been talking much of you. He is an enchanting person, so sensitive, so wise. I think you liked him when you met him in

London.¹ . . . I hear you have had Ramsay MacDonald at Bolpur—John & his boy are bosom friends at school & chatter I believe like two monkeys in their dormitory.² My congratulations on your doctor's degree—honours of every kind crowd in upon you, O poet, like uninvited guests whom the host is too kind hearted to turn out of doors.³ Macmillan write of publishing my drawings of you in the spring.⁴ I shall see them next week as I go up to London for the first time for some months, for a day or two. It is difficult to tear myself away from this dear place & from my work, but it will not be for long.

I hope Surendranath is getting on with his translations—it is most important that a decent collection of your short stories be published here. I trust the new books have sold well—you have a very eager & thirsty audience here now. . . . ever yours affectionately

W. R.

1. Edward Carpenter (1844–1929), Socialist philosopher. Rothenstein admired his affection for mankind but thought his achievements were limited. (See *MM* II, 346. But see also Hynes, *The Edwardian Turn of Mind,* pp. 134–138, 149–166.)
2. J. Ramsay MacDonald (1866–1937), in Bengal with the Public Services Commission. (See Letter 15, note 1.) Fisher wrote: "Next to Gokhale [MacDonald] is the most distinguished man on our Commission and you should see him make the officials sit up! He is a queer tempered chap however, full of temperament and susceptibility—and I never quite know how he will react. He hates Oxford . . . : but he has a fine warm heart and is adored by the Indians." (Fisher to Gilbert Murray, March 31, 1913. Fisher: Bodleian.) G. K. Gokhale (1866–1915), Maharashtrian Moderate nationalist, founder of the Servants of India Society in Poona.
3. On December 26, 1913, Calcutta University gave Tagore a Doctorate of Letters, *honoris causa.*
4. Rothenstein, *Six Portraits of Sir Rabindranath Tagore,* prefatory note by Max Beerbohm (London, 1915).

74
Tagore to Rothenstein

[February 1914]

. . . speeding across wild regions, making it impossible for me to guess his whereabouts.¹ Pratima is in Ranchi and our Calcutta house is deserted.

Suren has been translating one of my novels for the Modern Review. Do you read it?²

It will amuse you to learn that at a semi-public conference of the Mohamedan leaders of Bengal Valentine Chirol gave his audience to understand that the English Gitanjali was practically written by Yeats. Naturally such rumours get easy credence among our people who can believe in all kinds of miracles except genuine worth in their own men. It is annoyingly insulting for me to be constantly suspected of being capable of enjoying a reputation by fraud and it makes me wish that the chance had never been given to me to come out of the quiet corner of my obscurity. In your society the admiration that a poet or an artist can get is sometimes so alarmingly great that it is hardly pleasant for the recipient or healthy for the public. Too great uprush of praise makes the atmosphere thick with the dust of envy and antagonism and of what avail can be the honour to a poet when his readers' minds become clouded and simple enjoyment of his works become difficult. When there was no printing press and people had to copy their favourite poems in their own hands admiration was genuine. There should be some difficulty in securing things you truly love and they should not be thrust upon you before you are ready to receive them. However it matters very little whoever is the author of a particular work so long as it is good. We do not know who painted the Ajanta pictures or who were the architects who built the Konarak temple. You have read my poem about the man whose harvest had been taken in the golden boat of time but he himself could not secure a place in it. Our names can be spared but not our true works.³

One thing is troubling my mind which I must tell you. You know my sister Mrs Ghosal who is an author. She is one of those unfortunate beings who has more ambition than abilities but just enough talent to keep her mediocrity alive for a short period of time. Her weakness has been taken advantage of by some unscrupulous literary agents in London and she has had her stories translated and published. I have given her no encouragement but I have not been successful in making her see things in their proper light. It is likely that she may go to England and use my name and you may meet her but be merciful to her and never let her harbour in her mind any illusion about her worth and her chance. I am afraid she will be a source of trouble to my friends who I hope will be candid to her for my sake and will not allow her to mistake ordinary politeness for encouragement.[4]

Arya Chaudhuri, my grand nephew, has asked me to give him an introduction letter to you which I have gladly given. He was in England for some years studying architecture and he is going back there to finish his course. He has not any particular talent or ambition so he is pleasant and companionable. I should be glad if you speak to him kindly and introduce him to some people worth knowing.[5]

I am sure you are getting more and more surprised at the length of my letter. My letters to my English friends are usually short, not because of the shortness of my memory or thinness of my love or paucity of subjects. I know you will have no sympathy for me, for it is difficult for you to realise it, when I tell you your language is not easy for me to use. I know I am apt to make a mess of your prepositions and in my blissful ignorance I go on dropping your articles in wrong places or dropping them out altogether. Then I do not know set phrases which greatly economise trouble in sentence making and very often I do not know how to write simple matter of fact things in English. No wonder people can hardly believe that I had any hand in translating the poems of Gitanjali. You have the unfair advantage over me in not allowing me to answer your English letters in Bengali—that would be returning tit for tat. This is the principle of vicarious punishment and I have to suffer for your ignorance of my language and I do not know if you do not have to suffer for my ignorance of yours—for, as your poet says, little learning is a dangerous thing.[6]

I wonder if Mrs Rothenstein occasionally remembers the traveller from the far Eastern shore who one day sat dreamily in her balcony under the shadow of the blossoming rose tree. I must not be forgotten because I was quiet and gave her far too little trouble to leave a lasting impression in her memory. She must know that there is a chance, however remote, of my visiting her again when it will be shameful if she cannot recognise me. But I must keep her supplied with my latest photographs. Give my love to her and to the children. When I promised you to send you dolls I did not realise that our people have grown old unawares and dolls have become scarce in our

Alice Rothenstein

country. But do not despair; dolls are immortal and Children. They are somewhere in hiding just now and they will come forth. Yours

Rabindranath Tagore

1. First page or pages missing. "His whereabouts": perhaps a reference to Rathindranath.
2. Tagore, *Cokher Bāli* [Eyesore; literally, "sand in the eyes"] (1903), in *R-R*, III, 281–512: *Eyesore*, trans. Surendranath Tagore, *MR*, 15 (1914), 93–98, 207–214, 303–311, 426–436, 539–549, 672–680; 16 (1914), 79–87, 220–226, 315–324, 424–431, 479–485, 641–652: *Binodini*, trans. Krishna Kripalani (Honolulu, 1964).
3. Valentine Chirol (1852–1929), Director, Foreign Department of the *Times*, 1899–1912; author of *Indian Unrest* (see above, Introduction, note 29), was in Bengal with the Public Services Commission. This alleged charge with respect to *Gitanjali* remains undocumented, but Tagore kept the conviction that Chirol had said something of the sort.

"My poem": "Shonār Tori," *Shonār Tori* [Golden Boat] (1894), in *R-R*, III, 7–8: no. 17, *The Fugitive* (London, 1921): in *CPP*, pp. 332–333.

4. Svarna Kumari Ghosal, *Kāhāke?* [To Whom?] (Calcutta, 1898): *To Whom? or An Indian Love-Story*, trans. Sorona Devi [Mukerjee] (Calcutta [1913]). Mrs. Ghosal (1857–1932) was nevertheless an outstanding woman. She had had no formal schooling but benefited from the family's cultural activities and from her husband's encouragement of her literary interests. She was editor, novelist, dramatist, and philanthropist. Rabindranath intervened too late; she had already written to Rothenstein (see Letter 76) and, earlier, to Robert Trevelyan (February 12, 1914. Julian Trevelyan). She urged Trevelyan to put forth efforts on her behalf, since it was difficult to attract the attention of literati in England.
5. Arya Chaudhuri, son of Indira Devi and Pramathanath Chaudhuri.
6. Amiya Chakravarty observes that Tagore was not quite at home with the common man's diction: "[His] English was just as true, but it was rather in the grand manner. He never quite grasped the conversational and even colloquial challenge of, for example, James Joyce." Tagore, Dr. Chakravarty says, "just missed the modern touch" because he was so often spared the detailed chores and close contacts of daily life where the English language was used on a "nonintellectual" level. (Interview with Amiya Chakravarty, New York City, August 30, 1965.)

75

Tagore to Rothenstein

Shilida   March 1, 1914

My dear Friend

I have collected some dolls and ornaments which I send you by this mail. I am afraid, these dolls are not a success. The spirit of imitation is over them and not that of creation. They are the outcome of the eating of the fruit of Knowledge and they have been banished from the paradise of Childhood,— they are ashamed to appear in the nakedness of their divine absurdity and they flock to the tailoring establishment of Natural history. But you will find some exceptions in the collection I am sending you. However, I think the ornaments will gladden your heart. I must not tell you the price I have paid for them —for I should like to let my two princesses across the water imagine when they put them on that they have cost the seven kings of the Fairy tales their kingdoms. I think you have forgotten to send me the proofs of my brother's drawings—for since your last letter two mails have passed and I haven't got them yet.

Dr J. C. Bose will be in England some time next May and I have been wishing I could accompany him there. I haven't had much peace since my return to India and I miss my English friends very badly.[1] With love to you all   I am   My beloved friend   Ever yours

Rabindranath Tagore

1. Jagadish Chandra Bose (1858–1937), Bengali plant physiologist, engaged in research on nervous impulses in plants. (See "Dr. J. C. Bose's Discovery," *MR*, 14 [1913], 211–212.)

76
Rothenstein to Tagore

Far Oakridge   March 2, 1914

My very dear friend—it is long since I last heard from you. Rathi writes that at last, wearied of the unwelcome adulation of unceasing deputations, you have fled far from the market place to seek quiet & beauty on the waters & banks of the Ganges. . . . It is in some such place that I like to think of you. We are all of us, partly through our own early restlessness & intense curiosity caught up in the wheels of city life—we need to sharpen our wits against those of others, to absorb & to give out opinions & influences, but our hearts were from the beginning away from these things, though we did not know it. So after years of passionate interest & depression we all of us turn our eyes back to mother earth. It is disappointment with men, perhaps with ourselves too, that sends us back to nature & makes us invent & fashion our Gods—we expect too much of them & of ourselves too, & believe that we can win wonderful victories through our own good swords alone. It is not disillusionment which sends one to solitude, but perhaps a more sane realisation that we cannot without danger to ourselves & others interfere with the wheels of the steering gear. Men seem to talk & endlessly talk, but all the while, though we feel we could get the ship along faster, man has, despite his weaknesses & treacheries, an underlying sense of sanity & rectitude, & he does make use of the winds that blow in a very wonderful way, from port to port. I have not really been any simpler or wiser here than in London, but the conditions are simpler, if no less easy, & the leisure I get after work is an infinite delight to me. I was not made for committees & drawing rooms. Some wicked fairy gave me an evil energy & a fictitious appearance of wisdom, which has involved me over & over again in needless worry, when all I wanted was peace of mind & reasonably decent relations with my neighbours.

Now that I have settled down here I am leading a much more satisfactory life, & I have not been to a single meeting, apart from village ones, since you left! Not even the India Society, my own nursling! but on the other hand we have produced a play here, played by the villagers themselves admirably.[1] We have just made arrangements to let our London house, keeping one or two rooms only, so this means, my wife has at last made up her mind that I am not to be lured back again....

Your sister Mrs Ghosal has written me this week, & I have just read her book. I do not know what it is like in Bengali. I have no doubt there is much beauty in the language; but the translation is so bald that we here must miss I fear its intrinsic charm—as it stands it cannot arouse much interest. The peep into a girl's heart is touching enough, but its psychology is a little too unsearching for an European audience —we have gone so far in the study of the human heart in our novels by our own authors that this simplicity, robbed of its natural charm of language, stands for very little. I hope to hear from you soon— . . . ever your friend

William Rothenstein

1. "The Village Wedding," unpublished play by Charles McEvoy (1879–1929), playwright and producer. In 1910 he built his Aldbourne Village Theatre. (See *MM* II, 342.)

77
Rothenstein to Tagore

Far Oakridge   March 9, 1914

My dear friend—a letter from you follows hard upon the heels of one I have just written to you. I am glad to have news of you once more, glad to hear that your own soul finds its old home with you again, undisturbed & at peace. I dislike breaking in upon your tranquil life by answering the many things you write of in your letter—many weeks will pass between its sending & my answer—& your mood will have gone by & my reply will seem tedious & perhaps unnecessary. What am I to say to you? To begin with I am away from everyone, & I can only write & find out what has gone wrong. Poor Fox Strangways! & poor India Society! indeed it is possible this last is not generous. I have heard nothing of the arrangements made over Chitra—I was only enchanted to read this much loved work of yours in so beautiful a form, to find it in print for others to read, & I saw only your own joy in the dress of this child of yours. Indeed you should have as many copies as you wish—is not the lovely book your own?[1] But that poor Fox Strangways should be blamed for the Society's remissness! surely that is a little hard. And to me it all seems so strange, when I look back & remember the not far distant day when scarcely a soul cared for the beauty & honour of anything Indian—it was all China & Japan. How we started the little society, how we devoted our time & our small means to its bringing forth & how I fought for fruitful statement of Indian genius in place of criticism of our long neglect & crude misrepresentation, friend & foe against one, & at last, through the devotion of a dozen generous artists & scholars, we do succeed in triumphant demonstration of the greatness of your country.²

But, dear friend, it is not Fox Strangways, it is Prof. Lethaby, who has written of Indian craftsmen as few have written, it is Laurence Binyon, it is Walter Crane you are complaining of, not to mention friends nearer home—surely our generosity, small though it be, is not to be weighed against a few copies of your noble book more or less.³ If you knew how hard the fight has been—it has not really been a selfish work. And if Fox Strangways had not been a very bull dog with Macmillan, I do not think you would ever have had the material position with the publishers that is yours to-day. And so with your French translation—it was he who wrested it from the charlatan de Rosen & gave it into the hands of a poet. It hurts me to have you write of him in this way—I know the man, I believe, & a better friend no one could have, though there are many more sympathetic & more attractive. I am only sorry in a way that I have neglected my own duties of late so far as the India Society goes. You ask me what I think about Kabir, whether you should not put the matter in the hands of Macmillan, leaving him to deal with the Society. Well, to be frank, I think that would not be a good thing to do. The India Society proposed publishing Ajit's translations, you nobly took them up & practically rewrote them, in fact, left them to retranslate from the Bengali text yourself, & left the copy with me, with the understanding that the Society was not to publish until (a) Mrs Stuart Moore had contributed her introduction (b) you had ascertained what royalty should be given to Kshiti Mohan Sen for his important share in the translation, & what acknowledgement should be made to Ajit for his initial effort. Of these things Macmillan can know nothing.⁴ It seems to me that the wish of the society to publish an edition similar to Gitanjali & Chitra, strictly limited as in their case, is a perfectly reasonable one; Macmillan can then have the work, & you & Mrs Stuart Moore can make the terms you wish.⁵ I have written Mrs Stuart Moore & sent her your own views on the matter, & also given her mine. It is my own hope that the Kabir translations will appear in the form I myself care for so much—then when the work on Ajanta has appeared we can all of us wind up the India Society, for our work will then have been done. I should be a hypocrite if I pretended that this work has not been most fruitful. I believe the society came into existence at the psychological moment, & that the endless worry & the great amount of time given up to carrying on its work has not been wasted. We shall have the books on our shelves & the worry will be forgotten; the fight is half won, & the complete victory depends upon others; your own noble work & your visit to us here has made our share very easy. As for what some one may from time to time say of you, can you expect to escape that strain of envy that shows like a scar at moments of excitement, when one amongst many is singled out for signal praise?[6] At all of us who devote our lives to some form of beauty mud is thrown, but no one living has had more respect & honour shown him, & more deservedly than yourself. I have found these woods "more free from hatred than the envious court" & have found in consequence greater peace & happiness here than I can expect so near London as Hampstead is. We have let the lease of our house, but my wife has arranged to keep a couple of rooms there, one being the room where you sat with us so often, & dreamed away so many hours on the balcony. I should hate to think that your visit to us here was marred by vexations which follow on the heels of fame. I have so many moving memories of your visit; we spent so many moving hours together. Neither you nor I are really ourselves talking & writing of Macmillan & copyright & the like. We get dragged into these things against our wills, but it is when the sun rises over the other side of the valley that you stand beside me in spirit, & I can see you now, alone in the evening on the broad river as the shadows deepen on either hand. The children talk of you so often, & your love for them is so dear to me. We send you our greetings & our love. Ever your friend

W. R.

1. Rothenstein's response to the missing pages of Letter 74.
2. Reference to Rothenstein's letter to the *Times* and his cosignatories. (See Introduction, note 7.)
3. W. R. Lethaby (1857–1931), in 1900 appointed first Professor of Design, Royal College of Art. Walter Crane (1845–1915), book illustrator, writer, a leader in the crafts revival in England.
4. Macmillan did know about Kabir. Fox Strangways, according to his agreement with Tagore, notified George Brett that "some time this year, not in the next two months, this Society will publish 100 poems of

Kabir (16th cen[tury] or so) translated by *Tagore* with introduction by *Mrs. Stuart Moore (Evelyn Underhill).*" (Fox Strangways to Brett, January 19, 1914. Macmillan Papers: New York Public Library.) Tagore told the London firm about this plan and asked them to confer with Mrs. Moore about terms and credits. He stated that the Bengali version, translated from Kabir's Hindi, was K. M. Sen's, and that Ajit Chakravarty used this as basis for his English version from which Tagore and Mrs. Moore had worked. Tagore added that Ajit felt it inappropriate for his name to appear, as so little of his work remained. Tagore, however, asked Macmillan to tell the India Society that he wished all contributors to be credited. (Tagore to Macmillan, February 25, 1914. MP:BM.)

5. Tagore apparently changed his mind about the Society's publishing Kabir at all. Fox Strangways heard that Evelyn Underhill, at Tagore's suggestion, had approached Macmillan. As Secretary of the Society, he then wrote: "I am rather puzzled by this, as these poems were definitely given by Mr Tagore to Mr Rothenstein last summer for publication by the India Society, . . . I have now . . . to warn you that I must hold you responsible for any agreement entered into, with regard to this matter, without the concurrence of that Society." (Fox Strangways to Macmillan, March 17, 1914. MCP.) Tagore then stated that he wanted Macmillan to publish Kabir *after* the Society's edition sold out. (Tagore to Macmillan, April 2, 1914. MP:BM.) In June, Fox Strangways commented testily that if the Kabir agreement seemed "elaborate," it was because "the lady (1) wrote a certain letter to the author which was intended to oust that Society from its rights in the matter, and (2) has thought fit to impound and keep the Society's property. I expect that if you had been making an agreement yourselves under these conditions you would have seen that there was no loophole." (Fox Strangways to Macmillan, June 16, 1914. MCP.) Between November 1913 and September 1914 Evelyn Underhill's only reference to Kabir was that "The India Society have been pressing me very hard to let them be printed at once but I have refusd to do this till I have your permission." (Evelyn Underhill to Tagore, November 16, 1913. R-S.) The New York firm remained in the dark about these maneuvers and, thinking that British publication was imminent, went to press with Kabir, then had to retrieve the premature shipments to preserve the British copyright. New York asked London to explain to Mr. Fox Strangways the "importance of simultaneous publication." (E. D. Marsh, for Macmillan, New York, to Macmillan, London. December 11, 1914. MP:BM.)

6. Here Rothenstein's letter picks up the truncated text of Letter 74 with its reference to Chirol.

78
Rothenstein to Tagore

Far Oakridge   March 20, 1914

My dear friend—since last writing you I have been in London & seen many friends, as I had an exhibition of my work there before giving up the studio.¹ There has been a great deal of trouble about Kabir, Mrs Stuart Moore writing that you had quite definitely put the matter into her hands, entirely, & wished her to offer the book to Macmillan.

She is good enough to write to me and say, that her responsibility begins & ends with this desire of yours, & that she knows nothing of any other past arrangements. I fear the secret of her attitude has come out quite simply & easily—her husband who is a lawyer has made it a condition that her name is to appear with yours, equal in importance, as translator, & on this condition only will she be willing to give up the text. The committee are dealing with this lady, whose mysticism is reserved for her books, I think rather than for practical life.² Evidently it was her fear that this might not be done by the Society which made her anxious to put it straightway into other hands. She is not the first who wishes the India Society at the bottom of the sea—it is somehow inevitable that those who work for others rather than for themselves should be suspected of evil motives—perhaps this is a fair view to take, & we are all better employed doing our own business. Then people know where they & others stand. At any rate some of us feel that the Society has already done the work it was founded to carry out, & others may now continue this in their own way. Being unduly nervous, the work is at least impossible for me; & one of my few links with London committees will be happily broken.

Andrews has been here & I was lucky enough to catch him. He tells me he wishes to devote himself to your service, so you will have some one in India who can take some of the burden of negotiating with people here off your shoulders.³ He is heart & soul devoted to you & to the cause of India, & I know you find him most helpful & sympathetic. He evidently helped the cause of your countrymen in S. Africa with great devotion & efficiency & I can understand how grateful your feelings towards him must be. He & Fox Strangways lunched with me & I think are going together to Macmillans. You know my own high opinion of [Fox Strangways]. I think he has done his work for you with the greatest efficiency & has given your affairs a more solid colour with Macmillans than a less dogged & combative nature could have effected, & I have always thought that you were more affected by his distinctly Anglo-

Pearson at Santiniketan

Indian outside than by the real beauty & stability of his inner nature.⁴ It is difficult for you to realise how many people cultivate you in order that something of value may accrue to them—from the first Fox Strangways was entirely disinterested, & I, who can see something of what goes on, have never known him claim any credit for himself.

He is at present engaged in his last battle on behalf of the India Society—with the Stuart Moores. I think the calm way in which this lady has tried to carry off the rights of the Society in your name has a little shocked most of us. In your last letter to me you gave me a very different feeling.⁵ You seemed to think the Society might feel some compunction over publishing work of yours for the third time, & you were good enough to ask my opinion as to whether the book should be offered to Macmillan if this were the case. This opinion I gave you in my last letter & when Andrews comes to you perhaps he will be able to give you all the facts of the matter.

Now I want to know of your being more tranquil in mind. I have a great longing to see you personally, to sit with you & to make you feel how really trifling this opposition of which you write really is. Chirol can be answered by Yeats, by Fox Strangways, by Andrews or by myself at any time—unfortunately no report of the kind has reached any of us. My own view you know, & that is precisely the opposite to what you suggest Chirol carried. I went carefully through both Chitra & the children poems, & felt more & more how much better your own version is than after its amendment by Sturge Moore.⁶ Here & there (as when he alters tank into pond) he fails to understand your own images. I don't think you need have any doubt as to your own power of saying what you mean in your own way in the case of the songs. The matter is a little more difficult in the stories—there I do sometimes miss the beauty of actual material which is necessary to a work of art. Prose is a very difficult matter—it is a question of raising the reader to untroubled levels at times, so that nothing shall interfere between your work & the reader. This is a long & wearisome letter. I can only repeat that I wish I could get *at* you. Your fame has brought you worry & little else to make you happier, & with all the world acclaiming you I can imagine a sense of solitariness which must settle like a cloud upon your soul at times. Here you have countless friends, each more devoted to you than the other. Yet when we are in need, even our friends are of little assistance. It is neither friendship nor sympathy we want, but more nobility & more rectitude from man. I find the stroke of man's little mean ways, his pushing & shoving more difficult to envisage than the harder knocks of the Gods. Something of this you must be feeling. But at any moment our spirits may happily rise superior to these things, & caught up in the great higher currents of life, go winging in exaltation, the earth below stretched out a radiant vision & nothing but space about us. You, more than most men, have this power, so I shall not sympathise too much with your other moments, when this mood refuses to lay hold of you, as it does with the rest of us more often than we care to admit.

To-day it is snowing, & as I write, I think of that wonderful improvisation you made for your boys,[7] & I send you my greetings across this whiteness, & all my affection. Ever yours

W. R.

1. With the National Portrait Society, Grosvenor Gallery, London.
2. Evelyn Underhill acted on Tagore's instructions. Her goddaughter recalls that Stuart Moore, a specialist in medieval law and antiquarian property rights, did manage his wife's business affairs meticulously, but this was his way of taking part in her work and expressing his pride in it. (Interview with Gillian Wilkinson, London, September 22, 1969.)
3. Andrews' mother died while he was in South Africa; he returned to India via England.
4. "Anglo-Indian outside": the Fox Strangways family's connections with the Indian Civil Service.
5. Reference to missing portions of Letter 74.
6. Rothenstein's holograph notation on incomplete manuscript with autograph revisions by Tagore: "The original ms of the 'Crescent Moon,' before the poems were more or less rewritten by Sturge Moore, not always to the advantage of Tagore's own translations, even though the English be more correct." (Tagore: Houghton.) An incomplete typescript has autograph revisions by both Tagore and Sturge Moore (TSM).
7. Tagore, *Phālguni* [Spring] (1916), in *R-R*, XII, 81–145: *The Cycle of Spring*, trans. C. F. Andrews and Nishikanta Sen, rev. by the author (London, 1917): in *CPP*, pp. 265–323.

79
Tagore to Rothenstein

Shanti Niketan   March 29, 1914

My dear Friend

I have come back from my retreat and have joined my school, though I am not in a mood to work. This is the season when with me moral enthusiasm of all kinds reaches its lowest level, and I feel misgivings about efficacy of toiling for the good of humanity. Spring is the time when one should completely surrender one's nature to the mysterious influence of the creative energy that stirs life into love and beauty. Unfortunately man has to maintain a uniformity in his work all the year round and behave as if the difference of seasons does not exist for him except in changing his clothes. However, summer vacation is near and I am planning to go to the hills directly I am free.

Dr Seal is about to leave India for England with his daughter. He is anxious that you should know her. She is a widow though very young, and she has written a book in Bengali which is a remarkable production, destined to take a very high place in our literature.[1] She wants to carry on her education in England and she should be glad to get your advice on this matter.

Pearson is with us and he sends you his love. He has joined me in my school work at a great sacrifice. His service will be very valuable to us no doubt, but his beautiful nature is something which is beyond all calculations of benefits. You must have met Andrews by this time, for he is in England and we are soon going to have him also in our midst. This is the best reward I have won from the West, the friendship and co-operation of noble hearts.

I send you a cutting from W[estminster] Gazette.[2] I never had invitation from Berlin, never intended going there, have no friends in that city and consequently have written no letter to anybody giving my reasons for cancelling my engagement. Will you contradict this rumour in your papers? Yours ever

Rabindranath Tagore

1. Sarayubala Das Gupta, *Basanta-Prayānna* [Passing of Spring] (Calcutta, 1914), a prose elegy for her husband, Basantaranjan Das Gupta, who died while a student in England.

2. A clipping, dated March 1, 1914, from the *Westminster Gazette* (London), quoting the Berlin *Tägliche Rundschau* to the effect that Tagore "had abandoned a European tour on account of adverse criticism caused by his winning the Nobel Prize." Tagore denied knowledge of this rumor or its source; meanwhile invitations were arriving from Berlin. (See Rabindranath to Jyotirindranath Tagore, Bengali letter [March 1914], *Cithipatra*, V, 16.) Fox Strangways also received inquiries and wrote Tagore: "I have said you are not leaving India. But if you hanker after lecturing you have only to let me know." (Fox Strangways to Tagore, January 2, 1914. R-S.)

80
Rothenstein to Tagore

Far Oakridge   April 2, 1914

My very dear friend—your last letter was so much happier in spirit than your two previous ones, that I feel pretty sure that the weeks of rest you sought for on the Padma you found & that you are refreshed in body & mind. . . .

The good Andrews came here for a couple of days to see us. It was a very real pleasure to have him—his is a sweet & gentle soul, affectionate & devoted. I was glad to have him to myself—London is not a fair place for getting to know people, when they come to see one with others going in & out, & I saw here how sincere & devoted a nature Andrews has. His devotion to you is beautiful & touching—you seem to have brought some kind of order & clearness into a troubled soul. . . . He told me that the poor & touching fanatic Petaval is with you. His help, poor soul, must be a risky asset. If meaning well were gold he would be a Croesus. Beyond this he never impressed us as you know; could you not encourage him to go on a mission to the Amazon? It was the excellent Edward Carpenter who set this mechanism going wrong—I am sure the good fellow was in his right place in the 44th Engineers.[1]

I am glad to hear that you are working on your own stories, as well as Surendra. It would be an excellent thing to carry out your idea of publishing a book of these as your next volume. I think they will come as a revelation to people who do not realise how complete is the instrument you have made—your short stories were my own first love & gave me some idea of what lay behind them. It was in the Postmaster I first saw mirrored a corner of that world of your creation in which I have now wandered so far & wide, thanks to your help, & I have a strong sentimental attachment to them in consequence, as well as a certainty of their profundity of vision.[2] Poets are expected to have an abstract devotion to nature & to mankind; but few have shown the sympathy & understanding for their fellows your prose stories bear witness to in your case, & it is as well people over here should have the chance of getting a nearer acquaintance with this side of your genius. . . .

. . . Ever, dear friend, your affectionate

W. R.

I see in The Times there is at last to be some notice taken of Indian students & some effort made for their reception among families here. But it is all to be done in connection with Cromwell Rd., & the names are all high & glittering ones which figure on the committee. Peers & great lawyers, cabinet ministers, but no simpler people, no mere men of culture or lovers of Indians seem to find a place on the list. I hope some day something will be done from your side, a good well-managed club as a meeting place, supported by the best of your people financially & otherwise, neither under the India Office umbrella, nor the political agitators, but in touch with the better elements both here & in India.[3]

1. However, see J. W. Petaval, "Rabindranath Tagore and Social Reform via Educational Reform," *The Asiatic Review* (London), n.s. 4, 3–4 (1914), 306–311, a well-reasoned argument for combining practical and theoretical education. Tagore introduced Petaval to Sir M. C. Nandy, Maharaja of Cossimbazar, Calcutta, who had opened a Polytechnic Institute where students could earn while learning. The Maharaja installed Petaval as Principal.

2. Tagore, "Postmāstār" [Postmaster] (1894), in *R-R*, XV, 411–417: "The Postmaster," trans. Debendra Nath Mitter, *MR*, 9 (1911), 36–39: in *Mashi and Other Stories*, "translated by various writers" (London, 1918), pp. 157–169.

3. See "Hospitality for Indian Students," *Times* (London), March 30, 1914, p. 7.

81
Tagore to Rothenstein

Shanti Niketan   April 21, 1914

My dear Friend

Andrews is here and he is full of you. It is such a great pleasure for me to hear from him all about you and the dear children and the delightful days he spent in your beautiful home. It makes my heart ache with a longing to knock at your door and see you happy under that tender grey sky and amidst the green swells of hills swept by fugitive lights and shadows. I know this is not a mere dream of mine, surely a day will come when you will receive a telegram and hurry to Chalford Station to be assured that it was not altogether a hoax. Everything will be pretty much the same only, I am afraid, the children will go on growing in the meanwhile not waiting for me at the crossing where the Fairyland has its last fingerpost pointing to the country of the Common Sense. Andrews missed seeing John which I regret very much. You know how I won his confidence, simply because he never could entirely believe in the rumour that I was a mere poet. It was perfectly touching to see how up to the very last he had enough respect left for me to condescend to discuss with me all the intricacies of aerial navigation. Do give my love to the children and thank them for me for the delightful pictures they have sent to us. You may be sure I will preserve Billy's picture most carefully till he grows up a famous painter when I shall have my chance.

Andrews is a perfect Godsend to me. My burden has been growing very heavy and I do not know what I would do but for his help. I am foolish in a world where most people are wise and my foolishness consists in imagining them to be no better than I am. It is surprising to know how a man can survive all the blunders he creates, one should have been killed in accident long before he had chance to breathe. I hope Andrews will be able to keep me from harm's way, though I have my doubts. Anyhow, his friendship is a clear gain for me which, I am sure, will last through all my disasters. We are planning to make ready for publication my short stories during this summer vacation. Yours ever

                              Rabindranath Tagore

82
Tagore to Rothenstein

               Ramgarh, Kumaon Hills   June 2, 1914

My dear Friend

Your letter gave me great joy, because it is your letter and because I got it when I had regained my peace of mind under the kindly care of the Father Himalaya. I have been wishing everyday since I came here that you were here. This is just the place in the world for you. My house here will wait for you even if it is in vain. I cannot imagine that you will never visit Shanti Niketan and this little nest of ours among the hills. It seems perfectly absurd to think that you have never seen *Shilida* and never lived in boats with us in the lonely sandbanks of the Padma. But, my friend, if you fail to come to share with us this feast of colour and light and love you will have to pay for it in your next birth. I do not know what your punishment will be—possibly you will have the heart of a *yogi* and yet be born again and again in London. I know you and your own atmosphere—I have seen you alone and in crowds, I have sat with you in your dinner table and sat to you in your studio, I have walked with you in the unimaginable shady lanes of Hampstead and in the solitude of your Gloucestershire forest, I have drunk your words sparkling with wit and wisdom and I have shared with you the silence of the sunset sky in that beautiful terrace at Oakhill Park, but I came to you like an apparition blurred and out of focus—at best like a statue, somewhat unreal, because bereft of all atmosphere. Do you not think it is unfair to me and that you should bring me out of the casket where my fate carefully placed me while sending me oversea—that you should hold me in the light turning me round to have a fair valuation of my personality? Very affectionately yours

                              Rabindranath Tagore

83
Tagore to Rothenstein

Calcutta   June 15, 1914

My dear Friend,

Our vacation is over and I am on my way to Bolpur to resume my work. Andrews is accompanying me and I am looking forward to our cooperation with great joy. Financial difficulties being somewhat slackened I am going to introduce some costly improvement in my school this year. Your Nobel prize and the successful sale of my English works have made me reckless and I am spending in anticipation of an income which may fail to keep pace with my expensive schemes. It is for the insolvent Alnashkars to be extravagant in their mere dreams but solvent Alnashkars are extravagant while wide awake.[1] In all my calculations I am fairly moderate but in carrying them out my spirit takes delight in pushing them aside and running ahead of them. Is it not sweet to have just the reasonable amount of assurance to enable one to be fearless in his undertakings with just enough reasonable doubt to give it a picquancy? I am sure you know what it is when you find it hard to stop improving and altering your house at Oakridge. But surely the claims of our truer life are great and we are cowardly misers when we hesitate to respond to its urgent calls, ever careful of a tomorrow which knows no end. Strangely enough I had a strong sense of the presence of death this time in the hills which gave me a clearer perspective of things enabling me to come away with a realisation of freedom I seldom had before. I have a strong hope that henceforth my works will be truer and my dedication of self more complete.[2]

Andrews is trying to persuade me to try my hands in translating some of my short stories but you know prose is so difficult and after all I am an interloper whose intrusions into your literature must not be too often, and in my unseemly greed I should not let your warm welcome of a guest degenerate into sullen tolerance or what is worse into angry hostility.[3] Ever your friend

Rabindranath Tagore

1. Alnashkar: the glass merchant in the *Arabian Nights* who stirred in his sleep and smashed his own wares while dreaming of future profits. By August, Tagore was asking advances on both American and Continental royalties, to finance school expansion. (Tagore to Macmillan, through Andrews. August 10, 1914. MP:BM.)
   2. See Tagore, *Letters to a Friend*, ed. C. F. Andrews (London, 1928), pp. 42–45.
   3. Tagore had already told the London Macmillans that he would try to translate the stories under Andrews' advisement. (Tagore to Macmillan, April 16, 1914, MP:BM.) Andrews told George Brett, however, that they could not be ready before Christmas, as the Poet was very tired but still wanted to do the translating himself. This would cause delay, but Brett might advertise the books as being in preparation. (Andrews to Brett, June 21 [1914]. MP:NYPL.)

84
Rothenstein to Tagore

                        Far Oakridge   June 16, 1914

My dear friend—I have to thank you for a delightful photograph of yourself—your room at Calcutta I fancy, for I see your Bolpur appointments simpler even, in my mind's eye. My craftsman's eye notices the charming design & workmanship of the furniture in the room—presumably made sixty or seventy years ago; above all I was glad to see you wearing the garb I first saw you clothed in. . . . Dr Seal sent me Basanta Prayanna, a most beautiful work for a young woman to write, but alas, not very satisfactorily translated.[1] Now I see that the King of the Dark Chamber is out & I shall hope to see a copy soon. This is, you know, one of my favourite works of yours. The wonderful boldness of the personification of God himself always delighted me. And how noble the relations between him & the Queen! Lovely as are the old Radha poems, not one has been translated, at any rate I have come across none, so human & profound as this play of yours. Do you remember the evening you read it in my studio? How few there were who understood it, but how enthusiastic were these few! Now that the play is in print, I fancy a good many will follow you well enough. What a joyous sheaf of translations you have set up—now it only wants the prose stories to bind it together. . . . Please greet many good friends, Andrews & Pearson, & our dear Pratima & Rathi. Ever yours

W. R.

 1. See Letter 79, note 1. Dr Seal, with Edward Thompson, translated *Basanta Prayānna* in Cambridge. Thompson had reported that Macmillan might publish it, "*provided* that Mr. Ravindranath Tagore's Introduction be allowed to be published." (Seal to Rothenstein, June 3, 1914. RP:HL.)

85
Rothenstein to Tagore

Far Oakridge June 29, 1914

My very dear friend—Ernest Rhys has just left me. He is preparing, as you doubtless know, a book upon your work & came to "talk Tagore."[1] What a dear fellow he is, so unpretending & sincere, with much more talent & perception than many who cut greater figures in the literary world. He is very "seeing" & has, to my mind at least, as sane an appreciation of your work as any man I know. I hope he will cover the whole field—as you know it is not the so-called "mystical" side of you that seems to me the most significant; it is the extraordinary sympathy with the whole expression of the human heart—its most exalted strivings & its most touching weaknesses—which you show, the depth of your psychological insight & your understanding of its sensitiveness, which is the crown & glory of your work. You have touched life so largely & comprehensively at so many points, & always where you touch it you have given yourself with absolute passion to its truest interpretation.

 I have just been rereading "The King [of the Dark Chamber]," admiring alike the profundity of its religious teaching & the wit of its character drawing. It is always as mystic that the reviewers treat you, but to me you seem so much more. Is that why you tease me, as you do in your last letter, about "turning you round in the light in order to have a fair valuation of your personality"? You of all men need have no fear of the light. . . . Blemishes! are there not rocks and caves, as well as anemones & silver & golden scales? No, my friend, it is because you are a man, with a man's rich gifts of human strength & weakness that I love you, not because you are a saint. Your affection & friendship has been to me what it has been to many others, a rare privilege & a real heartening, & you need not be afraid that I chaffer as to the value of these things. You have so many people devoted to you, you who have the secret of drawing the best out of all men you meet, but I believe you know that the queer ugly little man at Oakridge is bound by one slender thread to yourself which will he believes last as long as his own thread of life. Was not the thread woven upon sacred soil? soil that has nourished me, a poor alien, in the most miraculous & generous fashion, so that, though ignorant & without scholarship, a little speck of Indian soul was given me, a mere grain of dust, but fruitful & precious beyond words. I have just been living in the memory of Ajanta & have, Heaven be thanked, finished my little note for the book which is to be ready in the autumn.[2] . . .

Rhys left me yesterday, expressing himself as enchanted with Oakridge, & what praise goes nearer to my heart? I miss the children, living here alone during alterations, but like the very simple life I lead by myself. Yes, do not fear, I hope to walk once more upon Indian ground, & to sit with you all at Bolpur. Ever yours affectionately

W. R.

1. Ernest Rhys, *Rabindranath Tagore: A Biographical Study* (London, 1915). Rhys wrote: "Your letter is stimulating and makes me realise pretty keenly what a Tagore book ought to do, and how far I am likely to stray from the reality in doing it. . . . My task is to get at the reality, and not to minister to any cult: but it is, as you surmise, hard for an outsider to penetrate the Indian confines, and get home there." (Rhys to Rothenstein, June 18, 1914. RP:HL.) He told Tagore: "As I go on with the book, it starts difficulties that were certainly not foreseen when it was begun. However it will do me good to finish it, whatever the public and critics may eventually think of it. That it will quite satisfy you is too much to hope; but you will credit it with more than [that which] lies in the printed page." (Rhys to Tagore, June 27, 1914. R-S.)

2. Rothenstein, "The Import of the Ajanta Paintings in the History of Art," in Herringham et al., *Ajanta Frescoes*, pp. 22–23.

86
Tagore to Rothenstein

Shanti Niketan   July 8, 1914

My dear Friend

I was rather surprised to receive from Macmillans copies of The King of the Dark Chamber. I had no idea that they were going to bring it out so soon and I was not prepared for it. The manuscript that you had with you was the first draft and in the later ones the translation had undergone such a vast deal of alterations that it is quite a different thing now. So I was rather put out at the sudden appearance of this book with all its crudities, but it cannot be helped. But the worst of it is that I am not the translator—it was an Indian student, Kshitish Chandra Sen, who translated it for me. I have cabled to Macmillans to make correct announcement—please see that it is done properly. It places me in a very awkward situation with Mr Sen.[1]

Andrews is with me working in my school and trying hard to learn Bengali. We regularly sit together to translate some of my short stories—I think we have done some decent work and we hope to have a manuscript ready for publication before the Christmas season.[2] Ever yours

Rabindranath Tagore

1. The New York firm was equally surprised; Brett first learned of the publication from an advertisement. (Brett to Frederick Macmillan, June 15, 1914. MP:BM.)
2. But see Letter 90, note 3.

87
Rothenstein to Tagore

Far Oakridge   August 4, 1914

My dear friend—I knew something had gone wrong over "The King." Fox Strangways wrote & asked me if I had a copy, saying Macmillan wanted it. I sent mine on at once, of course, thinking Macmillan was going to consider future publication; my surprise was great when I saw the book announced, & I was certain that the translation was not yours. I told this both to Ernest Rhys & Fox Strangways; had Macmillan told me, or had I heard at all, that the book was to be published at once, I would have told them. But the real point of the whole matter is this—everything which now bears your name is gold to Macmillan, so that, in spite of the fact that he is guardian of your literary honour, he cannot tell the difference between your workmanship, & that of a very different hand. You remember you left the ms with me, on account of the Nation suggestion, which Macmillan would not sanction.[1] What puzzles me is that you should get no proofs, not be considered at all & be in fact in absolute ignorance of the intended publication.[2] Well as your business interests may now be fortified, I cannot help regretting that the old arrangements, whereby some such friends as Rhys, Yeats, Fox Strangways & perhaps myself were to form a sort of literary advisory committee to take charge of your works did not remain in being. All a publisher naturally cares about is that a book shall sell; your own interest in your work is not by any means a financial one, certainly this is only a pleasant & subsidiary interest, coming long afterwards, & when you were here, you were at one with us in wanting your work to appear in the best form & at the most appropriate moments. As it is, the sense of the world for these things is not very delicate. Chitra, one of the most perfect pieces of literature in the world, did not have a very understanding reception; the King, one of your profoundest & noblest conceptions, appears in a form few of us care greatly for, & it is excellently reviewed, its English I believe was greatly praised, & no one seems to have suspected it was not your own translation. I hope another form of this noble work of yours will appear; I confess to an immense admiration for it, but the slang and other weaknesses of the translation always worry me a little.[3]

In future, if I am asked for any of your works, I shall refer Macmillan to you. We all of us thought you a little mistaken in giving them the management of your affairs. Some of us have, alas, unalluring features, but we make good watch dogs. However, [George] Macmillan having found his literary sense less perfect than it might be, will be more cautious in future. I have just had the proof of my little note on your brother's drawings, as well as the title page—after how many months!

Now, I write at a tense moment of our history. I have always been a passionate anti-war man; I have always argued that to suspect Germany of monstrous intentions was unworthy & unseemly, but to-day it is difficult not to believe that she has long cherished & developed most sinister plans. The horrors of war I am not likely to see; but to my surprise something of the intense passion of it has come upon me as upon others. For the first time I would leave palette & brushes & go where I could help, & I see & feel all the time the extraordinary democratic spirit which prevails at these moments of danger & sacrifice. Heaven knows that, when one realises the German soldiers are dear touching men, with mothers & children like our own (mine was German) one wishes them no harm; but the insupportable bullying of the German military-political leaders has gone too far, & one longs to have this insolent power, which is always threatening Europe & the world, humbled & curbed, so that one's whole nature is tense with the hope that neither France nor ourselves are going to be crushed. You may be a little shocked to find me writing like this. If you were here, at this rich & peaceful moment of the harvest, knowing that we are now all plunged into discord & hatred, you would excuse the intense rancour we feel against this cruel & cynical power that is the present Germany's aim. I honestly believe we have done our best to keep peace in Europe; now we are deep in financial disaster & shortly thousands of dear bodies will lie rotting in the fields. I am sure you will all feel for us, & that India, like Ireland, will at such a moment forget all the bad things & see only the decent things we have done for her.

Please tell Andrews I will write him next week. Ever yours—

W. R.

1. See Letter 55, note 2; Letter 58.
2. The puzzle can be solved—up to a point. Evidently in reply to a Macmillan inquiry, Fox Strangways stated that *The King of the Dark Chamber* "is one of four [plays] which were to be included in your proposed volume." He will try to find a copy. (Fox Strangways to Macmillan, March 8, 1914. MCP.) He wrote Rothenstein: "Macmillans now pro-

pose to bring out the plays separately. The *Post Office* and *Chitra* are accessible, but have you got the *King of the Dark Chamber*? If not, who has? And there was a talk at one time of a fourth; what was the title of that? and who has it? or was there no such thing?" (Fox Strangways to Rothenstein [April 10?, 1914]. RP:HL.) When he had no word from Rothenstein he wrote: "I think it unlikely that the Americans [*i.e.*, Brett] would have a copy of the play; but anything may happen with an Oriental. I should certainly warn them about the use of such." (Fox Strangways to Macmillan, April 17, 1914. MCP.) A few weeks later he mailed "a large envelope, the best I can now give," evidently Rothenstein's copy of the play. (Fox Strangways to Macmillan, May 7, 1914. MCP.) Both he and Macmillan may have assumed that this, like other works released through Rothenstein, was formally submitted. If Kshitish Chandra Sen's contribution had been formally acknowledged from the outset, that difficulty at least would have been avoided. Rothenstein may have "told" Rhys and Fox Strangways about this, but at the most crucial stage of the exchange none of them could communicate easily with Macmillan. Rothenstein was in Gloucestershire, Rhys in Devon, Fox Strangways at Torquay. Rothenstein's crucial question remains: who *did* read proofs? Even here past procedure suggests partial explanation, for Tagore often instructed Macmillan to send proofs to his various English collaborators.

3. One reviewer wondered whether "a sprinkling of inadvertencies in his hitherto faultless English" meant that the author did not really care for this play; this reviewer generally reversed Rothenstein's estimate of its critical reception. (See review, *"The King of the Dark Chamber,"* *The Athenaeum* [London], July 25, 1914, p. 128.) *Chitra* was the work of "a poet in the full sense of the word." (Review, *"Chitra,"* ibid., January 17, 1914, p. 99.)

88
Tagore to Rothenstein

Srinagar, Kashmir   October 14, 1914

My dearest Friend

After many a change of plans I have come to Kashmir. You know its beauty is celebrated, which is a great drawback. Unless you discover a country it is not your own. I suppose it is the same with a poet—celebrity makes him stale—and the reader tries to pose himself as a discoverer by proving him to be a star of a lesser magnitude than as noted in the catalogue....

Hironmoy Roy Chowdry is here, in the vain attempt at securing an appointment. He asks me to request you to speak for him to some India Office authorities. Abanindra has resigned his post of the vice principal of Calcutta Art School and Hironmoy wants to fill the vacancy. But as this post commands comparatively high salary and with the solitary exception of Abanindra, has been held by Europeans, there is very little chance for him unless specially favoured by the higher powers. His qualifications are not inferior to those of the present principal, but you know, India is not for Indians and therefore he is trying to approach India Office people, hoping against hope.[1]

We have paid Walker's bills to the full but the book does not seem to be forthcoming. Ever yours

Rabindranath Tagore

1. Hironmoy Roy Chowdhury, distantly related to Tagore by marriage, was the first Indian with a diploma of Associate of the Royal College of Art, London. After Havell's departure Abanindranath was Acting Principal until 1909, when Percy Brown (1872–1955), who had been in the Indian Educational Service since 1899, became Principal. Abanindranath reverted to Vice-Principal, his post under Havell, and resigned in 1914 after a disagreement with Brown. The situation recalled Havell's 1910 plea before the Royal Society of Arts; when questioners in the House of Commons asked whether qualified Indians were passed over in favor of English appointees for art schools in India, the explanation given was that Abanindranath was passed over in 1909, "as he was not held to be qualified and he himself agreeing that the supervision and development of the school on its industrial side would be better left in other hands." He was passed over, in other words, because he was primarily an artist, not an industrial designer. (*The Parliamentary Debates* [*Official Report*] [London, 1914], series 5 [C] [May 5, 1914], vol. 62, col. 112.)

89
Rothenstein to Tagore

Far Oakridge   October 22, 1914

My dear friend—it is long since I heard from you. Fortunately Andrews keeps me informed of your welfare. I have not myself been a very regular correspondent. That I know, the house & the mess that has to be cleaned after the building has taken up my spare time, & at night I am too weary even for reading. I have seen little of Indians; I go up to London more and more rarely, & none come to see me. . . . But in spite of this, the thought of India is not often out of my head, & your own name comes to our lips daily. As you can imagine, we are all of us anxious enough in these days of strife. . . . But the habits of life are so binding, & every day my feet take me into the studio, & there, over my work, I ruminate, chafe, forget, lose myself & find myself, do good or indifferent work, & then in to lunch with the children, & only the newspaper tells me what is happening a couple of hundred miles away. Life goes on pretty much as usual here, & the world seems to be as peaceful & lovely a place as any one might wish to dream of. Only something sounds hollow in the spirit, & there are days of deep depression. . . .

For India at least there is nothing but appreciation; one hears & reads of something in the nature of fraternal feelings for the first time; only the reasons given are different from those we, old lovers of your country, have been swayed by. . . . I am glad you were spared any sign of this swift disaster when you were among us. . . . Ever your friend—
William Rothenstein

90
Tagore to Rothenstein

[Santiniketan]   December 29, 1914

My dear Friend

I send you the translation of a poem of mine suggested by the letter I got from Rachel. It gave me the right perspective and I saw all the simple things of the world in their proper significance in spite of the din and smoke of this terrible war.[1]

The Trumpet was written a fortnight before the war broke out—but the poem I am sending you now gives you my idea about war as inspired by the delightful letter of Rachel.[2]

When this reaches you I shall be sailing for Japan and following the track of the rising sun I may reach your door some sunny day of summer.[3] With my love to all the dear people in your house   Yours
Rabindranath Tagore

You are at liberty to do whatever you like with this poem.

1. Tagore, no. 22, *Balākā* [Wild Swans] (1916), in *R-R*, XII, 43–44: "The Freedom of Separation," *The Nation* (London), 16 (1915), 421: no. 10, *Fruit-Gathering:* in CPP, p. 143.

2. "The Trumpet": no. 4, *Balākā*, in *R-R*, XII, 6–8: no. 35, *Fruit-Gathering:* in CPP, pp. 152–153. Tagore sent "The Trumpet" without comment; Rothenstein acknowledged it on October 27, 1914 (R-S). Rachel had written, "Billy and Betty have some lovely caterpillars! but they are all turning into chrysalises." (Rachel Rothenstein to Tagore [October 24?, 1914]. R-S.) Andrews wrote of their delight in her refreshing sense of proportion and values as displayed in her "caterpillar letter." (Andrews to Rothenstein, December 28 [1914]. RP:HL.)

3. Tagore planned to visit Japan, China, and the United States, and the short stories would again be delayed. He promised to try to finish them while traveling and send them to Brett or to the London firm for preliminary revisions. (Tagore to Macmillan, through Andrews, December 28 [1914]. MP:BM.) This trip was postponed.

IV   1915   Letters 91-107

Hesitations and Losses

1915 was a year for pause and reconsideration. The realization that the war was not just a bad dream hung over everyone and everything. Tagore had settled down uneasily at Santiniketan. Rothenstein, living away from London at Oakridge, fought doggedly and alone his personal and artistic battles. From Oxford, Robert Bridges, Poet Laureate since 1913, posed the question still unasked in relation to Tagore's works: what are the rights and obligations of translators, co-translators, and retranslators?

Rothenstein had introduced Bridges and Tagore in 1912. They met again at Oxford in 1913, when, as Bridges told Tagore, "your presence there gave reality to the honest but vain profession of the University to be a home for all creeds and nations." He did not send congratulations, Bridges wrote, "when that mysterious committee of international judges crowned you with bank notes," but he wrote now because he had just met, for the first time, "the young Scotch missionary, [Edward] Thompson." Thompson had described Tagore's mode of life at Santiniketan, and "it is his telling me of it that has given me confidence to write as I do; for I guess from what he said that you are likelier to overvalue my sympathy than to underrate it."[1]

The two poets had a way of life in common, for Bridges had fled from London to Boars Hill, high above Oxford, to a solid, square-cut house on a wooded hillside with a long view to the valley below. "Another time," he told Tagore, "if you are here ever again, you must if possible be my guest for at least a part of your visit, up on the hill, where I live in a seclusion which is the more real (at least so I think) for being simply personal and domestic. No monastery was ever quieter and more secluded than my library, and the wood behind the

---

1. Bridges to Tagore, June 7, 1914. R-S. Robert Bridges (1844–1930) retired physician and practicing poet; Poet Laureate, 1913–1930.

house is as solitary as any in the world, though when you come to the end of it you can see the City towers in the valley, and hear the bells."

Bridges and Tagore seemed to share ways of thinking, as well, particularly religious thinking. The letter continued:

> Of all the advantages that I have found in my poetic attitude towards life none compare with the pleasure which its friendships have brought me; and the best and most intimate of them have been religious friendships— I mean with religious minds. In my early life I was a devoted churchman, but when I saw the folly of exclusiveness and fixed creeds, I wandered off into all kinds of mental wildernesses, and am now settled down in a nest of home made psychological and metaphysical convictions, which I do not find many to share, and I fancy that your theism is something that I should be more able to envy than profess. I am almost afraid that you would regard me as a profane layman, . . . But I am nevertheless rather envious of you. There is no luxury in envy, and I am luxuriously given—the envy in any case may witness to the sympathy which it is my wish to spare you of.[2]

When war began, Bridges wrote, "I wonder how you are taking all this. . . . I was terribly smitten down at first, with something like rage, but I hope that I am getting more placid. . . . the confidence of our nation, though tarnished with democratic vulgarity, is beautiful."[3]

This beauty of confidence springing from suffering and forgiveness was the theme of Bridges' proposed anthology, *The Spirit of Man*. He intended it to demonstrate "various moods of mind, which are allowed free play." The sequence of these moods might be rearranged "without damage and perhaps with advantage; but, . . . the main implication is essential, namely, that spirituality is the basis and foundation of human life."[4]

2. Ibid.
3. Bridges to Tagore, October 20, 1914. R-S.
4. Bridges, *The Spirit of Man: An Anthology in English & French from the Philosophers & Poets made by the Poet Laureate in 1915 & dedicated by gracious permission to His Majesty The King* (London, 1916) [pp. i–ii].

It was not Bridges' way merely to cast about for poems that were sufficiently "spiritual." They must speak to his condition and to the condition of England, and he would choose with conviction or not at all. He considered several new poems that Tagore had sent to Rothenstein, finally settled upon three from *Gitanjali* and eight from the Kabir volume, then asked Tagore's permission to use these with slight "verbal alterations."[5] The effect was that of a transparently calm day turned suddenly murky.

The entire episode of *The Spirit of Man* might be written off as an editorial flurry, had it not raised those fundamental questions about translation and translators. It revealed the dangers of joint editorial procedures and the full extent of Tagore's dilemma as translator and as public figure. That his poems were lyrics offered no ground for dispute. Bridges' early poems, some of his loveliest, are lyrics, but he was a thoroughgoing classicist who equated beauty with form, and form with simplicity and order. Personal emotion is a source of beauty only if it is restrained by form. Tagore's Bengali lyrics, although rich with strongly disciplined rhyme and meter and every sort of assonance, became free verse in his English versions, and Bridges considered free verse unpardonably formless and unrestrained. The title of his 1922 essay on the subject tells the story: "Humdrum & Harum-Scarum: A Lecture on Free Verse." Bridges believed that "free verse is good and theoretically defensible only in so far as it can create expectancy without the old metrical devices. If it fails to effect this, it seems to me but a broken jerky sort of bad prose; and the old fluent prose needs not me nor any one else to defend it from those who would cut it to fragments and call its fragments verse."[6]

---

5. Bridges' phrase: "This is the correspondence: letters from Tagore, Macmillan, Rothenstein and Thompson which resulted at last in my having permission to make verbal alterations in the English of Tagore's original poem, (and in his translations from Kabir,—) for the Spirit of Man." Bridges crossed out the reference to Kabir. (Holograph note, n.d. Bridges Papers.)

6. He specifies "adverse conditions" that threaten free versifiers: "(1) Loss of carrying power. (2) Self-consciousness. (3) Same-ness of line structure. (4) Indetermination of subsidiary 'accent.'" "Humdrum & Harum-Scarum: A Lecture on Free Verse," *Collected Essays, Papers, &c. of Robrt Bridges* (London, 1928), II, 47. Published also as "A Paper on Free Verse," *The North American Review*, 216 (1922), 647–658.

The controversy finally focused upon Number 67 of *Gitanjali*. Bridges' notation reads: "It stands between Plato and Aristotle [in *The Spirit of Man*], and it was necessary for the solidity of my book that it should not stumble in that place."[7] When Bridges' and Tagore's versions are laid side by side it is plain which parts Bridges considered stumbling blocks. The poem apostrophizes an Eternal Being; Bridges sharpened the hallmark of the genre by maintaining the ecstatic opening tone to the end of the first line: "O Thou Beautiful! how in the nest thy love embraceth the soul with sweet sounds and colour and fragrant odours!" He restructured several lines to eliminate syntactical indiscretions and awkward usages. He gave consistency to the diction. Twice in the opening line Tagore had used "thou art," then reverted to the familiar form of the pronoun so that the lofty tone of his first two lines sinks abruptly to the more prosaic tone of "There comes the morning with the golden basket in her right hand." Bridges' verbs, however, follow throughout the pattern set in the first line by Tagore's "Thou art the sky."

Whether Bridges' changes preserve Tagore's tone is another matter. Tagore was apparently unaware of the extent to which twentieth-century English-speaking readers, conditioned by the diction of the King James Bible, habitually distinguished between certain forms as archaic and others as modern. In many Bengali lyrics Tagore intentionally established the informal relation, characteristic of Vaishnava lyrics, between the poet and the Eternal Being addressed; he used the familiar form of the second-person pronoun and a corresponding informal verb inflection—a very important distinction in Bengali. But, by mixing formal and informal English verb and pronoun forms, he left room for doubts about his original intention for the tone of the poem.

The fundamental difficulty lay in the fact that Bridges and Tagore had different sets of poetic values. The classical form without which, in Bridges' opinion, no English poem could be truly beautiful, did not claim priority in Tagore's. This becomes quite clear in the final lines of the two versions. Bridges disposed of the dangling preposition "in," then knitted

---

7. Tagore, no. 81, *Naibedya*, in R-R, VIII, 63: no. 67, *Gitanjali*: in CPP, p. 25. Bridges' holograph notation, n.d. BrP.

C. F. Andrews, M. K. Gandhi, and W. W. Pearson in South Africa

Tagore's last sentence into the stanza: "wherein is neither day nor night, nor form nor colour, nor ever any word." But, by letting this stand alone, Tagore achieved one of his most haunting English lines: "There is no day nor night, nor form nor colour, and never, never a word." Bridges' version is more correct; Tagore's is made memorable by the cadence of that last line. Neither has the form and cadence of the line in Bengali.[8]

Obstacles to agreement, however, were not literary or even commercial, but sentimental. Bridges was not dealing, as he supposed, with his friend Tagore, but with Andrews. Andrews was distressed, not primarily because of literary objections to Bridges' "verbal alterations" but because he objected on principle to any changes in anything of Tagore's.[9]

Bridges duly reported to Rothenstein Tagore's first response: "[Tagore] says (1) *that I may take anything from his works, or from his translation of Kabir's poems. But that the right of permission 'rests with my publishers,* WHO, I AM SURE WILL NOT REFUSE YOU.'" Tagore himself begged off: he had no critical understanding of English prosody, he claimed. He appreciated the help of those who did, and Bridges' version was beautiful, but the reading public preferred the *Gitanjali* version it had learned to love. Therefore, Macmillan, as his agent, must rule on the matter. "If," Bridges told Rothenstein, "I may not deal with the English of the Gitanjali poems I shall not use them. And I shall therefore ask only permission to use the one [Number 67] of which Tagore speaks in his letter." Bridges had rewritten the Kabir poems "by collation with the originals in the B[ritish] Museum." He added, "I am afraid that Tagore's version was done without actual reference to the original Hindi."

8. Even transliteration conveys these: *"barna nāi, gandha nāi— nāi nāi bāni."*
9. Thompson wrote: "[Tagore] has been annexed as a private possession by C. F. Andrews, late of Delhi." (Thompson to Bridges [July? 1915]. BrP.) Rothenstein wrote: "[Tagore] is I think under the influence of an English missionary, sweet and well meaning enough, but without any sense of literature and very little of the masculine side of life. He flatters the sentimental side of Tagore, and does not understand the more natural and humourous side of his nature—the best side, in fact." (Rothenstein to Bridges, July 20, 1915. BrP.)

Bridges then offered a plainspoken estimate of Tagore's position vis-à-vis the reading public in England:

> It is plain (with reference to the Gitanjali poems) that Tagore overestimates the familiarity which English readers have with his book. We are accustomed too to give great weight to the apology that is always made for those poems, viz. that the English does not do them justice: and that they are much more beautiful in their original language. Tagore's English book would, I think, only gain (if it was at all affected) by my procedure—and after what he has said I would only take that one poem. I am pretty sure that the Gitanjali poems will not gain more appreciation in England than they have already. If they are to extend their popularity nothing could help them more than their recognition in such a book as I propose to bring out.

Bridges went on to make a crucially important point: he would acknowledge debts to the [Sen-Chakravarty-]Tagore-Underhill version of Kabir, but, "it is plainly as open to me as to anyone else to translate Kabir." In view of the multiple identity of the Kabir translator and of the fact that no Kabir copyright existed, Bridges' position appeared a firm one. In a postscript to this same letter he stated: "It is absolutely certain that my use of Tagore's poem will *help* his book, especially with persons who (like Sir Walter Raleigh) now *laugh at it*. I have heard Raleigh run it down in his public lectures. That sort of thing would be met by my version."[10]

Andrews now raised the other point at issue: literary honor and Tagore's debt to Yeats. In an impassioned letter to Rothenstein, Andrews reviewed Tagore's literary and personal relations with Yeats and insisted that the latter would be outraged by changes in any poems that he had originally edited. Andrews' letter performs a very real service, for it projects a vivid picture of Tagore and Bridges (with Rothenstein and Frederick Macmillan caught between) pursuing quite different aspects of a problem and Tagore, at least, not

10. Bridges to Rothenstein, April 19 [1915]. RP:HL. Bridges' italics.

realizing that communication was less than perfect between them.[11]

Tagore was rightly if belatedly concerned about his literary honor, but instead of stating at the outset that his hesitations sprang from uncertainties about English usage, he shifted the responsibility onto Yeats, Macmillan, and that amorphous creature, the reading public. Tagore and Andrews assumed that fame once gained was fame forever assured, but Bridges knew the public's fickleness and had less faith in its undying devotion to Tagore's poems. He told Rothenstein:

> About the popularity of Tagore's poetry in England. Of course that will be a matter of fashion, and will not depend on the excellencies which a few admirers like yourself see in it. And I should expect a *publisher* to take that view; and there is no doubt that my presentation of that poem would help him. That seems to me to be the practical point.
>
> Raleigh's judgment is a very fair idea of the sort of taste that is likely to prevail. But though I feel pretty sure that Tagore's vein will not find much sympathy in England, there is no certainty—and one can only guess probabilities.[12]

Bridges' publisher, C. J. Longman, informed him that Macmillan had given permission on condition "that the extracts must be given in the language of Tagore himself."[13]

There the matter stood. Bridges appealed to the Society of Authors for "expert advice" on the rights of a retranslator.[14] The Society's Secretary, G. Herbert Thring, promptly cited another case in which an editor had had copyright trouble because he

---

11. Andrews to Rothenstein, April 5 [1915]. RP:HL.
12. Bridges to Rothenstein, April 28 [1915]. RP:HL.
13. Longman to Bridges, May 7, 1915. BrP. Bridges correctly interpreted this as "a definite refusal from [Macmillan] to [allow me to] use my version of Tagore's poem." He decided to drop the *Gitanjali* poem: "As for Kabir, I shall make new translations with [H. S.] Suhrawardy [Oxford student]." (Bridges to Rothenstein, May 8 [1915]. RP:HL.)
14. Bridges to Society of Authors, May 8 [1915]. Society of Authors Archives: British Museum. He stated plainly, "I cannot read Hindi but employ a very competent expert [Suhrawardy]."

had worked from a previously published edition, not from original texts in the British Museum. This procedure, Thring said, was

> the wrong way round, and from your statement it seems to me that you may be doing the same. If the translations come from the originals without any reference to Macmillan's translations [i.e., from the Kabir volume], then I think you would be entitled to publish them, the originals being out of copyright. . . . The point is as follows: if the originals are out of copyright, anyone can make translations, but any new translator must be able to show distinctly, if his title is challenged, that his translation is made without any reference to the translations of others. In other words, he may not use the work of others for his own advancement and pecuniary gain.[15]

Bridges' reply to Thring summarized every retranslator's predicament with regard to literary honor:

> The main principle of the law is admirable, but its application is hopeless. It rules that no one may retranslate anything of which he happens to have read a fairly competent copyright translation. For he must in most cases use many of the same words, and there can be no proof that they were not suggested to him by the earlier translation.
>
> In the question of indebtedness there is no real distinction between his having the copyright translation before his eyes, or in his subconscious memory when he retranslates: except this distinction, namely that he may use the copy under his eye to enable him to avoid consciously a [likeness] which he might unconsciously have fallen into. And it would be ridiculous to allow this (which might be mere dishonesty) and forbid the unconscious similarities.
>
> There seems to me to be no possibility of proving that a new translation is not influenced by an old one (and therefore does not "use the work of others") if the re-

15. Thring to Bridges, May 10, 1915. BrP.

translator has read the old one—much more it is to be proved that he was familiar with it and retranslated because he did not like it—as is my case.[16]

Nowhere in this voluminous dossier is there evidence that these fundamental questions received the attention they deserved, or that the comparative literary merits of Bridges' "verbal alterations" and Tagore's original English wording were systematically and dispassionately examined and judged by strictly literary criteria. The episode should have marked a turning point in Tagore's career. It did no such thing. On the contrary, it made quite clear the fact that what appeared to be Tagore's obstinate certainty about his translated texts was really the paralysis of uncertainty. Translation and publication went on in the old way as if predestined.

Bridges did not abandon the *Gitanjali* poem after all.[17] The correspondence became an almost farcical exchange among Bridges, Tagore, Rothenstein and Andrews; Edward Thompson, now back in Bengal; the Macmillans; and Yeats, who was not outraged in the least. The denouement, when it came, was bacterial: a cholera infection removed Andrews temporarily from the scene. Bridges' request was ultimately judged on sentimental, not literary grounds, and the principal immediate outcome of the whole affair was a great waste of the time and nervous energy of all concerned.

16. Bridges to Thring, May 13, 1915. Society of Authors: BM. The fair copy sent to Thring differs slightly in wording but is substantially the same in meaning as a draft transcribed for the editor by the late Lord Bridges. The word "likeness," bracketed in the second paragraph as quoted, is illegible in Bridges' holograph letter to Thring and is supplied here from Lord Bridges' transcription.
17. He used numbers 67, 92, and 31 from *Gitanjali*, in *The Spirit of Man* numbers 38, 282, 284; from the Kabir volume, nine poems, in *The Spirit of Man* numbers 17, 43, 57, 66, 175, 182, 397, 399, 415.

91
Tagore to Rothenstein

Shanti Niketan [January 5?, 1915]

My dear Friend

I have made some corrections in the poem I sent to you last week. I enclose the revised version herewith.

The war that is going on in Europe has sent its storm-clouds all over the world, and we are under the gloom of their shadows. In the modern age a complete connection of nervous system has been established in the body of humanity and we are sharing your sufferings across the sea. We hope this war is a fight against warfare—it is the birth-pang of a new era of peace. The brute, hidden in the heart of civilisation, must be discovered to be pursued and killed. It has shown itself in all its fierce hideousness and you cannot let it pass by. With love   yours

Rabindranath Tagore

92
Rothenstein to Tagore

Far Oakridge   January 12, 1915

My dear friend— . . . Since last writing I have lost my dear father, & this has entailed many letters & much correspondence with my family. It means the break-up of our old home, & the dispersal of all it contained, for there is no one left to occupy it. While my parents were alive children & grandchildren came together there. Now each of us has made his & her own centre, & we look up at the clock & see how long past mid-day it is—mid-day which seemed so long in coming! And this reminds me of Kabir, who has at last appeared, dressed in the same white garment as your own Gitanjali & under it also a noble heart beats. I can fancy the good Ajit will be the first to congratulate himself on having been the cause of our getting the precious work: you have indeed made a noble thing of the translation. It is a great delight to me to know another example of the peculiar genius of India shown to the world. There is a passionate conviction of the reality of God all through the poems which puts a sense of power & beauty to its simple statement which is most moving, & your translation seems to have kept the spirit of the man alive & blithe, as though he were still singing on the Panch Ganga Ghat [at Benares]; & I were listening to him, & seeing him there, with a crowd round him. I suppose a painter understands the pan-theistic attitude better than most people, because when he's painting anyone or anything, all the beauty in the world comes bursting out of the thing or person he is concentrated upon & he knows that this beauty has no aesthetic effect on him, but an overpoweringly human one, making him, while he is subjected to it, love man & beast & bird, field & sky & tree & hill with an all-embracing heart. I am not sure that we aren't very disagreeable the moment after, when we go into the house from the studio or field; that is why perhaps we are not often heroes to our valets—they don't see us until we want something to eat, or to wear, or until we have a headache or a cold. At any rate, I am content to know as little about the man himself as we know of the painters of Ajanta. I expect the India Society has expressed its gratitude for your help in the matter; I was glad to see that Miss Underhill's share was profusely acknowledged in the title page but with a due sense of her share in the book, compared with yours; also that Kshiti Mohan Babu's patient research & learning should be set down, as well as the good Ajit's initiative in sending over the first tidings.[1] When the Ajanta book is out we shall feel that the little society, launched on such stormy seas among so many rocks, will have justified its existence. If the wares it has brought from Eastern shores be few, they are rich & precious. . . . I was at Oxford for a week-end some little time ago, & saw Bridges in his charming home on Boars Hill, & we talked much of you—also some very intelligent Indian students, with whom I had a long chat.[2] Otherwise I stay faithfully here, painting & exercising in fields & woods. . . . Ever yours affectionately

W. R.

1. The Kabir project raveled out in desultory wrangling about credits and fees. Tagore instructed Macmillan to consult with Fox Strangways

about a fee for Evelyn Underhill. (Tagore to Macmillan, February 25, 1914. MP:BM.) Fox Strangways proposed that "K. M. Sen will be paid something *via* Tagore, also A. Chakravarty but I presume they will come into Mrs. M[oore]'s preface. What exercises me is ought we to pay Tagore anything for himself, and if so what. Our small [India Society] edition won't stand very much." (Fox Strangways to Rothenstein [April 10?, 1914]. RP:HL.) Later, with some asperity he told the Macmillans in London, "There has been a longwinded business about the *headlines*— in the way now, I believe, to be settled—but any text that you have has probably got them wrong (i.e. according to the experts)." (Fox Strangways to Macmillan, November 24, 1914. MCP.) Evelyn Underhill had asked Tagore how he wished "our various shares in the production described on the title page? I thought we might say that this version was 'based upon that of Ajit Kumar Chakravarty.' And do you wish anything said about him in the introduction? and if so, what?" (Evelyn Underhill to Tagore, November 16, 1913. R-S.) (See Kabir, *One Hundred Poems of Kabir*, pp. xxvi–xxvii.)

2. See *MM* II, 299.

93
Tagore to Rothenstein

Shilida February 9, 1915

My dear Friend

If the following translation of a Bengali poem of mine be acceptable to any of your papers please have it published and out of its proceeds buy something for our soldiers in the trenches. With love.   Yours

RabindranathTagore

Summer's Pioneers
Tired of waiting, you burst your bounds,
Impatient flowers, before the winter had gone.
Glimpses of the unseen comer came into your wayside watch
And you rushed out running and panting,
O restless jasmines, O troop of riotous roses!

You were the first to march to the breach of death.
Your clamour of colour and perfume troubled the air.
You laughed and pressed and pushed each other,
Bared your breasts and dropped to the ground in heaps.

The summer will come in its time
Sailing in the floodtide of the south wind.
But you never counted slow moments to be sure of him.
You recklessly spent your all in the road in terrible joy of faith.

You heard his footsteps from afar
And flung your mantle of death for him to tread on.
Your bonds break even before the rescuer is seen,
You make him your own ere he can come and claim you.[1]

You know I am not sure of your English punctuation and grammer, please make corrections if needed. We sail for Japan early next month—I shall give you my address before starting. Give my love to all your dear people.

1. Tagore, no. 21, *Balākā*, in *R-R*, XII, 42: "Summer Pioneers," *The Fortnightly Review* (London), 103 (1915), 846: no. 52, *Lover's Gift:* in *CPP*, pp. 209–210. This MS draft of poem has slight autograph revisions by Rothenstein. (Tagore: Houghton).

94
Tagore to Rothenstein

Calcutta   February 18, 1915

My dear Friend

My visit to Japan has been postponed a few months longer. In the meanwhile I am thinking of spending my summer in Kashmere. I need rest, and going into a new country is rather disconcerting. Lowes Dickinson's Essay on The Civilisations of India, China and Japan has made me feel sad. Not only he is entirely out of sympathy with India but has tried to make out that there is something inherent in Englishman which makes him incapable of appreciating India—and to him India by her very nature will be a source of eternal irritation. Of all countries in the world India is *the* East to him—that is to say an abstraction. Possibly he is right in his observations—but then it is a hopeless misery for India till the end of this chapter of her history and it is utterly bad for those who have come merely to govern her from across the sea. I only hope Dickinson is not right and that it was heat and hurry and dyspepsia that blotted out the human India from his sight leading him into the blank of a monotonous mist of classification.[1]

I am sending you another translation of my poem. I hope this may be instrumental in bringing to our soldiers some little comfort to remind them of the anxious love of their countrymen in the distant home. With my best love   Yours ever

Rabindranath Tagore

1. G. Lowes Dickinson, *An Essay on the Civilisations of India, China & Japan* (London, 1914), his 1913 report to the Albert Kahn Foundation on whose traveling fellowship Dickinson, accompanied part of the way by Robert Trevelyan and E. M. Forster, visited Asia. Dickinson did prefer China to India and said so repeatedly in private and in print. (See Forster, *Goldsworthy Lowes Dickinson* [London, 1934], pp. 135–154.) Trevelyan's son Julian recalls his father's saying that when he landed in Bombay he was struck by the classical look of the people. At Chhatarpur, Dickinson fell ill, and Trevelyan whiled away the time by trying to learn Persian; Julian Trevelyan recalls books in the family library that his father could not read but enjoyed as reminders at hand of older civilizations. (Interview with Julian Trevelyan, London, August 5, 1969.) Dickinson saw nothing Hellenic in dress or anything else Indian. In China he found all that he had missed in India: simplicity, repose, good taste, and above all, a secular atmosphere. He does seem to isolate India, for he draws a line not between East and West, but between India and the rest of the world. He did not claim perfect understanding but said: "East and West in my mind wove a web whose pattern I cannot trace. But a pattern there is. And some day historians will be able to find it." (Dickinson, *Appearances: Being Notes of Travel* [London, 1914], p. 31.)

95
Rothenstein to Tagore

Far Oakridge   March 15 [1915]

My very dear friend—your last poem has just reached me—also the news that you have not been well & have given up your intended trip to Japan, sad news, for this means I fear that the long pointed buds of our beech trees will unroll themselves & turn from bright green to orange red without being seen by you. I had built many castles for many summer days. Instead you are to wander in the valleys of Kashmir, that land of the Arabian nights of which so many travellers tell. This means at least that you are in flight from the importunities of men. Our neighbours give us heavier blows at times than our enemies,[1] for they give them to our faith & hope; it is not the big whacks that hurt, but the little meannesses, the want of imagination for fairness & helpfulness, which hurt us & make us miserable so often. I think I can detect something of this in your last poem—The Freedom of Separation.... Robert Bridges has the other two & is making suggestions. The "Judgement" he does not understand altogether—he writes "in the last section is it meant that forgiveness is punishment or that punishment is forgiveness? That is, must the sinner be shattered before he becomes contrite or is his contrition his shattering? or again thus—is divine pardon the most powerful produce[r] of contrition greater even than natural beauty (1st stanza) & than spiritual beauty (2nd stanza) or is punishment the sign of forgiveness," but perhaps you would prefer to give your explanation which may be a very different one from any he suggests.[2]

We each have our own feeling about a poem as [about] a picture—a good poem has this quality of life about it, & I don't think it is necessary to discover precisely what was in the poet's or painter's mind, for he does not always know that himself.

I have been trying to get out of Emery Walker the cause of the delay in your brother's book. I find he is now good enough to pretend that he was waiting for me to give the order to the printers! I have written to tell him that the work was put into his hands by your son to carry out completely.[3] I passed the proofs & wrote the preface months ago; if this happened in India, how we should batter the poor Indians!

... I hope this mood of yours which has brought me the last 3 poems is still on you, & that others will follow. It is so necessary in this confusion for some of us to set certain things down clearly.... You in Kashmir will only get vague rumors of these things, but as you wrote, we have now one great nervous system & all peoples have learned that now at any rate. Indeed the distinction between the dreaming East & the active West, in which I have never believed, is being blotted out, if it ever existed. Japan has not acted for nothing, & in the dim future one can imagine, alas, other wars & bitternesses in which perhaps equally or more passionate hatreds will be awakened & spend themselves. In the meanwhile every decent thought helps to stitch the wounds of the world. I have no faith in beauty without wisdom & soundness. The best sentiments & ideals are without

Rabindranath Tagore, drawing by Jyotirindranath Tagore

value unless they are passionately meant—this is what education must mean if it is to help men. . . . Ever yours affectionately

W. R.

1. Immediately after the outbreak of war, Rothenstein was reported to local police as a German spy. He had been seen painting a picture of the railway tunnel; a newly laid concrete barn floor must be a gun emplacement; large numbers of telegrams and packing cases came and went at Iles Farm; and of course his name and parentage were German. It transpired that the rumors had originated in nearby Stroud, and Oakridge neighbors apologized. Nevertheless, on April 4, 1916, Charles and Albert Rothenstein changed their surname to Rutherston; at the moment of decision, William found himself profoundly unwilling to take this step. (See *MM* II, 288–289; Speaight, *William Rothenstein*, pp. 267–268, 278–280.)

2. Rothenstein quotes a letter from Bridges, March 13 [1915] (RP: HL). Bridges had "Summer's Pioneers" (see Letter 93) and "Judgment" (no. 11, *Balākā*, in *R-R*, XII, 27–30: no. 36. *Fruit-Gathering:* in *CPP*, pp. 153–154). He considered "Judgment" "difficult to deal with because I could not be absolutely sure of the poet's intention. And for that reason I like the other poem better: and the thought is so simple that I am surprised that no one (so far as I can remember) has ever made the same use of it. If my little wit should return to me in a day or two [after illness], and I am able then to understand all the Judgment Poem, I will let you know. But I do not think I shall like to tackle that one—I should like to have the other in my book." (Bridges to Rothenstein, March 12 [1915]. RP:HL.)

3. Rathindranath had left Walker with the impression that Rothenstein was in charge. (Walker to Rothenstein, March 17, 1915. RP:HL.) The book continues its elusive ways. A drawer-by-drawer search of papers remaining in Emery Walker's former London residence failed to yield information about it, and no library visited or consulted by the editor has been able to produce a copy of the book or a record of publication. Pulinbehari Sen, Tagore bibliographer, states that its title is *Twenty-Five Collotypes from the Original Drawings of Jyotirindranath Tagore* and that it has a Preface by Rothenstein and was published in London in 1914. However, Walker ordered its binding in 1915, and Andrews wrote appreciatively of it in 1916. (Andrews to Rothenstein [Autumn 1916]. RP:HL.)

96
Tagore to Rothenstein

Shanti Niketan   April 4, 1915

My dear Friend

I give up Japan, at least, for the present. Not for any sudden failure in courage or enthusiasm but for the same blessed reason that brings a modern war to its halt. My finance is hopeless, mainly owing to the European complications.

I got a letter from Dr Bridges with his own version of a Gitanjali poem. I cannot judge it. But since I have got my fame as an English writer I feel extreme reluctance in accepting alterations in my English poems by any of your writers. I must not give men any reasonable ground for accusing me,—which they do,—of reaping advantage of other men's genius and skill. There are people who suspect that I owe in a large measure to Andrews' help for my literary success, which is so false that I can afford to laugh at it. But it is different about Yeats. I think Yeats was sparing in his suggestions—moreover, I was with him during the revisions. But one is apt to delude himself, and it is very easy for me to gradually forget the share Yeats had in making my things passable. Though you have the first draft of my translations with you I have unfortunately allowed the revised typed pages to get lost in which Yeats pencilled his corrections. Of course, at that time I never could imagine that anything that I could write would find its place in your literature. But the situation is changed now. And if it be true that Yeats' touches have made it possible for Gitanjali to occupy the place it does then that must be confessed. At least by my subsequent unadulterated writings my true level should be found out and the faintest speck of lie should be wiped out from the fame I enjoy now. It does not matter what the people think of me but it does matter all the world to me to be true to myself. This is the reason why I cannot accept any help from Bridges excepting where the grammar is wrong or wrong words have been used. My translations are frankly prose,—my aim is to make them simple with just a suggestion of rhythm to give them a touch of the lyric, avoiding all archaisms and poetical conventions.

I am sending you some more of my translations—keep them with you till we meet, if you have any doubts about their fitness. I still cherish the hope of seeing you and the dear children in your green solitude and bury there under the fallen leaves all the artificial laurels lurking in my wreath. With love   Yours affectionately

> Rabindranath Tagore

Andrews does not admire the alterations made by Bridges but that does not affect me. In fact I am not so much anxious about mutilations as about added beauties which I cannot claim as mine.

R. T.

97
Tagore to Rothenstein

Shanti Niketan   April 13, 1915

My dear Friend,

Poets are not reliable commentators of their own writings but to my mind the meaning of the last verse of "Judgment" is so simple that even the author of it may be credited of understanding it. When a moral law is grossly violated God's forgiveness comes not in the form of mitigation of pain but in the form of mitigation of evil. Three forces are acting towards destroying evil at its root—one is beauty, the other is love, the third is the clear realisation of the fearfulness of evil which can never be possible until we fully see its tremendous consequences. When we truly know that evil is ugly, that it hurts love, and that it upsets balance of things then we can be sure that we are forgiven. Forgiveness is not in blissful ignorance, not in avoidance of retribution, but in gaining the purity of consciousness at the cost of all else.

You know I want to send you my poems because I love you to read them and to think that I think of you and the very least of all because I want them published. With warmest love. Yours affectionately

Rabindranath Tagore

98
Rothenstein to Tagore

Far Oakridge   April 30, 1915

My very dear friend— . . . Now let me tell you how delighted I am to see such welcome signs of activity on your part. For each one of the poems I care immensely. I am not as you know a literary man & in consequence it is insight into life which I look for in the written word. There I find you impeccable, of a sincerity which people who don't try to create have no conception of. In the Freedom of Separation I think I discern a noble lesson learned from your own experience which has touched me very much, & I am deeply moved by the conception of how "our efforts stiffen into bricks & stones, & thus the city of man is built." . . . Often I long for an order into which I can escape all the shame social difficulties bring on one so constantly—how well I can understand your sannyasis & our monks & friars. Happily something written here & there, something said & done, brings one's sanity back again, but the war has shown us the quicksand upon which our wellbeing is built & I don't think we can ever feel quite the same about things again. I think we have understood a good deal, we poets and painters, but our punishment has been in being right, not in being wrong. We have stood outside, that is our birthright, but we have also made use of the benefits & share in the responsibility. The consequence, for the time at least, is a sense of the thinness of the wall which divides life from death, & a something more than a determination to make the most fruitful & the least selfish use of the life remaining to us. I am not sure that this doesn't make one at times disagreeable & arrogant in one's desire to act straightly & think directly. You are further away, but I somehow fancy that I can feel something of a new power & determination in your new work. At any rate it has given me great joy & inspiration & I cannot help feeling that it will give inspiration to others.

Bridges writes that you are unwilling to let him change the form of the Gitanjali poems he intended using. I have written him that since Yeats went over the original translations, you naturally feel it would appear ungracious to him to allow any other hand to touch what he has passed & in some measure himself perfected, & he is apparently not able himself to agree.[1] He proposes, I think, using one of the poems & speaking to Macmillan regarding Kabir. But he will doubtless have written you himself. He is anxious to produce a great anthology of sacred literature & being high handed in his methods, he thinks all translations are fair game, so far as his own conception of form can improve them.[2] As you know, he has strong personal views regarding rhythm, & explained to me how great was the improvement he could make in the slight changes he proposed; as he holds his views with courage & conviction, I have always admired him, & it was a great delight to me to know of his admiration for your poems. I hope you will be able to come to some understanding with him, for it would be a pleasure to us lovers of Indian literature to find an ample place for your work in his anthology. He is an overbearing & masterful man, but a real poet & has a noble vision. For the moment my head is full of the war, & I am finding it more difficult to sit quietly aloof than before. There is a sense of shame in the comfort of home, when every day brings news of the loss of a friend, or of added misery & destruction. I fear your dream of coming to us this year will not be realised. The children remain my joy. They speak of you often & keep your memory fresh & shining.

I see a life of you announced, but I have not seen it yet.[3] I am a little shy of the greatness of my friends, & lives of the living never seem to me quite natural. I am sure Rhys will have done his work with delicacy & taste & I will have read it by the time I write you again. I will look after the poems, but I do not believe in publishing too many at a time.

My love to Andrews & Pearson.   Ever yours

W. R.

1. "He ... himself": Bridges. Rothenstein had suggested that Tagore feared offending Yeats. He added: "[Tagore] has lately sent me some new translations, all remarkable, it seems to me, in subject, but not very beautiful in form. I don't like to bother you with them, but if you have any curiosity to read them, and could further make some suggestions, I know you would be doing R.N.T. a favour. I delight in Raleigh's wit and wisdom, but his bad opinion of Tagore does not affect my own delight in his poems. I feel he has a psychological insight into the human heart which is very profound and always stirs me, however imperfect the expression in his own translations; and I find myself more and more judging pictures and books from this point of view." (Rothenstein to Bridges, April 26, 1915. BrP.)

2. Bridges' purpose seems to have been unclear in several quarters. Sir Frederick Macmillan called it an "Anthology of Consolation," perhaps thinking that this was Bridges' own phrase. (Frederick Macmillan to Lauder Brunton, June 4, 1915. BrP.) Bridges wrote, "I am not making an 'anthology of consolatory verse' whatever my publisher may think I am doing: but Tagore will *never* be in better company than he would be in my book: and I shall be very sorry if I do not get permission to put in that one poem. He will lose as much as I do—and I have written to him again about it. He was coming to stay with me this summer, but I fear that the

war is preventing him." (Bridges to Frederick Macmillan, June 8, 1915. MP:BM.)

3. Ernest Rhys, *Rabindranath Tagore: A Biographical Study.* (See Letter 85, note 1.)

99
Rothenstein to Tagore

Far Oakridge   May 12, 1915

My dear friend—your letter of April 13 has just come. It is not that poets & painters are not reliable commentators on their own writings & works: it is that a good work of art means to each person a buttress to his own experience. That is why so many readings are possible. Bridges, who has a searching & precise mind, had his own feelings about Judgement; mine were again different & now you send me your own interpretation. The variety pays homage to the pregnancy of the poem—at least such is my view. We deal with things & powers to which we are blindly obedient, if we be true artists, but which we do not of necessity ourselves understand. If I paint a tree, & follow with enough concentration the poise of the bole & the directions of the great spreading branches, I may indicate all the forces which have bent & twisted them & drawn them upwards, but my mind is innocent of all knowledge of these forces; any student of arboriculture knows these things, but by obedience & good use of my powers I may be able to make other people feel the tree-i-ness in a way the scientific man is unable to do. So with your poems; I do not mean that you have not an all-embracing intelligence; but the value of your work lies in your true obedience to the unchanging laws of balance. We are unbalanced at our ultimate grave risk, & unless an artist use his gifts with scrupulous judgement he is a danger to the village—that is at the root of the mistrust which so many good people feel towards the breed.

This war is the result of the greed of generations—states have to pay for their deafness to the small still voice just as individuals have—& this greed has ruined the constitution of Europe & each member of the family is flying at the face of his nearest

Rothenstein, "St. Martin's Summer."
Courtesy of Manchester City Art Gallery

relative. We shall feed on bread & gruel for a time; but the instinct to overload our stomachs & our purses is evidently a lasting one; Japan has thrown away for ever the pilgrim's staff & bowl & wants to live in a red brick villa like the rest of us & India, I fear, would, had she the chance, do the same. Rhys, good man, gives the impression that you, an Indian saint, regard this war with the wise & tranquil eyes of the East. But there are many men here who see the waste & the crime of this dreadful struggle as clearly as you do. I still feel there is too much of the Eastern & Western formulas in his book, which I have just read. The critical part seems to me excellent—clear & discriminating; the biographical portion will be less sympathetic to the more serious scholars; I think he would have been wiser to have given the relation between your inspiration & that of your forbears & contemporaries more fully & to have made less of the personal element. Much more knowledge of the more intimate life of India is needed than Rhys has got to make the biographical part convincing. He has made your personality too isolated & aloof from actual surroundings, for you are as much a part of your contemporary Indian world as your poems are & he has set you as a sculptor sets a Queen or a Viceroy or a public benefactor, on a marble pedestal, too unconscious of the working & living crowds of common people to satisfy the best kind of reader. This is perhaps inevitable in all lives of the living; but I like the old stern portraiture, where the artist does not try to flatter the features or to modify wrinkles or obesity, but gives to the great man the convincing construction of the common man, getting the indication of greatness rather through nobility of mien & simplicity of gesture than through any weakening of his own artistic probity. This kind of portraiture is, alas, of the past almost, but it is so much a part of my own vision that I cannot easily enjoy any other.[1]

Bridges writes that he has been in correspondence with Macmillan & is disappointed with the result. It is difficult, you being so far away, to explain matters clearly—distance, & the written word, are apt to exaggerate the sense of difference. Bridges feels your poems to be written in Bengali, in which language he believes them perfect. He holds there are people who do not understand their beauty, because to him, as to them, the beauty is imperfectly carried. "I will put one of them into perfect form, &

you will see how doubters will at once accept it" is his point. I can understand your hesitation, especially regarding Gitanjali. I am personally disappointed, as I was promised his cooperation in preparing, when necessary, the new poems for publication, & because I am naturally concerned about your welfare, & I consider Bridges, although pedantic & a little overbearing, one of the noblest & sincerest men living. You must, however, act as seems best to you & I do not wish to bring any personal views to bear upon you.[2]

. . . All send their love to you.   Ever yours

W. R.

1. Rhys knew his own shortcomings: "You know Tagore, and where he is strong and where he is weak, as no one else does in this country, I imagine; and it is good to think that my book satisfies you at all. That it will not please, or convince, the critics who are inclined to disbelieve in his reality, his art, and the rest, I know well enough. But I felt obliged to write about him cordially, one may even say, uncritically, giving way to the delight in a poetry that surprises one out of one's ordinary lukewarm feelings for contemporary half-inspired verse and prose. So let it be!" (Rhys to Rothenstein, May 16, 1915. RP:HL.)

2. Bridges wrote: "Of course if Tagore really objects to my version being published I cannot oppose his wish. But the effect will be that I shall not put Tagore's poem into my book. And I think that will be less satisfactory to him than if I put my version in."

He added: "It is really taking a *lower* estimate or valuation of his work to refuse various versions being made of it, than to allow experiments such as mine—and I only propose to deal with this *one* poem." He added a postscript: "The book is getting very enthusiastic encouragement from 'authorities' who have seen it in its present condition. MacM probably thinks it is an ordinary anthology." (Bridges to Rothenstein, May 8 [1915]. RP:HL.)

100
Rothenstein to Tagore

Far Oakridge   June 3, 1915

My dear friend—after the crown of bays come the gilt spurs— I do not know whether you will be happier for the wearing of them, for the steeds we ride carry us where they will & at their own pace, & they are apt to be mulish when we wish to apply force to make them move; it is for this reason the ancients represented the poet's mount as winged, & I think it is this steed you will always care for to the exclusion of all others, & when you are not on his back, you will be walking with naked feet through jungle & village, glad to feel nothing between yourself & the naked earth. Congratulations will pour in to you—I could wish myself that our people should not have been ignorant of you & of your work for nearly half a century & should wait for the recognition which came to you so quickly when you crossed the seas before acknowledging the splendour of your work. But this is the way of officialdom; & if it means, as it does mean, more recognition of your beloved country, then you will accept this personal homage as honour paid your countrymen. For all men cannot be knighted, & those upon whose shoulders garlands are set stand for the honour & dignity of their fellows. And this it is fitting you of all men should do, though I know what looks so light & flowerlike to others is a heavy burden for the wearer. We here live in obscured days & it is difficult not to carry a heavy heart within. I think of you too walking with a graver step, & I fear this summer will not see you here among us. If next summer the cloud is lifted, we may hope to welcome you; but I fear we shall be too exhausted & too anxious for some form of settlement to work out a perfect arrangement of the world's affairs, & that this will not be a war to end wars, as some optimists hoped at the beginning. Perhaps we are not meant to have lasting peace, as we do not find it mentally, but only in blessed snatches, seeking it always when our energies are disappointed, but forgetting the disappointment ever afresh, & rushing into action with renewed faith & meeting always with the same defeat. We send you, O noble knight, our most affectionate greetings. The children, when they return from their lessons, will jump for joy, for they love brave knights & fair women, having the best of taste & a profound sense of the flowerlike in life.[1]   Ever yours

W. R.

1. Rachel's congratulations were more succinct: "Dear Sir Rabinderanath, I am so glad the King has given you a knighthood. I hope you are well, all our pets are." (Rachel Rothenstein to Tagore [June 3, 1915]. R-S.) Tagore told Alice Rothenstein that this renewed rush of public attention had "some quality of asphyxiating gas in it, and I do not know any mask that can protect me from its effect. Love is for the living and honour for the dead, that is my motto." He added: "I have been feeling

restless to go and see you but this war has held me back. I was planning to go to Japan but the spirit of the Modern Japan repels me. Politics is selfish and hateful and full of lies in most countries but Japan is all politics without any redeeming features and it should be shunned by all poets. My heart is set westwards and I am waiting for the war clouds to clear up." (Tagore to Alice Rothenstein, July 2, 1915. RP.)

101
Rothenstein to Tagore

Far Oakridge July 1, 1915

My very dear friend—it is long since I heard from you, but happily the poems you send serve the purpose of letters & give me the best of news.... We have had Max Beerbohm & his wife staying with us. They are keen appreciators of your work, & he is writing a note on half a dozen drawings chosen from the ones I made of you which will appear, I believe, in the autumn.[1] It always warms my heart when people really care for your work, & Max, like all real satirists, is very sensitive to beauty & is not readily deceived by make-believe....

Did I tell you that I saw Thomas Hardy when I was away painting in Dorset, & he told me how much he cared for your writings?[2] The children speak of you often—I wish you could see them now.... We do want you back with us. Only this dreadful war must end before you will care to come back among us. I was sorry to hear from you that your finances too are in a bad way on account of it. I hoped that you had now no need to worry on that score, & that your books were bringing you in enough to take away all further anxiety regarding the financial side of the school. Here to-morrow is the unknown, & no one ventures to look 48 hours ahead. I hope all goes well with your people—Abanindranath wrote that he & Rathi have plans for a school.[3] We speak often of Rathi & our dear Pratima, whose picture adorns the nursery here. Our dear love to you all. Ever yours most affectionately.

W. R.

1. See Letter 73, note 4.
2. See *MM* II, 290. Rothenstein frequently smoothed rough edges from his friends' comments on Tagore's works. A later letter from Hardy is

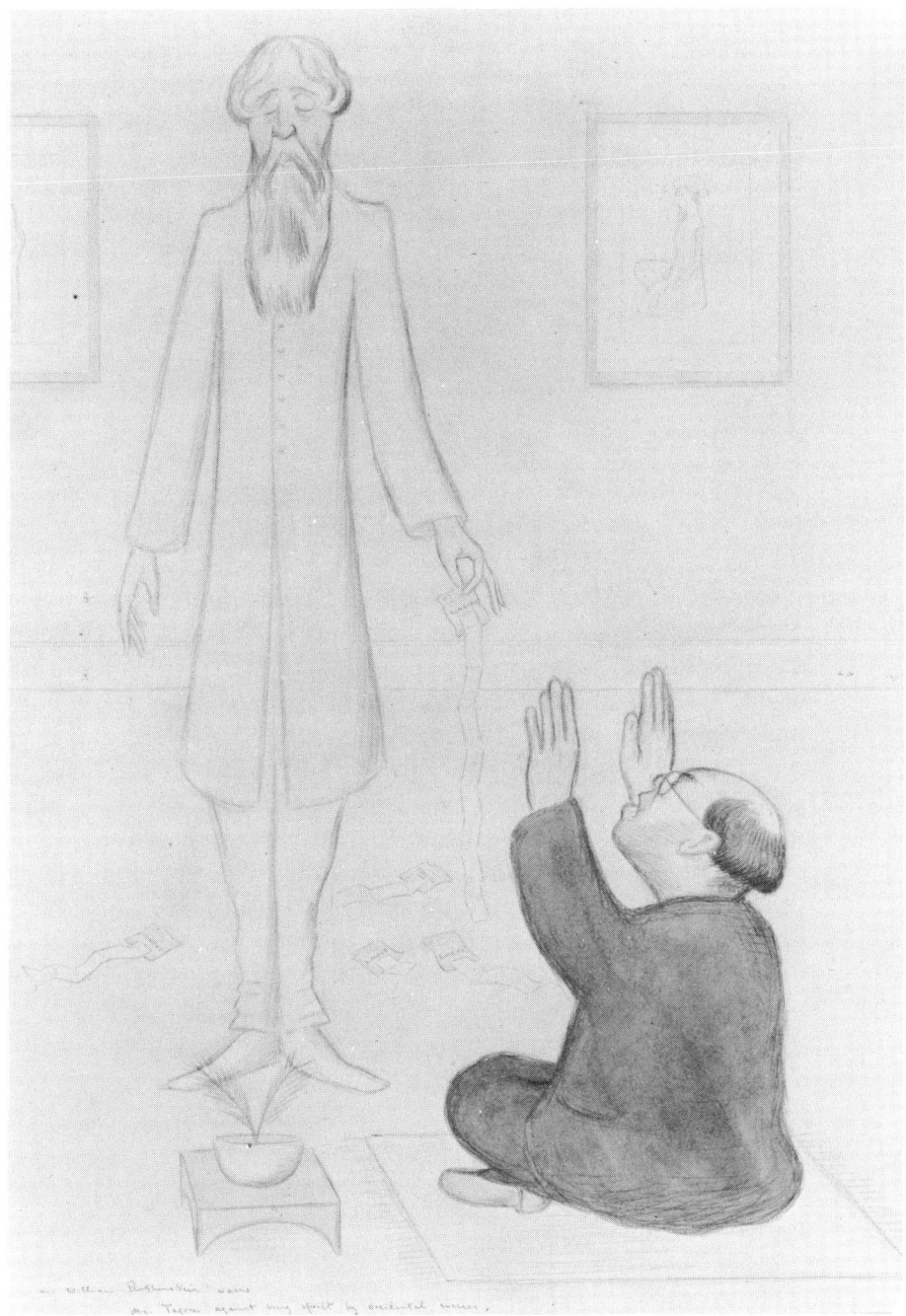

Max Beerbohm, "Mr. William Rothenstein warns Mr. Tagore against being spoilt by occidental success"

kind but equivocal. (Hardy to Rothenstein, February 23, 1916. RP:HL.)

3. Abanindranath wrote: "Work is going very slow here, so I am thinking of starting a sort of art club in my Uncle's House [Rabindranath's Calcutta residence] making Rathi take charge of it. We are going to begin in a very small way at first—just a place for meeting the artists and exhibiting their work, gradually we will try to develop our club into a regular Home for artists. This war has spoiled many things chiefly 'art.'" (Abanindranath Tagore to Rothenstein, April 27, 1915. RP:IOL.) The "sort of art club" became the Indian Society for Oriental Arts, still a focus for artistic activity in Bengal.

102
Tagore to Rothenstein

Shilida   July 22, 1915

My dearest Friend

Famine threatens Bengal. Men are so intimately linked together nowadays that the shells you are exchanging with your enemies cannot help striking us in our vital parts in some form or other. I was about to take a trip somewhere when the cry of misery reached me from our villages and I have come here to see what I can do to help these famished souls.[1] If I can get a remittance from Macmillans before long it will be very opportune. The usual course with them is to send money to their authors once a year about January but they agreed to make half yearly payments to me. If they do not forget to carry out their promise I shall get something from them before the end of this month. I have had a long break in my correspondence with you owing to this cloud hanging over Bengal.

I am busy with my tenants and I must cut my letter short. Yours ever

Rabindranath Tagore

To move is to meet you every moment, Fellow-traveller!
It is to sing to the music of your steps.
He who is touched by your breath never seeks the sheltered
   bank, he sets his reckless sails to the wind riding the turbulent water.
He who throws his doors open stepping onwards receives your
   greeting.

He stops not to count his gain or to mourn his loss; his heart beats the drum for him to march on, for to march is to march with you every step, Fellow-traveller!

Be ready for the sailing of the sea, my heart, and let those linger behind who must.
For your name has been called in the loud morning light!
    Wait for none!
The desire of the bud is for the shelter of the night to be fed with dew but the blown flower cries for the freedom of the day.
Burst your sheath, my heart, and come out![2]

    1. See Tagore, *Letters to a Friend,* pp. 64–65.
    2. Tagore, no. 95, *Gitāli* [Songs] (1914), in *R-R,* XI, 283: no. 13, *Fruit-Gathering:* in *CPP,* p. 145. This poem was written in the Bengali month corresponding to September–October 1914 and appears under the heading "Pujā" [Worship] in the collection of Tagore's words for songs. (See his *Gitabitān* [Song Collection] [Calcutta, 1960], p. 222.)

103
Rothenstein to Tagore

                        Far Oakridge   July 28, 1915

My very dear friend—Rachel was proud & delighted with her letter.[1] Few people realise what joy letters give to children; of the hundreds we write a year how few we do write to them. I think you understand the souls of children. When I go up for a day or two to London, & have to see people & perhaps sit through a committee meeting & I always come back a wreck; then the joy in being with the children again restores me & I keep well until some business calls me up, when I go always at my health's peril. The Gods who made me energetic & gave me a little passion & a little faith did me an ill turn when they made me ugly & charmless. Such as I men use for a certain fruitfulness of ideas & ready service in causes which appeal to us, but they quickly turn their backs once we have served our purpose, for the happy element of personal magnetism is wanting, & when sins are to be forgiven, they choose other company. I think this comes from a profoundly hidden instinct in us all &

is, despite its unkindness & painfulness, a really good thing. We all rightly love radiance & blitheness in people & in works of art—it is the spirit nature shows on her own lovely face & those who have the most of it come nearest to expressing her secret & do the greatest service to their fellows. When men give me pain I try to justify myself but at heart I know at odd moments how it happened, & that they would have given less [pain] to a blither spirit. There are moments, however, when I wish men were not quite so stupid.

Bridges writes again of an interview with Macmillan—he is very tenacious of his idea, & asks me to add my appeal to his. It is so obvious that I can do nothing.[2] Poor Andrews—I am so sorry to learn how ill he has been—has not the faintest idea of what the work & position of Bridges stands for among us here, & he is evidently set against your listening to him.[3] Further the good Andrews writes as though I were a naughty schoolboy, not to be blamed too much for my naughtiness, being young & unfledged, assuring me that you feel indulgent toward me & begs [me] not to take my faults too much to heart. The situation has a comic side, if you consider the remote & leonine Bridges, with his slender output resulting from his extreme standard of form, & yet for his lack of it the excellent Andrews sends him down to face his Maker in Hell—has he not written doth instead of does? Simplicity no one knows better than yourself is not baldness—it is a very much more resisting & passionate thing than an empty formula, the result of an intense desire to put thought into kingly dress, a slow undressing, regretful & often heartbreaking, & throwing away of ornaments which took weeks in the making, to get back to the divine nakedness in the end. I think Bridges has some of this simplicity & that his work is less cold & hard than most people think—but this is merely a personal opinion. Further I entirely concurred with what you wrote me & understood your reasons, clearly & simply stated, for your disinclination to fall in with Bridges' proposal. What I don't like is Macmillan's part in the business. Picture dealers & publishers are, in the present state of affairs, a necessity; but their power should be restricted to business concerning our work, & I don't like a man of the distinction & gallantry of Bridges to be snapped at by that man-trap mouth which terrifies me whenever I meet George Macmillan.[4] I gather from Bridges he has written you,

so tenacious is he of his idea, & I believe, from what I know of you, that you will at once respond to his appeal & that nothing I can write will influence you one way or the other. When you come back to us and meet your friends face to face these difficulties will not be. By next summer the war must be over & then I hope we may welcome you again. Of the kind you will get here you will have no doubt. The children have forgotten nothing of you. They long for news of Pratima, whose dear picture adorns their nursery. John comes back from school this week—he is fourteen now—how they grow! We had Mrs Cornford here last week—you remember her dear nut brown face, do you not? There are two volumes of Darwin letters I am reading which are delightful—they give a serene picture of family life a century & half a century ago which makes one look upon the near past as something miraculously safe & steady in this shaking & murderous time.[5] All our love to you.   Ever your affectionate
W. R.

1. Tagore to Rachel Rothenstein, July 2, 1915. RP. Quoted by Speaight in *William Rothenstein*, p. 283.
2. Bridges had asked Rothenstein to call on Macmillan: "I should not of course propose this if I did not know that you felt an interest in the matter. I do not like *writing* to them, lest I should get a final written refusal of Tagore's poem, *which I very much wish to use*." (Bridges to Rothenstein, April 19 [1915]. RP:HL.) Bridges' book was ready to go to press, but Tagore had written "that I should print my version of Gitanjali 67 'Thou art the sky'—and was sorry that Macmillan did not see his way to permit me. He enclosed a copy of his letter (to me) to Macmillan with instructions to M[acmillan] to refuse me." (Bridges to Rothenstein, July 26 [1915]. RP:HL. Tagore's letter to Bridges, March 22, 1915, forwarded to Macmillan on March 23, 1915. MP:BM.)
3. Andrews, who was in Simla recuperating from cholera, advised Rothenstein to forget the incident; he and the Poet were merely amused that Rothenstein should have taken Bridges so seriously. Andrews then reviewed the entire episode, charged Bridges anew with his stylistic sins, but expressed relief that "Judgment," Tagore's Christmas gift to Andrews, had escaped unscathed. Rothenstein must not feel guilty but must join in their amusement. (Andrews to Rothenstein, June 16 [1915]. RP: HL.) Rothenstein was not amused. He had wanted Tagore to understand why he admired Bridges as a man and as a poet. Edward Thompson, whom Bridges had asked also to intercede with Tagore, testified to Andrews' interference, for "Andrews last autumn held up letters, etc. of mine for 6 months, causing me great inconvenience, as some of them were business letters, written on Messrs. Macmillans' behalf and requiring immediate answer." (Thompson to Bridges [July? 1915]. BrP.)
4. Rothenstein had strong feelings about the role of publishers and art dealers, but in this case he was unfair. Sir Frederick and George

Frances D. and Francis M. Cornford in France

Macmillan acted throughout on Tagore's explicit instructions that "versions of translations of his poems which have already been before the public should never be published in altered forms." (Frederick Macmillan to Bridges. September 6, 1915. BrP.)

5. Henrietta Litchfield, *Emma Darwin: A Century of Family Letters, 1792–1896, Edited by Her Daughter, Henrietta Litchfield.* 2 vols. (London, 1915).

104
Tagore to Rothenstein

       Shanti Niketan August 20, 1915

My dearest Friend

 A spirit of restlessness is upon me and I have been longing to get away somewhere. I think it is my effort to get out of my outer skin which has grown dry and dead. I must feel myself afresh in a fresh sky. I am too much with men here who want me for various purposes. I fret against being obliged to make myself useful in all kinds of way to all manners of men. I want to know that man is more than a useful animal. Really one can give more when one is asked less. To be useful you have to adapt yourself to others and thus you kill your own truth. It is a fearful wastage.

 You do not know how I wish to be near you, my friend. I long to taste the pure joy of friendship free from all claims of narrow necessities. So often I dream of the deep quiet of your presence and the sensitive touches of your talk that used to surprise and satisfy me beyond measure. It was the breadth of freedom and depth of sympathy all about you that captivated me so much when I came to know you. And my mind always turns back to you whenever I feel the need of a perfect combination of solitude and company in one. But I must wait till this war is over and in the meanwhile forget that I have a soul.

 I got Dr Bridges' letter last week and the following is the extract of the concluding portion of my reply to it: "I think there is a stage in all writings where they must have a finality in spite of their shortcomings. Authors have their limitations and we have to put up with them if they give us something positively good. If we begin to think of improvement there is no end to it and differences of opinion are sure to arise. Please do not think that I have the least conceit about my English. Being not born to it I have no standard of judgment in my mind about this language—at least, I cannot consciously use it. Therefore I am all the more helpless in deciding whether certain alterations add to the value of a poem with which my readers' minds have already become familiar. I know, habit gives a poem its true living character, making it seem inevitable like a flower or a fruit. Flaws are there but life makes up for all its flaws."[1]

Why doesn't Dr Bridges try to translate some of my poems directly from the original with the help of his Bengali friends in Oxford?[2]

I have got ready two of my MSS. of poems for publication. One, of the type of the Gitanjali, I have named "Fruit gathering," and the other of that of The Gardener "Lover's Gift." I shall send typed copies to you next mail for your opinion.[3] This time I shall have to brave the risk of publishing them with all their imperfections unaltered, except errors of grammer and idiom. I think I should wait for the war to be over till they are published. Do you agree with me? My love to you all.   Yours ever
Rabindranath Tagore

1. Tagore said also that Bridges perhaps failed to realize how little he (Tagore) knew about publishing procedure in England and how dependent he was upon Macmillan as his agent. (Tagore to Bridges, August 19, 1916. BrP.) He had already told Macmillan that he hesitated because he felt unable to judge Bridges' alterations; Macmillan must therefore decide. (Tagore to Macmillan, August 13, 1915. MP:BM.)

Bridges had appealed to Yeats, who had already heard of the affair from Binyon and Rothenstein, had seen Bridges' manuscript, and was entirely cooperative (see Yeats, *Letters,* p. 598). On the strength of Yeats's appeal, Tagore now decided to yield—although he still insisted that he must rely on Macmillan and had put the matter in their hands. (Tagore to Yeats, August 31, 1915. Michael Yeats.) Yeats had written: "I should be sorry to prevent Robert Bridges from making the slight changes he wishes. He is at moments a most admirable poet and always the chief scholar in English style now living. His creative power is not great though very exquisite but no living man is so well fitted to measure and emend a detail of [speech?]. I have the same mother tongue that he has, but I would be grateful should he care to revise a poem of mine, certainly I would be ashamed if consideration for my revision should keep you from accepting his. I feel that he is the head of my craft in England and have felt so since the death of Swinburne, or from before it for Swinburne's abundant genius repelled me." (Yeats to Tagore, July 31 [1915]. R-S.)

Thompson reported from Bengal that Tagore "has written . . . to Macmillans, telling them to give you permission to do what you wish. If Macmillans haven't already let you know this, I have his letter by me, expressly saying he has given permission, and *if any difficulty arises I will forward it to you.*" (Thompson to Bridges, September 13, 1915. BrP. Thompson's italics.) Bridges soon heard from Macmillan and replied, "I was much surprised by your letter this morning. I had not quite despaired, but I had not written again to Tagore. I will now do so: and *I will certainly not do anything opposed to his wishes.* I will report to you later. Meanwhile let me thank you very much for your great kindness in tolerating my importunity." (Bridges to Frederick Macmillan, September 24 [1915]. MP:BM. Bridges' italics.) Sir Frederick expressed relief that the matter "should be taken out of our hands and left to you and Tagore." (Frederick Macmillan to Bridges, September 28, 1915. BrP.)

2. That Tagore suggested this at this time shows how little he understood the strength of Bridges' convictions. There is no evidence that Rothenstein forwarded the suggestion.

3. Tagore, expressing increased confidence in his command over English usage, sent copies also to Yeats. (Tagore to Yeats, August 31, 1915. Michael Yeats.)

105
Rothenstein to Tagore

Far Oakridge   September 16, 1915

My very dear friend—your affectionate letter found me on my return from Belgium—it was good to hear from you on coming back into the peace of this countryside after the sights I had been seeing at Ypres & other ruined towns & villages near the front.[1] . . .

How well I know what you mean when you say that a certain kind of public altruism is actually a thing one is ashamed inwardly to be connected with, & that only in one way can one give one's self to others—& that usually one which people know at first too little of to make any conscious use of: but that doesn't matter. I have been trying here to make some people realise that if some of the things said about art & letters be true, they are as true in time of war as in time of peace, & that so far from our energy being useless at such moments as these we are going through, it was never more wanted. . . . I think we find ourselves in muddy waters directly we try to help consciously as men; the instruments of our trade, under our concentrated use of them, have a wisdom & a sanity which is impeccable, if we really understand the laws of our craft, & it is in this sanity I do most passionately believe; & it is sadly wanting among most men at such times as these. . . .

What of your brother's book—I can't understand Walker's delay? . . . Andrews writes me again—I am glad to know he is himself again.² This will serve to carry you our affectionate greetings.   Ever yours

W. R.

1. Emile Vandervelde (1866–1938), Belgian Minister of State, took Rothenstein to the Belgian front to make a portrait drawing of King Leopold, reproductions to be sold for war relief. The King was unavailable, and Rothenstein drew Ypres instead. (See *MM* II, 303–306.)
2. See Letter 103, note 3.

106
Tagore to Rothenstein

Calcutta   December 10, 1915

My dearest Friend,

You are wonderfully right in your estimate of Hironmoy, who is no nephew of mine but a cousin of my late wife. He is somewhat foolish and his physical and mental indolence is far above normal.¹ . . .

I have done a great deal of writings lately and been generally successful in making myself fiercely hated by a large body of my countrymen. I know it is a rare distinction for me, far nobler than what I achieved from men's praises—but still it is a starvation—anyhow it is a diet of prickly pears upon which desert animals like camels thrive best, but not those who have more sensitive organs of taste and digestion. It is not so much the unpleasantness of making enemies that repels one, as the vulgarity of the whole thing. In the human world we have to fight with each other but unfortunately our weapons are different and one having muscle has to encounter another possessing a native supply of filthiness. However, it is no use denying the fact that human sympathy and appreciation are necessary for our hearts, and they can only be sacrificed for the higher interest of truth and humanity.²

I suspect the time is hard for Walker and the money that he got from us went down by a wrong passage. What I think was inexcusable for him was to ask from us a further sum of money for the binding expenses while he was far from being ready with the book. However, do not worry too much about this—surely, we shall be able to bear our loss much more easily than he his gain.³

The migratory impulse is in my wings now. I felt exactly this restlessness before leaving for Europe last time. Possibly it is some inner accumulation in me which wants bursting its pod to be scattered in the wind. Then I want to see you, and I feel that this time I shall be able to come still closer to you, for during these three years' separation our friendship has had time to send its roots into the deeper soil of our subconscious minds. Yours ever

Rabindranath Tagore

1. See Letter 88, note 1. A Rothenstein letter or message about Hironmoy is apparently lost.
2. Thompson wrote of possible cause and effect of Tagore's feelings of tension: "Rabi has greatly changed for the worse, in one respect. He was always very touchy under criticism; but now he is rabid if a word of disparagement is breathed, broods over it and resents it as injustice. He is spending his time writing and printing personal 'apologies,' in verse and prose." (Thompson to Bridges [July? 1915]. BrP.)
3. Tagore's insinuation is unjustifiable. See Letter 95, note 3.

107
Tagore to Rothenstein

Calcutta   December 31, 1915

My dearest Friend

Your book containing six portraits of mine has delighted my heart. Your love is there in those sketches, and that is what makes them so valuable to me. It is a lasting memorial of our friendship. Max Beerbohm's introduction is perfectly charming, and while reading it I was struck with the fact that you had been discovered long before I met you by your other friends. I have been entertaining in my heart a secret pride for having truly known you, but I am ready to give up that pride and shall be content to share my love for you with your other friends.

Macmillans are urging me to send them some translations of my short stories but I am hesitating for the reason that the beauty of the originals can hardly be preserved in translation.[1] They require rewriting in English, not translating. That can only be done by the author himself—but I do not have sufficient command of English to venture to do it. So while I am vacilating some of my countrymen in America are trying to publish unauthorised translations. I don't mind being robbed in money but the robbery is of a more serious kind, and I have not the power to stop them.[2] . . .

I am tired and am feeling the necessity of a change of environment. You cannot imagine how I am longing to go to you. I am like a migratory bird having two homes—and my home on the other side of the sea is calling me.   Yours ever

Rabindranath Tagore

1. Macmillan was urging because the stories were long overdue. (See Letter 83, note 3; Letter 90, note 3.) Tagore still wavered between disliking his own work and disliking that of others. Thompson was to translate some stories, but when Andrews arrived Tagore rejected Thompson's collaboration. Tagore apologized but maintained that the situation was now altered, and Andrews would work on the stories. (Tagore to Thompson, February 24, 1914. Edward P. Thompson Papers.) By March 1916 no stories had been delivered. Brett wrote: "We promised, in our announcement list last year, the publication of the volume of Short Stories, and we have had a great deal of inquiry for this volume and much disappointment expressed on the part of the trade on its nonappearance." (Brett to Frederick Macmillan, March 22, 1916. MP:BM.)

2. Brett told Andrews that Tagore *did* have power to stop them by getting his own translations into print. Brett was "daily in fear that a volume of these will be collected and published by some American pirating concern. These unauthorized publications of the stories not only damage Mr. Tagore's reputation, as the stories are often illy translated, but such publication has a tendency to decrease the size of the audience for Mr. Tagore's own volume when it appears." (Brett to Andrews, July 26, 1915. MP:NYPL.) When it was clear that the book would miss the Christmas trade, Brett appealed again: "Is it possible, perhaps, that Mr. Tagore has something else nearly ready for publication that we could include in our list of announcements for the spring publishing season of next year?" (Brett to Andrews, November 12, 1915. MP:NYPL.)

V 1916-1919 Letters 108-137

Marking Time

As one year of war followed another, Rothenstein's and Tagore's references to reunion had an increasingly hollow ring. The Englishman tried hard to discern moral patterns in the general misery, but these were overborne by the hideous particulars: "I used to find it hard to believe there could be good in the spirit of war, but I can see a great deal emerging; and there is a whole new world to recreate. Only it is very terrible to have to listen to village neighbours, when their sons are killed, or don't write home, and there is really nothing to be said in reply to their hatred of war."[1]

His reply was to throw himself more intensely into his work. In 1917 he became the first Professor of Civic Art at Sheffield University. That December he went to France as an Official War Artist, and Max Beerbohm drew a perky Private Rothenstein reprimanding a tall, austere colonel for organizational lapses.[2] Being at the Front was both exciting and profoundly depressing; he kept his spirits up by planning ways for artists to help disabled veterans.[3]

Meanwhile, some efforts were being made to improve relations between England and India. Edwin Montagu, Secretary of State for India, and Lord Chelmsford, the Viceroy, toured India together and made recommendations that would become the comparatively liberal Montagu-Chelmsford Reforms. A Royal Commission chaired by Rothenstein's friend Michael Sadler, Vice-Chancellor of Leeds University, investigated conditions at Calcutta University and recommended changes. Still, many Indians despaired of being heard at all after the Armi-

1. Rothenstein to Barbara Hammond, May 8, 1917. Hammond Papers: Bodleian Library.
2. *MM* II, 315. In Max's caption Rothenstein complains that a sergeant has said, " 'Oh, blow them Ajanta Frescoes!' "
3. Rothenstein to John Galsworthy, August 14, 1918. Galsworthy Collection: Birmingham University Library.

stice, resentment seethed over the repressions that culminated in the Rowlatt Acts of 1919, and Gandhian noncooperation gained momentum.[4]

Tagore's position was anomalous. He could be made into a splendid showpiece but also could be embarrassingly unmanageable, for he persisted in saying that self-government must be earned through responsible behavior. But now it was easier for Indian critics to blame his alleged disaffection on corruption by the West, whence came his knighthood and no small financial good fortune, and it was easier for him, when he felt misunderstood at home, to look to friends in the West who wrote repeatedly that they wished him back among them. The more he was criticized in India, the greater his longing for England; the more remote the possibility of travel across Europe, the more elaborate his schemes for circumventing the war. In 1914 Tagore considered trying to reach England via China, Japan, and the United States.[5] In 1915 he asked Harriet Moody, only half in jest, to meet him in Japan and proceed thence to Chicago.[6] He told Ernest Rhys that he felt "homesick for that corner of your sofa," and Yeats that peacetime would find him in England attending to his new publications and supervising Iseult Gonne's Bengali lessons.[7] At the end of 1915 and again at the end of 1918, he told the London Macmillans that he hoped to sail for England the following spring.[8]

None of these plans matured, but in May 1916 he did sail for

4. Edwin Montagu (1879–1924), Secretary of State for India, 1917–1922. For his account of this tour, see *An Indian Diary*, ed. Venetia Montagu (London, 1930). Frederic Thesiger, 1st Viscount Chelmsford (1868–1933), Viceroy of India, 1916–1921. On Montagu-Chelmsford Report, see S. D. Waley, *Edwin Montagu: A Memoir and an Account of His Visits to India* (New York, 1964), pp. 159–162; Broomfield, *Elite Conflict*, pp. 108, 109, 121, 130. Michael Sadler (1861–1943), Vice-Chancellor, Leeds University, 1911–1923. On Rowlatt Acts, see Broomfield, *Elite Conflict*, pp. 140–142.

5. Tagore to Macmillan, through Andrews [December 28, 1914]. MP: BM.

6. Tagore to Harriet Moody, February 18, 1915. University of Chicago Library. Quoted by Dunbar in *A House in Chicago*, p. 126.

7. Tagore to Rhys, May 19, 1915. Quoted by Rhys in *Letters from Limbo* (London, 1936), p. 168. Tagore to Yeats, August 31, 1915. Michael Yeats.

8. Tagore to Macmillan, November 15, 1915; November 5, 1918. MP:BM.

Japan and then for the United States. In Japan he reiterated his desire to see Rothenstein and England.[9] Andrews poured out his own feelings and those of Tagore: the Poet had hoped for solitude and leisure, but Japan had made of him a "Champion of Asia." The publicity would be even worse in the United States; and England was still inaccessible.[10]

The war forced the future to mark time, but Bridges' questions about the rights and obligations of translators and Tagore's concern for his literary honor need not have been held in abeyance. The year 1916 presented a second chance to deal with these, for Macmillan published *The Hungry Stones and Other Stories,* the long-delayed first volume of Tagore's short stories. Another collection, *Mashi and Other Stories,* was in preparation.[11]

Tagore's short fiction might have offered critics another chance to evaluate him as a serious writer and his publisher an opportunity to appeal to readers unattracted by his poems. Tagore's best stories maintain an extraordinarily high standard of quality for their time and place. Working quite alone, he had perfected methods that would come to be called "modern": swift, oblique characterization, implied questioning of specific situations that unfold to link the individual to the universal, inconclusive endings that force the reader onto his own resources for answers. The phrase "his best stories" must qualify any consideration of Tagore's short fiction. From one story to another, frequently within a story, quality is uneven. Fine characterizations become blurred or a wonderfully ironic situation dissolves in sentimental or philosophical digressions; this suggests that he was not always in control of his materials and did not always know why his best stories were his best. Discriminating selection was therefore essential, and almost the entire canon of his Bengali short fiction was available; he wrote most of his best stories before 1916.

The Hungry Stones and Other Stories suggests that selection,

9. Letters 111, 113. For his itinerary, see Stephen N. Hay, *Asian Ideas of East and West: Tagore and His Critics in Japan, China, and India* (Cambridge, Mass., 1970), pp. 52–81.
10. Andrews to Rothenstein, August 3 [1916]. RP:HL.
11. Tagore, *The Hungry Stones and Other Stories,* trans. "by several hands" (London, 1916); *Mashi and Other Stories,* trans. "by various writers."

like translation, was the work of "several hands." Whimsy, historical legend, the supernatural, personal anecdote, are mismatched with genuine drama and acerbic social and political commentary. Many characters are well-rounded, even heroic. Others remain as flat as the playing-card characters in one of Tagore's own fables.[12] His use of incident, his pacing and consistency of tone are less impressive here than in other stories left for later volumes or passed over entirely. Was this collection intended to exhibit Tagore's virtuosity or supply Western readers with cultural contexts for "unrest in India" (it does neither satisfactorily), or simply to fill up a volume? That this last was the case is indicated by another of Whibley's reports to Macmillan:

> I may say at once that these stories are far better than those which make up the volume, recently sent to press. They have a sharper point, and are infinitely better written and better proportioned. Moreover, the translation is more neatly done—by [word illegible] comparison.
>
> But I agree with you that it is better not to distribute the book, which is in preparation. I do not know how many pages you expect that book to make. If it turns out unduly short, one or two of these stories might be added to it. Otherwise I should recommend that they be held over, until Tagore has written enough fresh ones to make a volume. At the same time I confess that there seems a danger of Tagore's spoiling his own market by overproduction. However, if the people still continue to buy volumes of his stories, I suppose there is no reason why they should not have them. But what becomes of the legend of the exclusive and secluded poet?[13]

Whibley's question is easily answered. The exclusive and secluded poet was so caught up in the toils of travel, public appearances, private worries, and politics, that after 1918 he

---

12. See Tagore, "Ektā Āshāre Galpa" [An Implausible Story] (1894), in *R-R*, XVII, 172–180: "The Kingdom of Cards," *The Hungry Stones and Other Stories*, pp. 91–107: "An Implausible Story," *The Housewarming and Other Selected Writings*, trans. Mary Lago and Tarun Gupta, ed. Amiya Chakravarty (New York, 1965), pp. 21–29.

13. Whibley, Macmillan Reader's Reports [1916], vol. K, p. 107. MCP.

wrote few new stories, and few of those up to his best standard. Most of those coming to Macmillan were from the storehouse of the pre-Nobel years. Selection of the stories, as of the poems and plays, was done quite haphazardly. Correspondence in the files of both the London and New York Macmillan firms leaves a distinct impression that they were obliged to take what came and handle it as best they could. A member of the firm would be informed that certain works were being translated by Tagore, or by one of his relatives, or by an associate at Santiniketan, or by any one of a number of other persons. One day a draft, with or without Tagore's final revisions, would appear on a Macmillan desk. As early as 1917 George Brett told George Macmillan that he was "aghast" at the speed with which book after book arrived from Tagore, "with the evident expectation on his part that all could be published within a few months."[14] That the contents of *Gitanjali* were determined largely by accident is explainable in the light of circumstances, but there is no firm evidence that at any time thereafter a careful, comprehensive survey of Tagore's Bengali works, made available to all concerned, determined which should be presented to Western readers as representative of his best writings.

Tagore's uncertainties still encouraged rotating editorial procedures. The story collections leave an impression that the "various writers" whose translations were "revised by the author" each chose a favorite story or two and that the author added several to legitimatize the collection, which was then shipped to London or New York in installment lots accompanied by Tagore's statements that quality was uneven, that he was dissatisfied, and that Macmillan must select and correct.[15] The issue of Tagore's literary honor never again arose as urgently as in 1915.

In the conduct of his business affairs Tagore and his agents still made the simultaneous commitments that had so frustrated Fox Strangways and now filled Macmillan files with letters from would-be translators and foreign publishers who

14. Brett to George Macmillan, March 1, 1917. MP:BM.
15. Tagore to Macmillan, January 13, November 15, December 31, 1915. MP:BM. Whibley was to "see the book through the press," and Tagore, when informed of this plan, "left us a free hand in regard to revision." (George Macmillan to Brett, May 4, 1916. MP:NYPL.)

thought they had permission from Mr. Tagore himself.[16] Even during his 1916 American tour, Tagore had been concerned about royalties; George Macmillan had sent George Brett a summary of accounts, Brett talked with Tagore and wrote a new contract, and Tagore had returned to India apparently reassured.[17] In 1919 the subject of royalties revived with a vengeance. Tagore needed money for expansion of his Santiniketan school as Visva-Bharati University, an Indian center for international exchange of students, teachers, and ideas.[18] His American income, however, was dwindling. Brett heard that the manager of Macmillan's Calcutta depot had reported in London that Sir Rabindranath Tagore was dissatisfied with his American sales. "We must make allowances for a poet," Maurice Macmillan wrote, "and I do not know how far he is influenced by those around him; but Mr. Andrews has actually asked on his behalf if your accounts dealing with his books may be inspected by anyone appointed by Tagore himself. I do not know what you will say about this, but I imagine that you will write and tell the poet that the accounts are open to the inspection of any authorised persons, for of course there is nothing in them to conceal."[19]

Brett's dignified response conveys a tone of shocked surprise. He advised Tagore that such a matter should come to him directly, not relayed through Calcutta and London. Tagore, or Andrews, "if he is acting in your behalf," should list suspected

16. Vol. 55005. MP:BM.
17. George Macmillan summarized Tagore's London accounts as of November 1, 1916, and pointed out that Tagore's statements about royalties from the London firm "are not strictly in accordance with facts," for percentages were consistently higher than Tagore had reported them to Brett. (George Macmillan to Brett, November 1, 1916. MP:NYPL.) Two days later Brett had heard from friends in the western United States that Tagore had complained to them and had misquoted sums paid to him. "It has been somewhat difficult, I may say," Brett wrote to London, "to prevent Tagore from making arrangements with other American publishers for his forthcoming books notwithstanding the contract which was written in May of 1914 giving us the publication of his books here until January 1918." (Brett to Frederick Macmillan, November 3, 1916. MP:BM.)
18. "Visva": world-wide, universal. "Bharati": pertaining to wisdom, also "Indian," from the name of Bharati, Indian goddess of speech. Hence Visva-Bharati as "universal wisdom" and "the world and India."
19. Maurice Macmillan to Brett, May 20, 1919. MP:NYPL.

types of inaccuracies.[20] If there was to be an audit, Tagore must bear its costs. The trouble arose, Brett told Maurice Macmillan, "solely because, owing to Tagore's alleged activities in this country, and perhaps in India also, the American public made up its mind that he was pro-German, or pacifist, or both, and for a time ceased buying his books, in fact, the sales fell off to practically nothing, and we even had to take back from the booksellers considerable stock of Tagore's books previously sold to them, and for which they could find no sale."[21]

The end of the affair was a letter from Tagore, ingenuously expressing disinterest in commercial details. Never, he stated, had he investigated accounts, since all proceeds went to his school. If the Santiniketan finance committee were worried, they might communicate this through Mr. Andrews.[22] Andrews was indeed the person who had acted on Tagore's behalf in complaining to Macmillan's Calcutta manager. In a burst of belated logic he wrote to say that Brett's reference to the war and to suspicions of Tagore's involvement in pro-German plots helped to explain the reduced sales in America.[23]

Even after all of this, Tagore appeared to resist the realization that declining royalties were logically related to a war, to suspicions (however unfounded) of his loyalty, and to hastily done translations and adverse literary criticisms. Physically and emotionally exhausted, he prepared for a holiday in Australia and another American lecture tour that he hoped might replenish Santiniketan's depleted treasury.

20. Brett to Tagore, June 11, 1919. MP:NYPL.
21. Brett to Maurice Macmillan, June 11, 1919. MP:BM.
22. Tagore to Brett, July 22, 1919. MP:NYPL.
23. Andrews to Brett, July 21, 1919. MP:NYPL.

108
Tagore to Rothenstein

Shantiniketan   March 24, 1916

My friend, this will speak for itself.[1] War is everywhere. Differences require constant adjustments, differences of interests, of races, of positions. This gives rise to fightings in all stages of the history of Man. So please consider the present fight between our students and their European Teachers—the subject matter of this paper—as the manifestation of the same force, though in a much feebler degree, as the war that is going on in Europe.

I am naturally lazy, but I have the stupid knack of getting myself into a maze of works. I want to rest, but my fate is against me. I am losing my poet's birthright, which is leisure and detachment.

I have asked Macmillans to send you copies of my manuscript poems. Have you got them?

Give my love to the dear children.   Yours

Rabindranath Tagore

1. Written on a reprint of Tagore's article, "Indian Students and Western Teachers," *MR*, 19 (1916), 416–422 (RP:HL). Student protest strikes and violence at Presidency College, Calcutta University, evoked police action, disciplinary measures, investigation, and much debate. (See editorials, "Report of the Presidency College Enquiry Committee" and "Outsiders as Public Servants in British India," *MR*, 19 [1916], 601–611, 611–614.)

109
Rothenstein to Tagore

Far Oakridge   April 16, 1916

My very dear friend, you have been very much in my mind & I have more than once wanted to sit down to write you. I have had some trouble, but the wound is healing & I am becoming myself again.[1] When worry comes, it is as a bailiff who sits down on the threshold of one's brain & try as we will, we can't get rid of him. I hope you have not had too many worries; I get the impression from your letters that you have too many public duties forced on you to be quite happy, & that you long for an obscurer life. I rather think the old time court was a less exigent task master than our present demos; the Prince, if he forgot his purse too habitually, at least gave gracious thanks & robes of honour to his poets & painters; to-day we risk our soul's life if, in response to the pitiable call we hear from all sides, we leave our studies and studios to mix with the crowd & offer our knowledge & sympathy to our fellows. Pleasant the lives of those whose gifts are valued & accepted. With the rest of us what we so long to give is more often refused, & we feel the poorer always—are the poorer, for this refusal. I often feel my own life a failure, because I have not been one of the fortunate people of whom a great deal is asked. It is hard to make work for one's self—easy to accomplish a set task, for the first is often but a ploughing of the sand. . . . Andrews tells me you have been busy with old Bengali poems, & that Yeats has your translations.[2] I am expecting him here next Thursday & hope he may bring some with him. We had Newbolt with us last week, & I read him some of the poems from the new book which impressed him as they impressed me. He told me how glad he was that you are represented in "The Spirit of Man," Bridges' anthology. We both laughed over the fight, & the absurdity of Bridges' vanity; but in spite of this I hold Bridges to be one of our finest men, one of the rare poets with an unspotted soul. It is easy to laugh at a certain childish quality in him, to see he has always been a spoiled child in fact, but he really has a big & generous soul, & the introduction he has written to the book is a beautiful piece of writing. I remain unconverted regarding your contribution, & am delighted to know you among his company.[3] I read the second part of your reminiscences in the Modern Review—for some reason the number which contained the first chapters didn't come to me. Could you send me a copy?[4] . . .

We were to have seen you last summer—then this summer: but the war does not look like ending; there is little light to be seen. I need not say how often I wish you here. Our most affectionate greetings to you. I hope to hear from you soon—& to write you again before long.   Ever yours

W. R.

1. Rothenstein was rejected as an Official War Artist because of his German origins. A later application was accepted.

2. "Old Bengali poems": Tagore's poems for *Fruit-Gathering* and *Lover's Gift*. Macmillan sent Rothenstein typescripts and requested that he send promptly any revisions Tagore may have asked him to make. (Macmillan to Rothenstein, March 10, 1916. RP:HL.) Rothenstein replied that he could not accept this responsibility, although revisions were plainly needed. (Rothenstein to Macmillan, April 8, 1916. MP:BM.) Yeats grumbled (see his *Letters*, p. 612) but complied, with comments then and later. (Yeats to Macmillan, July 9, 1916; January 28, 1917. MP:BM. Quoted in part in *Letters to Macmillan*, ed. Simon Nowell-Smith [London, 1967], pp. 290–292.)

3. A statement either ingeniously or ingenuously ambivalent. Bridges wrote: "The book has sold very well. Of course I was tired of it six months ago and have now no opinion of its merits. But I was pleased when I did it, and was very glad to find that it turns out to be readable. At least I have done Shelley and Yeats justice." (Bridges to Rothenstein, February 21 [1916]. RP:HL.)

4. Tagore, *Jibansmriti* [Reminiscences] (1912), *R-R*, XVII, 261–432: *My Reminiscences*, trans. Surendranath Tagore, *MR*, 19 (1916), 1–8, 137–142, 285–290, 361–367, 475–480, 583–589; 20 (1916), 1–6, 121–127, 237–242, 353–361, 461–467, 577–582: *My Reminiscences* [trans. Surendranath Tagore] (London, 1917). Yeats had encouraged this project: "I believe it would be very successful if it came out at the close of the war and that it would help your fame more just now than any other book you could publish. Your readers know your poetry and your philosophy to some extent, and they are curious to understand its relation to your country and history. To judge too, by what I have heard of the book it might have political importance. If I thought the matter rested with [George?] Macmillan I would find some means (I do not know him personally) of urging on the publication." (Yeats to Tagore, July 31 [1915]. R-S.) Yeats told Rothenstein: "I too have had a letter lately from Tagore and have been urging him to bring out a translation of his autobiography before the poems come out. He thinks that it is too oriental but I tell him that the more we hear him, or overhear him talking to his own people the more we shall be interested. I feel that he must never seem to speak to us. I think too that when the war is over England will think differently about India, whether better or worse, I don't know, but differently and more, and that it is important that she come to understand that India has a public life of its own. So if he speaks to you of the autobiography, do not seem uninterested. Perhaps I am biassed because I believe it to point a moral that would be valuable to me in Ireland." (Yeats to Rothenstein [August? 1915]. RP:HL.) Tagore was happy to advance the revival of Irish culture but feared that the memoirs were too brief and personal, and Surendranath had not finished the translation. (Tagore to Yeats, March 5, 1916. Michael Yeats.)

110
Tagore to Rothenstein

Calcutta   April 28, 1916

My dearest Friend

I am sailing for Japan tomorrow night or the day after. I have been invited to America to lecture. I have not yet accepted their offer. I shall decide about it later on.[1] Doors are closing against us everywhere in the world. Indians going towards Japan or America are either disallowed or interned in Singapur. A student of mine was prevented from accompanying me but he, having some connection with the French Chandannagore, is going to join the Indian Volunteer corps to be sent by the French Government to France[2]

I earnestly hope that before I return to India the war will be over and I shall be able to come over to England and see you

Give my love to dear children   Yours

Rabindranath Tagore

My address c/o Thomas Cook & Son   Tokyo   Japan

1. The Keedick Agency of New York offered a lecture tour. Tagore refused because he hoped to speak to university and other select audiences, but he knew nothing about Keedick; he asked Brett, through Andrews, to suggest another agent. (Andrews to Brett, April 28, 1916. MP:NYPL.) Keedick's terms fluctuated throughout April. (Telegrams [copies], April 2, 8, 18, 30, 1916. MP:NYPL.) By June, Tagore had decided to visit America, and Andrews, from Yokohama, asked Brett to engage an agent. (Andrews to Brett, June 2, 1916. MP:NYPL.) Brett suggested the Pond Lyceum. (Brett to Andrews, June 9, 1916. MP: NYPL.) Tagore accepted; he and Pearson would reach Seattle, August 7 or 8, then go to Mrs. Moody's in Chicago. (Andrews to Brett, June 20 [1916]. MP:NYPL.) Pond's terms are cited as fluctuating from a round $12,000 for a continental tour to forty lectures at $500 each. (See Mukherjee. *Passage to America*, p. 74, note 44.) However, $12,000 for forty lectures is Keedick's April 30 offer, which Tagore declined. Brett does not mention Pond's terms and in fact refused to settle with Pond until Tagore was actually in the United States. (Brett to Andrews, June 28, 1916. MP:NYPL.)

2. Nowhere in the correspondence is this statement explained or substantiated.

111
Tagore to Rothenstein

[Osaka   June 2?, 1916][1]

Dearest friend

I am in Japan. Hope to reach you some day across America when the war is over. Give my love to the dear children.   Yours
Rabindranath Tagore

1. Letter written on clipping of undated article, "Sir Rabindranath Tagore in Osaka: A Criticism of Modern Civilisation" (RP:HL), from unidentified Japanese English-language newspaper quoting Tagore's Osaka address as reported in the *Japan Weekly Chronicle* (Kobe): "A Criticism of Modern Civilisation," June 8, 1916, pp. 921–922. Another editorial in this same issue of the *Japan Weekly Chronicle* states that Japanese reporters who boarded Tagore's ship at Hongkong had sent word that he would lecture in Osaka, and he had therefore done so "with a good nature that his persecutors did not deserve." Reporters at Kobe had scuffled disgracefully over Tagore on board his ship: "The unfortunate visitor, who had come to Japan in search of peace and quiet and recruitment of health, began to think that he had made a serious error in judgment." Readers were warned against unquestioning acceptance of these particular accounts of interviews with Tagore, for the reporters were so deficient in English that they could neither frame suitable questions nor understand Tagore's replies: "Accounts in the vernacular papers of what Sir Rabindranath Tagore replied must therefore be entirely apocryphal." (Editorial, "Sir Rabindranath Tagore in Kobe," *ibid.*, pp. 913–914.) Yet another editorial in this issue describes Tagore as "remarkable chiefly as expressing the soul of a people in a new form," and as a representative of an Indian revolt against literary and linguistic classicism, a revolt with numerous parallels in Japan. On the other hand, "Tagore preaches a broad humanity rather than any definite political ambition." (Editorial, "Rabindranath Tagore in Japan: Visit of the Bengali Poet," *ibid.*, p. 920.)

112
Rothenstein to Tagore

Far Oakridge   June 25, 1916

My very dear friend—since hearing of your intended journey to Japan I have been intending to write you daily, but Andrews' second letter comes to remind me of my neglect.[1] My excuse must be an unusual press of work—an exhibition of portrait drawings in London, for which many new drawings had to be made, & a decoration to paint for a forthcoming exhibition, which is to represent the Universities, & has necessitated my writing to 40 prospective sitters, who are to be incorporated in my processional portrait frieze.[2] Indeed I believe, if there is Heavenly indulgence, as there is human remissness, I deserve pardon for my unwritten letters, so much of my time being given to writing a proportion of those calling for a reply. Indeed did some of us employ the diligence we devote to careless letters to a more concentrated & consecutive motive, we non-writers would fill volumes, burying your professional output under their mass! and guilty as my conscience is, I am not sure that the debt is always on my side, O writer of charming epistles! But you are now a traveller, & so happily without a conscience. A traveller throws off the burdens he carries when he sits like a stock for troubles to settle on, as sparrows on a wire. He stays nowhere long enough to learn the meanness of men's souls; to him as dispenser of backsheesh all men are amiable, his feet leave every road before the entanglements are laid to trap them & from the face of everyone he meets the sun is gloriously & serenely reflected. Where the flowers grow most lush he goes, for he has no attachments, & the glory of the work of men's hands is everywhere to show what can be in men's hearts. I think I was as near to being a good man when I was in India as I am ever likely to be in this my pilgrimage through life. I still draw on the treasures I gathered there, more I think than you can imagine. Sometimes when I look through the drawings of people I met there I get a wild desire to go back, wondering whether it can really be true such people exist, & that by going to Cook's office, & eating fourteen dinners in a ship's saloon, I can in fact sit & draw them again.

Galsworthy, who has just been staying here, & who is very disillusioned regarding life just now, says he thinks the sense of humanity is really a sense of beauty, & only those with this sense can ever really feel for other people & other races; that it comes in fact with the sense of beauty & is therefore a negligible one, on which we cannot count in our plans & hopes for mankind.[3] I suppose it was the marvellous beauty of India & of Indians that gave me the exalted sense I was aware of when I was with you, & that I still get from glimpses & memories of things Indian. And so I wonder what, your own worries being shaken off by the simple turning of your back on artificial & unnatural responsibilities & claims, Japan & China are going to mean to you. Will they have the magic India had for my eyes & senses & will the Buddhist monks & sages move you with their beauty & serenity as your sannyasi moved me? What pilgrimages will you make, into what hills & groves, by what streams & cascades, into remote temple courts? For I don't see you visiting Japanese munition factories, with Andrews & Pearson as your guides. But perhaps you will linger in China before going to Yokohama; & all the time you are finding new & enrapturing ways I shall be treading only familiar ones, a little heavier hearted too for this long war with its complex emotions & unexpected promptings. If God is one, man is certainly not, & there are times when I can see the logic of the conception of many Gods & can imagine the world reinventing them, for what goes through a man's mind for a moment may be materialised for a thousand years. How many things one can be in a day—how many souls one can possess! Does a man of action shut his mind to all messages except one he hears clearly of set purpose or does the louder call really drown all others? I cannot myself say, for I cannot conceive myself not seeing the other way I might have taken, were it mine to be king or commander. But perhaps I am wrong, for in our crafts, where we are most alive, we see there may be many ways of writing & painting for others, but for us our way is clear.

. . . Write & let us know how you are faring, if you get an hour. This, so far as England is concerned, you will always regard as your home, & I like to think your thoughts come to it sometimes. My warm greetings to your fellow pilgrims. Andrews is so good in writing me.   Ever your affectionate friend

W. R.

1. Andrews wrote that they had paused in Penang, and that Tagore's thoughts were of seeing the Rothensteins and, if war ended, of going to England by the Siberian Railway or, if his money lasted, of waiting out the war in America. (Andrews to Rothenstein, May 12 [1916]. RP:HL.)

2. A successful show of forty-four portrait drawings, Leicester Galleries, London (see Speaight, *William Rothenstein*, pp. 275–276). "Decoration": large cartoon commemorating Oxford war dead. The Arts and Crafts Society showed it at Burlington House; it remained unfinished and is now at University College, Southampton.

3. Galsworthy was depressed by the harassment of Germans in England, by fears of eventual internment of his German brother-in-law and nephew, and by the hypothetical moral dilemma of whether he would volunteer if of military age. (See Dudley Barker, *The Man of Principle: A View of John Galsworthy* [London, 1963], pp. 170–185.)

113
Tagore to Rothenstein

Yokohama   August 2, 1916

My dearest Friend

I have nearly come to the end of my visit to Japan. I had my idea of Japan of the bookland—the Japan which had no soul of her own therefore had no difficulty in getting into the bodies belonging to others. I fully expected to find here one monotonous mist of the Modern everywhere and very little Japan behind it. But to my surprise I find that the mist is not continuous and Japan is still visible. Her features are distinct—and what more, she is human. She is not a mask of modern science and organisation with no living face inside. I can see that Japan has had all the advantage of the smallness of her area, security of her sea and homogeneity of her inhabitants. She is like a skillful gardener having a small piece of land, compelled to take recourse to intensive culture, making every inch of the ground yield its best. She has not been burdened with a bulk which breeds slowness and negligence. It is wonderful to see how the mind of a whole people has been trained to love beauty in nature and bring it out in art. It has been their conscious endeavour to make their daily life in all its details perfect in rhythm of beauty. There is no sign of oversight or vulgar display in their houses or their manners. The reticence in their taste shows their natural sensibility for the beautiful. Because their enjoyment is true, for them the enough is better than the more and right proportion than profuseness.

This has been made possible because for their expression they seem to have concentrated all their resources in the picturesque. Their genius has taken the course of the definite—they revel in the rhythm of proportion in lines and movements. But music is lacking in them and the deeper currents of poetry which deals with the ineffable. They have acquired a perfect sense of the form at some cost of the sense of the spirit. Their nature is solely aesthetic and not spiritual. Therefore it has been easier for them to make their ideals almost universal in their peoples. For these ideals are more in the sense of the decorum and deftness of mind and fingers than in the sense of the infinite in man—they are more of the dress than of the health. However, it is wonderful to see perfection achieved and made the common property of a whole race of men.

My next move is towards America where I shall spend my winter on a lecturing tour, hoping that by that time the war will be over and the next spring will find me in England. You know that I was not born for the career of the lecturer but life is a combination of what one is and what one is not, in which the latter predominates in quantity in the same proportion as the water is to the land in the composition of the earth.   Ever yours
Rabindranath Tagore

114
Rothenstein to Tagore

Far Oakridge   October 4, 1916

My very dear friend—I was delighted to hear from you again. Of your triumphs in Japan we have read, but I detected in your letter something of disillusion, of depression even, which makes me feel that the homage paid you has not given you any great satisfaction. You have been acclaimed as the hope & glory of the East; yet it is not because you were born in India that you have good things to say to men, but because you have a high probity & a sense of the beauty of the world you live in. You would say similar things had you been gifted with a similar sense here; and I doubt if the things you have to say to the men & women of Japan are any more open to them, should they have hard hearts & greedy eyes, than they are to us of the West. For I doubt whether they wish to lead more decent lives than we do. I fancy they have a similar desire to acquire all they can, perhaps with more patience & grimness than we have shown & with less sense of justice & seemliness in their dealings with their fellows.

I wish they would regard you as a sage, & believe themselves in what you believe. They will listen to you as men listen to anyone who can speak eloquently of things which are not real enough to them to shape their lives, or the policy of their government, but I think you may find Americans more genuine in their real desire to live as reasonably as possible than the Japanese. But I rather tremble for you among all these festivities, whether in Japan or in the States. I don't think you, or any real artist, can take any pleasure in mere fame & constant praise. We all grumble a little if nothing is given us, but a feeling of unreality always comes on us if we get it from the crowd. Opposition is not really good for us, but the reverse is so obviously bad for our peace of mind that we have got to believe opposition to be the healthier state. I am afraid you will grow weary of the publicity your visit brings you, & will find it, too, physically wearing. When you have given your lectures in America, do seriously consider the possibility of coming to us here. I don't fancy there is now any danger from submarines—certainly not in a neutral vessel, & you will find life going on here much as before. I am sure you will need a rest, & when you are refreshed you can renew your acquaintance with your many friends in London. . . . I wonder whether you will meet any of my friends in America. If you see Chapman tell him I have not forgotten him. Alas, one cannot write to all the good men one knows & admires. . . . Ever yours affectionately

William Rothenstein

We need no notice—only a letter so that we may get your room ready.

115
Tagore to Rothenstein

[San Francisco]   January 17, 1917[1]

My dear Friend

At last I am going home. My steamer sails today. Last three months my world of space and time was completely dislocated—my universe was shattered into bits dancing in a whirlpool. I had a hope that the war would be over by this time and I would go and see you. I can not tell you what a disappointment this has been to me. However with the advent of peace you will see me at your door. I wish you could come to us in India—I need you so much. Is it absolutely impossible? Can't you all come and accept my hospitality? I have not written to you for long—but your thought has been constantly in my mind.

    Give these stamps to Rachel and my love to dear children. Your affectionate friend

Rabindranath Tagore

    1. For itinerary see Hay, "Rabindranath Tagore in America," pp. 445–450; Mukherjee, *Passage to America*, pp. 74–85. This tour was hectic in the extreme. Tagore and Pearson, while they endured the rigors of an American lecture tour, tried at the same time to write, revise, and correct proofs. War slowed mails in all directions, and orderly correspondence with the Macmillan firms was impossible.

116
Rothenstein to Tagore

Far Oakridge   March 1, 1917

My very dear friend—I need scarcely tell you how disappointed we are that you finally tell us we cannot expect you here this year. The changed conditions of course gave me little hope of seeing you, for we could scarcely expect you to risk your life for the chance of sitting once more at our table & of seeing the moon rise over the valley opposite us. And your letters told us so little of your doings, & little more of your thoughts. Of your Harvard lectures I heard nothing—one newspaper, with a reproduction of one of my drawings of you, reached us here, from which I gathered you had been lecturing in The Carnegie Hall —a building in which, when I was painting portraits in New York, my studio was. But I had the misfortune to go to America a few months after my return from India, & the contrast, for a painter, was too great to allow of my losing any portion of my heart to America. No, I cannot, alas, think of India in these days. Not being a fashionable portrait painter I am hard hit by the war, & it is all I can do to keep things going, with John at school, & prices not very likely to come down, & mine not very likely to go up. But come back you must; I feel you have been too long out of touch with your English friends. I think we creative people need solitude first of all, & then we need the intimate ties a mutual desire for perfection gives our friendships. The crowd encourages a lowering of this, & of crowds I fancy you have had your fill. I used to say when I was in America that we are all Cinderellas, & when the clock strikes eleven we must each in turn return to our ashes, leaving the dazzling scene to the next wearer of the glass slippers America so charmingly provides—& how well American shoemakers fit our feet!

I can imagine you longing for Shantiniketan, & the company of those dear boys you teach, & the Indian plain & the scent of the burning timber & cow dung which, to me, was always so evocative, in the quiet evening. But perhaps you got more peace & quiet than I did in America, for I was staying with people all the time, in New York chiefly, & save for a week or two on the Hudson & in the Catskill hills, I got little time to myself. It is never overwork which hurts me, but underleisure. So I am glad to know you back at home, & this racketing pilgrimage over. What things you have done & what things seen, while all the time I have been looking across the self same little valley, at the same wych-elm in front of the house, over the same fields & hedges.[1] . . . I have volunteered under the national service scheme, & in a month, for all I know, may be sitting in an office tying up papers in red tape. In the meanwhile I paint, & when not painting, work on the farm. You will be amused to know, too, that I am now a Professor, the University of Sheffield having created a chair of civic art, which they offered to me, & which I accepted.[2] I hope, after the war, to paint something in the nature of a civic memorial in the University Hall. After the war! in the meanwhile one just accepts the material fabric of life, as always: something out of which a fine or a gross thing can be made. I believe it was to you I wrote, early in the war, that war is a monstrous exaggeration of what we call peace: of its virtues & its vices & crimes & injustices. I still believe this, & so find it gives the same opportunities to meanness & to generosity, to self-interest & self-sacrifice, to hasty & to sound judgement, stupidity & wisdom as all material life does. . . . The great thing, I think, is not to lose heart at the desolation & waste, not to get morbid about the evil that is in man. The Gods never make our lessons agreeable ones, or cheap in price, and as the memory of war is short, the lessons have to be repeated, it would seem, with unerring regularity. If the League of Nations can cure men of an atom of their greed, then we may hope for its efficiency. Such a League, like charity & other things, has to begin within us. That is why I have small sympathy with Indian politics, & with the young men's playing at Sinn Feinism. If it leads some of them to plot with Germans in America, how loathsome the means to an end, & until our pursuit of our ends is as decent & dignified as the ends themselves, we shall never attain them & not deserve to. You, I think, have a great chance in this direction, & I feel at bottom you can be of more fruitful service in your own beloved country, than in Japan or America, helping the young men to a sane vision of life.

. . . Ever your friend

William Rothenstein

1. Tagore cut short his New York tour and accompanied by Pearson went to Chicago to stay with Mrs. Moody. He then called off his Midwestern lectures because he had influenza, "but I hope he will be well enough to fulfil one or two more before he sails. I am thankful that he did not decide to stay on longer as I am sure his health would not have stood the strain." (Pearson to Brett, January 3 [1917]. MP:NYPL.) (See Hay, "Rabindranath Tagore in America," p. 449; Mukherjee, *Passage to America*, pp. 211–213.)
2. See *MM* II, 346.

117
Rothenstein to Tagore

London   June 20, 1917

My very dear friend, I am up in Town for a day or two. I must not put off writing to you, even though I have no writing paper, to tell you how excellent your last essays seem to me. The one on "Art," which presents an entirely new view of its meaning, is most inspiring—indeed the whole book is full of wisdom & a ripe & clear judgement. I have only one criticism to offer & that is of the photographs. They neither do you justice, nor do they throw light on the essays. The essay on "Woman" was delightful, full of delicate appreciation & a fine undercurrent of irony.[1]

I am glad to read that your autobiography is to appear, a book I have always wanted to read.[2] . . . I dreamed last night that I came to India, called on you & found you out & somehow came back the same night, & wondered at my folly, since I suddenly realised that to return the next day meant risking being torpedoed & I began to think of excuses in my sleep for not returning. Many people ask for news of you—you have myriads of friends throughout the world. I do want to hear something of your doings, & I cannot easily satisfy the many enquiries I get, both from the children & from friends. Your effect on Wells has been surprising—have you seen his new book on religion?[3] A lecture of mine is being published by Constable—I will send it to you directly I get a copy.[4] ... Ever yours

William Rothenstein

1. Tagore, *Personality: Lectures Delivered in America* (London, 1917). Photographs of Tagore as tourist in America suggest that his is the personality under discussion. "What Is Art?" pp. 3–38; "Woman," pp. 169–184.
2. Tagore, *My Reminiscences:* see Letter 109, note 4.
3. H. G. Wells, *God the Invisible King* (London, 1917), pp. 59, 159. Wells comments on Tagore as representative of the best in modern Indian theology.
4. Rothenstein, *A Plea for a Wider Use of Artists and Craftsmen* (London [1917]). Lecture delivered November 8, 1916, at Sheffield University and strongly reminiscent of Havell's plea for recognition of the fine arts of India. (See above, Introduction, note 1.)

118
Tagore to Rothenstein

Shantiniketan   July 6, 1917

My dearest Friend

Quite a number of your letters must have failed to reach me while I was rushing about in America howling away lectures to audience whose dimension was terrifyingly prodigious. I was assured that my presence was needed just at that moment in America and though there is a considerable amount of unreality in praise we receive still I had occasional satisfaction in feeling that I was not merely ornamental but necessary.

It was a very great disappointment to me not to be able to go to England after my adventure in the United States. The sudden reputation, which like a bombshell, has burst upon the once delightful obscurity of my solitude has not yet fully spent its force. It seems to have caused a permanent disturbance in the atmosphere of my life giving rise to a perpetual tornado of dust storm. I am struggling to fly away from this, but it has become a part of myself. The worst point in my complaint against this limelight illumination is that it has made my own country almost uninhabitable for me. My countrymen do not know how to forget me, which is unhealthy for them, as well as for myself. Houses are suitable for dwelling because their walls have neither eyes nor tongues. My surrounding walls are all eyes and they talk—not wisely, as you can well imagine. This makes me wish with a longing to take shelter with my friends in England where I can hope to be like a picture which has its proper perspective of distance and detachment. But I know my salvation lies in my being able to find out the peace and depth of the inner life which has its communication with the soul region of all the world. The outside has become too much for me and the balance has to be restored if I must not be upset by this continual misadjustment of burden. I am afraid the West has lost its foothold of the inner life and has been hopping with one leg, revelling in the very jerkiness of its difficult movement, because that has the appearance of power. Unfortunately the East has gone to the other extreme, and instead of using the inner life as the source of all harmonious movements has used it as a retreat for its practice of hibernation. But I, who have the amphibious duality of nature in me, whose food is in the West and breath air in the East, do not find a place where I can build my nest. I suppose I shall have to be a migratory bird and cross and recross the sea, owning two nests, one on each shore.[1]

1. Full text of surviving letter, which appears to have stopped short of the bottom of the page, without closing or signature.

119
Rothenstein to Tagore

[Far Oakridge July? 1917]

My very dear friend—a letter, which I enclose to show you you were not so neglected as you may have imagined, has just been returned to me—written during October last! How many more of my letters you failed to receive I do not know.[1] . . .

I have had Pearson's book on you & your school these last days—charmingly done & full of a deep regard for your aims & achievements. I will write him shortly.[2] But from India I get little news, & being cut off from London, I see nothing of Indians—not even of the delegates who have come to represent India at the Great Conference.[3] Sometimes the things said make one rub one's eyes—things many of us said years ago, when we were chid for our thoughts. Now the moment is riper, & I hope from my heart that the opinions we held which seemed rash & extreme ten years ago now seem sane & obvious enough. I believe, if only your young men will be patient, that your future is bound to be brighter. But not only must your young men be patient, but they must see to it that greater liberty & power shall mean in truth greater happiness for the Indian people. It may easily mean something different; better they should use their leisure thinking out some of the difficulties which have faced all states than in endless criticism & what our soldiers & schoolboys call "grousing." Certainly here there is a new feeling towards India, & I should be sorry indeed if the chance were not taken, by Indians as well as by our own people here, to bring about a new understanding.

I wish you would do what we talked of when you were here —form some kind of body to work with a similar body here.[4] I speak often with Fisher about Indian affairs: he is now, as you will know, President of the Board of Education, & of course in close touch with his colleagues, & any suggestions made for improving our inter-relations are welcomed by him most cordially. My own love for India is unchanging—only I fear that so many of the things I love India for will be swept away in the changes that are bound to come. I got a copy of your "stray birds" from America, for which I have to thank you; but I prefer the [London] Macmillan edition, with its simpler binding & printing. As for the picture, frankly, it is vile, & an eyesore in either edition. I think writers do well to induce their publishers to let pictures alone—they nearly always rob a good book of its dignity. At least the artist must be on the same level as the poet.[5] . . . When the war is over you will come to us—I believe you will find a visit to your friends here inspiring & fruitful, & you will certainly get a warm welcome. Not, I think, an American one; but that you will not want. Admiration there is on a vaster scale than anything of the kind can ever be here; but I fancy the more discriminating homage of a few people here is of at least equal value. . . . In the meanwhile all send their love, & I am, as ever, your affectionate friend

William Rothenstein

My brother Albert is now a 2nd Lieutenant in the Worcestershire regiment, expecting to be sent abroad shortly.

My letter of last October was not very prophetic about submarines![6]

1. Letter 114.
2. W. W. Pearson, *Shantiniketan: The Bolpur School of Rabindranath Tagore* (New York, 1916).
3. The Round Table Conference. (See Broomfield, *Elite Conflict*, pp. 96–97.)
4. An advisory board related to the school at Santiniketan.
5. Tagore, *Stray Birds*, with frontispiece by Willy Pogány (New York, 1916; London, 1917).
6. See Note 1.

120
Rothenstein to Tagore

Far Oakridge   August 25, 1917

My very dear friend—at last there comes a letter from you, a letter carrying with it an almost bodily sense of your presence, so like yourself is it. . . . & so when you write, I once more walk along the quiet Oakridge lanes, talking of life & death, of beauty & of India, as we used to do five years ago. Five years! & curiously enough we are having just such an August as we had then—rain & more rain. How living the memory of those days still is. Do you remember them as I do, how I came over every morning? & each time you had some new translation to read to me—the children's poems, the Princess Malini & the noble Chitra! What plans we discussed for production & publication, for the future of Indian art & of India & how deeply we were both moved by the beauty of the face of the world about us. . . . I can be disagreeable & unsympathetic; the Gods withheld their gift of charm from me; but I cannot hate, & I cannot train myself, so late in life, to see evil only in men's motives & actions. Habit & training have alike encouraged me to see, in any man sitting on a chair before me, only miraculous form & noble features; I know that if I put my pencil aside that less Godlike qualities will intervene. But I do carry a pencil always in my pocket, & this little round bit of wood enclosing a slender roll of graphite has kept my eyes sane & a great love in my heart for my fellows. It allowed me to see in your country only what is wholesome & comely. I am too old to throw it away, & to see ugliness, evil & untruth. So I remain entrenched at Oakridge, living with the children, their goats & rabbits, their cows & calves, painting these & trees & the clouds. I do believe in the eternal sanity of art, & do praise the Gods who put a sense of it in my heart. Does it not teach us respect for all men, a hatred of injustice & of meanness and an essential humility, however vain we may appear to others? If politicians could only fall in love with a tree, or a hayrick or an old cart resting under the shadow of a thatched shed, I believe they would be unable to face their tasks any more. Perhaps the tinkle of the temple bells, the sound of the anklets on the feet of your village women & the shapely forms & grave, chiselled faces of your men have touched the heart of our new Secretary of State [for India, Edwin Montagu], & so he is drawn to come back to you. May his coming bring something of what is near all your hearts. At least the things a few of us said a few years ago are becoming commonplaces on the lips of men to-day, & the war has taught hard lessons to many. Not the lessons which men expected to teach, are those they have had to learn, & some of the learners to-day look uncommonly aged & some of the masters strangely like children. No, dear friend, one can say nothing in letters. But you know something of the things that feed my heart, as I know much that fills yours.

That you feel the need of coming back to us delights me more than I can say. There is so much one wants to talk over. And life is short, & the wall between life & death is a very thin one. One of the things I look forward to is resuming the intimacy which filled my life with a rich plenty, in the peace & quiet of this green haven. When you do come, you must promise us a brief spell—then London shall have you & lay its gifts at your feet. But between us two there is, I do believe, something more sacred & intimate than exists between many men, & I believe too its flame has been kept burning in our hearths. . . . You will come back to us, will you not, as soon as the war ends? I am sorry you are so harassed in India—I can imagine where your difficulties come. The fact is we need repose; our life & wisdom, such as it is, has to be given to endow the things we make. . . . Do you remember how [William] Morris suffered, when he threw himself into practical socialism, & found himself caught in the toils of intrigue & the futilities of cleverness? . . . Do let me hear from you again soon. In the meanwhile I am ever yours most affectionately

William Rothenstein

121
Rothenstein to Tagore

Far Oakridge   September 19, 1917

My very dear friend—I was delighted with your book on nationalism. You have said, nobly & wisely, many things which need saying & I found myself in sympathy with you throughout. And your task was no easy one. A friendly public may turn into a hostile one for the same small cause which will make a private friend a secret enemy—and dealing as you do with an Indian, a Japanese & a European public you have been courageous in speaking what is in your heart. Nations respond to flattery always, even when it is flattery of themselves, but at a time like the present this self flattery becomes so tiresome & ludicrous that to one's surprise, a book like yours is welcomed in quite unexpected quarters. I think it admirable, from every point of view.[1] . . .

When [India] gets full control of her granaries, how much corn will she have garnered & kept? What is the Italy of to-day compared with Mazzini's dream? And if the 300,000,000 Gods are hurried out of India, can any one be sure that even one will be left? Yes, this I think one can be sure of. But I am frightened at the ruthlessness of broom handlers, scrubbers, & dusters when they get into laboratory or studio. The dirt goes, but other things are sometimes found cracked & damaged.

The sweeping & cleaning are best done by those who do the constructive work & must not be left to menials without souls.

... Ever yours

William Rothenstein

1. Tagore, *Nationalism* (London, 1917).

122
Rothenstein to Tagore

Far Oakridge   September 23, 1917

My dear friend—our friend Dr Sadler is coming out to India—I wish we sent many such ambassadors from West to East. I know it will give you more than usual pleasure to meet him, & I hope you will get him down to Bolpur. I believe he will be deeply moved by the beauty of your country & of its people, & I know you will do what you can to give him the chance of seeing something of the intimate life of Bengal. How I wish I were coming out with him! He will carry you affectionate greetings from us all & I hope he will bring back with him a great love for your country, for I know he brings a quick sympathy for it & its hopes with him.[1] Ever your friend

William Rothenstein

1. Michael Sadler was about to leave for India as Chairman of the Calcutta University Commission and asked Rothenstein for introductions: "If there is any Indian friend of yours to whom you would care to give me a letter of introduction, I should prize it. The memory of your seventeenth century Indian pictures is vivid with me and I feel that I learned a great deal from them as well as from your talk. Of course I have your lithographs of Tagore." Sadler had asked the Government of India to include Ajanta in his itinerary: "Binyon showed me the [Herringham] drawings on Wednesday and I felt that they were really fundamental to an understanding of the possibilities of India." (Sadler to Rothenstein, September 17, 28, 1917. RP:HL.)

123
Tagore to Rothenstein

Shanti Niketan   October 26, 1917

My dearest Friend,

It has given me deep pleasure to know that my last three books you like. I had my fear that my American lectures, especially those about nationalism, might give offence to my readers in England. Possibly to some extent they have done so.[1] But most of the reviews that I have seen in your papers are extremely mild. Some critics have taxed me with having misunderstood the meaning of the word "Nation". I suppose it is one of those words whose meaning is still in its process of formation. If you really mean by that word the peoples who have the consciousness of a common tradition and aspiration then why do you exclude us Bengalis from its category? for you are never tired of reminding us that we do not belong to a nation. When we try to understand you we find that our tradition and aspiration are of a different character from yours—it is more religious and social than political. Therefore it seems to me that the word nation in its meaning carries a special emphasis upon its political character. Politics becomes aggressively self-conscious when it sets itself in antagonism against other peoples, specially when it extends its dominion among alien races. This convulsive intensity of consciousness is productive of strength but not of health. The rapid growth of nationalism in Europe begins with her period of foreign exploration and exploitation. Its brilliance shines in contrast upon the dark background of the subjection of other peoples. Certainly it is based upon the idea of competition, conflict & conquest and not that of cooperation.[2] In human language there are very few words that have an absolute meaning. The unselfish people have not completely lost their self, only the selfish ones put stronger emphasis upon it and thus have a special designation. And the people with an aggressively emphatic politics is a nation. The man in his professional character has very often a special attitude of mind. There he feels an intense satisfaction if he can sell a lame horse at a price which is dear even for a sound one. Because in profession man has no other object before him but success. He may have an exalted standard of life in his private capacity and yet as a professional man his conduct may go entirely against that standard, without disturbing his appetite for dinner. Therefore it is not unusual to find rapacious landlords who are extravagant in their generosity. That grasping professional attitude of mind makes a nation of a people when it furiously pursues success and takes it to be a sign of sentimentalism to budge an inch from its reckless path of power at the dictates of humanity. What I have said in my lectures is that such an attitude of mind in a whole people of a country, such constant self idolatry by all kinds of ritualism and human sacrifice must go against moral providence of the world ending at last in a catastrophe.

By some unexpected freak of fate I was caught in a dust storm of our politics. I have just come out of it nearly choked to death. I am more convinced than ever that a poet might do worse than write mere verses. Try to be true to yourself by all means but not to be truer which is a hollow temptation set in our path by moral teachers.[3]

Give my love to dear children and tell them not to grow too fast before I come to see them. Because that will be unfair to me who can only grow older without growing at all. Ever yours

Rabindranath Tagore

1. British reactions varied, from a brief note that this was "a thoughtful book and one that Western readers will be the better for reading" (review, "*Nationalism*," *The Athenaeum* [London], October 1917, p. 522), to an elaborate assumption that he must be joking: "We need not perhaps take too serious a view of a poet's whimsical and partly humorous incursion into a field with which he is not familiar" (review, "The Neo-Hindu in America and Japan," *The Spectator* [London], 119 [1917], 386–387).

2. Not a new theme for Tagore. In 1905 he had said that English imperialism led toward inevitable calamity. He had reviewed the course of European imperialism, refuted Lord Curzon by name, and noted that imperialism and brutality always go hand in hand. (See his "Imperiyālijam" [Imperialism], *Rājā Prajā* [Ruler and Ruled] (1908), in *R-R*, X, 431–434.

3. After dispute over whether its chairman could dissolve a rowdy session of the Congress in Calcutta, Tagore was elected Chairman of its Reception Committee. He accepted, but arguments raged over the constitutionality of this as well. (See editorial, "Party Strife in Calcutta: A Few Stray Notes," *MR*, 22 [1917], 440–444; Broomfield, *Elite Conflict,* pp. 136, 138.) Rothenstein told his brother, "I see Tagore is being dragged

into Indian politics—a bad thing for a man with so little decision as he has." (William to Albert Rothenstein, November 25, 1917. RP:HL.)

124
Rothenstein to Tagore

Far Oakridge   April 5, 1918

My very dear friend—it is a long time since I last heard from you. I am just back from France & rather hoped to find a letter from you on my return. Instead of this I find a book of stories, which contains to my delight The Postmaster, the first writing of yours I ever read; it was published I think in the Modern Review.[1] It loses nothing from a second reading, & the little story will always have a particular value for me. The row of dark blue volumes is becoming a pleasantly long one. I found many men in France diligent readers of your books. . . .

But to return to this quiet corner of the world, & to my own dear innocent children is a strange thing too, after nearly four months at the scene of war. I cannot tell you how delightful the children are to me. Rachel & Betty have grown into young girls—they are no longer children—but they have really kept their innocence & impulses of love & devotion, & I think, when you meet them again, you will not be disappointed. . . . And you, what are you doing these days? I thought of you often while I was in France. I heard from Sadler that he had met you—a charming person he is, is he not?[2] But from you I have had no word since I last wrote & I hope before long to get news of you. Perhaps next year you will come to us. . . . Please give Gaganendranath & Abanindranath my very warm greetings. Are Pearson & Andrews with you?[3] The same, too, for them. Ever yours affectionately

William Rothenstein

    1. See Letter 80, note 2.
    2. Sadler and Tagore met in Calcutta on November 18: "Yesterday I saw Tagore for the first time and found that, thanks to your letters, he welcomed me very kindly." (Sadler to Rothenstein, November 19, 1917. RP:HL.)
    3. Pearson had left Tagore in the care of "an old friend of the family [who] joined us in America and is taking charge of him from here

[Yokohama] to Calcutta." Pearson stayed in Japan to write articles on India for a Japanese newspaper. (Pearson to Brett, February 14, June 11, 1917. MP:NYPL.) A year later Tagore heard that he had been arrested in China and imprisoned in Shanghai on political charges but was being returned to England for release. (Andrews to Rothenstein, May 31, 1918. RP:HL.) According to Mukhopadhyay, Pearson was arrested by the British Government in Singapore and also by "English police" in Peking (*Rabindrajibani*, II, 475, 509). In his next letter to Brett, Pearson wrote that he had been at home "nearly a month now" and was recovering from dysentery. (Pearson to Brett, August 9 [1918]. MP:NYPL.) In none of his surviving letters does Pearson mention arrest or deportation. Three members of the Pearson family to whom the editor applied for information had never heard of the alleged incident.

125
Tagore to Rothenstein

Shanti Niketan   June 1, 1918

Dear Friend, I have not written to you for long. Possibly it is because I find the channel of my correspondence clogged with crowds of letters that do not move—they are mere burden that has to be forcibly disposed of. They need dredgers to clear them up, and in the meanwhile they choke the living stream. Possibly I am growing lethargic like men living in an overcrowded room—my mind being crammed in a dense surrounding of small social claims that are inimical both to real work and to honest leisure. I have got into the habit of putting off writing letters to my friends till my mind regains its window and its easy chair; but the lengthening intervals of such inactivity produces the habit of non writing making the joints stiff of my letter writing personality.—For some time past I have been pining to go somewhere—it was like a homesickness for the far away. I planned all sorts of excursions in my mind—to the hills, to the southern India, to Ceylon—but one by one I gave them up like nuts whose kernels had perished. But I fear it was not the need of the change of places which I felt, but for me it was more like the strange case of an oyster trying to run away from its own shell. A crust has been formed round me, a crust of reputation and publicity which I can no longer shake off and find my freedom in the world of quiet delights. However, I have decided to start for America next autumn—it is but to take a desperate plunge into a violent change of surroundings. I hope this hateful war will be over sometime when I am there and I shall be able to come to England and see you.[1]

Something has happened to me lately which I find difficult even to mention. I very seldom speak about it to anybody. It is the death of my eldest daughter Bela. She was exceptionally beautiful in body and mind, and I can not but think that all things that are real in this world cannot afford to lose the intense reality of her life and yet remain the same. We can only see the one side of truth from the point where we live and miss the meaning of death, but there must be another side where it is in harmony with life, like the setting sun whose meaning is not in its disappearance but in the sunrise in the new morning outside our ken.[2]

I have met Dr Sadler and was greatly attracted by him. I do not know how much he will be able to accomplish, but he is one of those men who have rare power of vision and who can impart it to others. I believe he will be able to give a shock of life to our inert organisation and make people think. Along with much that is crude and inane he has come to know some of our best men like Dr Seal and I feel sure that will compensate him.[3] I am sending you by this mail a small book of mine named "The Parrot's Training" which has more meaning than words and a great deal more illustrations than the letterpress.[4] Your affectionate friend

Rabindranath Tagore

1. On June 2 Tagore wrote to Alice Rothenstein, "I hope the war will be over by the end of this year and I shall be able to spend the next spring with you and the children. Life is moving and we are unconsciously falling apart and after intervals we must renew our friendships, making alterations in our doors and windows of communication. Letters can carry words, but cannot make vital adjustments" (RP:HL).

Tagore had already asked Brett to arrange a 1918 lecture tour. (Tagore to Brett, cablegram, April 11 [1918]. MP:NYPL.) Brett cabled: YES POND OFFERS SAME ARRANGEMENTS DOUBTS POSSIBILITY ANY LARGE SUCCESS. (Brett to Tagore, April 12, 1918. MP:NYPL.) Brett then wrote: "Moreover, Mr. Pond and I are very much upset indeed because you have been accused in the press in this country of being what they called disloyal, a good many paragraphs having appeared from time to time indicating that you have had some connection with German agents or with certain disloyal elements in India." Brett had done what he could to counteract this and knew the charges were untrue, but "they still unfavorably influence the mind of many of our people." He would be pleased if Tagore came, as it might revive sales. (Brett to Tagore, April 15, 1918. MP:NYPL.) Andrews forwarded a letter from the Viceroy's office expressing regret that Tagore should be thus implicated and confirming that the charges were groundless. (Andrews to Brett, June 23, 1918. MP:NYPL.) However, Tagore soon abandoned the American plan. (Andrews to Brett, July 16, 1918. MP:NYPL.)

    2. Bela, thirty-two years old, died of tuberculosis.

    3. Sadler wrote, "A very great deal of what is best in my visit to Bengal is due to your kindness. . . . R. Tagore and Seal are very great and inspiring people. Your words on my behalf admitted me to their confidence much sooner than would have otherwise been possible." He added, "If only I could read and talk Bengali!" And added again, "Sometimes I can hardly bear to think of the cool, clear-outlined Cotswolds." (Sadler to Rothenstein, March 4, 1918. RP:HL.)

    4. Tagore, "Totā-Kāhini" [Tale of a Parrot], *Lipikā* [Sketches] (1922), in *R-R*, XXVI, 132–135: "The Parrot's Training," *The Parrot's Training and Other Stories,* trans. by the author (Calcutta, 1944), pp. 1–11. A delightful allegory about a Raja's pet bird that could sing but had no education and no manners. It was chained to its cage, pundits and administrators prescribed programs, but the Department of Education forgot it until a malicious faultfinder spread rumors of its death. It was dead indeed; it made no sound except the rustling of its "inner stuffing of bookleaves." In thirteen volumes, the report of Sadler's Commission tells the same story. (See Calcutta University Commission, 1917–19, *Report* [Calcutta, 1919–20].)

126
Rothenstein to Tagore

Far Oakridge   July 8, 1918

My dear friend—why have you become so silent? It is months since I last heard from you—. . . Happily there is a very different attitude toward India to-day. I hope Mr Montagu's report goes far towards the solution of difficulties long felt— I have not yet read the whole document but it looks as though a serious beginning is being made towards the carrying out of many of our hopes. I hope people in India will feel this to be the case. How much of the old India we love will remain, when all these changes come about, I wonder. But a country cannot live by the remains of its beauty; Italy has long felt this. And if men can be happier without it then it must go. But they cannot be happy always without it, & I hope a sense of beauty will come back to Indians, so that the dangers of the complete commercialisation of an old country like yours will not quite overwhelm the people who care for some of the finer things of life. Or were poet & artist always outcasts, having to put gold under men's pillows while they sleep? I was at my brother's [Charles Rothenstein, later Rutherston] house last week, & saw there the picture I painted of the Panch Ganga Ghat at Benares & when I saw it again, it seemed incredible my eyes should really have seen what I tried to set down; the palaces & the great flights of steps, the noble ghats & the crowds of enchanting people. If you go to Hardwar or Puri or Benares, spare a thought for one who loved India & cared for the welfare of Indians when many people were indifferent, & whose eyes would rejoice to see again for a brief space what you can look on throughout your life. Affectionate greetings from all the household.   Ever yours

William Rothenstein

127
Rothenstein to Tagore

Far Oakridge   August 20, 1918

My very dear friend—at last we get news of you & your spring gushes out in half a dozen streams. It is always an event to hear from you, for all the family. . . . I am sending you the latest photographs of the family, so that when you see my flock again you will be able to recognize it. Then when you have enjoyed either rest or a triumph in America, you will come back to us & be grateful once more for the peace of this golden vale. I believe a visit to England will prove a useful thing for you—to get into touch once more with men of your own trade of poetry will prove a joyful & fruitful thing for your spirit. And think of the drawings I will make of you! I have just been drawing André Gide, your French translator, who has been staying with us.[1] And now I am spending my last days at home for some time to come. I am being sent to France partly to make drawings & also to teach some of the 50,000 soldiers who are to form a kind of university behind the lines. I was called up by the military, &

was to be a Tommy; but Sir Henry Hadow appealed for me, & I am to work under him (he is Director of Education in France), these next months.[2] . . .

We were grieved to hear of the loss of some one very near to you. This is not the first you have had—I well remember how you told me of the death of your son, on a visit to a friend.[3] But death seems to have become a familiar of men. Not that he has ever stayed far from our haunts, but he has stayed among the shadows of the trees. But now he walks ever openly among men, taking the young by handfuls & putting them, as in the old children's stories, into his bottomless sack. It is we who invited him, so it would not be fair to call him shameless.

Be sure that, when the war is over, a chair will be ready for you at our table. In the meanwhile things are likely to be uncertain for me—not that they are not always so for all of us—until that time comes. For you, too, life must be full of uncertainty. I hope you will not allow the politicians to make use of you. I hope, too, that the Moderate party in India will not allow itself to be stampeded by the Extremists. An Extremist is but another genus of Jingo, who tries to hide his human doubts & instincts, as a poor Tibetan Devil-dancer might, behind the mask of a Superman.[4] Extremism, in life or in art, is trying to take a short cut to avoid the difficulties which make the crown of art & life. In the young it is but ignorance & warm hearted enthusiasm—in older men it is, even at its best, blind obstinacy or vanity; an audience will always applaud the man who appears to have nothing to say to half measures. But until the sense of man gets kinder by a hair's breadth, neither whole nor half measures will cure our hearts of the grief the unkindness of our fellows brings us. . . . Let us have examinations in human understanding, patience & sympathy for our civil services, if examinations we are to have at all. I doubt whether present-day Indians would pass much higher, or in greater numbers, than the people they complain of; if they can prove me wrong, then they are worthy to rule the world.

. . . Ever yours

William Rothenstein

1. On Gide at Oakridge, see *MM* II, 341–345. Rothenstein's drawing, in *The Portrait Drawings of William Rothenstein 1889–1925*, comp. John Rothenstein (London, 1926), plate 56.

2. Sir Henry Hadow (1859–1937), Precentor of Westminster Abbey; Honorary Chaplain to Queen Victoria; Vice-Chancellor of Sheffield University, 1919–1930. Rothenstein went instead to Cambridge to lecture to Australian Education Officers.
3. Tagore's son Somendranath died of cholera in 1907, aged eleven.
4. See Broomfield, *Elite Conflict*, pp. 169–203. During bureaucratic delays in implementing the Montagu-Chelmsford Reforms, Bengali Extremists became, if not well organized, better organized than the Moderates, who suffered disastrous losses in the 1923 elections.

128
Tagore to Rothenstein

Santi Niketan   September 25, 191[8][1]

My friend, we have to put up with many interruptions in life's amenities during this war time and, I suppose, it is of no use to complain if our letters do not reach our friends. My last effort at correspondence with you was some months ago when I sent letters to Mrs Rothenstein, Rachel and yourself by the same mail.[2] I am sure they did not deserve destruction, being friendly letters carrying some love and some laughter. However, let me take my chance once again with the hope that the time is not far away when I shall meet you in person.

In my last letter which was lost I gave you the news of my latest bereavement. I have lost my eldest daughter. She was young, and beautiful, and she had a deep love for flowers, animals, children and beauties of nature. Her observation of the human world which was expressed in a few short stories she wrote, was full of a delightful humour.

For the last few months I have plunged headlong into my school work. I teach three classes in the morning and the rest of the day I spend writing textbooks for my boys. These works that do not depend upon the fitfulness of inspiration are soothing, their unpretentious commonplaceness is restful to the mind like the monotonous green of the grass in the meadows round this place and crickets' chirp in the evening.

I have a genuine love for all young things. Feeding their minds with ideas and watching them grow give me great delight. As my method of teaching is not at all mechanical and is adventuresome it brings its surprises everyday keeping fresh my enthusiasm. I am sure you would enjoy watching me giving lessons to a class of quite young boys of the average age of fourteen, explaining to them in Bengali Shelley's Hymn to Intellectual Beauty and his Ode to the West Wind. I can assure you that now they understand those two poems in all their depth of truth and wealth of imagination. It is my experience that, if properly treated, the lessons that are difficult are more stimulating and attention compelling, and thus in a manner easier in the long run, than obviously easy lessons. The claim upon the students' mental concentration itself and their glow of pride in overcoming difficulties are of greater help for their growth of mind than anything that may be in the lessons themselves. However, of all the services to humanity teaching children is the most delightful one, provided it is done with the faith that their minds are living and therefore not to be moulded, but nourished. . . .

Before I conclude let me tell you we are all charmed with Dr Sadler, my only regret is that he has been so busy with his work and I had so few opportunities to meet him.[3] My affectionate greetings to Mrs Rothenstein and to the children.　Ever yours
　　　　　　　　　　　　　　　　　　　　　Rabindranath Tagore

　1. Plainly dated "1915," equally plainly an error for "1918."
　2. Letter 125.
　3. They met several times. See Michael Sadleir, *Michael Ernest Sadler: A Memoir by His Son* (London, 1949), p. 288. For Michael Sadler's summary of Bengal's educational problems, see pp. 304–305.

129
Tagore to Rothenstein

　　　　　　　　　　　　　　　Santi Niketan　October 7, 1918

My Friend, I am delighted to know that my last batch of letters has reached you after all, and my suspicion against my Kismet and other submerged agencies was groundless. . . .

One thing I forgot to mention in my recent letter to you—it is this, that I have altogether given up my idea of going to America. In fact, I cancelled my passage which had been booked. I had occasion to feel that in this war time men are in an abnormal state of mentality. When it costs them nothing to be cruel and unjust, and lies find their easy shelter and breedingplace in the widespread mire of suspicion. And this held me back to this quiet corner of the world to my peaceful work among children. I long to visit England and come in touch once more with my friends whose company was so stimulating to me and whose appreciation so precious, but I feel sure that this is not the time to tax you with claims of hospitality when the best part of your energies is engaged in one engrossing purpose. And in the meantime I am often visited by a profound feeling of mental detachment which I suppose is oriental. While in this state, I feel that it is of much greater importance to realise in beauty and truth the dualism in me of the Eternal and the Temporal, than to be going about picking men's words and scrambling for their attention at the cost of one's peace of mind and possibly of truth. It seems to me that in the West there is something undignified and unreal in the hustle and push of the marketplace of literature because of the material power it has acquired, and it gives me a feeling of shrinking pain and even of shame when I feel I am in the thick of this vociferous rush of the fighting crowd.

    The photograph you have sent me of the children has given me very great delight. Certainly they have grown, but they have not changed. I suppose, John must have begun thinking and judging and marking his white and black lines of classification across all mysteries of existence according to some very simple formula, partly borrowed and partly his own. But others are children, and I hope they will meet one of their own kind when they meet me.   Ever yours

                               Rabindranath Tagore

130
Rothenstein to Tagore

                    Church Army Recreation Hut, Ypres[1]
                    June 10, 1919

My very dear friend—for 6 months I have been on the Rhine & in the deserted area of France & Belgium, living the life of a troglodyte, cut off from my own world & so busy each day with my work that all correspondence, other than family letters, has been neglected. So it happens that I have neglected you as all my friends; though never have I thought more of them & needed them more & how could I help thinking of you during all these troubled days—troubled for India as everywhere. . . . We artists are by instinct with the builders; but fate has sent me into army spheres to paint destruction, & the planners are not here but at home. Hence socially I have not been exhilarated. But the beauty of places like Ypres is beyond words. I am constantly reminded of Chitor & Amber—will you not some day write an essay on the beauty of desolation? Where hands & voices were once busy, all is still, & nature seems to assimilate & take to her own bosom the work of our hands when it is shattered & make it her own, as though she refused it when it was a nest for our plots & schemes against her will, but accepted it when purified from our presence. I think you would care for some of the drawings I have made. Strife among men is not my subject—I have devoted myself entirely to poor remains of villages or the noble ruins of cities. . . . When are you coming back to us? . . .   Ever yours affectionately

William Rothenstein

1. Late in 1918 the War Office sent him to Bonn to work with Canadian War Artists on an artistic record of the war's aftermath. (See *MM* II, 355–361.)

131
Rothenstein to Tagore

Far Oakridge   July 11, 1919

My very dear friend—I have been profoundly moved by the beauty of "The Home and the World."[1] I don't know when you wrote it but it seems to me to contain your ripest wisdom. Only I am afraid that those alone who have been through the moral struggles which you have faced will realise how much truth there is in every page. I admire the book wholeheartedly. Indeed it has come at a moment when it has been of great comfort &

help to me. Few of us who have the creative sense could live through these years of war without being affected by the experience. I was what so many of us are, vaguely on the right side of things, generally moved by the gallant attitude to life, hating injustice & I hope generously inclined towards my fellows. But I realise—have realised more & more—how loose & untidy one's general condition has been, how undisciplined & indecisive. Indeed you have put the matter quite simply when you say that we have wanted to teach others while not having straightened one's self. . . .

Your book is a masterpiece of simple & uncompromising statement. And you have done the whole thing with a simple box of figures—not more than a Punch & Judy showman uses for his own little drama. Each character is clearly & sharply drawn, as are the characters of a Greek epic—and somehow to me Panchu brings with him the whole Indian scene as a background—the villages & the tanks, the temples & the peasant women in their dark red saris & those wandering mendicants who always fascinated me. It has been a great delight to read your book & to find your mind growing richer & even wiser than before.[2] Andrews' letter came as I was in the middle of it. He sent me a copy of your letter, printed in some Indian paper. How can I not approve of it? You have not put off, but have put on dignity.[3] . . . I too have had no easy task & know something of the difficulty of yours. We are expected to be pros or antis; as a matter of fact we can never be consistently either. . . . One hopes the years, be they few or many, still left to one will allow one to make up for past weaknesses. How to serve it is not always easy to see. And at the moment when our own needs are few the children grow into complex needs, and means have to come from somewhere when one's heart & mind are all for giving & have little taste for asking. . . . So you see it is not the time for me to put on the saffron dress, though all my instincts prompt me in some such direction. And England is not India. Are you for England? Be sure of a welcome when you come. In the meanwhile, though writing is a most unsatisfactory method of conducting friendship, it is our only means of communication. If I am remiss you will know how warm a place you have near my heart.   Ever yours

William Rothenstein

... I like to think I still am remembered by my friends in India; of Indians in England I now see nothing, greatly to my regret. Any one you may send will always be sure of a welcome.

1. Tagore, *Ghare-Bāire* [At Home-Outside] (1916), in *R-R*, VIII, 137–334: *The Home and the World,* trans. Surendranath Tagore, rev. Rabindranath Tagore (London, 1919).
2. Nostalgia for India attracts Rothenstein to Panchu, a minor character who represents Bengal's Common Man: a subtenant dependent on a landlord's whims, caught between Nationalist Moderates and Extremists. He comprehends issues on neither side and takes refuge in traditional observances that not only provide no relief but actually add to his troubles. Tagore saw India's Panchus as pawns in the hands of Nationalists like his character Sandip, a shoddy Extremist rabble-rouser whose ego is his principal investment in the cause.
3. Tagore resigned his knighthood in protest against the Amritsar Massacre on April 13, 1919. For his letter of resignation, see Thompson, *Rabindranath Tagore: Poet and Dramatist,* pp. 273–274.

132
Tagore to Rothenstein

Santi Niketan   July 25, 1919

Dearest Friend, your letter always gives me a sudden longing to go to England, just to have a few delightful days of quiet talks with you among those wooded downs under the soft grey light of your English sky. But the obstacle which I find against realising this wish is not external. Somehow my mind shrinks and refuses to get ready with enthusiasm. The first time when I went to England and found out my friends there and they found me out things were simple for me. For I was then a mere guest in your literary circle whose recognition of me depended upon the generosity of my hosts. But now unfortunately I have got a sort of sanctioned right and people do not have the freedom to ignore me. The fame that rests upon some public act of approbation carrying an authoritative warranty creates an unnatural situation vitiating the quality of both the praise and dispraise it excites. This makes me intently wish to go back to my former obscurity lighted only with the love of a few friends, and this makes me cling with all my heart to my work here outside the public gaze. One must have ample privacy and leisure to be fully true to oneself. Do you not think that the constant goading of criticism from the crowd to which all the creative souls of the modern age are subjected is demoralising? It is the subconscious mind which is creative—and to invade its silence with ceaseless chatter is to make it sterile. This is the reason why we find in the modern literature a straining after originality which is not true originality but merely novelty. The things that are original are as old as the hills and as simple as the morning breeze. But cheap criticisms originate from cleverness which is cheap and they only stimulate cleverness that has not the bloom of life but the finish of the manufactured article. In our country literature has not to live and grow under a blazing publicity as in the West and the man of letters is not constantly reminded that he is a literary man. This may not be stimulating but restful and I can say that for me restfulness is more important than the stimulant of a noisy public opinion. However, I should give anything to be able to take an Aeroplane flight and drop down at your door this moment. For I so want to talk to you about all manner of things! We have had our trials as you have had, but ours are all the more painful because it is not given to us to be able to take measures to redress our wrongs. We have to wait for a change of mind in others, wait under the menace of machine guns and the [Rowlatt] gagging act. What makes it intolerable for us is to know that truth will be suppressed scientifically, and those who have suffered injustice will also have to carry the burden of wrong judgment. It comes to me almost with the force of a new discovery that there is one thing which makes life worth living to us, it is doing some work, however small it may be, which is truly human, which has the beauty of the eternal about it and which may be safely and contemptuously ignored by the man gloating in the enjoyment of his unhallowed power. So, in order to forget that this life is a nightmare I have to serve these little boys I have gathered round me, teaching them elementary things and telling them stories. Their happiness, however momentary it may be, has an immense worth like the beauty of a flower that fades by the end of the day.   Ever yours

Rabindranath Tagore

133
Rothenstein to Tagore

Far Oakridge   August 15, 1919

My dear friend—Andrews writes that you are going to Australia & that there is really some solid prospect of your coming to us afterwards. We count upon your doing so—eight years is quite long enough to keep away. We shall hang banners from our castle turrets & maidens shall strew flowers before you all the way from Chalford to Oakridge. Further, besides the personal welcome, Sheffield University wishes to offer you a warm academic one. I hope you will listen to their proposals & will give them a lecture, or more. I suppose you will be lecturing in America too. You will like the Australians—they are keen & warm hearted people, eager in the pursuit of knowledge & responsive to those who, they think, can impart it. I was for a short time with their Education people at Cambridge, lecturing in lieu of military service & made many friends among them. One Bishop Long, of Bathurst, was their Head & a charming fellow he was. I hope you may meet him & others of my friends.[1] . . . Fox Strangways has just left us. He is proposing to edit a new musical quarterly which I feel sure will be very good.[2] The children now devote themselves wholeheartedly to music—you will I think be pleased with their singing. John goes to Oxford in October to read history. All send you affectionate greetings & look to seeing you next spring. Be sure of the welcome you will get from us all & not least from yours ever affectionately

William Rothenstein

1. Tagore accepted Australian lecture engagements and was to leave with Andrews in March 1920. (Andrews to Macmillan, July 20, 1919. MP:BM.) Almost at once the plan changed to an April 1920 departure, and arrival in the United States in the autumn. (Andrews to Brett, July 21, 1919. MP:NYPL.) The Rt. Rev. George Long (1875–1930), elected Bishop of Bathurst, 1911; Director of Education, A.I.F., 1918–19.

2. *Music and Letters* (London), edited by Fox Strangways, began publication in January 1920.

134
Rothenstein to Tagore

[Marl Bank, Worcester]   September 11, 1919

My very dear friend—I was glad to get your letter. But if you come to us you need not meet many more people than you saw before. Of course you will be pestered but you need not respond to all & sundry. . . . The news of your expected visit has caused joy at least in one household & you can always find a safe retreat from the crowd at Oakridge. I shall be interested to hear of your Australian experiences—I think you will find Australians large hearted & open minded—the best of them I mean. By the time you reach Europe I hope changes will have occurred. At present we are in a welter & painting is more than ever a solace. In fact any temptation one may have had to join in attempts at reform or rebuilding has gone—there are now so many cooks one feels no responsibility & one can devote oneself more quietly than ever to work. In our hearts we know this to be our normal state of mind—was it Yeats who said of some one we knew that he was too lazy to write a sonnet so he made a revolution? I know of no profounder saying.

I am at the moment staying in a musical atmosphere for the purpose of making a portrait of Sir Edward Elgar. He is anxious to meet you when you come over—but then, as you realise only too well, who isn't?[1]

John goes to Oxford next month & is reading hard. He promises well, I think, & has a very alert mind. Let me hear from you, if you can find time, from the Antipodes. In the meanwhile I am ever yours affectionately

William Rothenstein

1. Edward Elgar (1857–1934), composer. See *Music and Letters,* 1 (1920), 7. Rothenstein's drawing of Elgar was the first in his series of English composers, done at Fox Strangways' request, now in the National Portrait Gallery, London.

Sir Edward Elgar, drawing by Rothenstein.
Courtesy of National Portrait Gallery, London

135
Tagore to Rothenstein

Shanti Niketan September 18, 1919

Dearest Friend

This is the last hour of the last day this week when foreign letters should be posted and I come rushing to my desk to tell you that the last two letters I got from you have given me great delight. Your appreciation of my book I value more than all the favourable criticisms I read in the papers. For your insight reaches not merely the literary worth of a writing but its humanity.

I feel I cannot go to England just now. One of the reasons is that I cannot afford to bear the cost. But the most important one of them is that I cannot leave my school for any length of time. In India what we have is small and that has to be guarded with sleepless attention. Our scope for work is narrow and our resources also. And therefore we have to make our insignificant works great in spiritual value by dedicating our life to them and sacrificing our ambitions which distract our mind from them in the least. My school becomes a mere school, one among thousands, foolishly proud of its petty success, unless I impart my soul to it by giving it all that I have. You have in your country great institutions, standing high upon the basis of inherited magnificence, which expand your minds by mere association with them—but most of ours are in ruins and our field of new creations is pitifully limited, hedged in with restrictions. This is the reason why I feel it necessary to turn away my soul from its surroundings of sordid prospect by creating its own field of activity with utmost truth and devotion. It is a very small corner of the world where I have taken my shelter and I must make it great for myself by building the temple of my God in this spot. With my love to you all   Ever yours

Rabindranath Tagore

136
Rothenstein to Tagore

> The University, Sheffield
> October 21, 1919

My very dear friend—I was glad, as always, to hear from you. But of course we are all disappointed to learn that you have given up your plans for lecturing, for this robs us of the chance of having you with us, as we hoped, next spring. I am hoping you may change your mind between now and then. I understand your disinclination to leave India. But I do think, from more than one point of view, that a journey to England might be a fruitful one. What you feel about your school I can realise also —perhaps especially well at this moment. The air is noisy with schemes—the noise is no easier to bear because it carries the aristocratic name of reconstruction. One has more than ever before the certainty that to perform one's own task as well as possible is the only way in which one can live decently, & the smaller the place in which one can work the better. We are suffering from a loose & flabby amateurishness of spirit; Everyman has become a reconstructor, as he was a decadent thirty years ago, a pragmatist twenty years ago, a Morrisite or Whistlerite or a superman, a new woman or a Samurai.[1] There is the same lack of hardness & clearness of thought characteristic of all amateur yearnings. The world is like a school, promising in its advertisements attention to science & art, handicrafts, music, classics & the humanities, but employing slovenly minds to instruct & poor cooks to feed the bodies entrusted to it. The sense of the need there is for true service entices some of us into the hiring fair, but we must all soon creep back to our little corners, realising that to educate oneself & to make a few things well, so long as strength is with us, is our truest service. I can imagine what comfort your school gives you, for it is, as you say, your own, & the boys are your own children.

    I was pressed to speak about you for the opening lecture of the English Association here & I spoke & read some of your poems to a deeply attentive audience at the University yesterday. And my mind turned back to those early days, when Calderon's rendering of your story was just given in London.[2]

1. Samurai: see H. G. Wells, *A Modern Utopia* (New York, 1905), pp. 258–317.

2. Text ends here; this unfinished letter was forwarded with another note from Rothenstein on November 18, 1919 (R-S). "Calderon's rendering": *The Maharani of Arakan: A Romantic Comedy in One Act* (London, 1915), George Calderon's adaptation of Tagore's story, "Dāliyā" [Daliya] (1894), *R-R*, XVI, 312–320: "Daliya," *Housewarming*, pp. 13–21. First performed July 30, 1912, at the Royal Albert Hall, by the Indian Dramatic Society. Sturge Moore had thought the adaptation "all out of keeping. It should have been a naive and Puvis de Chavanny thing and instead . . . a touch of watered-down Shaw Burlesque." (Thomas to Marie Sturge Moore, October 14, 1912. TSM.) A revival at the Coliseum, June 19–July 8, 1916, starred Lena Ashwell, who had misgivings about the production, as well she might. (Lena Ashwell to Rothenstein, June 23 [1916]. RP:HL.) The play competed on a variety bill with such items as a "Naval Song Scene," motorcycling seals, a ventriloquist, and Alfredo the Vagabond Violinist. Calderon (1868–1915) was reported missing in action at Gallipoli and presumed dead.

137
Tagore to Rothenstein

Santiniketan December 9, 1919

My dearest friend, . . . I have given up the idea of going to Australia, for I feel that my school has come to that stage when my watchful presence and concentrated attention is necessary. Then again, I have developed a very strong distaste for creating anything like a noise in connection with myself. It is far better to leave the world indebted to you and go without claiming or receiving your dues than be dismissed with daily wages and a bonus at the year's end. I feel that there is something vulgar in receiving praise in the way praise is meted out in the modern marketplace. For the place is fearfully crowded and the atmosphere is turbid with din and dust raised by elbowing claimants and partisans. Fame nowadays has its immense money value, and it gets sleek and fleshy with prosperity [,] losing grace. I am sure, obscurity is necessary for those who have the gift of creation; it protects the unconscious bloom and delicacy of life from the rude handling of trade. Anyhow, I feel that my place is here in this remote corner of the earth with children for my companions, who never suspect in me any worthiness greater than or different from their own.

I must not approach your threshold without some gift for Rachel. Unfortunately, Andrews who used to collect postage stamps for me from the heavy mail I receive, is away in S. Africa. But I find I have some old Japanese paper money of historical value which I am sure will be appreciated by her—for she can earn the proud distinction of making a gift of them to some of your university museums. With my love to you all
Ever yours
           Rabindranath Tagore

VI   1920-1922   Letters 138-151

"A Passing Breeze"

Events between the years of 1920 and 1922 produced the rift that Rothenstein would recall as "a passing breeze."[1] For him and for Tagore 1920 marked a turning point. Rothenstein left his beloved Oakridge and returned to London as Principal of the Royal College of Art. Tagore became absorbed in plans for his new institution, Visva-Bharati. The painter and the poet were heads of conspicuous educational institutions and heirs to all the joys and tribulations thereof.

Their new roles should have forged a new bond between them, and for a time this was the case. Plans shelved since 1914 were taken up, but, just as the Nobel Prize had forced Tagore and his works along an apparently irreversible path, now Visva-Bharati seized control of its creator. The "passing breeze" was that only in retrospect. In the immediate event it was a genuine storm, the explosion of long-accumulated pressures. It stirred up the deepest feelings of both men about their relations to their respective arts, and it caused a lingering sea change in their friendship.

In 1920, when Tagore set out at last to see his English friends and, with a genuine sense of mission, to raise money for Visva-Bharati, he seemed oblivious to the storm whose signals had been plain on the horizon for several years. In correspondence with the Macmillan firms he remained apparently unaware of the lengths to which they had gone during the war to avoid damaging his reputation by reducing prices on his books or remaindering unsold stocks. Political affairs, also, he misjudged. The poet who understood so well the feelings of Bengali peasants and students, women and children, failed grievously to gauge the temper of the general public in the West. The United States was running full tilt into the twenties, a difficult time for

1. See Prologue.

idealists. Gandhi's activities alarmed even those Englishmen who attributed "Indian unrest" to nationalism's lunatic fringe; the fact that Gandhi, at Andrews' suggestion, had moved his Phoenix School from South Africa to temporary headquarters at Santiniketan in 1915 must have caused conservative officials to view the Visva-Bharati plan with some misgivings, and Tagore's courageous resignation of his knighthood in 1919 struck both officials and nonofficials as a deliberate insult to King, Crown, and Empire.[2]

In England, Tagore allowed himself and his old friends little time to recapture the spirit of his earlier visits. There was sporadic work with Sturge Moore on new translations of poems. There were proofs of a new volume of stories. A translation of his novel *Noukādubi* [*The Wreck*] was being passed glumly from hand to hand.[3] His days were consumed principally by

2. See M. K. Gandhi, *Speeches and Writings of Mahatma Gandhi*, 4th ed. (Madras [1933]), p. 191. See above, Letter 131, note 3.

3. "New . . . poems": three manuscript collections, *The Fugitive*, *The Wayside*, *The Farewell Curse*, from which poems were selected for the single volume, *The Fugitive*. (Typescript with autograph revisions by Tagore and Sturge Moore. TSM.) Final revision was left to Sturge Moore. (Sturge Moore to Macmillan [July 24, 1920]. MP:BM.)

"New . . . stories": *Broken Ties and Other Stories* [trans. various writers] (London, 1925). Tagore asked that credits not specify that only "Giribala" was his own translation. He had dictated drafts of the other stories to Andrews and Pearson but disliked their versions and had rewritten them. (Tagore to Macmillan, August 20, 1920. MP:BM.) However, see his "Mānbhanjan" [Appeasement] (1895), *R-R*, XX, 197–207: "Giribala," trans. "by the author," *Broken Ties and Other Stories*, pp. 177–192: "Appeasement," *Housewarming*, pp. 69–78.

"His novel": *Noukādubi* [Sunken Boat] (1906), in *R-R*, V, 165–432: *The Wreck* [trans. J. G. Drummond] (London, 1921). Macmillan had approved of several chapters of a translation by John Drummond (1884–1958), Indian Civil Service, Bengal, 1908–1936. (Drummond to Macmillan, April 10, 1920. MP:BM.) Tagore disclaimed ability to pass literary judgment on Drummond's work but found it otherwise satisfactory. (Drummond to Macmillan, August 6, 1920. MP:BM.) He told Macmillan, however, that it lacked the flavor of the Bengali text and requested revision by another writer. (Tagore to Macmillan, August 20, 1920. MP:BM.) Sturge Moore accepted, provided he not be "responsible in this case for more than slips of the pen and printer's errors and [I] am not to clear out any Bengali equivalents to Gallicisms which are so apt to disfigure these translations." (Sturge Moore to Macmillan, August 22, 1920. MP:BM.) Tagore then requested stylistic revision; Sturge Moore replied: "I am returning Dr. Tagore's novel, a great part of which I have read making a few slight corrections. To make it much better than it is would require a great deal more time than I can possibly spare." (Sturge Moore to Macmillan, August 30, 1920. MP:BM.)

speaking engagements, press interviews, and luncheons with miscellaneous assortments of eminent persons. Much of the time allotted to the Rothensteins was spent, not in long intimate talks at Oakridge, but in receiving other visitors who called on Tagore at the Rothensteins' London home. There was almost none of that idyllic atmosphere of the summer of 1912, when John Rothenstein leaned from his bedroom window at Oakridge to hear Yeats reading from the *Gitanjali* manuscripts on the terrace below.[4] Rothenstein had not asked time to stand still, but he felt the difference and told Max Beerbohm: "Tagore has just gone off to accept the homage of the neutral countries. He is to go on a long lecturing tour in America in October. Having seen a book of essays by his hand [*Personality*] illustrated by a hundred views of Tagore in America, I tried to persuade him to stay in Europe. . . . Alas, that the strong wine of praise, and the weak wine of worship, should have gone to this good man's head. It is a misfortune for a poet to be too handsome; . . . Perhaps adulation is a habit—I mean the receiving of it. At any rate, he is turning his back on the thin stream he can wash his feet in here, for the great gushing river he can bathe in in the New World."[5]

Tagore confirmed Rothenstein's feeling that he went away disappointed: "Our stay in England has been wasted," he told Andrews. Until October he fidgeted around Europe: "I came to Paris, not to stay here but to decide where to go."[6] Late in October he did go to the United States, in hopes of raising five million dollars for Visva-Bharati.[7]

Between October 6, 1920, and Tagore's return to England in March 1921, the correspondence with Rothenstein breaks off. That October 6 letter is an aggressive attempt to justify his actions and attitudes. He cast off the regimen of literary craftsmanship: "For a literary man the greatest joy is in the expression of his personality." He cast off England, for "my relationship with the Continental Europe is natural and unobstructed,

---

4. See John Rothenstein, *Summer's Lease: Autobiography, 1901–1938* (New York, 1965), p. 44.
5. Rothenstein to Beerbohm, August 5 [1920]. Rothenstein Papers: William Andrews Clark Memorial Library of the University of California at Los Angeles.
6. Tagore, *Letters to a Friend,* p. 90.
7. See Hay, "Rabindranath Tagore in America," p. 452.

Rabindranath Tagore in London, pastel by Edmond X. Kapp

being disinterested." He cast off Indian nationalism: "I have nothing to do directly with politics"—a statement he contradicted a few sentences later.[8]

He wished for freedom in an impossible separation, but he could no more cast off the demands of literary craftsmanship, or his indebtedness to England, or his involvement with Indian nationalism, than he could cast off his own nature. His letters from America record his progressive disillusionment.[9] There were bright intervals with old friends, but the tone of his letters, which Harriet Moody's biographer calls "the playfully wounded vein . . . as of a person who was persistently imposed upon by the universe," disguised a deepening depression and fatigue.[10] On March 19, 1921, he left for England, but he stayed only three weeks before rushing away again to the Continent.

His mood is caught by a drawing made during those weeks in England, not by Rothenstein but by Edmond X. Kapp, who drew Tagore in his robes and a tall black velvet turban. This is not the gracefully elegant figure of Rothenstein's drawings, but a lean and somber, almost gaunt Tagore, rigid and resigned. Rigid with fatigue he certainly was, as his letters show, and resigned to his growing obsession that the political might of Britain was arrayed against his embryo university, a Tagore not "playfully" but desperately wounded.[11]

Yet, in the United States, Tagore had literally walked away from one of his most generous potential supporters: Mrs. Dorothy Straight, widow of Willard Straight and benefactress of Cornell University. She asked Tagore to call and tell her more about his plans, but he made no effort to see her again. Soon afterward she met Leonard Elmhirst, then a graduate student at Cornell, and learned that he was going to India to take charge of Sriniketan, Tagore's rural reconstruction project near Santiniketan. Mrs. Straight told Elmhirst that she wanted to help Tagore but had found him very unbusinesslike. She finally gave Tagore a large sum of money for Sriniketan—on condi-

---

8. Letter 141.
9. Tagore, *Letters to a Friend,* pp. 98–150.
10. Dunbar, *A House in Chicago,* p. 177.
11. Tagore " 'chanted' " (i.e. recited) Bengali poems while sitting, and Mr. Kapp was unaware at the time of his perturbed state of mind. (Interview with E. X. Kapp, London, September 24, 1969.)

tion that Elmhirst administer it. One must wonder how many such opportunities Tagore missed when no Elmhirst was at hand!¹²

From November 1921 until July 1923 Elmhirst was in charge at Sriniketan, and his diary helps to fill some of the gaps in Tagore's interrupted correspondence with Rothenstein. In Elmhirst's affectionate but not uncritical view, Tagore is a man endeavoring to hold fast to sound original concepts that were in danger of being warped in the execution; to resist the attempts of Andrews (whom Tagore, somewhat wryly, dubbed "Sir Charles") to introduce Gandhian politics into Santiniketan affairs; and to keep bureaucratic obtuseness and Bengali resistance to self-help from hobbling the work at Sriniketan. "The Poet is not always a Philosopher," Elmhirst observed, "and sometimes his natural bitterness against certain gross aspects of British imperial behavior peeps out from under his normal philosophical calm. Among the British in Britain are still some of his very best friends, but as a nation they have never accorded him the kind of public ovations and popular enthusiasm that he met with recently on the Continent of Europe and especially in postwar Germany."¹³ Elmhirst has described Tagore as an "eminently grabbable person," who unfortunately allowed the wrong persons to grab him too often. He would refocus on his stated goals, and eventually reach them, but he frequently left behind a trail of confusion and consternation.¹⁴ The Tagore of this period whom Elmhirst characterizes thus is not the benign sage acclaimed on the Continent, but he is a more human, more understandable being: a lonely, affectionate man whose long-delayed reunion with his friends has somehow failed to rekindle the old fires, a prophet acclaimed in Europe but his honors diminishing in his own land and in the lands of his adopted mother tongue.

12. Interview with Leonard Elmhirst, Totnes, Devon, September 2, 1969. L. K. Elmhirst (1893–   ), Director, Institute of Rural Reconstruction, Visva-Bharati, 1921–1924; Founder-President, International Conference of Agricultural Economists, 1939–1953; Director, Dartington Hall Trust, Totnes. Willard Straight (1880–1918), United States Consular Service, East Asia, 1905–1909; founder, *Asia* (New York), 1900; after 1913 an associate of J. P. Morgan. He died in Paris, of pneumonia contracted during a mission related to War Risk Insurance.
13. Elmhirst diary, entry for January 18, 1922.
14. Interview with Leonard Elmhirst, London, August 14, 1967.

138
Rothenstein to Tagore

Far Oakridge   January 5, 1920

My very dear friend—I was delighted to hear from you. Only your letter comes at a moment when it serves to give an additional stab to my heart. For we are proposing to migrate, not to Egypt with the storks, but to London with the sparrows. The question of the children's education has become a pressing one —Rachel wants to study music, Betty is a promising musician too & a good artist in her way & Billy has to go to some sort of school. It is not a question of training the girls to be professional artists, but of giving them what no other teaching can do, an understanding of some of the beauty which many girls miss & a human view of men & women. I believe they are the better for having missed school life; but they now want more than a governess can teach them & I think they have done enough grammar and arithmetic. Music means so much to them, that I want to do all I can to get them good music. Billy is so clearly an artist, that he again needs no public school; so we have taken a house & studio in Kensington & move, if all goes well, next March. I doubt whether I can possibly keep two houses going. I, like yourself, cannot easily sell my wares in the public market place, & do not desire to make a large income—& in these days one house costs enough for any artist, without having to worry over the upkeep of a second one. So this beautiful place, which we have helped into being, will probably shelter alien souls & we hope at least we may find tenants who will appreciate it. But these seven years have been fruitful ones for the children. . . . And what a dangerous world all these young people have to face! Can it ever be anything but a dangerous world? Man's practical sense is so wanting that he seems unable to realise that evil is not likely to bring forth good, or untruth truth. When twenty years ago a few of us realised certain things regarding Indian affairs we were told that there was nothing wrong—only a few overeducated Bengalis were trying to make mischief. The same thing applies to Egypt. And if India gets the power she wants, she in her turn will be blind & deaf despite the eyes of a few of her own people. Could anything be more lamentable than the actual result of Mazzini's dreams & Garibaldi's endurance? And now what is called "Labour" here is beginning a new tyranny, forging new iron plates under which men's senses are to be imprisoned. So men are once again turning in despair of man towards the inner light, hoping as men have always hoped to find solace there. This is as it should be; but one cannot help wishing for true men who shall have the courage in public life good men have in their private lives. How many Gandhis have you in India—very few I fear. France in her bitterness has done us all great harm. Yet there are as many fine men there as anywhere else—such men as Anatole France, Romain Rolland, Henri Barbusse & others who suffer from their country's—& other countries'—folly & blindness. And in our own circle we only meet with humane & generous views of life. The difficulty seems to be to get a general expression of these views. In the meanwhile you have your school & I my bits of paper & canvas & we must make these mean as much as we can. I deeply regret your decision not to leave India—we all regret it—but I do understand what keeps you there. We all send most affectionate greetings. Ever yours—

William Rothenstein

139
Rothenstein to Tagore

[18 Sheffield Terrace, London]
March 14 [1920]

My dear friend—I open my letter to add a line in answer to a letter I have just had from Pearson. I am glad to read that you do really look forward to returning to us here. As for the Continent, I don't think you will want to make any plans for travelling. The bitterness & material ruin & desolation caused by the war will take long in healing. We shall all be too busy repairing what has been destroyed to think of travelling, & few people among us will have the means to do anything of the kind. No, you will know yourself welcome here whenever you come: such as it is our home here will be your home. But the future for us here is heavily veiled & no one can see beyond to-day. We have dark days to go through yet, & these are not days for making plans. So if you need a companion, you must think of someone else, for alas, I have neither the time, nor the inclination, for any wandering. My art is a long & difficult one, & needs all my devotion. I have not found anything else in life so consoling. I have my children, & my friends, & these are a prop & support to my courage & vision. I would not, even though I could, put my friendship with anyone to the test of travel; an artist leading an artist is the blind leading the blind. I am neither practical, nor business-like, nor strong enough in the nerves to envisage anything of the kind, but on the contrary, I am nervous & irritable, & much as I love France, I have not been there [in peacetime] for years on account of the discomfort of journeys of all kinds to me. So you may think yourself lucky in escaping my companionship abroad, if you really mean to consider anything of the kind. My own advice is "don't." Come to England & see your many friends here. Then when you tire of us you can think of going further afield. But the Continent will scarcely be a comfortable place for travellers for some time to come, I feel. None of us will want to go to Central Europe for many years to come, I fear, & France and Italy will need all our help towards reconstruction & refertilising, where her landscape is as a landscape in the moon.

In the meanwhile you will have the joy of returning to your own sheltered asram once more & the boys the happiness of having you back among them. Once more our affectionate greetings.

I enclose a letter of Rachel's, forgotten long since on my desk!

[William Rothenstein]

140
Tagore to Rothenstein

60 Kensington Palace Mansions [London]
July 31, 1920

My dearest Friend

We are busy preparing to leave England and I do not think I shall be able to come back here before I sail for America. The expenses of my stay here have been a great deal more than we calculated and can easily bear, and this has compelled us to book our passage from the French port which saves us more than a hundred pounds in Railway and steamer fare. I am desperately in need of raising funds for my school—and I see no other way but lecturing in America which is far more practicable for me than highway robbery or motor car raids, considering my training and other circumstances.[1]

It was fortunate for me to have been able to secure our lodging near your place and meet you once again as I believe this is going to be my last visit to this country. For I am growing old and things are changing fast making all communications difficult between different peoples. I am more convinced than ever that it is an intolerable presumptuousness for an individual to think that he has any special mission to do good. All that is claimed of him is to be true to himself and the good will come of itself unasked. So I must go back to my own place and my own work asking for no reward in the shape of success but only the inner guidance that instinctively finds its own goal.

I hope some day you will be able to come to India and see me among my boys. I always feel I cannot give a clear view of myself to my English friends, I am altogether out of perspective in this country.

Gorky's picture of Tolstoy is splendid in its brutal frankness but I cannot feel sure how much of it is Gorky and how much Tolstoy. It seems to me a composite picture in which both their features mingle. I feel that a true biography can only be written by a man whose nature is in harmony with his subject. I felt while reading this book that the instrument was wrong for the expression of the music, just as you felt when the Indian singer used piano for his accompaniment. Somehow the filthiness appears to me as out of proportion to the greatness of Tolstoy's character as depicted in this book, for which possibly the artist himself is responsible—for wrong emphasis may be stronger in its untruth than wrong words we use in our description.[2] With my love for you all. Ever yours

Rabindranath Tagore

1. Tagore had arrived in London on June 5, accompanied by Rathindranath, Pratima, and a grandniece. They had expected Pearson to arrange lodging for them, but this was done by the Rothensteins. Tagore soon began drawing heavily against future royalties. (Tagore to Macmillan, July 27, 1920. MP:BM.)

2. Maxim Gorky, *Reminiscences of Leo Nikolaevich Tolstoy,* trans. S. S. Koteliansky and Leonard Woolf (New York, 1920), in which Tolstoy appears robust and earthy. "Indian singer": Dilip Roy, Cambridge student, during a musical evening at the Rothensteins'. (See Roy, *Among the Great* [Bombay, 1945], p. 155.)

141
Tagore to Rothenstein

Grand Hotel Britannique, Brussels
October 6, 1920

Dearest friend, the continual enjoyment of sympathy and fellowship with which I have been surrounded since I came to the Continent makes it so difficult for me to sit down and write letters. I can hardly realise how it has become possible for me to have occupied the hearts of these people to which I could only find access through a very meagre and imperfect medium of translation. The welcome which has been accorded to me in all the countries that I have travelled in Europe has been deeply genuine and generous to the extreme. This makes it delightfully easy for me to give out the best that I have in me in an easy flow of communication. For a literary man the greatest joy is in the expression of his personality. It is a light which shines in its perfection of truth only where the atmosphere is transparent. I feel it clear that my relationship with the Continental Europe is natural and unobstructed, being disinterested. In England, I have distinctly felt in my last visit, it is obscured owing, I am sure, to the politics that ever stands between our people and yours, consciously or unconsciously. I have nothing to do directly with politics. I am not a Nationalist, moderate or immoderate in my political doctrine or aspiration. But politics is not a mere abstraction, it has its personality and it *does* intrude into my life where I am human. It kills and maims individuals, it tells lies, it uses its sacred sword of judgment justice for the purpose of massacre,[1] it spreads misery broadcast over centuries of exploitation, and I cannot say to myself, "Poet, you have nothing to do with these facts, for they belong to politics." This politics assumes its fullest diabolical aspect when I find all its hideous acts of injustice find moral support from a whole nation only because it wants to enjoy in comfort and safety the golden fruits reaped from abject degradation of human races. What hurts me most is the fact that your people are ready to judge others while they shield themselves from the judgment of history by all means of moral camouflage, by obliteration of evidence of misdeeds with scientific efficiency and farsightedness which were not within the means of our former rulers. But all the same judgement will come when the time is ripe; and because your politicians are conscious of that fact they are nervously busy in tightening their grasp upon the present situation, thinking that by doing so they will keep the future as their captive. I am sorry to be writing in this vein, but, I suppose, evil has its terrible fascination, and I cannot help reading newspaper in which the organised hooliganism of the Military Government in Ireland is daily being revealed and I daily wonder how can a Nation allow such things to pass or try to seek a comfortable hidingplace for its conscience behind thick walls of hypocricy and suppression of truth. It makes me almost physically ill and feel ashamed of comfort and freedom which as an individual I am allowed to enjoy. You have read the Esher Commission report and you know what it is going to be for our unfortunate country. More army, more expenditure, more taxation when the cost of living has risen higher than two hundred percent. This will make your Reform Bill a cruel mockery for us.[2] It is merely sweeping away the very little money the country has and then leave to her all the bills of the cost of education and other vital necessaries, to pay. The mockery will grow in cruelty enormously when after a few years you will blame us for not carrying out any constructive programme satisfactorily though opportunity was given. All this politics means untold misery to a people held forcible fixed to a state of helplessness for all time to come. But you must know that the downfall of your Empire is imminent when the moral downfall of your people is proceeding in a rapid pace. It is right and natural that you will put more and more faith upon brute force for holding together your unwieldy Empire, making it so monstrously ugly that the whole outraged world will pull it down in disgust. Your bloated prosperity is a barrier that prevents you to see what bearers of doom are silently marshalling their forces against you till the sudden signal is given from the dark.³

I hope you will be able to make allowance for any bitterness in my language in this letter which may seem to you as unwarrantable. Ever yours

Rabindranath Tagore

   1. Tagore struck out "judgment."
   2. The Indian Army was supported by taxes collected in India. Reginald Brett, 2nd Viscount Esher (1852–1930), had helped to reorganize Army Command in 1903–4; after 1905 he was a permanent member of a commission to examine the status of the Indian Army.
   3. This "sudden signal given from the dark" echoes Tagore's diary entry for September 19, 1890, a comment on cooperative activity as society's salvation. Europe, he felt, was pulling against itself, and he would not be surprised if the Africa of the future conquered Europe, for "the night comes out of Africa to overwhelm the bright day of Europe. . . . where darkness is gathering, there danger gathers strength in hiding." (Quoted by Mukhopadhyay in *Rabindrajibani,* I, 271.)

142
Tagore to Rothenstein

>Autour du Monde, 9 Quai du 4-Septembre
>Boulogne-sur-Seine   April 17, 1921¹

Dear friend, my short career in the sky was unobscured by clouds and luminous with the April sunshine. The only thing to which I could take objection was the deafening noise which followed me from shore to shore and made me glad to be back to the earth again where one has the choice of diluting all noise with silence as much as it is available.

Let me remind you of our conversation about the International University. It was decided that a committee should be formed in England which would help the committee in India about the selection of teachers and students belonging to Europe and about other matters which would be more convenient for them to deal with. I hope it will be possible for you with the help of Mr Montagu Lord Carmichael and other sympathisers to make a draft of rules and a list of names of those who will be likely to join us.² I have reasons to hope that some oriental society in this country can be persuaded to represent us in France and work in our behalf.³ A considerable number of books have been gathered and sent to our library from here and I feel certain that I can count upon the sympathy and co-operation of some influential persons in this country.⁴

I am afraid I shall have to be extremely busy the few days that I spend in Paris, in fact, all through my tour in the Continent. But I shall be able to bear the strain knowing that my appeal will find response in all countries of Europe.

You will be glad to learn that the French translation of my Home and the World has, as I am told, gone through six editions within a very short time.⁵ Affectionately yours

Rabindranath Tagore

1. On April 19 and 21 Tagore and Rathindranath called on Romain Rolland, who noted that Rabindranath, despite his charming manner, seemed convinced of the moral and intellectual superiority of the East, and of India in particular, over Europe. (See Rolland, *Inde: Journal [1915–1943]*, rev. ed. [Paris, 1960], p. 20.) For Tagore's itinerary, October 1920 to April 1921, see Hay, "Rabindranath Tagore in America," pp. 452–456; Mukherjee, *Passage to America,* pp. 85–92, 214–215.)

2. Montagu was still Secretary of State for India. Thomas Gibson-Carmichael, 1st Baron of Skirling (1859–1926), Governor of Madras, 1911–12; Governor of Bengal, 1912–1917. Rothenstein hoped to recruit Herbert Fisher and Michael Sadler as well, altogether a group impressively influential, well-disposed, and well-informed. Tagore had asked James Woods to help start a similar committee in the United States. (Tagore to Woods, December 14, 1920. David G. Williams.) Neither committee materialized.

3. Perhaps the Société des Amis d'Oriente, Paris.

4. The London Macmillans had already given the Santiniketan library a large collection of books. (Tagore to Macmillan, April 8, 1921. MP:BM.)

5. Tagore, *La Maison et le monde* [*The Home and the World*], trans. F. Roger-Cornaz (Paris, 1921).

143
Rothenstein to Tagore

Royal College of Art   April 23, 1921

My very dear friend—I was glad to hear news of your arrival & of your journey through the sky. Of this I was a little envious—were this form of transit open to me I would often visit the City of Light.¹ I went to dine with Lord Carmichael last night, to talk over your great scheme. He fully realises the importance of it & believes important things will come of it. He feels, as you know, as strongly as I do that a committee of Trustees should first be formed. This committee will primarily rid you of much personal responsibility & will give responsible backing to your project. Until you have something of the kind it will be difficult for you to get the people you want, true scholars, to go out to India, & as things are now, there is the danger of people whom you don't want streaming in. Of all things you have to guard against anything like Adyar.[2] The young Austrian-Slovakian lady came to see me yesterday to ask if I could help her to get a passport for India. But Lord Carmichael tells me that, however willing Mr Montagu may be, & other people in the India Office, to help you, the Foreign Office, at this particular time, is most unlikely to issue passports to any foreigners, save those having clear reasons for going to India & the backing of their embassies so far as their appropriateness is concerned. When things have settled down in India, there will not be the same difficulty; in this particular case I believe you owe me a cock. For I have saved you from the results of an invitation which the recipient, had she been quite worthy of it, would not have [been] quite so ready to accept. One wants more than a single meeting, on either side, in such important affairs. Perhaps I am unduly suspicious of the softer sex. But when great things have to be carried through, I doubt whether it is wise to encumber yourself with almond eyed ladies, however devoted to stupas & Boddhisatras.[3]

I think you should return, after your European tour, & see Sadler.

Carmichael tells me all sorts of people are coming over regarding Calcutta University & that, if you could put your scheme clearly before people here, such as Sadler, it is precisely the moment for doing so.[4]

I could wish the difficulties less apparent & above all, the presence by your side of someone who would take them on his own shoulders, leaving it to you to inspire men with the strength of your own convictions—some one used to administrative problems, whose vision & judgement would commend themselves to men of affairs.

Until you have found this rare but still obtainable bird, I would venture to counsel caution, so far as actual promises & invitations are concerned. You don't want to entangle yourself. It will take time before a scheme is formulated, buildings equipped, & you are ready to receive scholars. All sorts of questions will have to be threshed out before you can get your ship under weigh & there would be confusion if an attempt were made to start before charts & compasses were provided.

None of your friends wish to see you snowed under by a thousand details best left to less capable minds but more practical heads than yours. To impress caution on others is never an heroic role; but I must play it, seeing that the great parts are more easily filled.

I send you my warmest greetings: it was a great delight to have you back among us for a short time. I could wish you here again, with leisure to talk quietly over many things; but for the minutes we snatched from the many "people of importance" who claimed your time I am grateful. There are few men with whom talk is more peaceful & inspiring than with yourself & we have, you & I, much, I think, in our view of life, in common. Ever yours affectionately

W. R.

1. At this stage, principally a matter of nerves, but perhaps related to the heart condition diagnosed in 1925.

2. Theosophical Society ashram and headquarters near Madras.

3. The lady was Dr. Stella Kramrisch (1898–   ), Professor of Indian Art, Calcutta University, 1923–1950; Lecturer, Courtauld Institute, London, 1937–1940; Professor to Emeritus Professor of South Asian Art, University of Pennsylvania, 1950–   ; Curator of Indian Art, Philadelphia Museum of Art, 1954–   ; editor, *Journal of the Indian Society for Oriental Art*, 1932–   .

4. Those coming to London on behalf of Calcutta University went virtually unrecognized in Parliamentary debate. Two years later Herbert Fisher asked what was being done to implement the findings of Michael Sadler's Calcutta University Commission, and the Under Secretary of State for India replied in flawless bureaucratese: "Owing to financial and other difficulties it has not so far been possible to give effect to the proposals of the Commission in regard to the University of Calcutta, but the complex problems involved are receiving most careful consideration by the Government of Bengal." (*The Parliamentary Debates* [*Official Record*], series 5 [C], [April 11, 1923], vol. 162, col. 1228.)

144
Tagore to Rothenstein

> Autour du Monde, Boulogne-sur-Seine
> April 24, 1921

My dear friend, when I sent my appeal to Western people for an International Institution in India I made use of the word "University" for the sake of convenience. But that word not merely has an inner meaning but outer associations in minds of those who use it, and that fact tortures my idea into its own rigid shape. It is unfortunate. I should not allow my idea to be pinned to a word like a dead butterfly for a foreign museum. It must be known not by a definition, but by its own life growth. I saved my Santiniketan from being trampled into smoothness by the steam roller of your Education department. It is poor in resources and equipment but it has the wealth of truth that no money can ever buy. I am proud of the fact that it is not a machine-made article perfectly modelled in your workshop—it is our very own. If we must have a university it should spring from our own life and be sustained by it. You may say that such freedom is dangerous and that a machine will help to lessen our personal responsibility and make things easy for us. Yes, life has its risks and freedom its responsibility—and yet they are preferable for their own immense value and not for any other ulterior results. Now I am beginning to discover that it was more an ambition than an ideal which dragged me to the gate of the rich West. It must have been the vision of a big undertaking that lured me away from my seclusion in search of big means and big results. And I am being punished deep in my heart. So long I have been able to retain my perfect independence and self respect because I had faith in my own resources and proudly worked within their sovereign limits. This is the first time in my life when I have come to the foreign door asking for help and co-operation. But such help has to be bought with a price that is ruinous, and the bird has to accept its cage if it must be fed with comfort and regularity. However, my bird must still retain its freedom of wings and not be turned into a sumptuous nonentity by any controlling agency outside its own living organism. I know that the idea of an International University is complex, but I must make it simple in my own way. I shall be content if it attracts round it men who have neither name nor worldly means, but who have the mind and faith, who are to create a great future with their dreams. Very likely I shall never be able to work in harmony with a board of trustees, influential and highly respectable, for I am a vagabond at heart. But the powerful people of the world, the lords of the earth, may make it difficult for me to carry out my work. I know it, and I had experience of it in connection with my Santi Niketan and also in my tour in America. But am I afraid of failure? I am only afraid of being tempted away from truth in pursuit of success. The temptation assaults me occasionally I admit, but it comes from the outside atmosphere—my own abiding faith is in light and life and freedom, and my prayer is: "Lead me from the unreal to Truth."

This letter of mine is only to let you know that I free myself from the bondage of help and go back to the great Brotherhood of the Tramp, who seem helpless, but who are recruited by God for his own army. Ever yours

Rabindranath Tagore

145
Rothenstein to Tagore

18 Sheffield Terrace, London
April 28, 1921

My dear friend—indeed I am neither a believer in machines, nor an Inspector of Schools, nor an enemy of freedom; yet you write as though I were all these things. I think you mistake not myself only, but your own self too. For I believe you to be a poet, an inspirer of noble motives, a friend to all the gallant things that man has made & thought, a lover of the common things of life. I do not believe you to be a man of action & of affairs & I foresee many difficulties in your path if you take that dusty road. Your letter does not change my foreboding. To me you should point the way, but others should organise the road making—people who can deal with labourers & contractors better than you or I can do. I felt, when you were here, that some one must stand first of all between you & the quick sympathy of your heart. You say you do not want the learned & powerful; but likewise you do not want the campfollowers— of the arts & of the artists: these last are not the lowly & simple of heart. No, by no means.

Secondly, the life of man is short, but he can build fabrics which endure. And if you build well now, the foundations you are laying should support walls to outlast all of us now quick & strong. I still believe you need men of capacity & integrity to take certain responsibilities from your poet's shoulders. But you need not choose Europeans. Further, unpleasant & humiliating though it may be, the fact has to be envisaged that you cannot approach European scholars & leave English people unconsulted. If these last are not considered, you are making further difficulties for yourself. That is why I suggested you should return here before actually inviting foreign guests to stay with you in India.

But I realise that it is an ignoble thing to be sober when one's fellow guests are intoxicated; it is an attitude above all others hateful to me. You must admit you have taken full advantage of your jug of wine! My prayers will be for your noble venture. I think I know something of the vision that holds you & of the passionate desire to give rather than to take which possesses great hearts. So my blessing on your pilgrimage. No more sensible words shall come from me to irk your spirit. You shall lay the foundations of your city with your desires; these will make good mortar to hold the bricks & stones together. Ever yours

W. R.

All send affectionate greetings.

146
Tagore to Rothenstein

Geneva   May 8, 1921

My dear friend, when I was in America the British Agency thwarted me in my appeal to the people for the proposed University. An American friend, who is struggling against obstacles to raise funds for this object has lately informed me that the British Consul in his town is hindering him.[1] I am not trusted. How can I be certain that this mistrust which has nearly killed my mission by its antagonism will not kill it by its help? But possibly your point is that trying to be independent will not further my cause. That is true. It would be presumptuous for me to imagine that my project can thrive against suspicion lurking in the minds of British authorities. At the same time I feel strongly that it is far better to allow it openly to be strangled by that mistrust than to be fettered by its help. I remember your suggesting to me once in course of conversation that exuberant protestation of friendliness towards me on the part of the Continental people of Europe was easy because they had no responsibility with regard to such demonstrations. You were right. For disinterested relationship is the only pure channel through which sympathy and cooperation can have a clear flow. Possibly these very people would also be wisely suspicious in a similar case where they had their own interest to consider. I have often heard that when the French people tried to be hospitable to our Indian soldiers in the late war the British officers in charge of them were alarmed. It was easier for the French to be human and grateful towards those foreigners who came to fight for them than for the British officers who had their own anxieties about these soldiers which were not purely human. Similarly when I, who belong to a subject race under British rule, am too warmly received in America or in other Western countries, the British agency may feel uneasy—for their interest in me and my cause is not purely human and simple. Your contention is that the man who is sober in his mind accepts such facts as facts and deals with them accordingly and that it is a sign of moral drunkenness to be able to think that one can ignore them in pride of his self-sufficiency. But of one thing you may be certain that I have a natural power of resistance in me against intoxication produced by praise, and my mind at the present moment is not in a dazed state of drunkenness. I am not in the least oblivious of the fact that the breath of official suspiciousness can blight in a moment my cherished scheme. But I have already told you in my last letter that I try to follow the teaching of *Geeta* according to which all idealism should spurn to seek their value in success, but only in truth. So long as my motive is true, my method is honest and the process of my work open to the view of all comers from all countries I shall not be afraid ashamed of the meagreness of result,[2] poorness of appearance, or afraid of an utter failure at the hands of a ruling power which would hesitate to allow us freedom for giving expression to our higher nature. With love to you all   Ever yours

Rabindranath Tagore

1. Perhaps James Woods, but Tagore's letters to Woods make no mention of this. "British Agency": Criminal Investigation Department. Neither this nor similar subsequent charges are substantiated by evidence in any correspondence examined by the editor.

2. Tagore struck out "afraid."

147
Rothenstein to Tagore

Royal College of Art   [May 1921][1]

My dear friend—your letter saddens me. I believe you mistaken in your belief that the British authorities wish to hinder your project & I think it unkind to your friends here to suggest that their help will be would be as harmful to your scheme as their antipathy. I still think you are making needless difficulties for yourself—that you will have quite enough incalculable ones without these.

No one here wishes to prevent your giving expression to your higher nature: on the contrary, no one's higher nature is more admired than your own. But you have other people's needs to consider, not least those whom you are inviting to devote themselves to various tasks in India. You have funds to administer, & you have to consider the donors & helpers who are to assist you in setting up your ideal university at Bolpur.

Are you sure you are not taking away some of the freedom of these others, in seeking to pursue your own? There are many ways of following the teaching of Gita. Perhaps some of us too put truth before success even more as humbly & unobtrusively than as a great poet. For I do not feel your last letters are written from a friend to a friend, but seem as though written for other eyes than mine. It is clear you have no need, or rather, feel no need, for the counsel I can offer. I hope you wiser than I believe you to be without English cooperation but when you

I have enough freedom to. An artist always has sufficient freedom if he can shut himself in the prison of his workshop; it is when he opens his own studio door that servitude comes in & walks out into the open that his freedom is limited.

But I feel your letter to be less letter of a friend to a tried friend   So I shall shut myself up, & leave you, dear friend, to your own way great self. It is not I who wish to give counsel, but others that seek it too over-much for my peace of mind; & if you have no vanity I have not the strength or the health that many believe. Your letters are not   You should continue   may your wisdom prove better than mine, is the wish of yours ever

W. R.

You have now many friends & many counsellors and I have more tasks than I can fulfill before the sun sets. Ever yrs

Is it fair, if they are ready to answer your call, that you should put extra   should refuse to smooth some of the difficulties in their way?[2]

   1. Undated draft letter, apparently not copied or mailed. RP:HL.
   2. The draft is extensively revised. Rothenstein struck out "will be" in the first paragraph; "more" and "than" in the third sentence of the third paragraph, and the remainder of that paragraph from "For I do not feel . . ." He struck out the incomplete sentence at the beginning of the fourth paragraph, and the phrase, "that servitude comes in." In the fifth paragraph he struck out the incomplete sentence at the beginning, "way" in the next sentence, "too" and "if you have no vanity" in the next. "Your letters . . . is the wish" is struck out, and, in the second postscript, "put extra . . . some of the."

148
Rothenstein to Tagore

18 Sheffield Terrace, London
June 1 [1922]

My dear friend—it is long since I heard from you. Indeed the last letter you wrote me was to ask me not to do what you had previously pressed me to perform. I have no doubt my reply

Sylvain Lévi and Rabindranath Tagore at Santiniketan

showed some of the irritation I felt. But this scarcely seems a reason for the dropping of a friendship which was begun & continued, certainly with great gain & happines to myself & which you were used to assert was not altogether fruitless for yourself. I think it would be a pity if, travelling in triumph through Europe, you gave up for the praise of all men, the affection of a single friend. "For he had great possessions" I often feel means, or should mean, a great deal more than worldly goods. It is also possible that you are too busy to write; but it would seem a little ungrateful if you had no thought for one who had so much of your confidence when you were here & with whom you discussed your Bolpur plans so intimately. Of the fruit I have heard nothing, beyond the bare fact that your University is in being & that the most charming and distinguished of Professors & orientalists, Sylvain Lévi, is with you.[1] Such a man is worth a dozen of any other helpers I could think of & I have no doubt you will appreciate him to the full.

I suppose the many letters I had to write to get Dr Kramrisch into India are not to be worth one from herself; but she was so enthusiastic a pilgrim that I looked forward to hearing of her actual happiness, for I know how much more inspiring the Indian scene is than it is even in the excitement of one's imagination.[2] And if India is inspiring wherever one finds one's self, how much more must Bolpur satisfy one's hopes, Bolpur which I am never likely to see with my own eyes. I am told that India is no longer what it was when I paid my own eventful visit eleven years ago; but I imagine the changes to be more political & social than physical, though, alas, both East & West are at one in their creative weakness & we both look upon beauty as a thing to be preserved rather than created. Happily literature is still as active a force as ever & your own work has done more for India than all the archaeology of the schoolmen. I liked your last book very much.[3] Some day I hope to read translations of more novels.

Here our poets seem more gifted than our prose writers— a new Hardy volume has just come to enrich our store.[4] John spent his Easter holidays in Vienna & tells me how full the shops are of your books. We have Gordon Craig here, a brilliant and inspiring personality, in connection with an exhibition of theatrical art at S. Kensington Museum.[5] I think you met him when you first came to England. We miss Oakridge very much; but by keeping to one's work & daily duties one can live a fairly natural life in London. There is room everywhere for the exercise of one's good & one's bare faculties; four walls always leave one enough freedom to be generous or mean, Godfearing or careless, & he who rails against his material circumstances needs a doctor for his soul. The pursuit of truth through the practice of an art makes life a full & ever interesting thing, & when one has the privilege of constant intercourse with students, as both of us happily have, the day is all too short for what one would like to do. Let me have a line to give me news of yourself. I hope Pearson & Andrews are well & full of work. I expect to meet Lord Ronaldshay shortly, & to hear news of your artist nephews.[6] Ever yours affectionately—

William Rothenstein

1. Sylvain Lévi (1863–1935), distinguished French orientalist, at Santiniketan during a 1921–1923 tour of Asia.

2. Dr. Kramrisch apologized for her silence during months "spent in suspense and work. I often thought of what you had told me, still I feel that having gone through the fire has made me clearer. . . . I could not see much of the country up to now, but living in the nearness of Dr. Tagore makes me realise India in full intensity." She now lectured at Calcutta University and "the public seems to take a great interest in their own art which is quite unknown to them. . . . I sincerely hope that the Visva-Bharati will grow and develop. We all try to serve it with all our power and it has no other basis than its ideal and our surrender." (Stella Kramisch to Rothenstein, August 30, 1922. RP:HL.)

3. Tagore, *Creative Unity* (London, 1922), essays and lectures revised by Ernest Rhys after the usual confusion about arrangements. (Rhys to Tagore, June 15, 1921. R-S. Andrews to Macmillan, September 15, 1921. MP:BM.)

4. Thomas Hardy, *Late Lyrics and Earlier, with Many Other Verses* (London, 1922).

5. See Edward Craig, *Gordon Craig: The Story of His Life* (London, 1968), pp. 314–315.

6. Lawrence Dundas, 2nd Marquess of Zetland, Earl of Ronaldshay (1876–1961), Governor of Bengal, 1917–1922; Secretary of State for India, 1935–1940.

149
Tagore to Rothenstein

Santiniketan   July 13, 1922

My dear friend

When I was last in the United States trying to raise funds for my proposed university the British propaganda party tried their best to frustrate me and succeeded in their mission. I realised more strongly than ever before how we and our work are suspiciously watched and judged by the ruling race principally from the point of view of British interest. I was in a bitter state of mind in consequence of this when your letter came to me with the suggestion that a board should be appointed in England with the object of selecting the students and lecturers who were to come to us from the West. I believe we had some animated discussions about this in our letters which added to the feeling of irritation from which I was suffering at that moment. I was afraid that such a board would be dominated over by bureaucrats whose policy is to view all our doings with distrust. My idealism has hardly helped me in my relationship with the authorities in India. I suppose they consider it to be more dangerous from their standpoint than clamorous politics and vulgar self assertion of patriotism. Possibly they are right, but my mind refuses to go out of its way to make with them a prudent alliance of mutual adjustment in order to achieve success. Such an attempt at adjustment with the party in power is likely for us to be a great deal more costly than for them. But all this is not to discuss the subject but to offer you an explanation of my conduct. Now that is given it helps me to feel ashamed and sorry for having indulged in a fit of fretfulness for so long and to resume the natural thread of our friendship too precious to be allowed to weaken for any cause whatever. The interruption in our relationship has been growing a burden to me and I am deeply grateful to you for being the first to break it. When once an obstruction is formed in the stream of a communication which was natural and deep flowing it takes some time to discover how thin it is and made of debris that are casual and incongruous.[1]

After my return from the west I found the atmosphere of

my country most unfavourable for my institution. Our people in a fanatical mood of resentment were ready to repudiate the West altogether and any proposal of cooperation with the Western humanity in any form was considered almost as an act of sacrilege. I made myself conspicuously hateful to my countrymen by protesting against such an irrational outburst of passion. It was an irony of fate which while it drew upon my venture the mighty power of suspicion of the British Government also aroused antagonism in my own people against it. The onslaught of non-cooperation fell on me from both the opposing sides.² It has left my scheme stranded in a desolate sand bank financially unfertile which looks grey and bare but whose vastness is made all the more evident because of its isolation. Its atmosphere is healthgiving for the very reason of its being uncontaminated by the breath of popular approbation. From every other point of view it is thriving and the response which it has met from the western continents has exceeded my expectation. Professor Levi has been a great inspiration for us. He is not only a scholar but a personality and an ideal teacher in a higher sense of the word. We are expecting Dr Winternitz next cold season, and the next year Dr Geiger of Vienna University will come to help us. I hope some day we shall have adequate means to be able to invite from England someone like Prof. Gilbert Murray who has the detachment of mind of a scholar and a broad outlook upon life full of human sympathy.³ I shall send you our prospectus which is in the press and the Constitution of our University which I am sure will interest you. If you can help us in establishing its connection with your people in England in any possible way I shall be grateful. Will you remember me kindly to Mrs Rothenstein and give my love to the children? Ever yours

Rabindranath Tagore

1. Andrews, who had sensed something amiss, was about to write to Rothenstein when his letter arrived, and Tagore was soon himself again. (Andrews to Rothenstein, October 2 [1922]. RP:HL.)

The Government of India undoubtedly kept itself informed about the school, but Elmhirst recalls that "on one occasion Tagore sent me down to see the Governor's Private Secretary [W. R. Gourlay] and to find out what the official feeling was in the police department about Santiniketan and Tagore. I was sent by Gourlay with an official letter to interview the Chief of Police but he seemed blissfully unconscious of anything treasonable." (Elmhirst to the editor, February 13, 1970.) However, the idea died hard with Tagore, who later felt himself suspected of trying to establish an Indo-Chinese entente. (Tagore to Elmhirst, February 1, 1925. Elmhirst personal papers.)

2. Tagore took issue with Gandhi over extremism in the Swadeshi movement. (See Kripalani, *Rabindranath Tagore*, pp. 289–299.)

3. Moritz Winternitz (1863–1937), Austrian Indologist, ethnologist, authority on ancient and medieval Indian literature. He later visited Visva-Bharati, but the invitation to Bernhard Geiger (1881–1964), Professor of Indo-Iranian Philology, University of Vienna, 1919–1938, does not seem to have been followed up. Gilbert Murray did not go to Santiniketan.

150
Rothenstein to Tagore

Achenke, Austria   September 1, 1922

My very dear friend—your letter came to me here, at long last. I need not say how welcome it was. We should not allow misunderstandings between us—there is so much wanton indifference to the welfare of others throughout the world. We do stand for tolerance—indeed I think for something more than tolerance. I have been travelling among the old south German cities, with Rachel & Betty, on our way to Austria & coming among Germans & Austrians we are aghast at the failure to find a solution which will at least allow men & women to use the ordinary privileges of life. Surely men of good will, not to speak of men as closely bound by ties of friendship & affection as ourselves, should not allow differences to affect our relations. I rejoice at the quick & warm response to my letter. Indeed what you tell me of your own portion in India must help you to understand mine. For I, like yourself, shy at extreme positions. You know I have never been backward in expressing myself regarding the rights of Indians & our duty towards Indian life & Indian thought. But I believe there have been many noble minds, devoting themselves to the task life has set them, among Englishmen in India, in a selfless spirit; & when your irritation against bureaucratic management caused you to invite Frenchmen, Hungarians & Germans & not my countrymen to help you at Bolpur, I too, in a moment of weakness, showed irritation. But again like yourself, I believed nothing of the kind would have happened had we spoken, instead of written, words. But the mood has passed & once more the ferryman rows his boat from shore to shore. Your news of Bolpur is welcome. . . . We go back this month & get into harness again. I am rather overworked, with Kensington on my shoulders—a big task to take on them. You will have been glad to hear that Mukul [Dey] got his A.R.C.A. Diploma—I think the second Indian to gain this distinction. He is inclined to be desultory in his work & mind & I was afraid he would fail; but he pulled himself together at the end; & I think he has another year's grant from the Government of Bengal.[1] You will have read of the death of our beloved Hudson. He was with us up to the time of our leaving, constantly at the house, & though clearly failing, his mind was as keen & delightful as ever. To me he was one of the rarest of men—I admired the directness & integrity of his spirit & loved the man dearly. We shall miss him sorely.[2] The leaves drop one by one—sometimes in a shower—when one reaches half a century & more, but young eyes don't notice them. I see your works in all the bookshops here & in Germany—also in Tauchnitz. My warm regards to Pearson & Andrews—also my greetings to Dr Kramrisch & Mr Hnevkovsky, & to yourself my affectionate good wishes, as of old.[3] Yours ever

W. R.

1. Mukul Dey (1895–), Abanindranath Tagore's pupil, 1911–1915; Government scholarship student at the Royal College of Art, 1920–1922; Principal, Government School of Art, Calcutta, 1928–1943.

2. W. H. Hudson (1841–1922) had been the Rothensteins' close friend since at least 1901. (See *MM* II, 160–165.)

3. Jaroslav Hnevkovsky, Czech painter, an engineer who turned to art in 1909 and spent five years painting in the interior of Ceylon. He exhibited at the Leicester Galleries in March 1921, then visited Santiniketan, but he was shy to the point of inarticulateness, and little is known of his personal life.

151
Tagore to Rothenstein

                           Colombo, Ceylon   October 20, 1922

My friend, your letter has gladdened my heart. It has been delayed in reaching me owing to my uncertainty of address. It is my mission which does not allow me any rest but drives me across long distances to strange surroundings. For over a month I have been travelling from place to place in southern India till at last I have reached Ceylon. The time is not at all favourable in India for me to persuade our people of the importance of the reconciliation of the East and West. They all seem to think that it can wait till we are powerful enough to negotiate with the West on equal terms, till the Western people are compelled for the sake of expediency to come to a mutual understanding. It is the pride of nationalism which stands in the way of a spiritual ideal. It is very much like saying that until we are rich we need not be honest, that first we must have material power and then we shall be in a position to seek for spiritual perfection. Unfortunately such has been the brutal lesson of facts in the history of all powerful nations in the world, and the idealists have to fight against tremendous odds when they have to assert that there are truths which transcend all facts. There was a time when it was acknowledged that the physical survival is not the highest form of survival for human beings. But in the present age we have lost our faith in the path of immortality and the only path which we have accepted as real is the path of the Struggle for existence. But I strongly believe that races, even as individuals, may attain their fulfilment of life by giving up life for the cause of truth. However, I do not expect people to take me seriously when I ask them to rise above all injuries and indignities through one's constant and unflinching faith in higher realities of life. When we are assailed by the brute it is not the hurt which matters so much as the fact that we pay it our best compliments by accepting its methods. Since science has taken place of religion Man has been cultivating his faith in the brute and arming himself for the struggle for existence which is the process of the natural selection for the survival of the brute. All the same the fact is that man is man and we must keep him reminding of it by constantly appealing to his humanity. I have taken that task in my country though the time is unfavourable the minds of the people being overcast with storm clouds of resentment. I have occasional doubts in my mind as to whether I have not strayed away from my own true vocation; if that be so I have come too far off my track to be able to retrace my steps. I must jog on to the end of my days even though I feel weary and homesick for the solitude where my dreams had their early nest. Ever yours

Rabindranath Tagore

VII   1923-1935   Letters 152-193

The Teacher and the Traveler

When they resumed their correspondence in June 1922, Rothenstein and Tagore had settled into the routines of their new work. Both men had left quiet retreats to perform the difficult feat of pursuing a creative art while carrying out administrative duties. Both had clearly defined but unorthodox educational goals that involved them in controversies with more conservative forces. While thus engaged, both received invitations, barely touched upon in their letters, that were symbol and summary of their friendship: the Government of India asked Rothenstein to go to Delhi, and Tagore was asked whether he would come to Oxford to receive an honorary degree.

Once again Rothenstein found himself involved in the turgid internal affairs of art education in India. Indian students at the Royal College of Art found little scope for their talents when they returned home, and their prospects showed few signs of improving. Abanindranath Tagore was now Professor of Indian Fine Arts at Calcutta University, but he wrote to Havell in the tones of a brave man who fights a losing battle:

> I am giving regular art lectures in the Calcutta University, but you know Bengal is so sleepy. I feel as if I am addressing the pillars and the Book-cases of the University. Still I am hopeful Bengal is the place where the tree can grow. One thing I feel very much, viz. I am growing old and can not last and I do not see who will take my place. Nandalal [Bose, a former pupil] is not a fighter. So I want to finish all the fighting work before I leave so that I may leave the field fit for the corn. Send me your blessings, the battle is not yet over. I have to do so much writing that I hardly find time to paint but this cannot be avoided.[1]

1. Abanindranath Tagore to Havell, September 5 [1923]. Havell: IOL.

Rothenstein knew what it was to languish for lack of encouragement. He asked the India Office to persuade Government to put Indian artists to work at New Delhi. The new capital was the most publicized, most controversial building project in India, but arguments over the choice of building style or styles dragged on acrimoniously in England and India.[2]

In 1927 Rothenstein was asked to visit Delhi and help select artists who would decorate the finished buildings. But he had discovered in 1925 that he had a chronic heart condition, and his doctor forbade the journey. With deep regrets somewhat assuaged by second thoughts about the political aspects of the invitation, he declined.[3]

Indian artists eventually did no decorating at all on Government buildings in New Delhi.[4] Another opportunity presented itself when India House was built in London as headquarters for the Indian High Commission. Sir Atul Chatterjee, the High Commissioner, proposed interior murals by artists selected in an all-India open competition, and Rothenstein was to choose four artists to work under his supervision at the Royal College of Art.[5] This project set an outstanding example of the Indian cultural parochialism that Havell knew so well, for a great hue and cry issued from the Bombay School of Art: of the four artists selected, three were Bengalis and one was from Tripura state adjacent to Bengal. Obviously, Sir Atul's and Rothenstein's personal preferences for Bengalis were being indulged!

2. See, for example, editorial, "The Permanency of British Rule," *MR,* 11 (1912), 118.

3. See Rothenstein, *Since Fifty: Men and Memories, 1922–1938* (London, 1939), pp. 173, 174–175.

4. Lutyens refused the services of Indian artists, but his current biographer states that this was "not on racial grounds. He was prejudiced against all artists! One of the most characteristic things about his architecture (in England) is that he employed as few sculptors and painters as he possibly could—relying on abstract architectural forms. . . . Lutyens was always concerned to prevent paintings and sculptures being introduced into his buildings, except on his own stringently architectural terms." (Nicholas Taylor to the editor, December 12, 1969.) Baker liked decoration and agreed with Rothenstein's advocacy of "the need to risk immature efforts, if any advance is to be made." (Baker to Rothenstein, March 12, 1924. RP:HL.)

5. The office of High Commissioner, representing the Government of India in London, was established in 1920 to handle India Office agency work.

On April 6 and 10, 1931, these charges were prominently aired in the *Times of India*. The Bombay Art Society jumped into the fray with complaints that it had been slighted by The India Society in London.[6]

Finally, Alan M. Green, Deputy High Commissioner for India, wrote confidentially to Gilbert Wiles, Collector at Bombay, to explain "the agitation . . . [all] founded on a series of rather extraordinary misconceptions. There is no mystery at all about the mural decorations of India House. Our proposals were submitted to the Government of India . . . ; but I suppose it would be too much to expect a journalist to acquire correct information from public records before writing his leading articles!" Green then summarized "the history of the affair as briefly as I can"—in five single-spaced pages. The artists were all Bengalis, but only one came from Calcutta, a second was from Lucknow, a third from Delhi, and the fourth from Tripura. The suggestion that The India Society might have meddled with the selection machinery was "extraordinary . . . The India Society had nothing to do with the scheme; Lord Zetland and Lord Lytton had nothing to do with the scheme; Mr. Laurence Binyon had nothing to do with the scheme; none of them was even consulted." Sir Atul was involved only as High Commissioner, and "Sir William Rothenstein was consulted *not* as a member of the India Society but as the head of a Government art college. . . . I do think it monstrous that a Bombay paper should publicly accuse Sir Atul of rigging the market in favour of Bengal, and I do trust that you will use your influence to put this wrong right." Green had put it right where Rothenstein was concerned:

> Here may I explain that Professor Rothenstein is not a freelance with a school of his own; he is a distinguished Government servant serving under His Majesty's Government as head of the Royal College of Art. That College has a class of mural painting which has become, to say the least of it, well known and highly esteemed. The artists paid the regular fees to the College—or rather the Government of India paid the fees for them—but Professor Rothenstein not only

---

6. See editorials, "The India Society," "The India Society Again," *The Times of India* (Bombay), April 6, 1931, p. 8; April 10, 1931, p. 8.

gets nothing from the Government of India but has declined even to accept an honorarium for generally supervising the work of the artists at India House after leaving the College. As you are no doubt aware, Rothenstein is a very great admirer of Indian art and culture, and he considers it an honour to be associated in any way with Sir Atul's scheme. From the start he has given every assistance to the scholars, but has been most careful to avoid influencing them in any way.[7]

For his contribution to Indian art and culture Rothenstein received, as thanks for two years of extra work and worry, "a brief note of thanks from the Government of India and much abuse from other quarters." He received also renewed requests to obtain Royal Society honors, knighthoods, and publishers for aspiring Indians.[8]

This episode does much to explain Rothenstein's noticeably less permissive attitude toward contemporary Indian artists, as expressed in letters to Tagore. Rothenstein was acutely conscious of his responsibility for a new generation of artists, and also of limitations on his strength. He remained stubbornly idealistic, but ill health forced him to be more cautious in investing his physical and financial resources; he tended to turn to projects that offered working partners rather than passive beneficiaries.

Tagore, for his part, spent his reserves without stint for Visva-Bharati, whose idealized concept was grounded in principles of free exchange and useful application of ideas. After his meeting with Tagore in 1917, Sadler had told Rothenstein, "He has gone to the fundamental questions of our inquiry. The root of the matter lies in an attitude of mind towards education, which in its turn must be coloured by an ideal of life & of personal duty. Indian education, as we have to come

---

7. Green to Wiles, May 7, 1931. Crown-copyright. India Society Papers: India Office Library. Sir Alan Green (1885–1958), Indian Civil Service, 1909–1936. Victor, 2nd Earl of Lytton (1876–1947), Under Secretary of State for India, 1920–1922; Governor of Bengal, 1922–1927; Viceroy and Acting Governor-General, 1925.

8. *SF*, p. 175. Green wrote the "brief note." (Green to Rothenstein, June 14, 1932. RP:HL.) Rothenstein seems not to have known of Green's efforts on his behalf.

across it, is remote from what you or I would wish to have for our children. The river is choked with sand. How we are to blow up the sand is the problem."[9]

Despite his rapport with Sadler, Tagore dreaded the sterile institutionalism represented by the monolithic Calcutta University. In 1921 he had shied away from the very term "university." In the late 1920's he rejected help from the Government of Bengal, almost certainly fearing that it would compromise his educational philosophy. Sir Arthur Dash, then Secretary to the Government of Bengal in the Education Department, recalls that he and a colleague went to Santiniketan, "in the course of an official visit to ascertain if the Poet's University needed any financial assistance and would accept any from the Government of Bengal." They were graciously received, and, although the school gave them an impression of helter-skelter activity more poetic than practical, they placed their proposal before Tagore:

> He was just finishing the rehearsal of a children's play and advanced to meet us, holding the hand of a little girl of 7 and patting the head of another with the spare hand before using it to shake ours. He radiated charm and poetry in every gesture and remark. We sat and talked to him for about an hour and it was a moving experience. His voice was melodious and his choice of English and his diction wonderful. He could raise any amount of money for his schemes in America or Europe but little or nothing from his own countrymen. He was a prophet sadly without honour in his own country.
>
> We enquired gently about the welfare of his University. He told us frankly what the financial position was but when we asked if there was any way in which the Government of Bengal could render assistance, we were told with incredible softness that there was none. He knew they were in financial difficulty. He knew he was surrounded by all sorts of designing persons eager to batten on uplift. He did not mention uplift but explained that there was no mirage in his keeping before himself a sure hope of raising his countrymen in spite of faults and failings.

9. Sadler to Rothenstein, November 19, 1917. RP:HL.

It was indeed a moving interview and we went away sorrowful . . .[10]

Sir Arthur's description is itself moving; it so plainly bespeaks the emissaries' good will and Tagore's devotion to the beliefs for which he was literally wearing himself out. Like the sorcerer's apprentice he must "jog on to the end of my days" at an ever-accelerating pace.[11]

While Rothenstein stayed close to the Royal College of Art, Tagore's devotion to Visva-Bharati took him more and more away from it, and imperial politics followed him everywhere. He had assumed that being a poet exempted him from editorial chores; now, as he traveled and lectured to keep Visva-Bharati alive, he found again and again that the roles of poet and public figure were not always interchangeable. Sometimes, with curiosity essential in a poet but hazardous to a public figure, Tagore obdurately pursued situations with grave political aftereffects. One of these was precipitated by his determination to visit Mussolini in 1926. Elmhirst, who went to Naples to meet Tagore, pointed out that this was a propaganda trap, but Tagore insisted that he must see this political experiment. He was taken in hand by a pair of Mussolini's representatives, who plainly knew that Elmhirst recognized what they were and tried to evade this troublesome Englishman. Elmhirst, whose patience had limits, left the train. Mussolini's invitation was a propaganda trap, but Tagore did not fully comprehend this until some days later when Romain Rolland enlightened him in Switzerland. Then remorse, retractions for the press, and the fact that he was only a poet provided scant refuge.[12]

Tagore's letters in these years are a touching but wearying alternation of flights from and returns to reality; there is a general impression of great diffusion of time, energies, and

10. Arthur Dash to the editor, June 9, 1969. Sir Arthur Jules Dash (1887–), Indian Civil Service, 1910–1942.
11. See Letter 151.
12. Interviews with Leonard Elmhirst, London, August 14, 1967; August 13, 1969. Mr. Elmhirst recalled that he had told Tagore, "Gurudev, I'm in your way—you're going to Rome whether I advise it or not, so I'm leaving." Tagore later admitted his error to Elmhirst, but maintained that a poet must see things for himself; he had had to see Mussolini. (See also *Rolland and Tagore*, ed. Alex Aronson and Krishna Kripalani [Calcutta, 1945], pp. 89–95.)

affections. Traveling and lecturing for Visva-Bharati was a vicious circle; the more he traveled, the less time he had for new writing and translation. When editorial problems arose in London or New York it was even more difficult to find the author, who might be in China or Hungary or Canada or any of a dozen other places. Sometimes he tried, as in his letter of November 26, 1932, to recapture the ambience of those first summers with Rothenstein, but rather than dispassionate literary analysis, this letter seems an attempt to justify the course of events since 1912.[13] All that Tagore says in it has been said before, will be said again, and is part of a repeating pattern: the bird hurries back to the Indian nest, only to find it in disarray. After 1921 fewer of his works were translated into English, and more of these were travel diaries, letters, and lectures abroad. He wrote few new short stories. He published eight slender volumes of Bengali poems, among them some of his best later work, but no major volume appeared in English.

The hard fact, borne out by royalty figures, is that the English-speaking public in the West was not interested. The stereotype that fitted so neatly in 1912 now bored many who knew Tagore in no other guise. Much more serious was the disaffection of some who had been genuinely stirred by *Gitanjali* but had grown away from it as they matured: Ezra Pound, whose defection from the ranks of admirers should have been an early warning of danger ahead, and Yeats, whose work had gained steadily in discipline and variety. Frances Cornford spoke for them all when she told Gilbert Murray: "I suppose all that—'I am the bath and the bath-taps, I am the Tumbler and the Tooth-paste, I am the Sponge and the Sponger etc. ad lib—was once new to us—but now . . . can't only little dots express how all-too-familiar? I do think you're the man, for the briefest possible foreword about Tagore as the most remarkable *whole* man he was."[14]

Respect for the man outlasted the magic of the poetry, but in 1926 Tagore turned his back on a respectful gesture by Robert Bridges, who almost succeeded in getting for him the

13. Letter 186.
14. Frances Cornford to Murray [1954?]. Murray Papers: Bodleian. "The briefest . . . foreword": for Tagore, *A Flight of Swans: Poems from Balākā*, trans. Arabinda Bose. 2nd ed. (London, 1962).

Oxford degree denied by Curzon in 1912. For six months Bridges conducted a circumspect correspondence with Oxford's Hebdomadal Council; by October prospects seemed favorable although the degree could not be conferred before November 9. But Tagore, who left England in August for a lecture tour, wrote from Prague to say that his engagements were proliferating, that he would be in Europe six weeks more but needed rest and could not come to Oxford. He was grateful to his English friends, but the honor must await another day.[15]

The tone of this letter is curiously masked and casual. The lecture schedule was appallingly rigorous, but his letter makes it plain that these were ad hoc rigors accumulating as he went. On November 9, the day the degree might have been conferred, he was in a Hungarian sanatorium, trying to recoup his strength in order to finish his tour. An old acquaintance at Oxford suggested that Tagore feared political innuendoes like those that had followed his Nobel Prize and his knighthood.[16]

Tagore seemed to view his friendship with Rothenstein as part of a halcyon past debarred from the present by undefined, undefinable obstacles. Yet Bridges had defined them in 1915, with his questions about the ethics of translation. It was unlikely that Tagore would answer these now. His works were more and more left to retranslators.

The fault was partly England's, as Edward Thompson told Rothenstein, for "caring so little about Indian thought and literature."[17] It was also Tagore's, for casting off the literary craftsmanship that he found "cold blooded," but that in actuality demands the utmost in emotional commitment. Only fine craftsmanship, not mere remembering, could renew the literary satisfactions of that summer of 1912—but the working day was fast approaching evening.

 15. Tagore to Bridges, October 9, 1926. BrP.
 16. Estlin Carpenter to Bridges, October 8, 1926. BrP.
 17. Thompson to Rothenstein, March 16, 1927. RP:HL. Quoted in part, incorrectly dated 1931, in *SF*, p. 45.

152
Rothenstein to Tagore

Far Oakridge   April 6 [1923]

My dear friend—I have commenced more than one letter to you, which has not been finished. The worst of being back in London is, not that one overworks but one underleisures. People are shameless in begging for one's time. Here we have again a few days we may almost call our own. . . . The old house is in other hands; but we—Betty, Billy & myself—find a haven in John Drinkwater's small cottage, which we found for him here some years ago.[1] My wife is in London, to be near our dear Rachel, who has been ill for many months.[2] . . . We have had a very anxious time. You yourself have been through much anxiety & have suffered heavy losses. I hope, after your arduous wanderings, you are now finding peace again at Santiniketan. We hear of you from various sources. Yeats was in London recently & we spoke much of you. He is now a Senator, & this high office necessitates six soldiers sleeping in his house at Dublin. I think he was glad to find himself in England & was reluctant to return.[3] Goloubew was here, too, this year, lecturing for the India Society. He has gone to Angkor.[4] Binyon, Foster & myself are acting as official advisers in the matter of Indian representation in the Fine Art section at next year's Exhibition. We feel that if your nephews could send over their collection of paintings we could show a portion of them & give our people here a chance of seeing the extent & quality of the portfolios. Then it might be possible to acquire them for a national museum.[5]

I wonder how your own plans prosper & what place the creative arts take in them. The Indian students at the College are inclined to slacken just when they should put forward their greatest energies; but perhaps this is true of a proportion of all students. And I fancy money difficulties have a good deal to do with the matter; they certainly seem to absorb a great amount of their time. Lutyens & Baker both need active assistance, but I have so far hesitated to recommend either [former R.C.A. pupil, S.] Chowdhury or Mukul Dey for positions of responsibility over other people. Nor do I know how much active creative power remains among your people: here it is growing perceptibly less, and I doubt often whether the William Morris view that art springs from the peasantry is true. It certainly, in these days, comes from the middle class, which still shows astonishing fertility. I should like to see what your nephews are doing, both in their own work & through their influence as teachers. But I doubt whether I shall ever see India again. The work I have taken up here is now very near my heart, & the years pass quickly. But you may be sure little is forgotten of the precious months spent in your country & so far as I am able, I keep my mind in touch with its spirit. I still wish it were possible to have some true centre of Indian culture in England, where, as with you at Bolpur, Eastern & Western artists & scholars could meet. There is no link between us—we know nothing of what your craftsmen are doing to-day & little of your literary & scholarly activities. Lawrence tells me he is coming to India & my friend Somervell, who was with the Everest expedition, is going out as a medical missionary. I hope you will meet him—he is a splendid fellow.[6] Of your own work I hear little, but I know your time fruitfully spent & given & your life full. Ever my affectionate greetings—yours,

William Rothenstein

1. The Drinkwaters rented the cottage in April 1917.
2. Rachel won a scholarship at the Royal College of Music in 1922, but required surgery soon afterward and was still hospitalized.
3. See Yeats, *Letters*, pp. 695–696.
4. Victor Goloubew (1879–1945), photographer, archaeologist, collector, specialist in Indian and Indochinese art.
5. Sir William Foster (1863–1951), Registrar and Superintendent of Records, India Office, 1907–1923. "Exhibition": British Empire Exhibition, Wembley, 1924. (See [India Society, comp.] *Examples of Indian Art at the British Empire Exhibition, 1924* [London, 1925].) In December 1922 Rothenstein had asked Montagu to help find a possible London purchaser for the "Tagore Collection." Montagu approached both the Board of Education and the British Museum, but without success, and he was dubious about raising a sum as large as the Tagores' purchase price. He suggested that a London exhibition might stimulate public interest. (Montagu to Rothenstein, January 10, 1923. RP:HL.)
6. According to Rathindranath Tagore, his father met T. E. Lawrence in London in 1912 and 1920. (See his *On the Edges of Time*, pp. 115, 131.) Lawrence did not go to India until the autumn of 1926. T. H. Somervell (1890–   ), physician, artist, mountaineer, member of the 1922 and 1924 Everest expeditions, medical missionary in South India, 1923–1949.

153
Tagore to Rothenstein

Santiniketan   [October 1?, 1923]

My dear friend, I feel myself lost in the work I have taken up and there is a constant longing in me to be rescued and restored to my own true world. Yet it is a work to which I have been drawn irresistably. Only there come moments when I cannot help wondering whether the cost of the sacrifice which I offer to it is not too extravagant. I very often suffer from a feeling of homesickness for the rich leisure which I had when I was not burdened with a mission, when my duty was fully to live my own life.

Lately I have taken to travelling in different provinces of India on a campaign of raising funds. Chasing after money is the surest means of growing aged; it has had its effect upon me; I know that I am fast losing my store of youth with an inadequately poor compensation for it in the shape of material gain.

I do not know if you have heard of Pearson's death from accident in Italy.[1] It is a great loss to our Ashram and to me personally, to which it will be hard for us to be reconciled.

I have an invitation to China where I shall go in the beginning of March next year. I shall have to be away for about six months or more. I do not yet know whether the change of environment will give me rest and detachment which I need so much or whether the strain will be too much for the present state of my health.[2]

Our institution is growing in its scope and attracting helpers round it. The lecturers from Europe whom we have been able to secure for our students have proved to be of very great help to us both as teachers as well as friends. They have contributed to the ideal of this place and strengthened our faith in it. We have a young Englishman—Elmhirst by name—working with us for some time whose service has been very valuable in building up our village reconstruction work. He is a Cambridge graduate but he is in intimate touch with America, where he had his training in agriculture.[3]

When I was in England I had asked Ernest Rhys to come and

join us, to give our students some taste of English literature. He seemed to me willing, but Mrs Rhys pleaded ill health and the idea was given up. Some time ago I wrote to Sturge Moore inviting him to our Ashram but he has his work which keeps him tied to his own country for another four years.[4] We badly want a teacher who is not a mere scholar but who has the gift of imagination and expression.

I am glad to learn that dear Rachel is gradually regaining her health and I hope to see her restored to her cheerfulness and music if I ever have the opportunity to visit England once again. Ever yours

Rabindranath Tagore

1. Pearson died September 26, 1923, after a fall from a train near Pistoia, Italy.
2. For origins of this invitation see Hay, *Asian Ideas*, pp. 136–143.
3. See Elmhirst, *Rabindranath Tagore: Pioneer in Education* (London, 1961), pp. 18–43.
4. After Tagore left England in 1921, Rhys wrote, "I look back with wonder and regret to your coming and going. Would India and Shanti Niketan were possible for me. 'I long for peace,' as Heine said, and in London none is to be had." (Rhys to Tagore, July 18, 1921. R-S.) Mrs. Rhys was in fact ill; she died in Washington, D.C., in 1930. Tagore had told Sturge Moore that if he would come, the school would try to pay his expenses. (Tagore to Sturge Moore, February 7, 1923. TSM.)

154
Rothenstein to Tagore

13 Airlie Gardens, London   October 2, 1923

My very dear friend—I have thought of you much these last days. The news of dear Pearson's death came as a great shock. A few weeks ago he was discussing his plans & hopes & fears— and as you may imagine these all centred round India. No one was ever more devoted to your country than he was, or indeed, to yourself & to Bolpur & its school. He seemed to have a peculiar love for Bengal & its children—when I first met him at Calcutta I was struck by this devotion. You have lost a true disciple & friend. I know you valued his loyalty & affection deeply. And I am sure you need both these things. . . . We are both desperately busy people & writing becomes difficult—writing at least to the people one wants to talk with, I mean. It is long since I heard directly from you. But I should like you to believe that your welfare is very near my heart & though we can write little & may not even meet again that my affection is yours always. You know how much I should love to come to India once more. I see little chance of this being possible. I have accepted my reappointment at Kensington for 3 more years. This ties me to Europe. But my third eye looks often along the ghats by the Ganges; the scent of wood & cow dung often hangs before my nostrils & I hear again the silver tinkling of the russet browed women as they walk up & down the Temple steps. Ever yours—

William Rothenstein

155
Tagore to Rothenstein

Genoa   January 21, 1925

Dear friend, you must have heard from Rathi about my invitation to Peru. I fell very ill on the steamer, and for two months in Argentina, under doctor's advise, was solely occupied cultivating, what they call perfect rest. However, this gave me an opportunity to know what genuine feeling the people of that country had for me.[1]

I have just arrived in Italy. I hope I have strength enough to be able to respond to the reception awaiting me in this country. If I were not tied by my promise I should have straight gone back to India.

I have arranged for sailing home on the 15th of the next month which will just allow me to reach India before the hot season. I had thought of visiting England quietly for a few days but I have given up that idea, for I am still tired longing for my accustomed corner in Shanti Niketan. The evidence of my old age has suddenly become too strong for me to ignore it and I must gradually adjust my life to its claims. For the last few months I have been dreaming of a retirement full of a rich solitude like the night that has its stars. But I am afraid I shall only reach the dusk of a twilight and not the depth of that great dark that reveals its endless lights. My love to you all. Ever yours

Rabindranath Tagore

1. See Victoria Ocampo, "Tagore on the Banks of the River Plate," in [Sahitya Akademi, comp.] *Rabindranath Tagore: A Centenary Volume, 1861–1961* (New Delhi, 1961), pp. 27–47. This invitation was generated in Tokyo in 1924 when diplomatic attachés of five Latin American embassies called on Tagore, pointed out that he had visited every continent except South America, and asked whether he would welcome an invitation to visit there. (Interview with Leonard Elmhirst, London, August 13, 1969.) Tagore was to attend Centenary celebrations of the Republic of Peru, and he and Elmhirst sailed from Cherbourg on October 18. Tagore fell ill in Argentina, and by the time he was well enough to travel, Peru's celebrations were over. Rathindranath and Pratima were in France and England, but Rabindranath decided not to join them there, to Rothenstein's disappointment. (Rothenstein to Tagore, January 18, 24, 1925. R-S.)

156
Tagore to Rothenstein

Milan   January 27, 1925

Dear friend

What I did fear has happened. I have fallen ill. I almost feel guilty that it should have been so—for I have been met with such an outburst of welcome that it grieves my heart not to be able to respond to it in an adequate manner. Twice I have been able to appear before the public and the enthusiasm of the people has made me feel humble—I only wish I could do something to them to deserve this. But I have not even the strength to leave my bed and appear before them to say how grateful I am. I am sailing back to India on the next Monday. But I am sure to come back to Italy either next autumn or in the following spring.

Pratima sends her grateful regards to you. She is full of praise of her teachers who helped her to learn a great deal in a very short time. I myself on behalf of our institution am very thankful to you for giving her this opportunity.[1]

I am sorry that dear Rachel is still suffering from ill health. Give her my love and tell her that her thoughts have visited my mind often in a most irrelevant manner. I hope I shall find her restored to her best health when I see her next.

    Day after tomorrow we go to Venice and from there we take our ship. With love to you all   Ever yours

Rabindranath Tagore

    1. Rothenstein admitted Pratima as a special student in pottery classes at the Royal College of Art. Mukhopadhyay mentions only that she had pottery instruction in Paris. (See his *Rabindrajibani,* III, 197.)

157
Rothenstein to Tagore

13 Airlie Gardens, London   April 26 [1925]

My dear friend—John tells me that the stupid error made by the New Statesman caused you to think pen & brushes for ever laid aside. Happily I am still to be allowed to look at things for a while; days, months or years, who knows? This was made clear in the succeeding number of the New Statesman, which I hope met your or Andrews' eyes.[1] But John tells me a more disturbing thing than the report of my demise—that you yourself have been ill. I hope by the time this reaches you that the trouble, of which Andrews writes, will have expended itself, & that rest, sorely needed after your long travels, will have brought you back strength and renewed energies. You, like myself, want to look as long as you may at the loveliness of the face of the world. It is perhaps the least deceptive, & not the least profound, vision of reality vouchsafed to us. . . . I was grieved to hear of the death of your brother, whose drawings I so much admired.[2] I remember you telling me of him, of his devotion to philosophy & of his deep knowledge of many subjects. You will, I hope, allow yourself to be free from some of your many cares & charges, & give yourself rest, mentally & physically. You have done your share, & more than your share, of work. I think creative work, exhausting as it often is, is less so than doing things for which nature, which decrees us to be artists, does not fit our spirits. . . . My voeux for a peaceful convalescence. Ever yours—

William Rothenstein

1. John Rothenstein requested information for a catalogue raisonné of his father's portrait drawings, and the editor headed the letter, "The Late Mr. Rothenstein," a demise that John had not implied. (See *New Statesman and Nation*, January 24, 1925, p. 444; January 31, 1925, p. 470.) By a bitter irony, pains he had thought indicated indigestion were diagnosed a few months later as a heart condition which worsened steadily and caused a "long spell of silence" (see Letter 158).

2. Jyotirindranath Tagore died on March 4, 1925.

158
Tagore to Rothenstein

Santiniketan   April 14, 1926

My dear friend, how very nice to get your letter after such a long spell of silence. It deeply touches my heart, especially, in the present state of my existence when I seem to be living in the dusk of a dimmed existence. The memory of the dawn of a friendship in a strange horizon revealing an unprobed depth of radiance in its wealth of colours that struck my mind with wonder moment after moment often comes back to me when I sit alone on my easy chair with no other claim of the world upon me but to be supremely lazy and forget all my absurd pretentions to be its benefactor. When a person is too much obsessed with the importance of his usefulness he is apt to cut himself from the access to the stream of simple enjoyments that flows across his life and thus to produce a dryness of soil which may be good for laying foundation of all kinds of things but never for the cultivation of living beauty of creation. With the breaking down of my health I have lost my occupation while gaining back the leisure which constantly reminds me of the natural field of my life now lying buried under the debris of my work. It brings today to my memory all the surprises of that fruitful time of rich idleness, that epic era of divine inutility to which your thoughts belong so intimately. It may be too late for me to conjure it up again but it is good to know that I had once upon a time the full opportunity to live my own true life which was glorious for me and may be for others. Ever yours

Rabindranath Tagore

159
Rothenstein to Tagore

13 Airlie Gardens, London   June 15, 1926

My dear friend—I cannot tell you how relieved I was, after getting your last letter, to hear you were in Italy. For the world is a beautiful place & one is reluctant to shut one's eyes on it forever. And I am thankful for each day of life. I feel now that our roles are reversed. You still have the energy to travel, to speak with all & sundry, to go from one lovely scene to another. Italy seems to me to come nearer to the beauty of Indian towns than any European country. To-day we can still see much of it as it was in the days of its glory. Now its glory lies in its engineering genius, & our children's children will not, I fear, be able to see the life which the country folk & the small townsfolk still lead. I did not think I should have the good fortune to see you again. I am sorely stricken in health, but not in spirit, & your visit will mean much to me. I do trust you will not overtire yourself. Ever yours affectionately

William Rothenstein

160
Tagore to Rothenstein

Dolder Grand Hotel, Zurich   July 5, 1926

Dear Friend

My engagements in Italy had been of a strenuous nature—it had nearly brought me to the brink of a breakdown. I was obliged to take a week's rest in Villeneuve in Switzerland and the beauty and peace of that place have done me good. I have come to Zurich, invited by the University, and shall leave this place for Viena where I intend to consult some specialist about my weakness.

My experience in Italy has convinced me that I should be careful about spending my physical resources which have come to the point of exhaustion. It may be that doctors will compel me to accept the Martial law of medical treatment and keep me confined for some time in some nursing home. It makes it difficult for me to give you the time and the date when I shall be able to come to England. I do not know if you have any plan of going out to the country this summer—for, I hear, you also have not been well. However, I am sure, we shall meet somewhere and sometime before I leave Europe. If you do not delay too long in giving me information about your own health and plan, which I wish to have, write to me to the care of Dr Winternitz, University Prague. With love to you all   Ever yours

Rabindranath Tagore

161
Tagore to Rothenstein

Hotel Regina [London]   August 7, 1926

My very dear friend

I wish I had the same leisure that I possessed when I first came to know you—those days full of profound enjoyment and daily surprises of friendship. Unfortunately for me I have lost the place that I once chanced to gain in the heart of your country and today I feel that I merely drift here on the current of the crowd, a superficial existence that tires me every moment. But one thing I have discovered lately that my love for you has sent its roots in the underground depth of my being and it is sure to survive all the changes of outward circumstance. My heart aches today when I remember our close and constant companionship in the early days of our acquaintance so richly endowed by the unstinted generosity of your love. I am immensely thankful for this experience and also for the help you rendered unexpectedly in introducing Europe to me in whose shore, like a migratory bird, I have my second nest.

It is unlikely that I shall visit England again but I carry the touch of your hand with me and the remembrance of our last meeting which was short but poignantly full of tender recollections. With love   Ever yours

Rabindranath Tagore

I am leaving this morning for Dartinghall Parsonage, Totnes where Elmhirst lives.[1]

1. Tagore came to London on July 30, but by August 7 he was in Totnes, Devon. Leonard Elmhirst and Dorothy Straight had married and had purchased Dartington Hall to be made into a community center and school. Here Tagore means the Old Parsonage at Dartington, where he stayed because the Hall itself was not ready for visitors. Similar errors and confusions in an earlier letter from France testify to his state of mental and physical exhaustion. (Tagore to Rothenstein, July 29 [1926]. RP:HL.)

162
Tagore to Rothenstein

Hotel Rose, Wiesbaden   September 22, 1926

Dear friend

The termination of my lecture tour is not yet in sight. The path is going on lengthening itself and I see that during the end of October I shall find myself in the heart of Poland.[1] Everyday it is growing doubtful whether I shall be able to go back to England before I leave Europe. My steamer will start from some European port about the third week of November and the promises which I have made to different parties in different parts of the world will make me busily engaged all this time—unless I choose to be wayward and claim the privilege of a poet to break his engagements.

Rathi is in Berlin. He has gone through his operation and is doing well. I shall be back there on the 25th of this month.[2] With my love to you all I am   Yours affectionately

Rabindranath Tagore

It would have given me great pleasure if I could do anything to help the Poetry book shop—but I am afraid I shall not have the chance.[3]

1. He fell ill in Budapest on or about October 25 and never reached Poland. This is the tour that prevented his receiving the Oxford degree. (See Introduction to Part VII, "The Teacher and the Traveler.")

2. Rathindranath's operation was apparently a minor one. According to Mukhopadhyay, Rabindranath was in Dusseldorf on September 25. (See his *Rabindrajibani*, III, 260.)

3. Harold and Alida Monro's Poetry Bookshop, London, a rallying place since 1913 for poets and poetry-lovers.

163
Tagore to Rothenstein

[Lake Balaton, Hungary]   October 23, 1926

Dear friend

I had my invitation from Russia and was preparing to visit that country when I was taken ill and I am still confined to bed. May be it is providential and the people who have the inborn gift for making mistakes in spite of repeated lessons should be thankful to visitations of sickness if they happen in right moments. My doctor advises me to choose some warm place in southern Europe where I can have enough of the sunny climate and perfect idleness. I am not in a fit condition to brave your November in England. I wish I could see you once again before I sailed for India, but I dare not try it. If I can secure a suitable place in south of France may I ask you to spend a few days with me there. My friend Mon. [Albert] Kahn has a beautiful villa in Mentone—If it is not already occupied by some of his friends I am sure he will be glad to allow me to stay there a few weeks. You know nothing will give me more pleasure than your company in this place. I am going to write a letter to Mon. Kahn today if his villa is available for me.

It may be that you know I had a long programme of lectures in several towns in Germany. It was a severe trial for me owing to my weak state of health, but it caused me a constant surprise of joy to find that the people there have a strong feeling of regards for me. The glimpses they may have had of my works and personality could be nothing more than meagre and fragmentary and I do not know how these could have won for me such a warm recognition. It is not unlikely that this is an epidemic of a passing fancy which will bring about its own reaction—for Europe seems to be nervously afraid of making a wrong selection in her intellectual favourites and in times of doubt claims back from them as indemnity a great deal more than she had paid to them. But I am not afraid, for I am sure that in my own language I have an asset a fraction of which has not yet been touched by the western public, and I hope that I do not delude myself when I think that I have enough to pay for my place in the memory of man, a place which may not be extensive but true.

If you have done with the manuscript of the story which Rathindranath had sent to you before coming away please return it to me, for it is required by a continental publisher. If you send it to the care of the American Express Co., 11 Rue Scribe I shall find it.[1]

I deeply regret, my very dear friend, that I shall not see you this time before I leave—but I hope it will be possible for me next year to visit you and find you restored to health. With love

Rabindranath Tagore

1. Probably *Cokher Bāli* [Eyesore] (see Letter 74, note 2). No Continental edition appeared, and Macmillan had planned no new volume of Tagore's fiction after *Gorā* [Gora] (1910), in *R-R*, VI, 109–572: *Gora* [trans. W. W. Pearson, rev. Surendranath Tagore] (London, 1924). In 1921 Tagore, who had asked Surendranath to translate *Gorā*, instructed Andrews to submit it to Macmillan. (Andrews to Macmillan, August 11, 1921. MP:BM.) However, a note signed "Translator" gives Surendranath credit for final revisions only. After publication Tagore complained from Peking that Pearson's work was inaccurate and that Macmillan had rushed the book. (Tagore to Sturge Moore, May 20, 1924. TSM.) Later Andrews wrote that Tagore did not object to an abridged Swedish translation since the English version itself needed abridgment. (Andrews to Macmillan, July 26, 1925. MP:BM.)

164
Rothenstein to Tagore

13 Airlie Gardens, London   March 15, 1927

My dear friend—many thanks for the kind thought—the little radiant fireflies gave me much pleasure.[1] I have also lately read some translations made by Edward Thompson of some of your poems: previously unknown to me. "Noon" & "Sea Waves" I thought especially beautiful.[2] I was disappointed not to see you again. I hoped you were coming to get the Oxford degree, of which you spoke to me. I suppose you got entangled in Continental engagements.[3] At any rate, it was a great pleasure to have had you here. I fear I was very ill at the time . . . from acute poisoning from my teeth. . . . I read your article in Keyserling's marriage book.[4] I am always impressed by the vigour of Indian representations of the Indian woman. In your last novel (by the way, I hope the typed copy I sent on to you in Paris reached you) I felt the strength of the women compared with the men. Hardy has something of this quality in his novels. But that subtle admixture of gravity & sensuousness in all sculpture, & in Indian paintings is equally illustrated in your literature. It is a unique thing—the apsaras type has remained throughout Indian history, & still survives in your poems. It has also been revived in the paintings of the Calcutta School. Only I feel a little lack of inner & outer dynamic vitality in the drawings, generally. All art is really representative—has never been anything else—expressed sometimes with more, sometimes with less imaginative or illustrative elements. The images of Buddha, of Vishnu & Shiva were not less, but more massive than men models, & the paintings of Ajanta, when they were freshly done, must have been startlingly realistic & alive.

. . . Yours ever affectionately

William Rothenstein

1. Tagore, *Fireflies* (London, 1927). (See Elmhirst, *Rabindranath Tagore: Pioneer in Education*, pp. 15–16.)
2. Tagore, "Madhyāhra" [Midday], *Caitāli* [Of April; also, the last rice gleaned in April] (1896), in *R-R*, V, 11–12: "Noon," trans. Edward Thompson, *Rabindranath Tagore: Poet and Dramatist*, p. 144; "Shindhyatorang" [Sea Waves], *Mānashi*, in *R-R*, II, 157–161: "Sea Waves," trans. Thompson, *ibid.*, 79–82.
3. Rothenstein knew the facts; Thompson's letter (see *SF*, p. 46) is plainly a response to one from him.
4. Tagore, "The Indian Ideal of Marriage," *The Book of Marriage: A New Interpretation by Twenty-Four Leaders of Contemporary Thought, Arranged and Edited by Count Hermann Keyserling* (New York, 1926), pp. 98–122.

165
Tagore to Rothenstein

Visva-Bharati, Bengal
April 20, 1927

Dear friend, I am glad to know that you have reached the cause of your illness and that has helped you. I have come back to my institution and am attending to its claims some of which are material in their character and most exhausting. My work being non-political fails to attract help from my countrymen, and this loneliness heavy with a spirit of antipathy is a difficult burden for me to bear. I have not the gift of the moral asceticism which some of my countrymen have, and I never pretend to say that I can dispense with human sympathy.

From your letter it is evident that you have read Thompson's book about myself. It is one of the most absurd books that I have ever read dealing with a poet's life and writings. All through his pages he has never allowed his readers to guess that he has a very imperfect knowledge of Bengali language which necessarily prevents him from realising the atmosphere of our words and therefore the colour and music and life of them. He cannot make distinction between that which is essential and non-essential and he jumbles together details without any consideration for their significance. For those who know Bengali his presentation of the subject is too often ludicrously disproportionate. He has been a schoolmaster in an Indian school and that comes out in his pages too often in his pompous spirit of self confidence even in a realm where he ought to have been conscious of his limitations. The book is full of prejudices which have no foundation in facts, as for instance when he insinuates that I lack in my admiration for Shakespeare—or that I have an antipathy against Englishmen.[1] Of course, I have my grievances against the British Government in India, but I have a genuine respect for the English character which has so often been expressed in my writings. Then again, being a Christian Missionary, his training makes him incapable of understanding some of the ideas that run all through my writings—like that of the *Jeevan-devata,* the limited aspect of divinity which has its unique place in the individual life, in contrast to that which belongs to the universe.[2] The God of Christianity has his special recognition as the God of humanity—in Hinduism in our everyday meditation we try to realise his cosmic manifestation and thus free our soul from its bondage of the limitedness of the immediate; but for us he is also individual for the individual, working out, through our evolution in time, our ultimate destiny. On the whole, the author is never afraid to be unjust, and that only shows his want of respect. I am certain he would have been much more careful in his treatment if his subject were a continental poet of reputation in Europe. He ought to have realised his responsibility all the more because of the fact that there was hardly anyone in Europe who could judge his book from his own first hand knowledge. But this has only made him bold and safely dogmatic, affording him impunity when he built his conclusions upon inaccurate data.[3]

How I wish you had known Bengali! With love   Ever yours
Rabindranath Tagore

   1. Tagore seems to have taken offense at Thompson's statement that "the Englishman finds in its pages [*Balākā*] a tribute to Shakespeare, from this unlikeliest of admirers." (Thompson, *Rabindranath Tagore: Poet and Dramatist*, p. 244.) Tagore missed Thompson's intention, which was to compliment the variety and richness of the poems.
   2. See *ibid.*, pp. 110–124. Thompson's thesis is Tagore's own: the *jiban-devatā* [life-god], a personal god who is part of the poet's inner life, merges with the universal through exercise of his creative faculties. (See also S[arvepalli] Radhakrishnan, *The Philosophy of Rabindranath Tagore* [London, 1918], pp. 130–133.)
   3. Thompson's book is not, nor does it pretend to be a complete study, but he applies to Tagore's poems and plays some of the standards of that literary craftsmanship that Tagore had rejected. Thompson's attitude toward India, again akin to Tagore's own, was an intense and frequently exasperated affection, summed up in his semi-autobiographical novels, *An Indian Day* (New York, 1927) and *A Farewell to India* (London, 1931).

166
Rothenstein to Tagore

            13 Airlie Gardens, London   September 16, 1928

My dear friend—it was disappointing to hear that you were not after all coming over this autumn. I hope your health is improving. You do not spare yourself. An artist, though he should be, is not usually miserly with his strength & passion. I marvel always at your energy. I greatly enjoyed your late articles—the one on Bali especially.[1] But of course I only see your occasional English writings—doubtless you pour out wisdom in Bengali, to the delight of your fellows. What an interesting time you must have had on your Javanese & Bali pilgrimage; what I have read & heard of Bali has always fascinated me; but your

Rothenstein painting at Far Oakridge

account is the most living & intimate I have read. We are just back from Germany, where I went for a cure again—to Nauheim. It does wonders for one's heart: I am almost a normal person again. But having been near the brink was a great experience.

I still think often of India; I am told of great changes; hotels where there were none, quantities of tourists, new roads & much Westernisation. This is inevitable. An era of history is closing & a fresh one opening. Small wonder the times of travail are difficult. Perhaps later there will be less bitterness against England felt in India. We can all see the faults; but there are qualities too. Finally we are judged by our best: I still think the standard of social conduct set up by England has set a higher one throughout the world & that some day this will be more generously acknowledged. You once wrote me a letter which I felt to be less generous than your wonted ones, & I answered, I fear, with some show of irritation.[2] I think this made a tiny rift in relations which, to me at least, were very beautiful ones. This is part of the disharmony which follows from the distorting of men's energies. Yet how rich in many ways has been the relationship between East & West. I for one disbelieve in the ideal East & the material West, & I doubt whether the future will bear out the cliché. In the meanwhile it is difficult enough to be a decent man anywhere, & as difficult to be a decent artist. I am grateful to have been given a little talent, for it has helped me to see the beauty of the face of the world & to understand, at least, true work. To you have been given great gifts & you can look back on a life of exceptional fruitfulness. I send you my affectionate greetings. Ever yours

William Rothenstein

1. The articles were a series by Kalidas Nag, "Greater India Revisited" (*MR*, 42 [1927], 68–74, 219–224, 389–398; 43 [1928], 83–88). Between July 20 and October 27 Tagore and his party worked their way down the Malay Peninsula, made two separate stops in Java with a side trip to Bali, and went on to Bangkok. This was a marathon round of receptions, lectures, and entertainments. Tagore was to have left Calcutta on May 12 to give the Hibbert Lectures at Manchester College, Oxford, but he fell ill in Madras. He rested for ten days in Ceylon, but his health did not improve; he returned to Calcutta, and his lectures were cancelled.

2. See Letters 138–151.

167
Tagore to Rothenstein

Calcutta   February 22, 1929

Dear friend,

In connection with the decoration of the India House, London, the High Commissioner for India has submitted a scheme for the award of scholarships tenable in Europe to enable Indian artists to obtain further training in Europe. I am sure you have a voice in the selection of candidates and I have no hesitation in sending my recommendation of a student . . .[1]

I am preparing for a voyage in Canada where I have to represent India at the National Conference on Education to be held in Vancouver in April. I have accepted this invitation in the hope that the long sea voyage across the Pacific will do me good though I have my misgivings about my ability for fulfilling the expectation of my hosts owing to my physical weakness. On my way back home I shall take in England and see my friends if my health permits.[2] . . . I wish you could come to India on some mission or other and see what we are doing in Santiniketan where we have formed a centre of art culture in Bengal. If I ever have an opportunity I should like to show you some pictures that I have done myself with the hope of once again being startled with your appreciation as in the case of Gitanjali. With love. Ever yours

Rabindranath Tagore

1. The timing of this request could not have been worse, in view of the controversy over the India House mural painters. (See Introduction to Part VII, "The Teacher and the Traveler.")
2. See Hay, "Rabindranath Tagore in America," pp. 457–458; Kripalani, *Rabindranath Tagore*, pp. 342–343.

168
Tagore to Rothenstein

Villa Kahn, Cap. Martin   March 30, 1930

Dear friend

Surviving series of mishaps on the way we have at last arrived in Europe after a prolonged voyage of 26 days. I intend to spend some weeks in south of France till it gets warmer when I am expected in Paris. I suppose you know I have my invitation to lecture in Oxford possibly in the beginning of June when I hope it will be tolerably warm in England.[1]

I find that you already know that of late I have suddenly been seized with the mania of producing pictures. The praise which they had won from our own circle of artists I did not take at all seriously till some of them attracted notice of a Japanese artist of renown whose appreciation came to me as a surprise. Some European painters who lately visited our *Ashram* strongly recommended me to have them exhibited in Berlin and Paris. Thus I have been persuaded to bring them with me, about four hundreds of them. I still feel misgivings and I want your advice. They certainly possess psychological interest being products of untutored fingers and untrained mind. I am sure they do not represent what they call Indian Art, and in one sense they may be original, revealing a strangeness born of my utter inexperience and individual limitations. But I strongly desire to have your opinion before they are judged by others in Europe. I do hope it is not utterly impossible for you to come to this beautiful villa and stay with us for a few days. I shall only be too happy to bear your travelling expenses and shall do my best to make you comfortable. Ever yours

Rabindranath Tagore

1. The postponed Hibbert lectures were rescheduled for May 19, 21, 26. An exhibition of his paintings opened at the Galerie Pigalle, Paris, on May 2; in July works dated from 1928 to 1930 were shown at the Gallery Ferdinand Möller, Berlin.

169
Rothenstein to Tagore

13 Airlie Gardens, London   [April] 3, 1930

My dear friend—I was delighted to get your letter; not only because it told me you were in Europe, but also because it breathed a happy spirit. I hope this means that you are enjoying good health. It is charming of you to ask me to stay with you in France: how I wish that I could! Nothing would have pleased me more than to spend my Easter vacation with you: writing is a poor means of intercourse & there is much I would like to hear from you. And to be together would be like old days. Alas, I have to go to Nauheim next week, for my cure. I go there every year now; the treatment seems, in my case, to have worked wonders. . . .

I hear you have been writing much, & beautifully, in Bengali. I have only been able to read your articles in your cousin's [Modern] Review, which I always enjoy.

I am seeing much of your young Indian artists—charming young people they are. And I believe they will do their work well. There is, in much contemporary Indian painting, an element of weakness which can be challenged with benefit to the artists. I am sure they will gain something, & need lose nothing, by coming to Europe.

I am glad that you are staying in France, & that I shall be back when you come to England. Everyone here will be happy to see you again. You will find this house a busy hive. I send you my affectionate greetings; & do believe how much I regret my tedious Nauheim Easter. Ever yours—

Will Rothenstein

170
Tagore to Rothenstein

Villa Dunnre, Cap. Martin   April 7, 1930

Dear friend, I feel a great desire to be able to enjoy once again a real talk with you not in a hurry of a casual visit, but with proper intervals and in the atmosphere of a generous leisure. I can never forget the inspiring conversation which I used to have from you in the golden age of our first acquaintance. Unfortunately history, specially of a happy character, rarely repeats itself. Since that time my life has been too much burdened by responsibility and my mind which once had its superfluity is encumbered to its last limit. This is not the condition for the best harvest of friendship to mature and I often feel with regret that I have not been just to myself while trying to be wastefully prodigal for the sake of others.

However I shall meet you in London where I am likely to be about the end of May, and then I shall have the chance to show you my pictures. They are so different, one from the other, that I do not know which are the characteristic ones that may enable you to form your opinion of these vagaries of mine. With love   Ever yours

Rabindranath Tagore

171
Tagore to Rothenstein

7 Rue de l'Université, Geneva[1]
August 24, 1930

Very dear friend

To be reconciled to the inevitable with good grace is wisdom. So let me in a spirit of resignation accept the fact that you must have an undisturbed opportunity to produce your pictures while I nourish a desperate hope in my mind to find some rent somewhere in the closely knit days which hold me captive—and to play truant to all obligations that are compulsory. The rich luxury of leisure is not for me while I am in Europe—I am doomed to be unrelentingly good to humanity and remain harnessed to a cause. The artist in me ever urges me to be naughty and natural—but it requires good deal of courage to be what I truly am. Then again I do not really know myself and dare not play tricks with my nature. So the good for nothing artist must have for his bed-fellow the man of a hundred good intentions.

In Germany my pictures have found a very warm welcome which was far beyond my expectation. Five of them have got their permanent place in Berlin National Gallery, and several invitations have come from other centres for their exhibition. This has a strange analogy with the time which followed the Gitanjali publication—it is sudden and boisterous like a hill stream after a shower and like the same casual flood may dis-

appear with the same emphasis of suddenness.² With love
Ever yours

Rabindranath Tagore

The appeal for help which Andrews intended to publish in your papers never had my sanction and I have stopped it.³

    1. The Geneva address of Tagore's American supporter, Miss Josephine Storey. He and his party (Rathindranath, Pratima, and a secretary) had reached London on May 11, with Tagore still eager for Rothenstein's advice about his pictures. (Tagore to Alice Rothenstein, May 9, 1930. RP:HL.) Rothenstein and Sturge Moore rallied once again and tried to arrange an exhibition at Curtis Moffat's Gallery in Fitzroy Square, since it was "impossible to get [any other] gallery in London at this time. The drawings are extraordinarily vital: they show none of the weakness of the revivalist schools which stand for modern Indian art. But of course they are mostly 'abstract' in character." (Rothenstein to Sturge Moore, June 6, 1930. TSM.) Tagore was in Birmingham, where his paintings were on display during June at the City Museum and Art Gallery. No London show was arranged through Moffat. On July 8 Tagore was in Devon with the Elmhirsts, and on July 10 he left for Berlin.
    2. There is no record and no catalogue listing since 1930 of works purchased from Tagore. (Marjan Rinkleff-Reinders, Berlin National Gallery, to the editor, March 26, 1970.)
    3. Laurence Housman told Rothenstein: "A letter is being prepared for the press with about 12 proposed signatories—yours among the number—asking support for a fund to help Rabindranath Tagore's work at Santiniketan. I have been put on to collect the signatures. I have got C. P. Scott's, and am writing to Gilbert Murray, Masefield, Sir Michael Sadler, and the others that have been proposed. Will you sign with us, if the thing can be got through?" Later he wrote: "Holiday time causes difficulty and delay. At present only about half the signatures we are asking for have come in. The old man has been told of the effort that is being made for him, and is greatly cheered." (Laurence Housman to Rothenstein, July 28, August 19, 1930. RP:HL.)

172
Tagore to Rothenstein

7, Rue de l'Université, Geneva
[September 1?, 1930]

Very dear friend

    The world in which I find myself today has its light rays which do not touch the artist—he does not exist. I feel homesick for that paradise for the lazy minds which is somewhere not very far from the Bolpur Station. I have been tempted and banished from it, lured away from the flower of beauty to the fruit of work, and I am dreaming of my salvation at the end of my term of trial—but the time is not near.

H. G. Wells came to see me yesterday and I was delighted. I felt that his thoughts are being grouped on a large background of history and his thoughts stimulated my mind.[1]

You will be surprised to hear that I am getting ready to visit Russia from where I have received invitation. I am eager to meet the people who are working at, not a new chapter, but a new volume of the history of man which is not merely for their own country but for the whole world,[2]   Ever yours

Rabindranath Tagore

1. Sudhin Ghose, Bengali writer, was present, made notes on their conversation, and published them in "Three Conversations: Tagore Talks with Einstein, with Rolland, and with Wells," *Asia*, 31 (1931), 139–143, 196–197. This angered Wells, who felt that the occasion had been turned to Tagore's publicity purposes. In 1931 Wells flatly refused to contribute to *The Golden Book of Tagore: A Homage to Rabindranath Tagore from India and the World in Celebration of His Seventieth Birthday*, ed. Ramananda Chatterjee (Calcutta, 1931). (Wells to Rothenstein, August 26, 1931. RP:HL.)

2. See Hay, *Asian Ideas,* pp. 173–174. The Rothensteins were at Carutza, Caux sur Montreux, and begged Tagore to join them. To a letter from Alice Rothenstein ([August 31, 1930] R-S) he replied that, although her letter tempted him, he dare not break his engagements: "I have to prove, so long as I am in the west, that Indians are also punctual in their habits and know the value of time and in the language of their conducts they observe the same accents and idioms as you do. In fact, we have to translate ourselves—otherwise you do not understand us, or what is far worse, misunderstand. If I were the original Rabindranath of the east I could come to you this moment and my people would laugh and say the fellow has forgotten the date. But the translation has to observe a different grammar and be very correct." (Tagore to Alice Rothenstein [September 1?, 1930]. RP.)

173
Rothenstein to Tagore

Carutza, Caux   September 2, 1930

My dear friend—what an interesting time you will have in Russia! Had I been strong enough, I would have gone to see for myself what is, after all, one of the most significant experiments of our time. Indeed I understand how drawn you feel to the people who get from men like yourself what so few have to give. True poets are rare; but poets who give themselves as well as great poetry are rarer still. But I, who thought myself cut off from work, am grateful for a few years of gardening. Each thing begun that I am allowed to finish makes me feel grateful for the privilege of life. And since strength has been so unexpectedly given back to me, I feel it a duty to use it fruitfully. But these lake mists have been very trying—there are impatient intervals of waiting. We have a guest here just now—someone who thinks life without Betty would not be worth living. So I do not think we shall keep Betty at home much longer.

What golden days these have been; golden, & high up where we are, cool, too, as gold. I hope you haven't suffered from the heat in Geneva.

You don't tell us how long you expect to stay: we may remain here for another 10 days. Affectionate greetings from yours ever—

W. R.

174
Tagore to Rothenstein

Hotel Algonquin, New York   November 6, 1930

My dear Friend

I have passed through a physical crisis—my doctor looked serious—but I am out of it. I ought to have run back home but I dare not. I have struggled for thirty years unaided to build up a scheme which could be my own best offer to my country's need. It has won praise from our people and our Government but very little more that is substantial, till at last my days have come to this end and I am driven against my will and my ill health to come to this country with my beggar's bowl. I can not afford to go back home empty handed at this moment when sufferings are cruel and universal in my country and starvation is inevitable. My trial here is certainly much milder than that which a very large number of our men and women are passing through and it would be cowardly for me to complain even if my health completely fails me.

I assure you I shall try to be very careful for I must live a few more years for the sake of my own cause which must not be orphaned and lost.

I do not know when I shall be able to find my release and go back to my own corner for *I* can not be the chooser. With my love to you all   Ever yours

Rabindranath Tagore

175
Rothenstein to Tagore

13 Airlie Gardens, London   [November 1930]

My dear friend—I was distressed to read of your being laid up in America. Indeed you take too much upon your shoulders—so do many of us, but you load yourself, like a station porter, with luggage only a porter can carry. I too have played the porter, to my cost, but am ten years your junior. Russia, & then the States—'twas too much to undertake. I envied you your Russian experience, I confess. Were I strong enough I should like to see something of this extraordinary experiment in democracy. But I shouldn't dash off to America afterwards. But rest does wonders, & I hope they are insisting on perfect quiet, & keeping idealists away from you—American idealists are the most exhausting experience that can happen to one.[1] . . . There is an exhibition now on at India House of Solomon's Bombay followers—there is great merit in Western art & great merit in Eastern art, but none in bad art, whether of the West or the East.[2]

Perhaps later, with renewed strength, but enforced leisure, you will take up pencil & brush again. Meanwhile complete rest is what you need. May it bring you complete refreshment. We hope to see you here before your return to India—perhaps you will spend a few quiet days with us. Every one here sends you warm greetings, & voeux for your speedy recovery. I know your wonderful recuperative powers. Ever yours—

William Rothenstein

1. Tagore was in Russia from September 11 to September 25, when he went to Germany. He describes the tour in his *Rāshiār Cithi* [Letters from Russia] (1931), in *R-R*, XX, 269–349: *Letters from Russia*, trans. Sasadhar Sinha (Calcutta, 1960). He sailed October 3 for America. (See Hay, "Rabindranath Tagore in America," pp. 458–461; Mukherjee, *Passage to America*, pp. 99–107, 215–216.) His literary affairs were being conducted extemporaneously; Rathindranath, who was in England, instructed Macmillan to send all payments to him, as his father was continually on the road. (Rathindranath Tagore to Macmillan, September 24, 1930. MP:BM.) Rabindranath told his niece that his illness began in Paris, where he tried in vain to ward off the attack. Returning home was impossible, he told her, and if a truth were self-evident in this episode, it was that men were not immortal. (Tagore to Indira Devi Chaudhuri, Bengali letter, October 25, 1930, *Cithipatra*, V, 76–77.)

2. W. E. Gladstone Solomon (1880–?), Principal of the Government School of Art in Bombay, whose students exhibited at India House in October 1930. India Society scrapbooks for 1930 (India Society: IOL) mention no connection with this event, which may have been sponsored by the Indian High Commission.

176
Tagore to Rothenstein

Hotel Regina, London   January 9, 1931[1]

Dear Sir William[2]

I am leaving today. I have asked my friend who is in America to bring all my pictures to you. Will you thank Mr Evelyn Shaw on my behalf and arrange with him the exhibition?[3] I had hoped that I should stay on for some few more days and meet you once more but I decided that it would be wiser for Rathi's sake to start from London instead of taking the overland route. I earnestly hope that you may come to us in India and meet me in my own surroundings. With love to you all. Ever yours

Rabindranath Tagore

1. Tagore left the United States on December 18, reached England on December 23, returned to Calcutta by January 31.
2. Rothenstein was knighted in January 1931.

3. Sir Evelyn Shaw (1882–) Honorary General Secretary, British School at Rome, 1912–1947. "America . . . my pictures": show of Tagore's work in November 1930 at The Fifty-Sixth Street Galleries, New York City. The catalogue contained a Foreword by Coomaraswamy and a note by Tagore, "The Language of Pictures." Rothenstein and Shaw discussed the possibility of a Tagore exhibit at the Imperial Institute in London in October, but Rothenstein also pointed out that Tagore must bear gallery and framing charges. (Rothenstein to Tagore, March 5, 1931. R-S.)

177
Tagore to Rothenstein

Santiniketan   March 24, 1931

My dear Friend

The present economic condition in Bengal is severely critical. The jute which is the mainstay of our peasants remains unreaped in the field owing to an abnormally low price. We who mainly depend upon our income from the land are desperately devising curtailment of expenditure to an extreme limit. In such an atmosphere of compulsory self-immolation I do not feel the least enthusiasm about spending money over my picture exhibition. However, let me know the probable cost if I venture to proceed about it. The pictures which are in the American gallery waiting to be brought to you are all mounted and only require framing. I hardly feel sanguine about their sale and my empty pocket cannot afford to be reckless. The money that I had earned in previous exhibitions has vanished like raindrops upon an arid land—and therefore I cannot help asking you to be wisely cautious in your advice. . . .

You will be surprised to learn that I hardly know anything about the recent political development in India. I do not read newspapers for I have my own work which I consider to be important and I cannot allow my mind to be waylaid by discussions that are outside my scope. My love to you all   Ever yours

Rabindranath Tagore

178
Rothenstein to Tagore

13 Airlie Gardens, London   [May 1931]

My very dear friend—do you refer to a diary? I don't. So the date of your birthday slipped my memory. The anniversary has a special meaning for me too, for it spans just 20 years of our friendship. You were 50 when we met, & I forty save one year—both young, to our present way of thinking. It was a significant meeting: I little thought, as I asked shyly whether I might make a drawing of you, how closely our lives were to be connected. The friendship has been an asset in my later life; indeed, I cannot imagine these years without your place in them. I have been re-reading your letters, so full of wit & wisdom, &, during the war years, of pain & disillusion too. . . . Jute is not your harvest; I see golden sheaves in a long perspective, rows of them, which you have set up, from seeds you have sown. In my eyes, you are to be envied. It is on the fulness of your years I congratulate you, not on their number. . . . Would that I could greet you in person, in your beloved Bolpur. India I can only revisit in my mind; I count as one of the chief misfortunes of a damaged heart that I cannot come to you in person. But if minds, as I believe possible, can & do commune across space, you will know something of what is in mine. But we must meet again—your last visit gave us so much happiness; it is for you to be generous, & to put my fewer years to shame. . . . Ever your friend

William Rothenstein

179
Tagore to Rothenstein

Santiniketan   May 16, 1931

My dear friend

I have just got your most fascinating book while I am lying on bed with fever and on the eve of a voyage to Persia from where I have an invitation. I have decided to go for in spite of some risk to my health I can not resist the temptation. It is like playing the bad boy anticipating the punishment that lies in store for me.[1]

I wonder if my publishers have sent to you my Religion of Man. I am afraid it is too personal, with an idea in its centre which is almost incommunicable specially in a language which is foreign to me. It seems from some of the short notices that my English readers are either unable or unwilling to meet me half way. But to my great surprise General Smuts of South Africa has written a highly appreciative letter about it to Andrews describing this book as the best that I have ever written.[2]

I am to start in a day or two if in the meanwhile my state of health does not make it absolutely impossible for me.

From some newspaper clippings it seems that my friends in America have started an Exhibition in Boston and the critics are unhesitating in their praise which is unusual in that country about things belonging to art.[3] With love   Ever yours

Rabindranath Tagore

1. The trip had to be postponed. "Fascinating book": Rothenstein's *Men and Memories, 1872–1900*.
2. See "General Smuts on Rabindranath Tagore's 'The Religion of Man,'" *MR*, 49 (1931), 730–731. Tagore, *The Religion of Man* (London, 1931), his Hibbert Lectures (see Letter 168).
3. An exhibition and sale of his works at the Museum of Fine Arts, and at the Doll and Richards Gallery, Boston, in October.

180
Tagore to Rothenstein

Darjeeling   June 26, 1931

My dear friend

The materials and tendencies are no doubt important in our history but when some unexpected push of an accident startles them into a final form it seems to carry a purpose of a creative providence. Of all the facts in my life the fact of my meeting you in London in 1912 was most amazing in its consequences in the opening up of a prospect for me so utterly different from my former environment. Your discovery of a few meagre pages of my manuscript brought me out from my seclusion into the heart of a large world and turned me into a migratory being that has its two homes in the two opposite shores of the sea. This present celebration of my 70th birthday has its significance in the fact that I have won my right to claim a recognition as the poet who has had his two births, one among his own people and another in the freedom of humanity. This great fact has its intimate relation to your own friendship which had been offered to me when I was still in the shadow of obscurity. Others are sending me today greetings of praise along with their felicitations from all parts of the world but you anticipated this event, and your homage, as coming from a representative of world culture, was the first one that I received in my life. With my best love to you and to yours

Rabindranath Tagore

I know that during my contact with you I occasionally displayed moods that must have caused you pain, but I hope you realise that they never represented my deeper normality, that they were provoked by some jerks of time which for the moment was passing over a road badly out of repairs.

181
Rothenstein to Tagore

Royal College of Art   July 15, 1931

My very dear friend—your letter warmed my heart. My visit to India (21 years ago! is it credible?) & my meeting with you, were Providential. Your friendship has enriched my life: be sure it has been deeply valued. Indeed it has been no ordinary one; something in my nature responded, from the beginning, to your own, has since always responded, & whenever we have met, face to face, I have felt ours to be a perfect friendship. But Tagore disciples are not Tagore. I have never loved followers as I have the master; & sometimes the followers prejudice people, & create a reaction against the master himself. Only lately I was asked to join a Tagore society: I said, politely I hope, but firmly—no. When I can stand before the handiwork of an artist, what need have I of chromo lithographs? Has not the portable organ driven the sweet Indian stringed instruments from the hearth? . . . It is for the gift of ourselves that we are most grateful—those who rob us of our sincerity are bad company, mean, lousy, cut-purses & cut-throats, treacherous, ill living, false, stinking, underhand, ill-conditioned, ungodly persons, to be avoided at all costs.

I gather that you are not to go to Persia—a wise decision, surely. A journey thither I gather to be by no means without hardship; & from what you write you owe reasonable care to yourself. . . .

I send you my warmest greetings; your letters are always welcome. I value your last more than I can tell you. Ever your affectionate

Will Rothenstein

182
Tagore to Rothenstein

Darjeeling November 15, 1931

My very dear friend

The whole country is under the gloom of the Economic depression, on the top of which, a large part of Bengal is devasted by floods. Visva Bharati is in a sorry plight, for we have nearly come to the end of our tether. A very long period of suffering is before our people, the continual strain of which is sure to drive a number of our young men to desperate deeds of violence creating a vicious circle of an alternate repression and defiance.

Your suggestion of a secretary is tempting but hopelessly beyond our means at a time when public beggars like us have lost their trade and borrowing is not encouraged.[1]

I have come to Darjeeling in search of health and peace of mind, but the latter has run out of stock in the present day world and I must not complain. Kindly remember me to Lady Rothenstein and accept my love. Ever yours

Rabindranath Tagore

1. Rothenstein had asked whether Tagore could employ an English secretary who wanted a position in India. (Rothenstein to Tagore, September 28, 1931. R-S.)

183
Rothenstein to Tagore

13 Airlie Gardens, London   January 15, 1932

My very dear friend—I have only lately been reading the letters sent to me during the last 2 months or more. I had an attack of pneumonia, & all letters were withheld, yours among them, until convalescence was over. To my surprise my heart stood the strain without giving me trouble & I feel none the worse. But O, the waste of weeks! I am glad to know you have been away in the mountains: glad too that you have avoided the loud-speaker, so crude, so deafening, of the political gramophone. I kept away from Gandhi while he was here. The truth can only be courted in solitary places; even then how rarely won! I would prefer that Gandhi had sworn seven days silence, rather than he should have got caught in the coils of words. No, it isn't my India I see now, nor do I imagine it to be yours. That is my fear, that when you get India into your own hands something very precious may have gone—an essence, a perfume, a vision that may escape.[1]

I gave that large decoration I painted—Evening at Benares—do you remember it, with yourself in the foreground, to India House.[2] I tried, too, to interest various Round Table Deputies in the work of Barman & his friend, but in vain. Barman left last week & promised to carry you my greetings. The paintings are among the best I think, of any Indian mural paintings; & these young men have learned something, I think: how to work together. They should prove useful men in the future. But I wonder often how much aesthetic sense there is in truth among your countrymen.[3] I hope what I read here, that your peasants are melting down their beautiful gold ornaments, is not true. Jewellery is the last of the Indian arts that remains in its purity among the people—or am I wrong? I wonder often what you are doing, what writing, what painting too. The sight of your handwriting is always welcome. I send you my affectionate greetings for a fruitful year. I heard from Yeats not long ago, who told me he had written to you.[4] He remains ever a loyal friend—wise & steadfast. Sturge Moore & Binyon have both appeared as accepted poets, in volume form.[5] But poor Binyon has been very ill, & is to go away for some time. Ever yours,

William Rothenstein

My warm greetings to Rathindranath & his dear wife—& to your nephews, if they still remember me.

1. Rothenstein disliked Gandhi: "Madame Naidu used to come and beg William to draw [Gandhi]—but William who had met him years before—made some charming excuse of being busy etc. etc." (Alice Rothenstein to Flora Russell [March 1945]. By permission of Mrs. Noel Blakiston.)

2. "Sunset at Benares" now hangs in the India Supply Mission, Bromyard Avenue, London W. 3.

3. Herbert Baker shared this misgiving: "What I did see of their colour [at India House] I did not think very good. It seems to me that all Indian painters make the vital mistake of following the colour scheme of Ajanta, where, accidentally, I think, and due to decay, browns prevail. Do you not think they ought to keep more to the primitive colours, particularly where there must be so much brown in the human skins?" (Baker to Rothenstein, January 22, 1931. RP:HL.) Barman: D. K. Dev Barman (1902–   ), one of the India House mural painters, a student at the Royal College of Art, 1929–30.

4. Rothenstein was pursued by requests to remind Tagore's famous friends to contribute to *The Golden Book of Tagore*. Yeats replied that he would felicitate Tagore in his own time and fashion. (Yeats to Rothenstein, September 4 [1931]. RP:HL. Quoted in part in *SF*, pp. 178–179.) He did so promptly. (Yeats to Tagore, September 7, 1931. R-S. Quoted in *The Golden Book of Tagore*, p. 269.)

5. Sturge Moore, *The Poems of T. Sturge Moore*, 2 vols. (London, 1931–32). Binyon, *Collected Poems of Laurence Binyon*, 2 vols. (London, 1931).

184
Rothenstein to Tagore

13 Airlie Gardens, London   April 15, 1932

My very dear friend—I received a handsome present from India—a Golden Book, beautifully printed & illustrated, an universal paean to yourself. It is a model of what a good Indian book can be—I was often critical of your Indian printing in the past. I would gladly have sent photographs of the 1st & last drawing I made of you; but the good Ramananda said nothing of reproductions when he first wrote to me.

I hear that you are again in better health, & that you are again thinking of a visit to Persia—by air-plane![1] I envy you your energy & adventure, as I envy Shaw's. I saw him yesterday, hale as ever, after a visit to S. Africa. Yeats, too, is in Town, wiser & wittier than ever, quite recovered from his illness. We spoke much of you, & of India. He, of course, is all for separation; he is much more uncompromising than I. My feelings are ever for the bottom dog—& now, so far as I can gather, the English officials & business men seem to be that![2] Seriously, I am deeply concerned about the present state: I ask of those returning from India about conditions there, & I get contradictory accounts. A lady, to whom I gave a letter to yourself, tells me that Shantiniketan was the one hopeful place she visited. But it is not in India alone—everywhere the noise is so deafening. I have shut my studio door on the confusion, & found peace in work. Yesterday I dined with Sturge Moore & we, too, talked of you. Mukul [Dey] had sent him a booklet of your drawings—some excellent ones among them. How is Mukul doing? I hear nothing from him. I was often critical of him & I hear he "scandalises me" as Paul Robeson would say. I confess one of the happier results of years is indifference to the arrows of men; indeed, on the whole, I would say I am happier now than in my younger days. At the moment, I feel like a convict released, for my 2nd vol. of memories is out of my hands & my spare time my own again. But one book for 20 years! I have left out, perforce, so much I wanted to say—a good deal that I did say; and how difficult to write about contemporaries![3] Sugar ornaments on the birthday & the wedding day are accepted, but for everyday sustenance, something less rich for the stomach. By the way, Yeats was full of an autobiography of a sadhu who is over here, one of the remarkable books ever written, he thinks. I forget his name—do you know anything of him?[4] . . . I send you affectionate greetings. Ever yours—

W. R.

1. Tagore flew to Iran on April 11, accompanied by Pratima, preceded by two secretaries. He returned to Calcutta on June 3.

2. A few months later Yeats and Shaw busied themselves with founding the Irish Academy of Letters. (See Yeats, *Letters*, pp. 800–802.)

3. *Men and Memories, 1900–1922*.

4. Purohit Swami, *An Indian Monk: His Life and Adventures* (London, 1932). At first Yeats declined to become involved with this book. (See *W. B. Yeats and Thomas Sturge Moore: Their Correspondence 1901–1937*, ed. Ursula Bridge [London, 1953], pp. 168–170.) He then agreed to write a preface. (See his *Letters*, p. 806.) Sturge Moore also edited the Swami's work, the sequel being a spate of correspondence between Marie Sturge Moore and Mrs. W. B. Yeats about Yeats and the Swami. (Box 31, items 188–198. TSM.)

185
Rothenstein to Tagore

13 Airlie Gardens, London   November 4, 1932

My dear friend—it is long since I last heard from you. Now Andrews tells me of your loss—a beloved grandchild. You have suffered many such losses—but the seeming waste of a promising young life always seems the hardest of fate's knocks to bear. I scarcely realised that the young Ganguli I knew (I haven't seen him for some time) had a son of 19.[1] From Andrews I heard, too, that you had flown to Persia—when I last heard from you you had given up the idea of this visit. How much of the world you have seen![2] I envy you less now than I would have done formerly. In a world distracted I find comfort in quiet corners. This summer I visited my old home; & the beauty of the scenes I knew as a boy touched me deeply —so much, that I felt I had done better to have painted what I understood better than any foreign subjects—& was better fitted to interpret than others. Do not think that my love for India is not what it was. But I find myself unable to understand the complexities of the many interests; while sympathising with the natural urge for freedom, I dislike the exaggerations & untruthfulnesses involved in a struggle, & am without the knowledge required for fair judgment. Men like Shastri seemed to me rare among the delegates I met during the Conference.[3] . . .

Yeats was in London recently—he has grown wise—& witty too—with the years. He thought I had somewhat underestimated the help he & Sturge Moore gave you on your translations: that you could not discern the finer shades between used & unused phrases as they could. But you would be the first to admit that: I only wanted to rebutt the malicious suggestions made in India—never here. You have no more loyal admirers than Yeats & Sturge Moore.[4] I have just heard that Barman has got work to do in India;[5] this I was pleased indeed to know; but I was surprised to find that 2 of his colleagues at India House are back again. I hoped they would all get work in their own country. Surely there is something wrong if 2 gifted young artists can find no employment in India. I hope in time your painters will get closer to Indian life, as the old painters did, than is now the case. Do they really care so much for your mythological tales, & so little for the beauty of everything under the light of the sun?

Indian traditions—European traditions! there is so little difference, au fond, between them. But European artists have had more curiosity, surely, & have explored fresh avenues, in the last 2 centuries especially, than Eastern ones. (I must except Japan—with Hok'sai & Outamaro.) Surely Indian painters can learn from Europe without shame. The real trouble is that they have seen the worst examples of commercial art in India, the worst furniture & pictures in European bungalows. I am all for the interpretation of the true Indian spirit, but revival is scarcely creation, & I think a visit to Europe should often prove stimulating to an ingenuous spirit.

. . . Of your recent work I know nothing—who, without Bengali, can follow it?[6] I send you my affectionate greetings & am, as ever, yours—

William Rothenstein

1. Nitindranath Ganguli, Tagore's only grandchild, died of virulent tuberculosis in Germany in August 1932.
2. Rothenstein forgets that he has heard this. See Letter 184.

3. V. S. Srinivasa Shastri (1869–1946), Moderate leader, member since 1906 of Gokhale's Servants of India Society and its President 1915–1917; Member, Viceroy's Legislative Council, 1916–1920; elected to Council of State under Montagu-Chelmsford Reforms; Member, Moderate Delegation to England, 1919; representative to Imperial Conference, 1920.

4. See *MM* II, 262–271, 282–286. Rothenstein had told Yeats: "I am of course telling the story of Tagore's first visit to England, and of the preparation of Gitanjali in which you had so large a share. Incidentally this gives me a chance of correcting the unfair statements frequently made in India that you had to re-write a great part of Gitanjali before it was fit for publication." (Rothenstein to Yeats, August 19, 1931. Michael Yeats.)

5. Barman applied for a post as Inspector of Drawing.

6. Tagore's only imaginative writing recently published in English translation was *The Golden Boat,* trans. Bhabani Bhattacharya (London, 1932), miscellaneous poems and prose sketches (not to be confused with Tagore's Bengali volume, *Shonār Tori*). When Tagore heard that Bhattacharya had included several poems already in *Fruit-Gathering* and *The Fugitive,* he lodged a strong protest. (Tagore to Macmillan, February 17, 1932. MP:BM.)

186
Tagore to Rothenstein

                        Visva-Bharati, Bengal   November 26, 1932

My dear friend,

Your letter has given me deep joy. I have suffered much in life and my grandson's death was one more poignant sorrow for me. He was a lovable boy, and that his fresh young life should be taken away from us was hard indeed to bear. I have now recovered from the shock: experience widens our realization of life which includes death as well.

Persia was a great inspiration to me. It is splendid to find a nation courageously throwing off the stranglehold of inert tradition and relentless foreign exploitation, and emerging with fresh and rebellious life into the sunlight of freedom. I felt a stir of new consciousness in the air of Persia, which harmonised so well with the beauty of the land and the great culture of its people.[1]

Coming back to my country I find things getting worse in India—a deepening gloom which has been relieved by the vigorous social reforms set in motion by Mahatmaji's great fast. Not being a politician I cannot presume to devise means and methods which may bring in better days for our peoples but I suffer with them. As you say there is exaggeration on both sides and I shrink from the aggressiveness inevitably produced by litigants both of whom are to blame for the present condition. The party whose voice is smothered by every means at the command of an efficient scientific power naturally attach too much importance to events which are inconsequential when seen in a wide perspective of truth. It is a pity that Sastri whom you rightly praise has been ruled out from the Conference in London.[2]

Your letter has the subtle atmosphere of Art evoking many coloured images of reality. Who would leave them for the harsh assertiveness of facts that carry no meaning in themselves and must wait for the inner mind to be related to significance?

You remind me of those early days of Gitanjali.

Poets are proverbially vain and I am no exception. Therefore if I cherish even an exaggerated notion of the value of my own poems which are in Bengali I am sure you will half humorously tolerate it. But I am no such fool as to claim an exhorbitant price for my English which is a borrowed acquisition coming late in my life. I am sure you remember with what reluctant hesitation I gave up to your hand my manuscript of Gitanjali feeling sure that my English was of that amorphous kind for whose syntax a school-boy could be reprimanded. The next day you came rushing to me with assurance which I dared not take seriously and to prove to me the competence of your literary judgment you made three copies of those translations and sent them to Stopford Brooke, Bradley and Yeats. The letter which Bradley sent to you in answer left no room for me to feel diffident about the merit of those poems and Stopford Brooke's opinion also was a corroboration. These were enthusiastic as far as I remember.[3] But even then I had no doubt that it was not the language but the earnest feeling expressed in a simple manner which touched their hearts. That was amply enough for a foreigner and the unstinted praise offered to me by those renowned critics was a great deal more than I could ever expect. Then came those delightful days when I worked with Yeats and I am sure the magic of his pen helped my English to attain some quality of permanence. It was not at all necessary for my own reputation that I should find my place in the history of your literature. It was an accident for which you were also responsible and possibly most of all was Yeats. But yet sometimes I feel almost ashamed that I whose undoubted claim has been recognised by my countrymen to a sovereignty in our own world of letters should not have waited till it was discovered by the outside world in its own true majesty and environment, that I should ever go out of my way to court the attention of others having their own language for their enjoyment and use. At least it is never the function of a poet to personally help in the transportation of his poems to an alien form and atmosphere, and be responsible for any unseemly risk that may happen to them. However, you must own that you alone were to blame for this and not myself. To the end of my days I should have felt happy and contented to think that the translations I did were merely for private recreation and never for public display if you did not bring them before your readers. Please thank Yeats once again on my behalf for the help which he rendered to my poems in their perilous adventure of a foreign reincarnation and assure him that I at least never underrate the value of his literary comradeship.[4] Latterly I have written and published both prose and poetry in English, mostly translations, unaided by any friendly help, but this again I have done in order to express my ideas, not for gaining any reputation for my mastery in the use of a language which can never be mine.

It is sad that some of our artists should feel that they have little scope for creative work in our own land. Burman, as far as I know, is still in Tipperah State, and there is a danger of his wasting his talents for want of proper stimulation. European art, like European literature has its great message for us, and this can be truly realized only when we have developed our own individuality which can react to it and assimilate it into the living texture of its being. What is fatal for our creative workers is to get into the habit of depending upon the approbation of western critics and trying to come up to their expectations. The standard of critical judgment must be in the artists' own realizations and in the atmosphere which surrounds them. I feel that the present ferment in India's social and cultural life should open up new vistas before our artists, giving them abundant material wherewith to enrich their art. Nandalal [Bose] and others have already felt the need of a new orientation in their technique and subject matter and their recent works show a vigorous departure from traditions and that spirit of creative adventure which you speak of so beautifully. . . . Ever sincerely yours,

Rabindranath Tagore

1. Tagore describes the trip in his *Pārshyae* [In Persia] (1936), in *R-R*, XXII, 431–502.
2. "Mahatmaji's great fast": Gandhi's fast began September 20 at Poona, as protest against the Communal Award which split the Hindu community by making outcaste groups a separate electoral unit. (See Kripalani, *Rabindranath Tagore,* pp. 366–368.) "Sastri . . . ruled out": the Indian National Liberal Federation was one of the groups unrepresented at the Round Table Conference, thus eliminating Shastri as a delegate. (See editorial, "Pocket Purdah 'R.T.C.,'" *MR*, 52 (1932), 589–590.)
3. See Introduction, note 40; Letter 4, note 1.
4. It seems likely that Rothenstein's compliance with this request evoked Yeats's vehement response, dated "[probably 1935]" in his *Letters*, pp. 834–835.

187
Rothenstein to Tagore

13 Airlie Gardens, London   October 18, 1933

My dear friend—I don't know which of us wrote last: it seems long since I heard from you, though happily I hear often of you. . . . I was asked to join the initiating committee [of a suggested Indian Academy]. My one preoccupation was that if anything of the kind is founded in India (& I hope entirely by your own people) it should not be, like the British Academy, merely limited to scholars, but active in encouragement of the creative side of art & literature. To do is more important than to study what has been done. This is not to dismiss scholarship—only to give it its proper place. Indian painting is still timid & over-derivative. It is always surprising to me that the overwhelming vitality of Indian life should be so feebly repre-

William Butler Yeats

sented. It is perhaps a paradox that extreme nationalism is so ineffective in rousing the inner spirit. Perhaps that comes later.¹ I notice that Yeats, A.E. & other Irish friends have taken no political part in national affairs of late. Have you read Yeats's last book of poems? To my mind it contains some of the best work he has ever done.² Simplicity is not a formula but the gradual shedding of desired & desirable things—a final radiance; & that Yeats has achieved. It is our loss that Bengali is a closed book to us; otherwise we too would follow your own ripening. . . . I send you my affectionate greetings, in which the family joins. Ever yours—

William Rothenstein

1. The Indian Academy never came into being. A committee met in London on March 14, 1933, and proposed that such an Academy concern itself with both the natural sciences and the arts. However, since "the constitution of the proposed Academy would necessarily be worked out by a committee in India the matter was left without further specification." Tagore was one of the Indians suggested as members, "with a view to the required assurance of Indian countenance." (Untitled committee report, March 14 [1933]. Havell: IOL.)
2. Yeats, *The Winding Stair and Other Poems* (London, 1933).

188
Tagore to Rothenstein

"Uttarayan," Santiniketan   November 17, 1933

My dear friend,

The first encroachment of old age in our life is very much like our village road after the flood brought by rainy season subsides. The boat then is useless and walking over the mud is met with numerous unpleasant surprises at every step. But the last few miles in the road I am passing along is dry and grey and I am reconciled to its inefficient unevenness. I am cultivating the wisdom of indigence and I hardly ever now make mistake by claiming credit in my bank when the overdraft is fast reaching its limit. I have grown careful about the expenditure of my energy even though all disappointed parties blame me for deliberate miserliness. Only it hurts me when I suddenly realise that tied to my powerlessness my young helpers are robbed of their freedom and the pressure of my tired strength tires them. I never blame them if they desert me—my complaint is against the inconsiderate people who persistently refuse to make allowance for the natural disabilities of my present condition.

 What you have said in your letter about our modern artists I fully agree with. It has too often been evident in all departments of our life the fact that when we are pushed into a wider freedom from the narrow enclosure of our tradition that has become anachronistic we begin to build new walls and create another impasse before us. This happens almost in all countries but in India it has grown chronic owing to our utter lack of zest in life and inertia born of continual despondency. . . . With love to you all, Ever yours

           Rabindranath Tagore

189
Rothenstein to Tagore

    13 Airlie Gardens, London [December? 1933]

My very dear friend—a letter from you is always welcome; & in this case it was followed by a gift, that of a recent book of your poems. Would that I could read them! I can only look at the pictures, which interest me greatly.[1] . . . The return to an earlier tradition in Havell's time was a welcome thing, & a wholesome. But I cannot but feel this should be a passing phase & that something more living, nearer to the life & spirit of present-day India, should have emerged. Oddly enough, there is a note in your own drawings, poet though you be, which shows a fresh mood & a more vigorous handling. I should like to see something of this energy in the touch, & subject matter, of other Indian work. I appear to be accused of a bias in favour of the Calcutta artists; as a matter of fact I am somewhat critical of all my Indian artist friends.[2] There is a weak strain running through most of their work, which I cannot but see; while in Europe there is still infinite invention & virility through the arts, despite its long history. I say this to you, as I would to no one else. Indeed, I have recently written to the Viceroy again pressing the claims of Indian artists on public support.[3]

Your nice secretary was with us lately—I like him very much.[4] . . . We send you our warm greetings & wishes for the year. Ever affectionately—

William Rothenstein

1. Tagore, *Bicitritā* [Variety] (1933), in *R-R*, XVII, 1–46. Original edition illustrated by Gaganendranath and Abanindranath Tagore, Nandalal Bose, and others of the Calcutta School of artists.
2. See Introduction to Part VII, "The Teacher and the Traveler."
3. Rothenstein to Lord Willingdon, December 6, 1933. Copy. RP:HL. Rothenstein also reasserted his impartiality toward all schools of Indian artists. Freeman Freeman-Thomas, 1st Marquess of Willingdon (1866–1941), Governor of Bombay, 1913–1919; Governor of Madras, 1919–1924; Governor-General of Canada, 1926–1931; Viceroy of India, 1931–1936.
4. Amiya Chakravarty (1901–), at Oxford 1933–34 to write a doctoral dissertation on Thomas Hardy. (See Chakravarty, *The Dynasts and the Post-War Age in Poetry: A Study in Modern Ideas* [London, 1938].)

190
Tagore to Rothenstein

"Uttarayan"   October 12, 1934

My dear Friend,

Chakravarty came over for a couple of months and is now returning to Oxford to continue his researches. As he will tell you, I have been painting many pictures and sometimes I feel that you would like to see my new things which are done with that daring in technique and style that only an untrained and persistently impulsive dreamer can achieve. I have been wondering whether it would not be possible for me once for all to have an exhibition of my pictures in London so that they could be properly evaluated. In the gathering evening of my life I would dearly like once more to visit England to meet my friends—perhaps I could then take some of my pictures along with me.

Chakravarty has had talks with my cousin Abanindranath,

and with Nandalal about the exhibition of Indian Art which will soon be held in London. He will tell you in detail the reasons why most of our artists, who are as you know unable to spend money ahead on their pictures, have not been able to co-operate with the organizers of the exhibition. It will be a pity if the pictures of some of our best artists go unrepresented at an exhibition which claims to represent modern Indian Art. My love to you all,   Ever yours,

                                      Rabindranath Tagore

191
Rothenstein to Tagore

                      Far Oakridge   October 27, 1934

My dear Rabindranath—I am delighted to hear there is a prospect of our seeing you in the near future. You have so many friends here who will give you a warm welcome. And an Exhibition of your pictures! I am curious to see how you have developed your unexpected & very vital gift of hand. I went to see the Leicester Gallery people, & found that Sir Michael Sadler had preceded me there. You could not have a better person to press your claims, or a more suitable place of exhibition. But I cannot see how a show can be arranged at the same time as the India Society's, which I gather is to be seen shortly. They have not consulted me about this show, & I know nothing whatever about it. I resigned from the Committee 2 or 3 years ago & am no wise in touch with them. Indeed I am relieved that my co-operation was not asked for.[1] I seem to have been accused of Macchiavelism of some mysterious kind in the Indian Press regarding my interest in Indian painting. We had a visit from Stella Kramrisch, whom I was most pleased to see again. To my mind she has the profoundest understanding of Indian plastic art of any one I have met. I admire the whole hearted & selfless manner in which she has devoted herself to the art of India. . . .

    . . . I am thinking of retiring from the College, having served there for 15 years, when we shall be able to spend still more time here. I always associate you, in large measure, with this peaceful corner of the world. . . . Ever yours affectionately

William Rothenstein

1. No Tagore exhibition took place at the Leicester Galleries, which have no present record of these negotiations. The India Society Exhibition of Modern Indian Art, at the New Burlington Galleries, December 1934, was London's first all-India show of the kind. It attracted much favorable comment which made little mention, however, of William Rothenstein or of the Society's origins.

192
Tagore to Rothenstein

"Uttarayan"   November 28, 1934

My dear Rothenstein,

It was a great delight to get your letter and to know you welcome the idea of an exhibition of my pictures in London. Sir Michael Sadler has sent me a copy of a letter from the Leicester Galleries to him and my Secretary is writing this mail to the gallery direct to fix up details. As you know already it cannot be managed before the autumn next.

I am indeed flirting with the idea of a last visit to England where I have so many good friends like you who I know will give me a very warm welcome. But the flesh is weak and I am not quite sure if I could manage the trip at this time of my life. However I will try.

I have got a letter from Mr. Pieris, the artist whom you recommended to our Art Department. I am asking him to come out and join us.[1] With all good wishes,   Yours as ever

Rabindranath Tagore

1. Harry Pieris, of Colombo, Ceylon, a student at the Royal College of Art, was at Santiniketan on Tagore's invitation from August 1935 to March 1938. He did not teach because the Art Department was unprepared for his coming and seemed disinclined to make room either for him or for ideas about Western art aside from those of the British Royal Academy: "I went with great hopes of being helpful and useful but came away rather disillusioned. Poets can visualize and dream great dreams but it is very difficult for people with little poetic and artistic vision to carry out great ideas. I don't think those who were entrusted with Tagore's school at that time were capable of carrying out his ideas. I was

not impressed with the Bengal School of Art. Mere imitation never produced great creative work. But I am very glad that I had an opportunity of seeing what was being done and do not regret having gone there." (Harry Pieris to the editor, November 17, 1970.)

193
Rothenstein to Tagore

13 Airlie Gardens, London June 25, 1935

My dear friend—I get news of you from Indian friends who come to see us, recently from Pratima & Rathi, whom we were delighted to see again. Pratima's drawings gave me particular pleasure—I saw marked improvement in her design, a freshness too of outlook. . . . I have always tried to impress on the Indian students who have worked under me that tradition is a living, an *active* thing, not the lifeless one they practise. Think of the changes in form between Giotto & Michelangelo! and in building between the 11th & 14th centuries. The pale imitations of the vigorous painters who worked under Akbar & Jehangir have never seemed to me truly traditional; that is why, though often asked, I have hesitated to write on Indian painting. It is the vigour, the marvellous inventiveness & fertility of the Indian spirit which I have always admired, first at Ajanta, & later at Khajraho & Bhuvaneshvar; & lately Stella Kramrisch has sent me, out of the generosity of her soul, a carved apsaras, in which I can delight daily in one of the great inventions of the art of the world. What power, what subtlety, what ripe beauty of form lies in this fragment! Your painters have been led astray by the loose talk & writing about Indian spirituality. What can be more spiritual than power? It was through his power that Krishna saved the world, that Christ healed the sick, brought the dead to life, cast out devils.

Lately we have been celebrating Yeats's 70th birthday. I saw him when he was in London; A.E. too is here, not in good health, unfortunately, but like Yeats, grown wise & ripe with the years.[1] Muhammed Iqbal was to have come this June, but I am told he too is ill, & so prevented.[2] I hear that your fertility is unaffected by the years—that like Yeats's your latest poems are among your best. Alas, difference of tongues cuts us off from your writing.

Next month I say goodbye to my colleagues & the students at the Royal College, after 15 years among them. A great relief to me, in the hope that with all my time my own, I may use my freedom for a while before brushes & pencils have to be laid down. . . . I send you my affectionate greetings & am, as ever, yours

Wm Rothenstein

1. See *SF*, pp. 230–232.
2. Mohammed Iqbal (1873–1938), Muslim poet-philosopher, had been in London for the 1931 Round Table Conference. (See *SF*, pp. 46–48.) Thompson wrote after his death: "One of Iqbal's last letters to me was almost heartbreaking in its low key. He wrote of 'the confusion about to come on my vast, undisciplined, and starving country.' Isn't their English grand? 'vast . . . undisciplined . . . starving.' " (Thompson to Rothenstein, August 12, 1938. RP:HL.)

VIII 1936-1940 Letters 194-201

Afterthoughts

Rothenstein left the Royal College of Art in July 1935, and after 1935 Tagore made no more foreign tours. Their last letters have unmistakable modulations of disengagement, of coming to terms with the past. They are occasionally a little vague about whose turn it is to reply, a little absentminded about news last brought up to date. Rothenstein's India of 1910 and 1911, the Hampstead and Oakridge of the long, wet summer of 1912, belong to a prewar past. Figures from that past disappear one by one, and those remaining view it as from a great distance. "I am almost tempted now," Ernest Rhys told Tagore, "to tell you more about myself, and then to try and picture you exactly as you are at Shanti Niketan with a view to comparing your lot with mine. We have so much in common; both of us lasting on and as it were 'surviving our other selves,' and I am sure our thoughts even at a world's distance run to one tune, and strive to keep the great old music alive in this contrary world."[1]

Rothenstein asked Sturge Moore to write a text to accompany a drawing of Tagore, and Sturge Moore replied: "Should I chiefly insist that his work has not yet been judged and that the adequate judgment can only come from those who know Bengali as well as English? and that he is not an Asiatic Longfellow, but a new phenomenon of whom only a distorted shadow is shown by his work in English?"[2]

"I am very grateful," Rothenstein replied when he received the commentary. "What you say in your note needed saying. Tagore is clearly a great man; the shadow we know hints at the mass of fine work of which we hear. Your text is just what I hoped for: I am sending it off at once. I am suddenly re-

---

1. Rhys to Tagore, December 7, 1936. R-S.
2. Sturge Moore to Rothenstein, May 14, 1937. RP:HL. See Rothenstein, *Contemporaries: Portrait Drawings* (London, 1937), pp. 93–96.

minded that the drawing to be reproduced was made while you were talking with Tagore—discussing and reading translations—at a house in Hampstead some years ago. Do you happen to remember the occasion?"[3]

Administrative and commercial affairs impinge only slightly, as do also the urgencies and excitements of shared endeavor. Rothenstein, at Oakridge again, paints Cotswolds landscapes out-of-doors in all possible and impossible weathers. Tagore, the bird settled once and for all into the Indian nest, writes new Bengali poems in a new mode, less stylized, more personal, yet more austere than the poems known to readers in the West. Both men agree about shortcomings in the arts. Tagore had told Sturge Moore that he disliked the aggressiveness of modern poetry.[4] In his third and last volume of memoirs, Rothenstein wrote, "I hear it said that the strange grammar and syntax met with among some poets and painters is in accord with the confusion of post-war times."[5]

Their postwar times rushed toward an unthinkably new prewar time. When he wrote his last letter to Tagore, Rothenstein was again a War Artist, his uniform pockets bulging in unmilitary fashion with pencils and crayons with which to draw men of the Royal Air Force, the last pictorial record of many of them. The man with the damaged heart, who in peacetime hesitated to fly to Paris, now flew everywhere about Britain in open planes, snatched food and sleep when and where he could, and often sat up all night waiting to count returning planes and pilots. This was "an odd experience for a man nearing the end of his life," John Rothenstein wrote. "Yet I never heard him repine; he never wished himself a student in Montmartre again or a traveller to Benares. Likewise, devoted as he was to the Royal College of Art, he never regretted his retirement: his eyes were ever upon the present."[6]

Tagore, in the last year of his life, issued his somber statement, *Crisis in Civilisation*, a disheartened and disheartening view of the destruction that Western civilization had brought

3. Rothenstein to Sturge Moore, May 24 [1937]. TSM.
4. Tagore to Sturge Moore, June 11, 1935. TSM.
5. *SF*, p. 280.
6. John Rothenstein, *Brave Day Hideous Night: Autobiography, 1939–1965* (New York, 1966), p. 158.

Rothenstein in uniform of R.A.F. War Artist

upon itself. He was disillusioned with England in particular, of whom he had expected more because her literature, technology, and energetic example of achievement had promised so much of the good life. But life in Europe was not good in 1941 and not yet good enough in India. Yet England's shortcomings as a nation had not destroyed his faith in Man and in the "really largehearted Englishmen" whose example "would not allow me wholly to lose faith in the race which produced them." He mentioned by name only Andrews.[7]

Some of the other names had appeared in 1939 in a volume of Tagore's Bengali essays written in England during the first summer of *Gitanjali*. It is all there: bustling London and the cheerless Bloomsbury hotel; William Rothenstein and Alice, and their four children playing in the Hampstead garden while Tagore watches from the veranda and compares them with Indian children at play; Yeats, whose presence commands attention the moment he enters a room; Stopford Brooke and Tagore looking into the treetops of Manchester Square and speaking of literature and eternity and reincarnation; Henry Massingham and the *Nation* staff at their editorial luncheon table, while Tagore listens and meditates upon contrasts between journalists in India and in England. And, at the end, a letter from America, which speaks of prairie snow in the night and a quiet Midwestern Sunday. It is all there, and many descendants of Tagore's old friends have not known that these Bengali essays exist.[8]

Nevertheless, the paradigm of exchange exists. Tagore, peerless among modern Bengali writers, had singlehandedly ushered Bengali literature into the twentieth century. Rothenstein, singleminded in his "boundless reverence for the creative faculty,"[9] tirelessly rallying his friends to an artistic cause, brought Tagore into the circle of those who were in the very act of reforming English and American literary and artistic tastes. If, as Masefield pointed out, the plants selected did not always

---

7. Tagore, *Shabhyatār Shangkat* [Civilization's Dilemma], in *R-R*, XXVI, 633–641: *Crisis in Civilization* (Calcutta, 1941), pp. 14–16.

8. Tagore, "Landane" [In London], 513–516; "Bandhu" [Friend], 516–521; "Kabi Ietsh" [Poet Yeats], 521–528; "Stapphord Bruk" [Stopford Brooke], 528–533; "Emerikār Cithi" [Letter from America], 580–582, in his *Pather Shancay*, in *R-R*, XXVI.

9. John Rothenstein, *Summer's Lease*, p. 43.

transplant, experience shows the way to successful selection and cultivation. If, as Whibley had warned, "the half is greater than the whole," the whole is by no means diminished; even with all its confusions and false starts, it comprises a touching, intriguing, and enormously important chapter in literary history.

194
Rothenstein to Tagore

Far Oakridge   May 10, 1937

My dear Rabindranath—I do not know which of us last wrote to the other; but it is overlong since I heard from you. Of you I hear often, for I see no one from Bengal but I ask news of your doings & of your health. . . .

Sturge Moore, too, I see often; now that we live at Highgate we are near neighbours. I saw Ed. Thompson lately who told me of his remorse at mislaying Brajendranath's long poem. On this I remembered that I had a copy, sent me some years ago by Brajendranath, with additions & corrections, & looking among my papers I happily found it, & have sent it to the Vice Chancellor, as a gift to Calcutta University, in the hope that they may publish it. I hear the good old man is very ill. Alas, the years go by & one's friends close their eyes.[1] . . . Oakridge is as remote & unspoiled as when you were here—just 25 years ago! I hear that you divide your time between writing & drawing in fruitful production. What a mass of work you have put into the world! but I hear too that there is no one to follow you in creative vitality. Is India too political to have the necessary energy to give; like Ireland too preoccupied with self?

I send you & yours my affectionate greetings—you I wish I could give them in person! But India is too far away & work here too insistent with demands. I must think of her as of old, though I am told of great changes, not altogether to my own "visual" taste. But we may say the same of Europe. Ever, my dear Rabindranath, your old friend

William Rothenstein

1. "Brajendranath's long poem": a set of philosophical poems sent from Seal to Rothenstein, and from Rothenstein to Chesterton for an opinion. (See SF, pp. 113–115.) Thompson and Seal were later estranged for many years, not over this poem, but over Thompson's book, *Rabindranath Tagore: His Life and Work* (Calcutta, 1921), dedicated to Seal. They met once more: "Seal broke off an ancient and deep friendship because of my earlier smaller book on Tagore. For 20 years we had nothing to do with each other. Then, 2 years ago, Prasanta Mahalanobis suddenly led me into his presence. The old man, who has had several strokes, was being fed with milk like a child, the milk stroking all over his beard. He had no idea I was coming, and he started up with a wild cry, 'Ohhh!

Edward Thompson!' and broke down and sobbed. The rest is something I do not care to set down in a letter." (Thompson to Rothenstein, August 12, 1938. RP:HL.)

195
Tagore to Rothenstein

Almora, U[nited] P[rovinces]   June 11, 1937

My dear Rothenstein,

Your letters invariably bring to me the fragrance of the world, the shores of which are fast receding away from us. You, Sturge Moore, and Ernest Rhys are perhaps my only link with that world and I can quite realise that you do not exactly fit in with the modern scheme of things. I myself sometimes feel quite anti-dated in my country even though I try to keep abreast of modern tendencies in our world of thought and action; strange gods have been put on the altar, stranger incantations are being mumbled. But I do not grumble for each generation has its own problems to face and its own set of values. Only we are out of place.

You must forgive me if I am no longer an assiduous letter-writer as I used to be; a strange listlessness envelops me so often and my only shelter then is with my brush and the paints. With the ruthless freedom of an invader, I have been playing havoc in the complacent & stagnant world of Indian art and my people are puzzled for they do not know what judgment to pronounce upon my pictures. But I must say I am enjoying hugely my role as a painter.

The advent of old age I have to admit freely and its perhaps the first time that I have sought shelter in the hills frightened of the summer heat of the plains. Almora is far away from the beaten tracks of civilisation and here I am comparatively safe from meetings, receptions and interviews. I wish I could have stayed here for an indefinitely long period but Santiniketan has its exhorbitant demands and I am afraid I have to go back when the Institution re-opens early July. With warmest greetings, as of old,

Rabindranath Tagore

196
Rothenstein to Tagore

Far Oakridge   August 25, 1937

My dear Rabindranath—I was delighted to get your book, with its immediate evidence of your undiminished vitality. Alas, that I cannot read your language! For I know your wit as I know your wisdom, & I fancy the text sparkling.[1]

... I am reminded that it is just 25 years since you, & we, came here. Little did we think then of the place Oakridge was to take in our & our children's lives. Besides this cottage, we have built on to another & made it into a hostel for the children, now all married. Happily wives, husbands, brothers & sisters-in-law are devoted to one another, & we have a happy family circle. Betty has just had a daughter, & Rachel lives with her husband in Sheffield. Oakridge remains unspoilt & remote as when you knew it.

We heard much of you & your activities from Stella Kramrisch, that able & scholarly woman. ...

I have seen a good deal of Yeats this year—formerly he had the body of a butterfly, & the mind of a grub, he said, now he has the body of a grub, alas, but the butterfly's mind. He is writing remarkable poetry.

... I cherish my Indian friendships, & am always yours affectionately

William Rothenstein

1. Tagore, *Khāpchārā* [Inconsistent] (1937), in *R-R*, XXI, 1–56. Nonsense rhymes illustrated by Tagore.

197
Rothenstein to Tagore

High Point, Highgate Village, London
February 23, 1938

My dear Rabindranath,

Such a grief it was to hear of my old friend Gaganendranath's death. I have never forgotten his kindness to me when I used to come to your house during my visit to India. I carried away an impression of a nature of rare beauty and gifts of a high order. . . .

I hear of constant activity on your part and envy you the fullness of your creative vitality. I, too, find great happiness in daily work. Something new enters in to what one is doing and one wonders whether often in the past one hasn't taken a wrong path. We live a great deal at Oakridge now that I am free from all official duties and have only a flat in London. . . . With Yeats and Sturge Moore I often speak of you. Yeats, in spite of poor health, writes and talks better than ever. I see him whenever he comes to London from Dublin. . . .

I gather that much of your time is still devoted to drawing. I can imagine this to be a continual source of interest to you. I, alas, am an objective artist and must wait on direct inspiration from nature for my drawing and painting. . . . How fortunate we artists and poets are that in the confusion of life we at least have clear aims. I send you, as ever, my affectionate good wishes. Always yours

William Rothenstein

198
Tagore to Rothenstein

"Uttarayan"   March 12, 1938

My dear Rothenstein,

Thanks for your letter. What you write is quite true. It is a heavy price to pay for living long, this constant loss of one's dear ones. A long life, like many other acquisitions, is a blessing only if it is enjoyed by all whom one loves and cherishes. I was, however, reconciled to Gaganendra's death long before it actually came—ever since that fatal disease deprived him of his power of expression. Body had become literally a prison to his noble and adventurous spirit. Death has only released it.[1]

It is good to hear from you. Your letters recall many happy days and contacts for which one feels grateful to life. Oakridge will always remain associated with them. I am glad to hear it remains the same as it was. Here is another sad consequence of old age, that while age and distance enhance the charm of old associations, they disable one from renewing them.

My imagination is as restless as ever. I try to restrain myself, but hardly has one book come out when I am correcting proofs of another. It would amuse you to know that my last book on science has already run into three editions. My little book of poems written after illness is also selling well.[2] I sometimes wonder if what people admire as "creative activity" is not after all a kind of disease. And then this painting, it has become a regular playmate of mine, giving me just the distraction I need from literary talkativeness. It is like dreaming. . . . With my best wishes and affectionate regards,

Rabindranath Tagore

1. Gaganendranath was incapacitated by a stroke, ten years previous to his death.
2. Tagore, *Visva-Paricay* [World-Acquaintance] (1937), in *R-R*, XXV, 345–415; *Prāntik* [Borderland] (1938), in *R-R*, XXII, 1–19.

199
Rothenstein to Tagore

Far Oakridge   June 7, 1939

My dear friend,

It is overlong since I heard from you, though I hear *of* you from time to time. It is always a pleasure to know that you continue to pour out work, that your productivity is undiminished. I too find regular work a solace in my later years. We have given up our flat in London and this is now our permanent home. So although I go up to London now and again here I am more or less master of my time, which means largely master of the time to be idle; just to stare out across the valley and potter about the garden. Being here I see little of Indian friends, or strangers who come to London bringing letters from you and others. I have been using some of my leisure to write a third volume, a final one, of memories, in which I have allowed myself to include some letters of yours.[1] Needless to say they contain no reflections to which objection could be taken. I will send you the book when it appears in the autumn. You will have been moved, I am sure, to have heard of Yeats's death. He always spoke warmly of you and your work. No one appreciated more that for which you have consistently stood. I was in close touch with him up to the end.[2] Alas, I have come to the age of adieus. I was in Paris a month ago and found myself one of the few survivors from my early days there. I saw André Gide, by the way, your first French translator, and found him full of ideas and vitally alive as ever. I hoped to see Valéry and Duhamel but they were both out of Paris. Do you know Duhamel's Salavin?[3] I think it one of the most original among contemporary books. It is just 27 years since you spent the summer with us here. Do you remember how it poured with rain and how you said, where a stranger is it is always exceptional weather? That was two years before the war, then unimaginable. Now we are living in a fearful expectancy. Yet life goes on from day to day, the small and great troubles, the small and great pleasures still the basis of our thoughts and doings. Happily nothing can change the beauty of the face of the world which is to me a source of perpetual wonder. Ever, dear Rabindranath, your old friend,

William Rothenstein

1. *Since Fifty: Men and Memories, 1922–1938*. See pp. 43–44, 112–113, 175–176, 177, 288–289.

2. Yeats died on January 28, 1939, at Cap Martin. His last letter to Rothenstein was a request for Michael (Billy) Rothenstein to do embroidery designs based on several of his poems. (Yeats to Rothenstein, January 12, 1939. RP:HL.)

3. Georges Duhamel, *Journal de Salavin* (Paris, 1927): *Salavin*, trans. Gladys Billings (London, 1936). Tagore met Duhamel (1884–1966), physician, novelist, and poet, at Villeneuve in 1926. In 1930 he met Paul Valéry (1871–1945), poet and philosopher, in Paris, and, for the first time, André Gide. (See Kripalani, *Rabindranath Tagore*, pp. 328, 345.)

200
Tagore to Rothenstein

"Uttarayan"   June 25, 1939

My dear Rothenstein,

I thank you for your letter which recalls back to my mind the never-to-be forgotten memories of my stay in your village, where practically for the first time I had my real contact with the English country. It is now a quarter of a century that stands athwart my mind and yet I can almost see today the undulating downs and the luscious green of the meadows. Some times I have so irresistibly felt like visiting the places once again before I take my farewell but Europe today is a powder-magazine and I wonder if it has a place for a mere poet like myself. Anyway I would seem rather a weird figure in a gas-mask and therefore I must desist. In my country my people are steadily gaining in self-respect and faith in our destiny but I cannot be happy when I know that the very ideals which were the foundation of a great civilisation are daily vanishing.

As regards your using my letters in your third volume of autobiography, you have most certainly my enthusiastic consent but do be discreet about the material that you use. I have of course every faith in your judgment.

I have just returned after my summer holidays on the himalayas; the rains have set in and you have to see for yourself to realise the gorgeous beauty of the chasing raven-black clouds on the sky at Santiniketan. Yours ever

Rabindranath Tagore

201
Rothenstein to Tagore

>	as from Far Oakridge
>	Royal Air Force, Pembroke Dock, South Wales
>	April 8, 1940

My dear friend—you are often in my mind—how could it be otherwise. Lately I heard with pleasure that Oxford has at last done what it was more than once so nearly doing—offering you its Doctorate. Now I read of your great friend's death.[1] I know how devoted you were to him & how deep his allegiance to you. Alas, dear Rabindranath, we have reached the age of farewells. Almost daily I have to regret some old friend, & the perspective before one grows ever shorter. It is already 30 years since I was in India, & had the rare fortune to meet you. I am glad at least

I was in your wonderful country before it became altogether political. I write altogether, but of course I know that the general course of life runs apart from politics—that the touching ways of men, women & children continue, as goodness & evil continue—these are permanent qualities. I like to think of you, in your later years, living at least far from the passions which the war has again roused in Europe. No one, 20 years ago, would have believed such a state possible. At least so far we have been spared the wanton slaughter of youth which took place early in the last war—we believed it was *the last war*. . . .

I am again doing war work—this time drawing airmen; glad to be of some use with my pencil still. Indeed I find my work ever more absorbing.[2]

I have lately written something on Yeats for a symposium Macmillans are publishing. I expect they have asked you to write on him, too.[3] . . .

I hope you can find peace away from the dust & noise of the market place. I send you, as ever, my warm & affectionate greetings. Your old friend

William Rothenstein

1. On August 7, 1940, Tagore at last received Oxford's Doctorate of Literature, *honoris causa,* given *in absentia* at a special Santiniketan convocation. (See Kripalani, *Rabindranath Tagore,* p. 389.) Andrews had died on April 5, 1940.

2. See Rothenstein, *Men of the RAF* (London, 1942).

3. Rothenstein, "Yeats as a Painter Saw Him," in *Scattering Branches: Tributes to the Memory of W. B. Yeats,* ed. Stephen Gwynn (New York, 1940), pp. 35–54. Tagore is not represented here.

Epilogue

William Rothenstein
January 29, 1872–February 14, 1945

In one of his three books of memoirs, he suggests that strenuous men may be divided into two categories: the givers and the takers: on the one hand, men whose incentive is their own emolument and own prestige, and so on; on the other hand, those who love their work for its own sake and seek no reward but have such pleasure and profit as the world may derive from it. Will himself was assuredly a giver, a giver with both hands, in the grand manner.

      Max Beerbohm
      March 6, 1945[1]

I couldn't help wishing someone had spoken about India, . . . but didn't want to bring in politics . . . perhaps a mistake on my part—but when I see the letters here from Tagore and dozens of others from India saying "You have opened the door of the West for the East—you alone have done this"—it makes me feel so sad.

      Alice Rothenstein to Flora Russell
      [March 1945][2]

William was a big blow—but at eighty-six so much has gone that one has got hardened to loss. I mourn, and then turn away, because mourning's no use. Many wise things he said, and much truth, I thought, and he loved his friends more than ever he said.

      A. H. Fox Strangways to Albert Rutherston
      November 8, 1945[3]

 1. Max Beerbohm, "William Rothenstein," Address at the Memorial Service, London [1945].
 2. Mrs. Noel Blakiston.
 3. RP:HL.

Bibliography and Index

Bibliography

PRIMARY SOURCES

Manuscript collections cited by the editor:
Blakiston, Mrs. Noel. Personal Papers.
Bridges, Robert. Bridges Family Papers.
Chapman, John Jay. Houghton Library, Harvard University.
University of Chicago Library. Special Collections.
Deraniyagala, R. St. L. Personal Papers.
Elmhirst, Leonard. Personal Papers.
Fisher, H. A. L. Bodleian Library, Oxford.
Galsworthy, John. Birmingham University Library.
Hammond, John and Barbara. Bodleian Library.
Havell, E. B. India Office Library.
India Society. India Office Library.
Kripalani, Krishna. Personal Papers.
Macmillan Papers (London). British Museum.
Macmillan Company Papers (London). Macmillan and Company, Limited.
Macmillan Company Records (New York). New York Public Library.
Murray, Gilbert. Bodleian Library.
Rolleston, T. W. Honor Stopford Drysdale Papers.
Rothenstein, William. William Andrews Clark Memorial Library of the University of California at Los Angeles.
────── Houghton Library, Harvard University.
────── India Office Library.
────── Rothenstein Family Papers.
Society of Authors Archives. British Museum.
Sturge Moore, Thomas. University of London Library.
Tagore, Rabindranath. Houghton Library, Harvard University.
────── Rabindra-Sadana, Santiniketan.
Thompson, Edward J. Edward P. Thompson Personal Papers.
Trevelyan, Robert. Julian Trevelyan Personal Papers.
Williams, David G. Personal Papers.
Winters, Janet L. Personal Papers.
Yeats, Michael. Personal Papers.

WORKS BY RABINDRANATH TAGORE

"Appeasement" ["Mānbhanjan"], in his *The Housewarming and Other Stories*, pp. 69–78.
"At the Fair," *The Fortnightly Review* (London), 99 (1913), 790.
Balākā [Wild Swans], in his *Rabindra-Racanābali*, XII, 1–77.
"Bandhu" [Friend], *Pather Shancay*, in his *Rabindra-Racanābali*, XXVI, 516–521.
Bicitritā [Variety], in his *Rabindra-Racanābali*, XVII, 1–46.
Binodini [*Cokher Bāli*]. Krishna Kripalani, trans. Honolulu: East-West Center Press, 1964.
Broken Ties and Other Stories [trans. by various writers]. London: Macmillan and Co., 1925.
Caitāli [Of April], in his *Rabindra-Racanābali*, V, 1–58.
Chinnapatra [Torn Leaves]. Calcutta: Visva-Bharati, 1962.
Chitra: A Play in One Act. London: The India Society, 1913.
Chitra: A Play in One Act. London: Macmillan and Co., 1914.
Cithipatra [Letters]. 7 vols. Calcutta: Visva-Bharati, 1942–60.
Citrāngadā [Chitrangada], in his *Rabindra-Racanābali*, III, 157–200.
Cokher Bāli [Eyesore], in his *Rabindra-Racanābali*, III, 281–512.
Collected Poems and Plays. New York: The Macmillan Company, 1958.
Creative Unity [rev. Ernest Rhys]. London: Macmillan and Co., 1922.
The Crescent Moon [*Shishu*]. London: Macmillan and Co., 1913.
Crisis in Civilization [*Shabhyatār Shangkat*]. Calcutta: Visva-Bharati, 1941.
The Cycle of Spring [*Phālguni*]. C. F. Andrews and Nishikanta Sen, trans., rev. by the author. London: Macmillan and Co., 1917.
Dākghar [Post Office], in his *Rabindra-Racanābali*, XI, 379–406.
"Dāliyā" [Daliya], in his *Rabindra-Racanābali*, XVI, 312–320.
"Daliya" ["Dāliyā"], in his *The Housewarming and Other Selected Writings*, pp. 13–21.
"Ektā Āshāre Galpa" [An Implausible Story], in his *Rabindra-Racanābali*, XVII, 172–180.
"Emerikār Cithi" [Letter from America], *Pather Shancay*, in his *Rabindra-Racanābali*, XXVI, 580–582.
Eyesore [*Cokher Bāli*]. Surendranath Tagore, trans. *The Modern Review* (Calcutta), 15 (1914), 93–98, 207–214, 303–311, 426–436, 539–549, 672–680; 16 (1914), 79–87, 220–226, 315–324, 424–431, 479–485, 641–652.
Fireflies. London: Macmillan and Co., 1927.
A Flight of Swans: Poems from Balākā. Arabinda Bose, trans. 2nd ed. London: John Murray, 1962.

"The Freedom of Separation," *The Nation* (London), 16 (1915), 421.
Fruit-Gathering. London: Macmillan and Co., 1916.
The Fugitive. London: Macmillan and Co., 1921.
The Gardener. London: Macmillan and Co., 1913.
Ghare-Bāire [At Home-Outside], in his *Rabindra-Racanābali*, VIII, 137–334.
"Giribala" ["Mānbhanjan"], in his *Broken Ties and Other Stories*, pp. 177–192.
Gitabitān [Song Collection]. Calcutta: Visva-Bharati, 1960.
Gitāli [Songs], in his *Rabindra-Racanābali*, XI, 215–294.
Gitānjali [Song-Offering], in his *Rabindra-Racanābali*, XI, 1–124.
Gitanjali (Song-Offerings). London: The India Society, 1912.
Gitanjali (Song-Offerings). London: Macmillan and Co., 1913.
Glimpses of Bengal [*Chinnapatra*]. Surendranath Tagore, trans. [rev. Thomas Sturge Moore]. London: Macmillan and Co., 1921.
Glimpses of Bengal Life. R[ajani] R[anjan] Sen, trans. Madras: Natesan & Co., 1913.
The Golden Boat. Bhabani Bhattacharya, trans. London: Allen & Unwin, 1932.
Gorā [Gora], in his *Rabindra-Racanābali*, VI, 109–572.
Gora [*Gorā*] [W. W. Pearson, trans., rev. Surendranath Tagore]. London: Macmillan and Co., 1924.
The Home and the World [*Ghare-Bāire*]. Surendranath Tagore, trans., rev. by the author. London: Macmillan and Co., 1919.
The Housewarming and Other Selected Writings. Mary Lago and Tarun Gupta, trans., Amiya Chakravarty, ed. New York: New American Library, 1965.
The Hungry Stones and Other Stories. London: Macmillan and Co., 1916.
"Imperiyālijam" [Imperialism], *Rājā Prajā*, in his *Rabindra-Racanābali*, X, 431–434.
"An Implausible Story" ["Ektā Āshāre Galpa"], in his *The Housewarming and Other Selected Writings*, pp. 21–29.
"The Indian Ideal of Marriage," in *The Book of Marriage: A New Interpretation by Twenty-Four Leaders of Contemporary Thought Arranged and Edited by Count Hermann Keyserling*, pp. 98–122.
"Indian Students and Western Teachers," *The Modern Review* (Calcutta), 19 (1916), 416–422.
Jibansmriti [Reminiscences], in his *Rabindra-Racanābali*, XVII, 261–432.
"Kabi Ietsh" [Poet Yeats], *Pather Shancay*, in his *Rabindra-Racanābali*, XXVI, 521–528.
Kāhini [Tales], in his *Rabindra-Racanābali*, V, 61–162.
Khāpchārā [Inconsistent], in his *Rabindra-Racanābali*, XXI, 1–56.

The King of the Dark Chamber [*Rājā*]. [Kshitish Chandra Sen, trans.] London: Macmillan and Co., 1914.
"The Kingdom of Cards" ["Ektā Āshāre Galpa"], in his *The Hungry Stones and Other Stories*, pp. 91–107.
Kshanikā [Momentary], in his *Rabindra-Racanābali*, VII, 203–332.
"Landane" [In London], *Pather Shancay*, in his *Rabindra-Racanābali*, XXVI, 513–516.
Letters from Russia [*Rāshiār Cithi*]. Sasadhar Sinha, trans. Calcutta: Visva-Bharati, 1960.
Letters to a Friend. C. F. Andrews, ed. London: Allen & Unwin, 1928.
Lipikā [Sketches], in his *Rabindra-Racanābali*, XXVI, 91–177.
Lover's Gift and Crossing. London: Macmillan and Co., 1918.
La Maison et le monde [*The Home and the World*]. F. Roger-Cornaz, trans. Paris: Payot, 1921.
Mālini [Malini], in his *Rabindra-Racanābali*, IV, 137–178.
Malini [*Mālini*], in his *Sacrifice and Other Plays*, pp. 43–82.
Mānashi [She of the Imagination], in his *Rabindra-Racanābali*, II, 117–278.
"Mānbhanjan" [Appeasement], in his *Rabindra-Racanābali*, XX, 197–207.
Mashi and Other Stories. London: Macmillan and Co., 1918.
My Reminiscences [*Jibansmriti*]. Surendranath Tagore, trans. *The Modern Review* (Calcutta), 19 (1916), 1–8, 137–142, 285–290, 361–367, 475–480, 583–589; 20 (1916), 1–6, 121–127, 237–242, 353–361, 461–467, 577–582.
My Reminiscences [*Jibansmriti*]. [Surendranath Tagore, trans.] London: Macmillan and Co., 1917.
Naibedya [Offering], in his *Rabindra-Racanābali*, VIII, 3–75.
Nationalism. London: Macmillan and Co., 1917.
Noukādubi [Sunken Boat], in his *Rabindra-Racanābali*, V, 165–432.
L'Offrande Lyrique [*Gitanjali (Song-Offerings)*]. André Gide, trans. Paris: Nouvelle Revue Francaise, 1913.
The Parrot's Training and Other Stories, trans. by the author. Calcutta: Visva-Bharati, 1944.
"The Parrot's Training" ["Totā Kāhini"], in his *The Parrot's Training and Other Stories*, pp. 1–11.
Pārshyae [In Persia], in his *Rabindra-Racanābali*, XXII, 431–502.
Pather Shancay [Travel Notes], in his *Rabindra-Racanābali*, XXVI, 459–582.
Personality: Lectures Delivered in America. London: Macmillan and Co., 1917.
Phālguni [Spring], in his *Rabindra-Racanābali*, XII, 81–145.
"Poems," *Poetry: A Magazine of Verse* (Chicago), 1 (1912–13), 84–86.

Poems, trans. by the author "with the exception of twelve [previously unpublished] poems." Krishna Kripalani et al., eds. Calcutta: Visva-Bharati, 1942.
"Postmāstār" [Postmaster], in his *Rabindra-Racanābali*, XV, 411–417.
"The Postmaster" ["Postmāstār"]. Debendra Nath Mitter, trans. *The Modern Review* (Calcutta), 9 (1911), 36–39.
"The Postmaster," in his *Mashi and Other Stories*, pp. 157–169.
The Post Office [*Dākghar*]. Devabrata Mukerjea, trans. Dundrum, County Dublin: Cuala Press, 1914.
The Post Office. London: Macmillan and Co., 1914.
Prāntik [Borderland], in his *Rabindra-Racanābali*, XXII, 1–19.
"The Problem of Evil," *The Hibbert Journal*, 11 (1913), 705–716.
Rabindra-Racanābali [Rabindranath's Works]. 27 vols., 2 supp., and index. Calcutta: Visva-Bharati, 1964–66.
"Race Conflict," *The Modern Review* (Calcutta), 13 (1913), 423–426.
Rājā [King], in his *Rabindra-Racanābali*, X, 191–266.
Rājā Prajā [Ruler and Ruled], in his *Rabindra-Racanābali*, X, 377–484.
Rāshiār Cithi [Letters from Russia], in his *Rabindra-Racanābali*, XX, 269–349.
"The Relation of the Individual to the Universe," in his *Sādhanā: The Realisation of Life*, pp. 3–22.
The Religion of Man. London: Macmillan and Co., 1931.
Sacrifice and Other Plays. London: Macmillan and Co., 1917.
Sādhanā: The Realisation of Life. London: Macmillan and Co., 1913.
Shabhyatār Shangkat [Civilization's Dilemma], in his *Rabindra-Racanābali*, XXVI, 633–641.
Shāntiniketan [Santiniketan], in his *Rabindra-Racanābali*, XIV, 283–519.
Shishu [Child], in his *Rabindra-Racanābali*, IX, 1–96.
Shonār Tori [Golden Boat], in his *Rabindra-Racanābali*, III, 1–153.
Smaran [Memory], in his *Rabindra-Racanābali*, VIII, 77–101.
"Stapphord Bruk" [Stopford Brooke], *Pather Shancay*, in his *Rabindra-Racanābali*, XXVI, 528–533.
Stray Birds. New York: The Macmillan Co., 1916.
Stray Birds. London: Macmillan and Co., 1917.
"Summer Pioneers," *The Fortnightly Review* (London), 103 (1915), 846.
"Totā Kāhini" [Tale of a Parrot], *Lipikā*, in his *Rabindra-Racanābali*, XXVI, 132–135.
Utsharga [Dedication], in his *Rabindra-Racanābali*, X, 3–91.
"Visvabodh" [World-Knowledge], *Shāntiniketan*, in his *Rabindra-Racanābali*, XIV, 507–519.

Visva-Paricay [World-Acquaintance], in his *Rabindra-Racanābali*, XXV, 345–415.
"What is Art?" in his *Personality: Lectures Delivered in America,* pp. 3–38.
"Woman," in his *Personality: Lectures Delivered in America,* pp. 169–184.
"The Woman in Sorrow," *The Nation* (London), 13 (1913), 498.
The Wreck [*Noukādubi*]. [J. G. Drummond, trans.] London: Macmillan and Co., 1921.

OTHER WORKS

Ackerley, J. R. *Hindoo Holiday: An Indian Journal.* London: Chatto & Windus, 1932.
Andrews, C. F. "An Evening with Rabindra," *The Modern Review* (Calcutta), 12 (1912), 225–228.
———— "On Reading the Translation of *Gitanjali,*" *The Modern Review,* 13 (1913), 397.
———— "To Rabindranath Tagore," *The Modern Review,* 11 (1912), 292.
———— "With Rabindra in England," *The Modern Review,* 13 (1913), 70–75.
Archer, W. G. *India and Modern Art.* London: Allen & Unwin, 1959.
Aronson, Alex, and Krishna Kripalani, eds. *Rolland and Tagore.* Calcutta: Visva-Bharati, 1945.
"Art in India," *The Times* (London), March 1, 1910, p. 11.
Barker, Dudley. *The Man of Principle: A View of John Galsworthy.* London: Heinemann, 1963.
Beerbohm, Max. "Enoch Soames," in his *Seven Men,* pp. 9–51.
———— *Seven Men.* 1st American ed. New York: Alfred A. Knopf, 1920.
———— "William Rothenstein," Address at the Memorial Service held at St. Martin-in-the-Fields, London, March 6, 1945. London: privately printed at the Curwen Press [1945].
Binyon, Laurence. *Collected Poems of Laurence Binyon.* 2 vols. London: Macmillan and Co., 1931.
Bridge, Ursula, ed. *W. B. Yeats and Thomas Sturge Moore: Their Correspondence 1901–1937.* London: Routledge & Paul, 1953.
Bridges, M. M., ed. *Collected Essays, Papers, &c. of Robert Bridges,* vols. 4–10.
Bridges, Robert. *Collected Essays, Papers, &c of Robert Bridges.* 10 vols. London: Oxford University Press, 1927–36.
———— "Humdrum & Harum-Scarum: A Lecture on Free Verse," in *Collected Essays, Papers, &c of Robert Bridges,* II, 35–55.

——— "A Paper on Free Verse," *The North American Review*, 216 (1922), 647–658. Another publication of his "Humdrum & Harum-Scarum: A Lecture on Free Verse."
——— *The Spirit of Man: An Anthology in English & French from the Philosophers & Poets made by the Poet Laureate in 1915 & dedicated by gracious permission to His Majesty The King.* London: Longmans Green & Co., 1916.
"British Association: The Presidential Address: Sir O. Lodge on Scientific Dogmatism." *The Times* (London), September 11, 1913, p. 11.
Brooke, Stopford. "Mr. Stopford Brooke on the *Gitanjali*" (letter), *The Modern Review* (Calcutta), 13 (1913), 479.
Broomfield, J. H. *Elite Conflict in a Plural Society: Twentieth-Century Bengal.* Berkeley and Los Angeles: University of California Press, 1968.
"The Building of New Delhi," *The Modern Review* (Calcutta), 14 (1913), 212.
Burns, Cecil. "The Functions of Schools of Art in India," *Journal of the Royal Society of Arts*, 57 (1908–9), 629–641.
Calcutta University Commission 1917–1919. *Report*. 13 vols. Calcutta: Superintendent Government Printing, India, 1919–20.
Calderon, George. *The Maharani of Arakan: A Romantic Comedy in One Act.* London: Francis Griffiths, 1915.
Chakravarty, Amiya. The Dynasts *and the Post-War Age in Poetry: A Study in Modern Ideas.* London and New York: Oxford University Press, 1938.
Chapman, John Jay. "Coatesville," in his *Memories and Milestones*, pp. 225–232.
——— *Memories and Milestones.* New York: Moffat, Yard and Co., 1915.
Chatterjee, Ramananda, ed. *The Golden Book of Tagore: A Homage to Rabindranath Tagore from India and the World in Celebration of His Seventieth Birthday.* Calcutta: Golden Book Committee, 1931.
Chirol, Valentine. *Indian Unrest.* London: Macmillan and Co., 1910.
"Chitra," *The Athenaeum* (London), January 17, 1914, p. 99.
Chowdhury, K. C. "The Lewis Institute," *The Modern Review* (Calcutta), 11 (1912), 395–401.
"The Copyright Question," *The Edinburgh Review*, 212 (1910), 310–327.
Craig, Edward. *Gordon Craig: The Story of His Life.* London: Victor Gollancz, 1968.
"A Criticism of Modern Civilisation," *The Japan Weekly Chronicle* (Kobe), June 8, 1916, pp. 921–922.
Das Gupta, Sarayubala. *Basanta-Prayānna* [Passing of Spring]. Calcutta: Gurudas Library, 1914.

Davids, T. W. R. et al. "The Architecture of Delhi" (letter), *The Times* (London), December 17, 1912, p. 5.
Davidson, Jo. *Between Sittings: An Informal Autobiography of Jo Davidson.* New York: Dial Press, 1951.
de Bary, W. T. et al., comps. *Sources of Indian Tradition,* vol. LVI: *Introduction to Oriental Civilizations.* Records of Civilization: Sources and Studies. New York: Columbia University Press, 1958.
de Rosen, Jean. "Gitanjali (*L'offrande des chants*)," *La Revue* (Paris), 101 (1913), 499–503.
———— "Rabindranath Tagore," *La Revue,* 101 (1913), 496–498.
"Details of the Outrage," *The Times* (London), December 24, 1912, p. 4.
Dickinson, G. Lowes. *Appearances: Being Notes of Travel.* London and Toronto: J. M. Dent & Sons, 1914.
———— *An Essay on the Civilisations of India, China & Japan.* A Report made to the Trustees of the Albert Kahn Travelling Fellowships. London and Toronto: J. M. Dent & Sons, 1914.
Dimock, Edward C., Jr., and Denise Levertov, trans. *In Praise of Krishna: Songs from the Bengali.* Garden City, N.Y.: Doubleday & Co., 1967.
———— "Rabindranath Tagore, 'The Greatest of the Bāuls of Bengal,'" *The Journal of Asian Studies,* 19 (1959–60), 33–51.
"Dinner to Mr. Rabindra Nath Tagore: A Bengali Poet," *The Times* (London), July 13, 1912, p. 5.
"Dr. J. C. Bose's Discovery," *The Modern Review* (Calcutta), 14 (1913), 211–212.
Duhamel, Georges. *Salavin.* Gladys Billings, trans. London: J. M. Dent & Sons, 1936.
Dunbar, Olivia. *A House in Chicago.* Chicago: University of Chicago Press, 1947.
"Eastern Art Makes Events in the West," *The Modern Review* (Calcutta), 7 (1910), 517–519.
Elmhirst, Leonard. *Rabindranath Tagore: Pioneer in Education.* London: John Murray, 1961.
Forster, E. M. *Goldsworthy Lowes Dickinson.* London: E. Arnold & Co., 1934.
Fox Strangways, A. H. *The Music of Hindostan.* Oxford: Clarendon Press, 1914.
Fry, Roger. "The Art of Mr. Rothenstein," *The Nation* (London), 7 (1910), 382–383.
———— "Plastic Design," *The Nation,* 9 (1911), 396.
Gandhi, M. K. *Speeches & Writings of Mahatma Gandhi.* 4th ed. Madras: Natesan & Co. [1933].
"The Gardener," *The Athenaeum* (London), November 1, 1913, p. 485.

Garnett, David. *The Golden Echo.* New York: Harcourt, Brace & Co., 1954.
"General Smuts on Rabindranath Tagore's 'The Religion of Man,' " *The Modern Review* (Calcutta), 49 (1931), 730–731.
Ghosal, Svarna Kumari. *Kāhāke?* [To Whom?]. Calcutta: Srichandrabhushan Sarkar, 1898.
────── *To Whom? or An Indian Love-Story* [*Kāhāke?*]. Sorona Devi [Mukerjee], trans. Calcutta: S. K. Lahiri & Co. [1913].
[Ghose, Sudhin] "Three Conversations: Tagore Talks with Einstein, with Rolland, and with Wells," *Asia* (New York), 31 (1931), 139–143, 196–197.
"*Gitanjali (Song-Offerings)*," *The Athenaeum* (London), November 16, 1912, p. 583.
Gorky, Maxim. *Reminiscences of Leo Nikolaevich Tolstoy.* S. S. Koteliansky and Leonard Woolf, trans. New York: B. W. Huebsch, 1920.
"A Great Man from Bengal," *The Daily Mail* (London), October 29, 1913, p. 6.
Gwynn, Stephen, ed. *Scattering Branches: Tributes to the Memory of W. B. Yeats.* New York: The Macmillan Co., 1940.
Hardy, Thomas. *Late Lyrics and Earlier, with Many Other Verses.* London: Macmillan and Co., 1922.
Havell, E. B. "Art Administration in India," *Journal of the Royal Society of Arts,* 58 (1909–10), 274–285.
Hay, Stephen. *Asian Ideas of East and West: Tagore and His Critics in Japan, China, and India.* Cambridge, Mass.: Harvard University Press, 1970.
────── "Rabindranath Tagore in America," *American Quarterly,* 14 (1962), 439–463.
Herringham, Lady C. J. P. *Ajanta Frescoes: Being Reproductions in Colour and Monochrome of Frescoes in Some of the Caves at Ajanta after Copies Taken in the Years 1909–1911 by Lady Herringham and her Assistants, with Introductory Essays by Various Members of the India Society.* London: Humphrey Milford, 1915.
Holroyd, Michael. *Lytton Strachey: A Critical Biography.* 2 vols. New York: Holt, Rinehart and Winston, 1967–68.
"Hospitality for Indian Students," *The Times* (London), March 30, 1914, p. 7.
Howe, M. A. DeWolfe. *John Jay Chapman and His Letters.* Boston: Houghton Mifflin & Co., 1937.
Hynes, Samuel. *The Edwardian Turn of Mind.* Princeton, New Jersey: Princeton University Press, 1968.
"The India Society," *The Times* (London), June 11, 1910, p. 18.
"The India Society," *The Modern Review* (Calcutta), 8 (1910), 161–163.

"The India Society," *The Times of India* (Bombay), April 6, 1931, p. 8.

"The India Society Again," *The Times of India*, April 10, 1931, p. 8.

[India Society, comp.] *Examples of Indian Art at the British Empire Exhibition, 1924*. London: The India Society, 1925.

"Indian Public Services: A Royal Commission to be Appointed," *The Times* (London), July 25, 1912, p. 5.

"Indians in America," *The Modern Review* (Calcutta), 13 (1913), 492.

Kabir. "Certain Poems of Kabir, translated by Kali Mohan Ghose and Ezra Pound. From the edition of Mr. Kshiti Mohan Sen," *The Modern Review*, 13 (1913), 611–613.

────── *One Hundred Poems of Kabir*, Rabindranath Tagore, trans., assisted by Evelyn Underhill. London: The India Society, 1914.

────── *Songs of Kabir*, Rabindranath Tagore, trans., with the assistance of Evelyn Underhill. New York: The Macmillan Co., 1915.

Kalidasa. *Sakuntala: Prepared for the English Stage by Kedar Nath Das Gupta in a New Version Written by Laurence Binyon*. London: Macmillan and Co., 1920.

Keyserling, Hermann, ed. *The Book of Marriage: A New Interpretation by Twenty-Four Leaders of Contemporary Thought Arranged and Edited by Count Hermann Keyserling*. New York: Harcourt, Brace & Co., 1926.

"The King of the Dark Chamber," *The Athenaeum* (London), July 25, 1914, p. 128.

Kripalani, Krishna. *Rabindranath Tagore: A Biography*. New York: Grove Press, 1962.

Lago, Mary M. "English Literature and Modern Bengali Short Fiction: A Study in Influences," unpub. diss. University of Missouri, 1969.

────── "Modes of Questioning in Tagore's Short Stories," *Studies in Short Fiction* (Newberry, S.C.), 5 (1967), 24–36.

Litchfield, Henrietta. *Emma Darwin: A Century of Family Letters, 1792–1896, Edited by Her Daughter, Henrietta Litchfield*. 2 vols. London: John Murray, 1915.

Lodge, Oliver. "Continuity." (See above, "British Association: The Presidential Address: Sir O. Lodge on Scientific Dogmatism.")

Macaulay, T. B. "Minute on Education," in *Sources of Indian Tradition*, W. T. de Bary et al., comps., pp. 596–601.

Monroe, Harriet. *A Poet's Life: Seventy Years in a Changing World*. New York: The Macmillan Co., 1938.

Montagu, Edwin. *An Indian Diary*. Venetia Montagu, ed. London: William Heinemann, 1930.

"Mr. Tagore's Poems," *Times Literary Supplement,* November 7, 1912, p. 492.
Mukherjee, Sujit. *Passage to America: The Reception of Rabindranath Tagore in the United States, 1912–1941.* Calcutta: Bookland Private, 1964.
Mukhopadhyay, Prabhatkumar. *Rabindrajibani o Rabindrashāhitya-Prabeshak* [Life of Rabindranath and Introduction to Rabindranath's Literature]. 4 vols., rev. ed. Calcutta: Visva-Bharati, 1960–64.
Nag, Kalidas. "Greater India Revisited," *The Modern Review* (Calcutta), 42 (1927), 68–74, 219–224, 389–398; 43 (1928), 83–88.
"*Nationalism,*" *The Athenaeum* (London), October 1917, p. 522.
"The Neo-Hindu in America and Japan," *The Spectator* (London), 119 (1917), 386–387.
"New English Art Club: A Memorable Exhibition," *The Times* (London), November 23, 1912, p. 11.
"The Nobel Literature Prize: Honour for an Indian Poet," *The Times* (London), November 14, 1913, p. 8.
Nowell-Smith, Simon, ed. *Letters to Macmillan.* London: Macmillan and St. Martin's Press, 1967.
Ocampo, Victoria. "Tagore on the Banks of the River Plate," in *Rabindranath Tagore: A Centenary Volume, 1861–1961* [Sahitya Akademi, comp.], pp. 27–47.
O'Malley, L. S. S. *Bengal District Gazeteers: Birbhum.* Calcutta: Bengal Secretariat Book Depot, 1910.
"Outsiders as Public Servants in British India," *The Modern Review* (Calcutta), 19 (1916), 611–614.
Paige, D. D., ed. *The Letters of Ezra Pound, 1907–1941.*
The Parliamentary Debates (Official Report), series 5 (1909–   ). London: His Majesty's Stationery Office.
"Party Strife in Calcutta: A Few Stray Notes," *The Modern Review* (Calcutta), 22 (1917), 440–444.
Pearson, W. W. *Shantiniketan: The Bolpur School of Rabindranath Tagore.* New York: The Macmillan Co., 1916.
"The Permanency of British Rule," *The Modern Review* (Calcutta), 11 (1912), 118.
Petaval, J. W. "Rabindranath Tagore and Social Reform via Educational Reform," *The Asiatic Review* (London), n.s. 4, 3–4 (1914), 306–311.
"Pocket Purdah 'R[ound] T[able] C[onference],'" *The Modern Review* (Calcutta), 52 (1932), 589–590.
"The 'Post-Impressionists' at the Grafton Galleries," *The Academy* (London), 79 (1910), 546–547.
Pound, Ezra. *The Letters of Ezra Pound, 1907–1941.* D. D. Paige, ed. New York: Harcourt, Brace & World, 1950.

——— "Rabindranath Tagore," *The Fortnightly Review* (London), 99 (1913), 571–579.
——— "Rabindranath Tagore: His Second Book into English," *The New Freewoman: An Individualist Review* (London), 1 (1913), 187–188.
"Rabindranath Tagore in Japan: Visit of the Bengali Poet," *The Japan Weekly Chronicle* (Kobe), June 8, 1916, p. 920.
"Rabindranath's Return," *The Modern Review* (Calcutta), 14 (1913), 427–428.
Radhakrishnan, S[arvepalli]. *The Philosophy of Rabindranath Tagore*. London: Macmillan and Co., 1918.
Raleigh, Walter. *The Letters of Sir Walter Raleigh, 1879–1922*. Lady Raleigh, ed. 2 vols. New York: The Macmillan Co., 1926.
"Report of the Presidency College Enquiry Committee," *The Modern Review* (Calcutta), 19 (1916), 601–611.
Rhys, Ernest. *Letters from Limbo*. London: J. M. Dent & Sons, 1936.
——— *Rabindranath Tagore: A Biographical Study*. London: Macmillan and Co., 1915.
Rolland, Romain. *Inde: Journal (1915–1943)*, rev. ed. Paris: Albin Michel, 1960.
Rolleston, T. W. *"Gitanjali (Song-Offerings),"* *The Hibbert Journal*, 11 (1913), 692–694.
Rothenstein, John. *Brave Day Hideous Night: Autobiography, 1939–1965*. New York: Holt, Rinehart & Winston, 1966.
——— "The Late Mr. Rothenstein" (letter), *The New Statesman and Nation* (London), January 24, 1925, p. 444.
——— *Summer's Lease: Autobiography, 1901–1938*. New York: Holt, Rinehart & Winston, 1965.
Rothenstein, William. "A Basis for the Appreciation of Works of Art: A Lecture Delivered Before the Cambridge University," *The Modern Review* (Calcutta), 13 (1913), 125–136.
——— *Contemporaries: Portrait Drawings*. London: Faber and Faber, 1937.
——— "Fine Art in India" (letter), *The Times* (London), February 28, 1910, p. 6.
——— "The Import of the Ajanta Paintings in the History of Art," in Herringham, *Ajanta Frescoes* . . . , pp. 22–23.
——— *Men and Memories: Recollections of William Rothenstein, 1872–1900*. London: Faber and Faber, 1931.
——— *Men and Memories: Recollections of William Rothenstein, 1900–1922*. London: Faber and Faber, 1932.
——— *Men of the RAF*. London: Oxford University Press, 1942.
——— *Oxford Characters*. London: John Lane, 1896.
——— *A Plea for a Wider Use of Artists and Craftsmen*. London: Constable & Co. [1917].

―――― *The Portrait Drawings of William Rothenstein 1889–1925.* John Rothenstein, comp. London: Chapman & Hall, 1926.

―――― *Since Fifty: Men and Memories, 1922–1938. Recollections of William Rothenstein.* London: Faber and Faber, 1939.

―――― *Six Portraits of Sir Rabindranath Tagore.* London: Macmillan and Co., 1915.

―――― "Yeats as a Painter Saw Him," in *Scattering Branches: Tributes to the Memory of W. B. Yeats.* Stephen Gwynn, ed., pp. 35–54.

Roy, Dilip. *Among the Great.* Bombay: Nalanda Publishers [1945].

Russell, G. W. [pseud. Æ]. *Co-operation and Nationality: A Guide for Rural Reformers from This to the Next Generation.* Dublin: Maunsel & Co., 1912.

Sadleir, Michael. *Michael Ernest Sadler: A Memoir by His Son.* London: Constable, 1949.

[Sahitya Akademi, comp.] *Rabindranath Tagore: A Centenary Volume 1861–1961.* New Delhi: Sahitya Akademi, 1961.

Sen, D. C. *Sati* [Sati], 2nd rev. ed. Calcutta: Gurudas Chatterji & Sons, 1909.

―――― *Sati: A Mythological Story,* trans. by the author. Calcutta: Atul Chandra Chakravarty and Nagendra Kumar Ray [1916].

Seymour, Mayce. "That Golden Time," *Visva-Bharati Quarterly,* 25 (1959), 1–15.

"Sir Rabindranath Tagore: Death in Calcutta," *The Times* (London), August 8, 1941, p. 4.

"Sir Rabindranath Tagore in Kobe," *The Japan Weekly Chronicle* (Kobe), June 8, 1916, pp. 913–914.

"Sir Rabindranath Tagore in Osaka: A Criticism of Modern Civilisation." (See above, "A Criticism of Modern Civilisation.")

Speaight, Robert. *William Rothenstein: The Portrait of an Artist in His Time.* London: Eyre & Spottiswoode, 1962.

Stebbins, Joel. "Jakob Kunz, 1874–1938," *Popular Astronomy,* 47 (1939), 1–5.

Stock, Noel. *The Life of Ezra Pound.* New York: Pantheon Books, 1970.

Sturge Moore, Thomas. *The Poems of T. Sturge Moore.* 2 vols. London: Macmillan and Co., 1931–32.

Swami, Purohit. *An Indian Monk: His Life and Adventures.* London: Macmillan and Co., 1932.

Tagore, Devendranath. *The Auto-Biography of Maharshi Devendranath Tagore.* Satyendranath Tagore and Indira Devi [Chaudhuri], trans. London: Macmillan and Co., 1914.

Tagore, Jyotirindranath. *Twenty-Five Collotypes from the Original Drawings of Jyotirindranath Tagore.* London: [n.p.], 1914.

Tagore, Rathindranath. *On the Edges of Time.* Calcutta: Orient Longmans, 1958.

Thompson, E. J. *A Farewell to India*. London: Ernest Benn, 1931.
——— *An Indian Day*. New York: Alfred A. Knopf, 1927.
——— *Rabindranath Tagore: His Life and Work*. Calcutta: Y.M.C.A. Publishing House, 1921.
——— *Rabindranath Tagore: Poet and Dramatist*. London: Oxford University Press, 1926.
Underhill, Evelyn. *Immanence*. London: J. M. Dent & Sons, 1912.
——— unsigned review, "An Indian Mystic," *The Nation* (London), 12 (1912–13), 320–322.
Vail, Albert and Emily M. *Heroic Lives*. Boston: Beacon Press, 1917.
von Hügel, Friedrich. *Eternal Life: A Study of Its Implications and Applications*. Edinburgh: T. & T. Clark, 1912.
Wade, Allan, ed. *The Letters of W. B. Yeats*.
Waley, S. D. *Edwin Montagu: A Memoir and an Account of His Visits to India*. New York: Asia Publishing House, 1964.
Wells, H. G. *God the Invisible King*. London: Macmillan and Co., 1917.
——— *A Modern Utopia*. New York: C. Scribner's Sons, 1905.
Willis, E. "Contemporary Thought and Life: The Races Congress," *The Modern Review* (Calcutta), 10 (1911), 275–281.
Woolf, Virginia. *Collected Essays*. 4 vols. New York: Harcourt Brace & World, 1967.
——— "Mr. Bennett and Mrs. Brown," in her *Collected Essays*, I, 319–337.
——— *Roger Fry: A Biography*. London: The Hogarth Press, 1940.
Yeats, W. B. *The Letters of W. B. Yeats*. Allan Wade, ed. London: Rupert Hart-Davis, 1954.
——— *The Winding Stair and Other Poems*. London: Macmillan and Co., 1933.

Index

Abbey Theatre, 71
Academic Committee. *See* Royal Society of Literature
Achenke, WR in, 294
Adrianople, 92
Adyar, 281
AE (pseud.). *See* Russell, G. W.
Agra, 31
Ajanta Caves: paintings in, 123, 147, 154, 188, 243n.1, 320, 340n.3, 354; C. Herringham at, 12; WR and, 28, 169, 217n.2
Akbar, 354
Alastor, 17
Albert Kahn Foundation, 191n.1
Aldbourne Village Theatre, 153n.1
Alexandra College (Dublin), 141n.1
Allahabad, Coomaraswamy in, 31; WR in, 31
Almora, RT in, 363
Almy, G. M., 86n.4
Alnashkar, 166
Amazon, 162
Amber, 255
Amritsar Massacre, 257n.3
Anderson, J. D., 23–24, 50n.1, 109n.2
America, Americans: WR on, 31, 76, 89, 94, 101, 106, 233–235, 332; RT on, 57–58, 69, 100n.5
Andrews, C. F., 52n.1, 94, 100n.4, 125, 157–174 *passim*, 194n.3, 214–230 *passim*, 246, 256–293n.1 *passim*, 313, 342, 360, 369n.1; personality of, 136–138, 182; as RT's agent, 164–165, 182–184, 186, 195–196, 208, 248–249n.1, 319n.1, 329; RT's letter to, 269
Androcles and the Lion (Shaw), 127n.3

Angkor Wat, 307
Anglo Indians, 39, 157–159
Apsaras figure, 12, 354
Arabian Nights, The, 167n.1, 191
Aristotle, 180
Arjuna, 30
Arnold, Thomas, 57, 61, 104
Art, artists, 44; Continental, European, Western, 2, 5–6, 12–13, 353n.1; Indian, 2–8, 10, 32–34, 128, 299–308 *passim*, 325, 340n.3, 352–354; Asian, Eastern, Oriental, 4–6, 12; English, 5–6, 10–13; Chinese, 7, 153; Japanese, 7, 153; French, 9–10. *See also* Rothenstein, William, views on art, artists
Arts and Crafts Society, 230n.2
Ashwell, Lena, 264n.2
Asia (New York), 272n.12, 330n.1
Athenaeum, The (London), 20–21, 74–75

Babuananda. *See* Chatterji, Ramananda
Bahai faith, 70n.2
Baker, Sir Herbert, 128, 129, 300n.4, 307, 340n.3
Balākā (wild swans), 133
Balaton, Lake, RT at, 318
Bangkok, RT in, 324n.1
Barbusse, Henri, 274
Basanta-Prayānna (Passing of Spring), 162n.1, 167
Baudelaire, Pierre, 142
Baūl singers, 15
Bedales School, 145n.2
Beerbohm, Max, 8, 34, 204, 215, 217, 371; WR's letter to, 269
Benares, 123n.3, 188, 250; WR in, 10, 30–32, 80, 358; Stephen in, 31–32; Woodroffe in, 31–32

Benares, Maharaja of, 31
Bengal, Bengalis, 13–16, 95, 125, 206, 212, 253n.3, 273, 299, 338; partition of, 13–16; literature of, 15; as "political question," 39; government of, 282n.4, 295, 303
Berenson, Bernard, WR's letter to, 37
Berlin: RT in, 317, 329n.1; Rathindranath Tagore in, 317
Berlin National Gallery, 328, 329n.2
Bhadralok (cultured people), 13–14
Bhagavad Gita, 30, 286–287
Bhattacharya, Bhabani, 344n.6
Bhowanipur, Pearson in, 126n.5
Bhuvaneshvar, 354
Bible, Biblical, 19, 21–22, 180
Binyon, Laurence, 69n.6, 154, 212n.1, 243n.1, 307, 340
Birdwood, Sir George, 2–7 *passim*
Birmingham (England), 53, 121n.1; Tagore in, 329n.1
Birmingham City Museum and Art Gallery, 329n.1
Birmingham Repertory Company, 117–118n.2
Biscay, Bay of, 122
Blake, William, 18, 20
Bloomsbury, 38, 360
Board of Education, 11n.21, 40, 239, 308n.5
Board of Trade, 134n.3
Boars Hill, 177, 188
Boddhisatra, 281
Bodley Head, The, 9
Bolpur, Bolpur school. *See* Santiniketan; Visva-Bharati University
Bombay: WR in, 35; RT in, 37
Bombay Art Society, 301
Bombay School of Art, 300, 333n.2
Bonn, WR in, 255n.1
Bose, J. C., 151
Bose, Nandalal, 299, 347, 351–352
Boston, RT in, 88, 98
Boulogne-sur-Seine, RT in, 279, 283
Bradford (Yorkshire), 9, 50n.1; WR in, 50, 53
Bradley, A. C., 51, 59–61, 68, 345
Brahmans, 15
Brahmo Samaj, 16

Brett, George, 155–156n.4, 167n.3, 170n.1, 176n.3, 216n.1–227n.1 *passim;* RT's letters to, 223, 248–249n.1
Bridges, Robert, 177–202 *passim*, 212–213n.1, 219, 305–306; and *Gitanjali,* 180–186, 197–198, 209, 225; WR's letters to, 182n.9, 198n.1; RT's letters to, 211–212, 306
Bridges, Edward, Lord, 186n.16
British Academy, 11n.21, 347
"British Agency." *See* Criminal Investigation Department
British Association, 121n.1
British Empire Exhibition of 1924, 308n.5
British Museum, 185, 308n.5
British School at Rome, 334n.3
Brixton Gaol, 28n.2
Brooke, Stopford, 20, 51, 85, 93, 109n.1, 345, 360
Brooks, Morgan, 58
Brooks, Mrs. Morgan, 58, 68n.4
Broomfield, J. H., 14
Brunton, Sir Lauder, 198n.2
Brussels, RT in, 277
Budapest, RT in, 317n.1
Buddha, figure of, 5–7, 320; Buddhist, 230
Burlington House, 230n.1
Burns, Cecil, 4

Calais, RT in, 37
Calcutta, 6–8, 95, 121, 167, 301; RT in, 13, 15–16, 33, 128, 143, 166, 190, 214–215, 227, 246n.2, 324n.1, 325, 333n.1, 342n.1; WR in, 32–35; High Court of, 80; Sadler in, 246, 248, 249n.3; Pearson in, 310
Calcutta University, 57n.1, 146n.3, 224n.1, 281, 291n.2, 299, 303, 362
Calcutta University Commission, 243, 249n.4, 282n.4
Calderon, George, 263, 264n.2
Cambridge (Massachusetts), RT in, 98
Cambridge (England), 23, 38
Cambridge Brotherhood, 52n.1
Cambridge University, 38n.6,

50n.1, 52n.1, 309; RT at, 19, 49, 50n.1, 51; WR at, 109n.2, 252n.2
Cap Martin, RT in, 325, 327
Carmichael, Lord, 280–281
Carnegie Hall, 234
Carpenter, Edward, 145–146, 162
Carpenter, Estlin, 306n.16
Carutza, WR in, 330
Cashmere. *See* Kashmir
Catskill Mountains, 235
Cawnpore, 31
Chakravarty, Ajit, 125–126n.3, 154, 183, 187–189
Chakravarty, Amiya, 351–352; interviews with, 133, 150n.6
Chandernagore, "Chandannagore," 227
Chapman, John Jay, 55–98 *passim*, 233
Chatterjee, Sir Atul, 300–301
Chatterji, K. N. (son of R. Chatterji), 55n.5, 76
Chatterji, Ramananda, 55n.5, 64, 76, 94, 341
Chaudhuri, Arya, 148
Chaudhuri, Indira Devi, 150n.5; RT's letter to, 333n.1
Chaudhuri, Pramathanath, 150n.5
Chelmsford, Lord, 217
Cherbourg: Elmhirst in, 312n.1; RT in, 312n.1
Chesterton, G. K., 362–363n.1
Chhatarpur: WR in, 28–31; Dickinson in, 191n.1; Trevelyan in, 191n.1
Chhatarpur, Maharaja of, 28, 33
Chicago: RT in, 78–106 *passim*, 236n.1; Pratima and Rathindranath Tagore in, 78, 82
Chirol, Valentine, 14n.29, 147, 156n.6, 159
Chitor, 255; WR in, 28
Chitrāngadā, 129
Chowdhury, S., 307
Christ, Christianity, 120, 354
Christian Science, 99
City of Lahore, 119
Clifford's Inn, 8
Coliseum (London), 264n.2
Colombo, RT in, 296
Communal Award, 347n.2

Congress of Religious Liberals, 87
Congress Party, 245n.3
Constable and Co., 237
Cook, Thomas & Son, 38, 107, 227, 229
Coole Park, 41
Coomaraswamy, Ananda, 5n.6, 31, 33, 334n.3
Copyright, 97, 133–134, 184–185
Cornell University, 271
Cornford, Frances, 19, 51, 209, 305
Coronation Durbar, 13
Cossimbazar, Maharaja of, 163n.1
Cotswolds, 249n.3, 358
Craig, Gordon, 30, 58, 290–291
Crane, Walter, 154
Cranmer-Byng, L., 86
Criminal Investigation Department, 285, 287n.1
Croesus, 162
Cromwell Road Centre for Indians, 57, 109n.1, 163
Crystal Palace, 66n.1
Curzon, Lord, 13–14, 38–40, 245n.2, 306

Daily Illini (Urbana), 68n.4
Daily Mail (London), 128
Darjeeling: WR in, 33; RT in, 336, 338
Dartington Hall, 272n.12, 317n.1
Darwin family, 19n.38, 209
Das Gupta, Basantaranjan, 162n.1
Das Gupta, K. N., 68
Das Gupta, Sarayubala, 162n.1
Dash, Sir Arthur, 303–304
Davids, T. W. R., 8, 92n.2
Davidson, Jo, 117n.1, 118
de Chavanne, Puvis, 264n.2
Degas, Edgar, 9, 12
de Goncourt, Edmond, 9
Delhi, 13, 31, 81–82; Pearson in, 126n.5; Andrews in, 136; WR and, 299–302
"Delhi affair." *See* New Delhi
Dent, J. M. & Sons, 86n.3
de Rosen, Jean, 124n.4, 142, 154
Dev Barman, D. K., 339, 343, 346
Dev Burman, Somendrachandra, 37, 74, 78–79
Dey, Mukul, 295, 307, 341

Dickinson, G. L., 50n.1; RT's comments on, 190–191
Dinesh Babu. *See* Sen, D. C.
Doll and Richards Gallery (Boston), 336n.3
Donne, John, 20
Dostoievsky, Feodor, 28n.2
Drinkwater, John, 117, 307
Drummond, J. G., 268n.3
Dublin, 38; WR in, 141
Dublin theatre. *See* Abbey Theatre
Dunham, Carroll, 54, 59
Dunham, Edward, 61n.1
Duchess Home (London), RT at, 116
Duhamel, Georges, 367
Dusseldorf, RT in, 317n.2

East, stereotype of, 192, 201
East Bengal, 16, 37
Egypt, 32, 273
Eldest Son, The (Galsworthy), 69n.5
Elgar, Sir Edward, 260
Elite Conflict in a Plural Society, 14
Elmhirst, Leonard, 271–272, 293–294n.1, 304, 309, 317, 329n.1; RT's letter to, 293–294n.1; interviews with, 272n.12,n.14, 304n.12, 312n.1
Emerson, Ralph Waldo, 14
Emerson Hall (Cambridge, Mass.), 99
England and India, 39. *See also* Rothenstein, views on India, Indians
English Association, 263
"Enoch Soames," 8–9
Esher Commission, 278
Essay on the Civilisations of India, China, and Japan, 190–191
Eternal Life: Its Implications and Applications, 73n.4
Europe, Europeans, 86; WR on, 76; RT on, 318
"Evening at Benares." *See* India House, WR's gift to
Everest, Mount, 308n.6
Everyman's Library, 85–86
Extradition law, 27

Far Oakridge, 63, 73, 79, 84, 194n.1, 273, 291, 307, 357, 365–366; WR at, 25–366 *passim*; RT at, 52n.2, 118n.1; Edward Carpenter at, 145–146; Andrews at, 157, 162; Rhys at, 168–169; Beerbohm at, 204; F. Cornford at, 209; Yeats at, 269
Fergusson, Robert, 5
Fifty-Sixth Street Galleries, 334n.3
First Universal Races Congress, 57n.1
Fisher, H. A. L., 10, 61, 63, 146n.2, 239, 280n.2, 282n.4; WR's letter to, 10–11
Flexner, Simon, 55–63 *passim*
Ford, Walter, 40
Foreign Office, 281
Forster, E. M., 191n.1
Fortnightly Review, The (London), 103
Foster, Sir William, 308n.5
Fox Strangways, A. H., 38–43, 259; importance to RT, 8; and India Society, 8, 92n.2, 156n.5, 188–189n.1; as RT's agent, 46n.19, 71–111 *passim*, 122–142 *passim*, 153–189 *passim*; personality of, 136, 157–159; WR's letter to, 43n.15
Fox Strangways, Maurice, 39
France, French, WR on, 142, 274
France, Anatole, 274
Francis of Assisi, Saint, 5
Fry, Roger, 10–13 *passim*

Galerie Pigalle, 326n.1
Gallery Ferdinand Möller, 326n.1
Galsworthy, John, 68, 229; WR's letter to, 217n.3
Gandhi, M. K., 126n.5, 218, 268, 272, 294n.2, 339, 347n.2
Ganges River, 10, 128, 151, 311
Ganguli, Nitindranath, 343n.1
Garibaldi, Giuseppe, 274
Garnett, Constance, WR's letters to, 27–28
Garnett, David, 27, 28n.2
Garnett, Edward, 28n.2
Geiger, Bernhard, 294n.3
Geneva, RT in, 285, 328–330

Genoa, RT in, 311
George V, King of England, 13, 40
Germany, Germans, 236; WR on, 172
Ghosal, Svarna Kumari, 147–153 *passim*
Ghose, Kalimohon, 55, 61, 68, 76, 103, 117, 120, 122, 125–126n.3
Ghose, Sudhin, 330n.1
Gibraltar, Rock of, 120
Gide, André, 46n.19, 124, 142, 250, 367
Gill, Eric, 10n.20
Giotto, 354
Gita, Geeta. See *Bhagavad Gita*
Gitanjali. See Bridges, and *Gitanjali;* Tagore, Rabindranath, works of; Yeats, and *Gitanjali*
Gloucester, Gloucestershire, 53, 165
Goethe, Johann Wolfgang von, 47
Gogol, Nikolai, 28n.2
Gokhale, G. K., 146n.2, 344n.3
Golden Book of Tagore, The, 340n.4, 341
Goloubew, Victor, 307
Gonne, Iseult, 46n.19, 47
Gorky, Maxim, 276
Gosse, Edmund, 42, 43–44n.16
Gourlay, W. R., 293n.1
Grafton Galleries (London), 10, 12–13
Granville-Barker, Harley, 69n.5, 127n.3
Greece, 32
Green, Sir Alan, 301–302
Grosvenor Gallery (London), 160n.1
Gupta, Sir Krishna, 40
Gurudev, RT as, 128

Hadow, Sir Henry, 251
Hammond, Barbara, WR's letter to, 217n.1
Hampstead, 30, 155, 165, 357–358; WR in, 49–112 *passim;* RT in, 38; Sturge Moore in, 44
Hardinge, Lord and Lady, 81n.5
Hardy, Thomas, 204, 290, 320, 351n.4
Harvard University, RT at, 98–101, 234

Havell, E. B.: and art controversy, 2–7, 10, 31, 33, 174n.1, 237n.4, 300, 350; and India Society, 90, 92n.2
Heine, Heinrich, 310n.4
Hellenic tradition, Hellenism, 19, 191n.1
Herbert, George, 20
Hermione Lectures, 141n.1
Heroic Lives, 70n.2
Herringham, Christiana, 12, 28, 243n.1
Herringham, Sir Wilmot, 12n.26
Hibbert Journal, The, 64, 101, 103, 105
Hibbert Lectures, 324n.1, 326, 336n.2
Himalaya Mountains, 165, 368
Hindi, 125–126n.3
Hindus, Hinduism, 5, 14–16, 120, 321
Hindu Mahasabha, 28n.2
Hnevkovsky, Jaroslav, 295n.3
Hok'sai, 343
Holdich, Sir Thomas, 6
Hongkong, RT in, 228n.1
Hornell, W. W., 40
Hotel St. Andrews (New York), 59
House of Commons, 174n.1
Housman, Laurence, 329n.3
Howrah Station, 129n.2
Hudson, W. H., 295
Hudson River, 80, 235
"Humdrum & Harum-Scarum: A Lecture on Free Verse," 179
Hungary, 305
"Hymn to Intellectual Beauty" (Shelley), 253

Iles Farm, 52n.2, 68n.1. *See also* Far Oakridge
Illinois, 57, 63
Illinois Institute of Technology, 78–79n.1
Illinois, University of, 58, 68, 70, 86n.4
Imperial Institute, 334n.3
Impressionism, 9, 14
India, Indians, 27, 102–103, 109n.2, 163, 188, 224, 227, 236, 299; and the West, 1, 4, 6, 14; art education in, 2–8,

India, Indians (*cont.*)
  173–174, 295n.1, 299; universities in, 2, 142n.2; Government of, 4, 13–14, 28, 293–294n.1, 299–302, 321; English education in, 14; and England, 19–20, 39, 217–218; literature of, 24, 61, 61n.3; music of, 61n.3; Native States in, 134n.3; Yeats on, 226n.4; Education Department of, 249n.4. *See also* Art, artists; Bombay School of Art; Calcutta University
India House, 332; murals for, 300–302, 325, 343; WR's gift to, 339; WR's gift displaced, 340n.2
India Office, 27, 40, 41n.11, 57n.1, 163, 173–174, 281, 300, 300n.5, 308n.5
India Society, The, 7–12 *passim*, 21, 39–43, 73n.3–92n.2 *passim*, 123–126 *passim*, 144–159 *passim*, 188–189, 301, 307, 333n.2, 352. *See also* Fox Strangways, and India Society; Rothenstein, William, and India Society
India Society Exhibition of Modern Indian Art, 353n.1
Indian Academy, 347
Indian Army, 279n.2
Indian Art, Dramatic and Friendly Society, 109n.1
Indian Civil Service, 160n.4
Indian Dramatic Society, 264n.2
Indian Educational Service, 64n.3
Indian High Commission, 300, 333n.2, 325
Indian National Liberal Federation, 347n.2
Indian Public Services Commission, 11n.21, 142n.2, 145, 150n.3
Indian Society for Oriental Arts, 206n.3
"Indian unrest," 14, 27, 220, 268
Indian Volunteer Corps, 227
International University. *See* Santiniketan; Visva-Bharati University
Iowa, University of, 100n.1
Iqbal, Muhammed, 354

Ireland: WR on, 141; Yeats on, 226n.4; RT on, 278
Irish Academy of Letters, 342n.2
Italy, 242; WR on 249–250, 315

Jacks, L. P., 64
Jalgaon, WR in, 28
Japan, Japanese, 73; WR on, 201, 230, 232–233; RT on, 203–204n.1, 231–232
Jehangir, 354
Jhalawar, Maharaja of, 134n.3
Jhelum, Lake of, 133
Jivan-devatā, Jeevan-devata (life-God), 321
Jorasanko, 25
Journal de Salavin, 367n.3
Joyce, James, 150n.6

Kabir, poems by, 122 126, 136, 154–160n.2, 187–189
Kahn, Albert, 318
Kapp, E. X., 271; interview with, 271n.11
Karma, 108
Kashmir, 30, 173
Keats, John, 18
Keedick Agency, 227n.1
Kensington, 273, 311. *See also* Royal College of Art
Keyserling, Count Hermann, 319–320
Khajraho, 354
Kismet, 253
Kobe, RT in, 228n.1
Konarak, 147
Kramrisch, Stella, 282n.3, 290, 352, 354, 364
Krishna, 30, 354
Kshiti Mohan Babu. *See* Sen, K. M.
Kunz, Jakob, 86n.4; as "German," 69

Lausanne, Marie Sturge Moore in, 44
Lawrence, T. E., 308n.6
League of Nations, 236
Leeds University, 217
Léger, Alexis, 124n.4
Leicester Galleries, 230n.2, 295n.3, 352–353
Leopold, King of Belgium, 214n.1

Lethaby, W. R., 154
Lévi, Sylvain, 290, 293
Lewis, Edwin, 78–79n.1, 82–83n.1, 85, 88, 96
Lewis Institute, 78–79n.1, 85
Liverpool, RT in, 120n.1
Lodge, Sir Oliver, 121
London, Londoners, 37–38, 84, 129n.3, 155, 165; WR in, 9–364 *passim*; RT in, 37–333 *passim*; Pratima and Rathindranath Tagore in, 37–38, 276n.1, 329n.1, 354; Harriet Moody in, 46n.19, 120n.3; Seal in, 57n.1; Yeats in, 76, 343; Pound in, 93; Gordon Craig in, 290–291
London Missionary Society, 126n.5
Long, George, Bishop of Bathurst, 259
Longman, C. J., 134n.3, 184
Longmans Green & Co., 134n.3
Loti, Pierre, 142
Lucknow, 31, 301
Lutyens, Sir Edwin, 128, 129n.3, 300n.4, 307
Lytton, Lord, 301

Macaulay, Lord, 2
MacDonald, Ramsay, 146
Mackail, John, 40
Macmillan, Sir Frederick, 134n.3, 183–212–213n.1 *passim*
Macmillan, George, 136, 171–172, 208, 209–211n.4, 221–222
Macmillan, Maurice, 223
Macmillan Co., The (New York), 95, 97, 156n.5, 267. *See also* Brett, George
Macmillan and Co. (London), 21–280 *passim*, 319n.1, 333n.1, 369; WR's letters to, 84–85n.2, 226n.2; RT's letters to, 123n.2, 135n.4, 155–156n.4,n.5, 167n.1,n.3, 176n.3, 188–189n.1, 212n.1, 218n.5,n.8, 221n.15, 268n.3, 276n.1, 280n.4, 344n.6
Madras, RT in, 324n.1
Maeterlinck, Maurice, 22
Mahabharata, 129
Mahalanobis, Prasanta, 362–363n.1

Maitra, D. N., 55, 59, 63, 80
Manchester (England), 30
Manchester Square (London), 94, 360
Marseilles, RT in, 37
Masefield, John, 23, 54n.2, 329n.3, 360–361
Massingham, Henry, 112–125 *passim*, 360
Mayo Hospital (Calcutta), 55n.4
Mazzini, Giuseppe, 242, 274
Mentone, Seal in, 61, 63
Michaelangelo, 354
Michigan, University of, 100n.1
Milan, RT in, 312
Milton, John, 14
Missionaries, 120, 122, 321
Modern Review, The (Calcutta), 22, 64, 94, 102–103, 105, 147, 225, 246, 327; and art controversy, 7–8
Moffat, Curtis, 329n.1
Monro, Alida, 318n.3
Monro, Harold, 318n.3
Monroe, Harriet, 82–83n.1, 145n.1
Montagu, Sir Edwin, 217, 241, 249, 279, 281, 308n.5
Montagu-Chelmsford Reforms, 217, 252n.4, 278, 344n.3
Montmartre, 358
Moody, Harriet, 46n.19, 99, 100n.3, 101, 103, 117n.1, 118, 120, 123, 145n.1, 218, 236, 271; RT's letter to, 218n.6
Moody, William Vaughan, 46n.19, 99
Moore, Stuart, 157–159, 160n.2
Moore, Mrs. Stuart. *See* Underhill, Evelyn
Morris, William, 242, 263, 308
Mukhopadhyay, Prabhatkumar, 70n.1, 246–247n.3, 313n.1
Murray, Gilbert, 61, 63, 293–294n.3, 305, 329n.3
Murray, John & Co., 73n.3, 86n.3
Museum of Fine Arts (Boston), 336n.3
Music and Letters, 259n.2
Music of Hindostan, The, 39
Muslim, Muhammedan, 14–15, 147
Mussolini, 304

Mysticism, 20, 71, 130n.1, 157

Naidu, Sarojini, 340n.1
Naples: Elmhirst and Tagore in, 304
Nation, The (London), 11, 63–82 *passim*, 112–125 *passim*, 171, 360
National Conference on Education (Canada), 325
National Portrait Gallery (London), 260n.1
National Portrait Society, 160n.1
Nauheim, WR in, 324, 327
New Burlington Galleries, 353n.1
New Delhi, 90, 92n.2, 129n.3, 300, 302, 307
New English Art Club, 9, 64n.2, 68n.2, 73n.5
New Statesman, The (London), 313
New York, RT in: 54n.1, 56–57, 59, 63, 88, 98, 105, 331–332; WR in, 235
Newbolt, Sir Henry, 42, 225
Newcastle, Staffordshire, RT in, 51–53
Nivedita, Sister, 7
Nobel Prize for Literature. *See* Tagore, and Nobel Prize
Noble, Margaret. *See*, Nivedita
Noyes, Alfred, 105

Oakhill Park, 165
Oakridge. *See* Far Oakridge
Oakridge Lynch, 52n.2; RT in, 52n.2
"Ode to the West Wind" (Shelley), 253
Osaka, RT in, 228
Outamaro, 343
Outram, William, 52n.1, 53
Oxford, 38, 177, 299; WR in, 8–9, 61, 63, 188; RT in, 177; Amiya Chakravarty in, 351–352
Oxford University, 38–39, 146n.2, 230n.2, 305–306; Manchester College of, 64, 324n.1; RT at, 326

Padma River, 143, 162, 165
Palmer, E. H., 24

Panch Ganga Ghat, 188, 250
Paris: WR in, 9, 367; RT in, 37, 269, 280, 367n.3
Parliament, 13, 134n.3, 282n.4
Pearson, W. W., 125, 161, 227n.1–246n.3 *passim*, 268n.3, 274, 276n.1, 291, 309–310
Peking, 246–247n.3; RT in, 319n.1
Pembroke Dock, South Wales, WR at, 368
Perse, St.-John. *See* Léger
Persia, RT on, 344
Petaval, J. W., 162
Phoenix School, 268
Pieris, Harry, 353
Pistoia, Pearson in, 310n.1
Plato, 180
Poe, Edgar Allan, 142
Poetry: A Magazine of Verse (Chicago), 82n.1–98 *passim*, 145n.1
Poetry Bookshop, 318n.3
Polytechnic Institute (Calcutta), 163n.1
Pond Lyceum, 227n.1
Poona, 146n.2, 347n.2
Postimpressionism, 10–14 *passim*
Pound, Ezra, 42–44, 93, 95, 125–126n.3, 305; as RT's agent, 85, 87, 98
Prague, RT in, 306
Prague University, 316
Publishers' Association, 134n.3
Pugin, Augustus, 5
Punjab, 39
Puranic legends, 81n.3
Purdue University, 100n.1

Radha, 30, 167
Raleigh, Sir Walter, 183–184, 198n.1
Ramakrishna Mission, 7n.10
Ramananda Babu. *See* Chatterji, Ramananda
Ramayana, 75
Ramgarh, RT in, 165
Ray, Satishchandra, 70n.1
Reform Bill. *See* Montagu-Chelmsford Reforms
Rhys, Ernest, 127n.3, 133, 135, 168, 171, 172–173n.2, 198, 201, 218, 309–310, 357; as editor,

86n.3, 118, 291n.3; RT's letters to, 118n.2, 218n.7
Rhys, Grace (Mrs. Ernest), 310
Ritchie, Sir Richmond, 27
Robeson, Paul, 341
Rochester (New York), RT in, 87–88
Rodin, Auguste, 9
Rolland, Romain, 274, 280n.1, 304
Rolleston, T. W., 40n.9, 64; importance to RT, 8
Ronaldshay, Lord, 291, 301
Rome, RT in, 304n.12
Rothenstein, Albert (younger brother of WR), 30, 31, 194n.1, 245–246n.3, 371
Rothenstein, Alice (wife of WR), 51–55n.2 passim, 68–96 passim, 111–119 passim, 128, 140, 148, 252, 307, 340n.1, 360, 371; WR's letters to, 28–31; RT's letters to, 100n.5, 203–204n.1, 248n.1, 329n.1, 330n.2
Rothenstein, Betty (younger daughter of WR), 80, 176n.2, 246, 273, 294, 307, 331, 364
Rothenstein, Charles (elder brother of WR), 194, 250
Rothenstein, John (elder son of WR), 52n.2, 79, 80, 96, 145–146, 164, 209, 234, 254, 259–260, 269, 290, 313, 358; RT's letter to, 100n.5
Rothenstein, Rachel (elder daughter of WR), 80, 175, 203–204n.1, 207, 234–275 passim, 294, 307, 312–313, 364
Rothenstein, William: personality of, 1, 8–9, 12, 31, 34, 50–51, 59, 76–77, 112, 151–152, 157, 169, 207–208, 240–242, 282, 331, 341–342, 358, 371; and art controversy, 5–8; and India Society, 7–8, 10, 90, 92n.2, 123–124, 152–156 passim; as "Paris in Oxford," 9–10; Memorial Service for, 34, 371; as artist, 44; war experiences of, 194n.1, 217, 225n.1, 235, 250–251, 254–255, 358, 369; as art educator, 217, 235, 267, 355, 357; knighted, 333–334
and Tagore: nature of correspondence with RT, 1, 25, 35, 66, 93, 101, 153, 229, 234, 240, 269–294 passim, 299, 310–311, 324, 335, 347, 357–358, 362; friendship with RT, 1, 13, 20–38 passim, 50–81 passim, 94–133 passim, 144–169 passim, 239–294 passim, 310–311, 324–338 passim, 367–369, 371; importance to RT, 1, 8, 17–18, 360; as RT's agent, 46n.19, 84–85n.2, 103; RT's letters to, 49, 51, 53, 56, 57, 58, 62, 64, 65, 68–69n.4, 69, 73, 74, 78, 82, 85, 86, 88, 98, 101, 105, 106, 107, 110, 112n.2, 113, 116, 117, 118, 119, 127, 129, 131, 140, 143, 146, 150, 161, 164, 165, 166, 170, 173, 175, 187, 189, 190, 194, 196, 206, 211, 214, 215, 224, 227, 228, 231, 233, 237, 244, 247, 252, 253, 257, 262, 264, 275, 277, 279, 283, 285, 292, 296, 309, 311, 312, 314, 315, 316, 317, 318, 320, 325, 327, 328, 329, 331, 333, 334, 335, 336, 338, 344, 349, 351, 353, 363, 365, 367
travels of (considered or completed): India, 9–12, 15, 27–35, 80, 236–237, 364–365; United States, 9–10, 13, 37, 80, 234–235; Belgium, 213, 254–255; France, 217, 246, 250, 254–255, 275, 358, 367; Austria, 294; Germany, 294–295, 324, 327; Switzerland, 330–331
views on art, artists, 10–14, 32, 77–90, passim, 109, 115–116, 142, 153–155, 163, 188, 192–214 passim, 224–239 passim, 255, 274, 285–291 passim, 313–324 passim, 338, 358, 365; European, Western, 5, 290, 308, 332, 343, Indian, 5, 31, 90, 153–155, 307–308, 320–327 passim, 343, 347–351, 354, Chinese, 153, Japanese, 153, 343, Eastern, Asian, 290, 308,

398 Index

Rothenstein, William (*cont.*)
  332, 343; India, Indians, 27–
  37 *passim*, 80–81, 102–104,
  163, 229–257 *passim*, 273–274,
  290–302 *passim*, 335, 352, 362,
  368–369;
    religion, 66–67, 71, 109
    education, 95–96, 263, 273,
    281–285 *passim*, 299
    politics, 122, 192, 197, 199–201,
    217, 235–236, 251, 273–274,
    324, 341, 349
      works of: portraits, 9n.17,
      12n.26, 43n.14,n.15, 61–67
      passim, 81n.4, 146n.4, 215–216,
      230n.2, 260, 339, 357; exhibitions of, 11–12, 30, 64n.2, 156–
      157, 228–229; reviews of, 11–
      12, 64n.2
      as writer, 336, 341, 367, 369
Rothenstein, William Michael
  younger son of WR), 80, 164,
  176n.2, 273, 307
Round Table Conference, 240n.3,
  343, 355n.2; as "political
  gramophone, 339
Rowlatt Acts, 218, 258
Roy, Dilip, 277n.2
Roy, Ram Mohun, 16
Roy Chaudhuri, Hironmoy, 173–
  174, 214
Royal Academy, 9, 353–354n.1
Royal Air Force, 358
Royal Albert Hall, 68, 264n.2
Royal College of Art, 155n.3,
  174n.1, 267, 295–313 *passim*,
  340n.3, 354–358 *passim*
Royal College of Music, 308n.2
Royal Institute of British Architects, 129n.3
Royal Society, 302
Royal Society of Arts, 2–8, 13,
  174n.1
Royal Society of Literature, 42–44
Ruskin, John, 5, 12
Russell, Flora, 340n.1, 371
Russell, George William, 141,
  349, 354
Rutherston, Albert. *See* Rothenstein, Albert
Rutherston, Charles. *See* Rothenstein, Charles
Sadler, Sir Michael, 217, 243, 246,
  248, 253, 280n.2, 281, 282n.4,
  302–303, 329n.3, 352
St. Martin-in-the-Fields, Church
  of, 34
Sakuntala, 68
Samurai, 263
San Francisco, RT in, 233
Sannyasi, 67, 68, 230
Santals, 33
Santiniketan, Santi Niketan, 15,
  17, 33, 78, 95, 165, 268, 307–
  308, 311–312, 329–330, 341,
  357, 368; RT's school at, 15n.32,
  37, 55n.5, 65, 66n.1, 88–111n.1,
  passim, 119, 139, 166, 204, 222–
  223, 235, 239, 243, 262, 271–
  310 *passim*, 325, 329n.3, 353–
  354n.1, 363, 369n.1; RT at, 16,
  121–131 *passim*, 140–143 *passim*, 161–177 *passim*, 187–196
  passim, 211–213, 224, 237–265
  passim, 292–294, 309–322 *passim*, 334–354 *passim*, 365–368;
  Pearson at, 126n.5, 161; MacDonald at, 146; Andrews at,
  136, 164; Petaval at, 162
Sati, 80, 85
Savarkar, Vinayak, 27–28
Scott, C. P., 329n.3
Seal, Sir Brajendranath, 57, 63,
  68, 77, 104, 128, 161, 167–
  168n.1, 248, 362–363n.1
Seal, B. N., 64n.3
Seattle: Pearson in, 227n.1; RT
  in, 227.1
Sen, D. C., 80, 85, 128
Sen, K. C., 170, 172–173n.2
Sen, K. M., 125, 154, 183, 188–
  189n.1
Sen, Pulinbehari, 194n.3
Sen, R. R., 123n.2
Servants of India Society, 146n.2,
  344n.3
Seymour, Arthur, 58, 70, 88
Seymour, Mayce (Mrs. Arthur),
  58, 70
Shakespeare, 14, 321
Shanghai, 246–247n.3
Shantiniketan, Shanti Niketan.
  See Santiniketan
Shastri, V. S. S., 343
Shaw, Charlotte, 112n.1
Shaw, Sir Evelyn, 333

Shaw, G. B., 42, 111, 127n.3, 264n.2, 341, 342n.2
Sheffield University, 11n.21, 259; WR at, 217, 235, 237n.4, 263
Shelley, Percy, 17, 253
Shilaidaha, Shilida, 143, 165; RT in, 37, 150, 189, 206
Shiva, 109n.1, 320
Silex Scintillans (Henry Vaughan), 20n.40
Sinclair, May, 117n.1
Sinn Feinism, 236
Skrine, F. H., 134n.3
Slade Professorship of Fine Art, 10–11
Smuts, Jan Christian, 336
Société des Amis d'Oriente, 280n.3
Society of Authors, 134n.3, 184–185
Society for Psychical Research, 121n.1
Solomon, W. E. G., 332
Somervell, T. H., 308n.6
"Song of Solomon," 21
South Africa, 126n.5, 142n.2, 157, 265
South Kensington, 107. See also Royal College of Art
South Kensington Museum, 290–291
Spirit of Man, The, 178–180, 225
Srinagar, RT in, 173
Sriniketan, 271–272
Stephen, Sir Harry, 31, 35n.1, 81n.1
Stephen, Lady, 31
Storey, Josephine, 329n.1
Straight, Dorothy (later Elmhirst), 271–272, 317n.1
Straight, Willard, 271–272
Stroud, Gloucestershire, 52n.2, 53, 194n.1
Sturge Moore, Marie, 44, 46, 264n.2, 342n.4
Sturge Moore, Thomas, 17–18, 22, 118, 264n.2, 310, 329n.1, 340, 341, 357–365 *passim;* as editor, 44–47, 125, 159, 160n.6, 268, 343; RT's letters to, 310n.4, 319n.1, 358; WR's letters to, 329n.1, 358
Suez Canal, 4
Sufi poets, 123n.3, 124n.1

Suhrawardy, H. S., 184n.13,n.14
Surendra Babu. *See* Tagore, Surendranath
Swadeshi, 294n.2
Swami, Purohit, 342n.4
Swinburne, Algernon, Yeats's opinion of, 212n.1
Symbol, symbolism, 6; RT's use of, 15, 47; RT as, 19–20, 138

Tägliche Rundschau (Berlin), 162n.2
Tagore family, 14–18 *passim*, 25, 147
Tagore, Abanindranath (cousin once removed of RT), 4, 6, 12n.26, 25–35 *passim*, 92n.2, 173–174, 204, 295n.1, 299, 351–352
Tagore, Bela (Chakravarty; eldest daughter of RT), 248, 252
Tagore, Debendranath (father of RT), 15–17, 126n.4
Tagore, Gaganendranath (cousin once removed of RT), 4, 33, 126, 351n.1, 364–365
Tagore, Jyotirindranath (elder brother of RT), 64n.4, 68, 77, 127n.1,n.2, 151, 314; RT's letters to, 100n.1, 162n.2
Tagore, Mrinalini Devi (wife of RT), 17, 50n.2
Tagore, Pratima (daughter-in-law of RT), 25, 37, 51, 52–89 *passim*, 146, 209, 312, 342n.1, 354
Tagore, Rabindranath: personality of, 1, 15–19 *passim*, 33, 47–85 *passim*, 100n.5, 133–144 *passim*, 160–169 *passim*, 201, 215n.2, 224, 254, 264–319 *passim*, 328–332 *passim*, 349–350, 366; and Nobel Prize, 1, 131–144 *passim*, 162n.2, 166, 267, 306; education of, 15–16; stereotype of, 18–24 *passim*, 272, 337–338; academic honors for, 38–39, 146, 305–306, 317n.1, 319, 368; and India Society, 39–40, 153–156; death of, 25; as translator, 47, 123n.3–126n.3 *passim*, 148, 159–167n.3, 180–187 *passim*, 212, 216, 268n.3, 306, 343, 345–346; literary honor of, 183–184, 195, 219,

Tagore, Rabindranath (*cont.*)
221; and knighthood, 202–203, 256–257n.3, 268, 306; 70th birthday of, 336–337

reception of in the West, 1–8 *passim*, 17–25 *passim*, 61–77 *passim*, 111–112, 267, 285, 293–294n.1, 305, 346, 357–358; in India, 8, 25, 120–121, 128, 140–151 *passim*, 214, 218, 238, 242, 272, 292–305 *passim*, 321, 331–332, 343, 346; in England, 17–24, 50, 67–85 *passim*, 106, 109, 128, 144, 147, 159–167 *passim*, 183–184, 218, 239–242 *passim*, 257–272 *passim*, 316, 345–346, 360; in United States, 69–94 *passim*, 102–106 *passim*, 219, 223, 237–238, 269–272 *passim*, 303, 331–332; in Japan, 219, 228n.1, 232–233, 242; in Europe, 242, 246, 269–329 *passim*; in South America, 311

and Rothenstein: nature of correspondence with WR, 64–65, 82, 148, 247, 252–253, 287–288, 299, 304, 305, 357–366 *passim*; friendship with WR, 1, 52–66 *passim*, 127–130 *passim*, 140, 151, 164, 165, 196, 211, 215–216, 234, 257–276 *passim*, 292, 305–316 *passim*, 327–339 *passim*, 367–368; WR's letters to, 35, 50, 53, 54, 59, 61, 63, 66, 71, 76, 79, 83, 89, 93, 94, 97, 100, 102, 103, 106, 108, 111, 112, 115, 120, 122, 123, 125, 126, 128, 130, 131, 139, 140, 141, 144, 145, 151, 153, 156, 162, 167, 168, 170, 174, 187, 191, 196, 199, 202, 204, 207, 213, 224, 228, 232, 234, 236, 238, 240, 242, 243, 246, 249, 250, 254, 255, 259, 260, 263, 273, 274, 280, 284, 287, 288, 294, 307, 310, 312n.1, 313, 315, 319, 322, 326, 330, 332, 334n.3, 335, 337, 339, 341, 342, 347, 350, 352, 354, 362, 364, 366, 368

travels of (considered or completed): in England, 16, 37–48, 53, 88–89, 94–95, 101–112n.1, 203, 218–274 *passim*, 309–328 *passim*, 352, 368; motivation of, 17, 65, 119–120, 122, 139, 211, 216, 274, 304–305, 357; in Europe, 37, 88, 103, 118, 161, 271–290 *passim*, 304–331 *passim*, 367n.3; illnesses during, 37, 55–59 *passim*, 82, 89, 112–118 *passim*, 306–324n.1 *passim*, 336; in North America, 44, 53–107 *passim*, 176n.3, 218–254 *passim*, 269–284 *passim*, 325–333n.1; helplessness in, 53, 57, 89, 94–101 *passim*; in South Asia, 101, 173, 190–192, 247, 296, 309, 324n.1, 336–337; in East Asia, 175–176, 190–195 *passim*, 218–236 *passim*, 309, 312n.1, 319n.1; in Australia, 223, 259–264 *passim*; in South America, 311; in Southeast Asia, 322; in Russia, 330–333 *passim*; in Persia, 335–342 *passim*

views on: politics, 13–16, 187, 224, 244–258 *passim*, 272–297 *passim*, 321–344 *passim*, 360; education, 15, 25, 252–258 *passim*, 283–304 *passim*; literature, 15, 18, 133, 258–276 *passim*, 358; India, 17, 61–62, 82, 127–128, 174–191 *passim*, 326, 332–350 *passim*, 363; religion, 18, 120, 321; Eastern civilization, 238; Western civilization, 238; science, 296

works of: translated, 1, 18–22 *passim*, 35–49 *passim*, 65–87 *passim*, 105–129 *passim*, 146–177 *passim*, 195, 216, 219, 268, 305, 345–346; fiction, 16, 21–22, 123n.2, 129; poems, 17–22 *passim*, 30, 40, 44, 71, 84, 90, 96–97, 108, 110, 122–123n.1; non-fiction, 21–22, 65–71 *passim*, 87, 105–111 *passim*, 123n.2; dramas, 22–23, 47–74 *passim*, 96–97, 109, 117, 122–125 *passim*; *Gitanjali*, 17–24 *passim*, 57–80 *passim*, 92n.3–106 *passim*, 126, 144, 148, 212, 269, 305, 325, 328, 345–346; publication of, 18–22 *passim*, 55, 71–136

passim; 154–176n.3 *passim,* 204, 206, 216–239 *passim,* 305, 319n.1, 333n.1; quoted or paraphrased, 18, 21, 22, 49–50, 75, 83, 180–182, 192, 196, 206–207; reviews of, 20–23 *passim,* 44, 61–77 *passim,* 129n.1, 130n.1, 171, 244–246, 262, 336. See also Bridges, and *Gitanjali;* Yeats, and *Gitanjali*
  as composer, 13–14, 18, 22
  as artist: paintings, 326, 328, 345, 363; exhibitions of (contemplated or held), 326, 329n.1, 333–334, 336, 351–352; reviews of, 336
Tagore, Rathindranath (elder son of RT), 37–105 *passim,* 136n.5, 151, 194n.3, 204, 311, 317, 319, 333, 354; WR's letter to, 25
Tagore, Renuka (Bhattacharya; second daughter of RT), 17
Tagore, Somendranath (younger son of RT), 17, 251
Tagore, Surendranath (nephew of RT), 113n.2, 115n.2–129 *passim,* 146–147, 150n.2, 162, 319n.1
Tagore, Svarna Kumari (elder sister of RT). *See* Ghosal
Taj Mahal, 144
Tate Gallery, 12
Tauchnitz, 295
Taylor, Nicholas, 300n.4
Theosophical Society, 73n.3, 282n.2
Thomas, F. W., 40
Thompson, Edward J., 38n.5, 105n.3, 168n.1, 177, 182n.9, 186, 209n.3–215n.2, 306, 319, 321–322, 355n.2, 362; RT's letter to, 216n.1
Thoreau, Henry David, 14
Thring, G. H., 184–185
Times, The (London), 7, 25, 40, 61, 81n.5, 139, 150n.3, 163; enters art controversy, 5–6
Times of India, The (Bombay), 301
Times Literary Supplement, 61, 65, 66
Tipperah State. *See* Tripura State

Tokyo, RT in, 227, 312n.1
Tolstoy, Leo, 276
Torre Pelice, Marie Sturge Moore in, 44
Totnes, Devon, RT in, 317n.1, 329n.1
Toulouse-Lautrec, Henri, 9
Tower of Babel, 24
Trevelyan, Julian, interview with, 191n.1
Trevelyan, Robert, 17–18, 22, 150n.4, 191n.1
Trieste, 120n.1
Tripura State, 300–301, 346
Turgenev, Ivan, 28n.2
Twelfth Night (Shakespeare), 68

Udaipur, 31; WR in, 28
Underhill, Evelyn, 68, 77, 82, 112n.2, 123n.3–125 *passim,* 154–160n.2 *passim,* 183, 188
Unitarianism, Unitarian Association, 70n.1, n.2
Unity Club, 69
University College (Southampton), 230n.2
"Unrest in India." *See* "Indian unrest"
Urbana (Illinois), RT in, 65–105 *passim*
Utilitarian philosophers, 14

Vail, Albert, 70n.2
Vaishnavism, Vaishnava, 15–30 *passim,* 123n.3, 180
Vale, Mr. *See* Vail, Albert
Valéry, Paul, 367
Vancouver, RT in, 325
Vandervelde, Emile, 214n.1
Vaughan, Henry, 20n.40
Vaughan Williams, Ralph, 40
Venice, RT in, 313
Vickers, John, 117–118n.2
Vienna, John Rothenstein in, 290; RT in, 315
Vienna University, 293
Villeneuve, RT in, 315, 367n.3
Vishnu, 320
Visva-Bharati University, 222, 267–310 *passim,* 321, 328
von Hügel, Friedrich, 71
Vrindavan, 30

Walker, Emery, 64n.4, 126, 145, 174, 192, 194n.3, 214–215
Washington, D.C., Grace Rhys in, 310n.4
Watts, Mr. and Mrs. G. F., 67–68
Wells, H. G., 237, 330
Westminster Gazette (London), 161
Whibley, Charles: as Macmillan's reader, 21–22, 68, 73n.2, 220, 361; as editor, 221n.15
Whistler, James, 9, 263
Whitehall, 13
Whitman, Walt, 14
Wiesbaden, RT in, 317
Wiles, Gilbert, 301
Wilkinson, Gillian, interview with, 160n.2
Willingdon, Lord, WR's letter to, 351n.3
Winternitz, Moritz, 294n.3, 316
Winters, Janet, 79n.1, 86n.2, 145n.1
Winter's Tale, The (Shakespeare), 68
Wisconsin, University of, 100n.1
Wisdom of the East Series, 73n.3, 86n.3
Woodroffe, Sir John, 32, 81n.1

Woods, James H., 99; RT's letters to, 100n.5, 280n.2, 287n.1
Woods, Margaret, WR's letter to, 28n.3
Woolf, Virginia, 10
Worcester, WR in, 260
Wordsworth, William, 18

Yeats, Georgie (Mrs. W. B.), 342n.4
Yeats, W. B., 17–18, 23, 40, 42, 54n.2, 68–76 *passim*, 93, 118, 141, 171, 186, 218, 260, 305, 307, 340–369 *passim*; and *Gitanjali*, 21–22, 40–46n.19, 55n.4, 81n.4–104 *passim*, 147, 159, 183, 195, 197, 212–213n.1; as editor, 41–47 *passim*, 110, 226n.2; as RT's agent, 85; RT's letters to, 100n.4, 212–213n.1, n.3, 218n.7, 226n.4; WR's letter to, 344n.4
Yogi, 165
Yokohama: RT in, 227, 231, 246–247n.3; Pearson in, 246–247n.3
Ypres, WR in, 213, 254

Zetland, Lord. *See* Ronaldshay
Zurich, RT in, 315
Zurich, University of, 315